PREPARING *the* WORLD *for* JESUS

A Survey of the World Before Christ

Kevin Swanson

Printed in Korea by Four Colour Print Group, Louisville, Kentucky.

ISBN: 978-1-7332304-6-9

Artwork on Front Cover: *Journey of the Magi* (1894) by James Tissot. Public Domain.

Production management: Joshua Schwisow
Cover and interior design by Justin Turley

Published by
Generations
19039 Plaza Dr. Ste. 210
Parker, CO 80134
Generations.org

For more information on this and other titles from Generations, visit:
Generations.org or call (888) 389-9080

Contents

This book is dedicated to the Lord Jesus Christ,
who is Lord of All.
He is the Chief Shepherd of His church.

PREPARING *the* WORLD *for* JESUS

A Survey of the World Before Christ

Kevin Swanson

Introduction—The Desire of the Nations

For thus says the LORD of hosts: "Once more (it is a little while) I will shake heaven and earth, the sea and dry land; and I will shake all nations, and they shall come to the Desire of All Nations, and I will fill this temple with glory" says the LORD of hosts. (Haggai 2:6-7)

History should never be studied as if two separate stories existed within it—the secular and the sacred or the extra-biblical and the biblical accounts. The story of Augustus Caesar should never be presented apart from the story of Jesus Christ. History is utterly meaningless without Christ. It is He who always appears as the main event. He alone gives meaning to history. Without Him, nothing can be held together, and history itself falls to pieces. Thus the story of history is one story, all of it engagingly interwoven, intensely meaningful, and supremely thrilling. It is the story of God's working within His creation to accomplish His wondrous purposes.

History possesses meaning only when we view it from God's perspective. The story of Augustus Caesar should become familiar to us only because he represents the world into which the Son of God was born. Jesus Christ really came into the real world, to really die for real sins and to establish a real kingdom that will never end. Every Christian family across the globe who desires to be rightly educated in world history must look first to the biblical historical records as their foundation. These alone provide the emphases that must form the main points of history from a biblical worldview perspective. Meanwhile, the Egyptians, Assyrians, Babylonians, Persians, and Greeks provide the stage upon which the drama of biblical history played out.

Unbelieving, post-Christian historians tell us that biblical history is worse than unimportant and is entirely inaccurate—nothing more than a fairy tale. This assertion, however, is quite at odds with the truth. The dark eons of history hardly offer us any certainty, and worldly archaeologists are left to wild guesswork. The ancient tales of the Mesopotamians and Egyptians are patently cloaked in myth, and honest historians will admit they can scarcely make heads or tails of them. Only the Scriptures, the revelation of God recorded by His reliable prophets, can possibly provide us with a definite and certain framework for the rest of history. Thus, we must rely on Scripture for the true and certain facts of history. This must always be the foundation upon which our understanding of history is built.

Since Scripture is the infallible, inerrant Word of God, we should not be surprised at how much extant archaeological evidence increasingly validates the Bible's records. *Preparing the World for Jesus* will summarize the best, the most accurate, and the most important recent archaeological finds pertaining to biblical events. As we should expect, these secular accounts confirm time and again the reliability of Scripture:

- The worldwide flood really happened, and every tribe and nation in the world was impacted by it.
- Moses actually led God's people out of Egypt. And Pharaoh's armies really were destroyed in the Red Sea, toppling the Egyptian Empire.
- Joshua actually fought the battle of Jericho, and the walls really did come tumbling down.
- Nebuchadnezzar was truly humbled.
- Nineveh really repented.

- Cyrus the Great was actually named by Isaiah 300 years before he was born, and he did indeed help to rebuild the temple by the decree of Almighty God.
- Alexander the Great was really the horn of the male goat in Daniel's dream.
- Jesus, the Son of God, was really born in Bethlehem.

Archaeology upholds all of this. But, more importantly, each of these events were recorded in God's Word, and they are all essential to understanding His Story—the story of the world.

Until Jesus came, the whole world groaned and travailed under the weight of man's sin. Although they may not have realized it, all nations of the world looked forward with a life-or-death, desperate anticipation to the coming of the true Messiah of God.

These ancient civilizations record the stories of a Satanic rule over the nations of men, the nightmarish rule of evil, the failures of the god-state, and the endless wars, cruelties, and treacheries of the great men of the world. The optimistic pride and the accomplishments of men could only, always lead them to pessimism and destruction. No hope existed for ancient man—no hope outside of a miraculous intervention by God. Only the Savior of God could save man from this terrible predicament. Only God's King would bring the ultimate rule of true righteousness and peace. Only the arrival of Jesus Christ could bring meaning to the world and hope to the fallen race of mankind.

This is the only way to study the history of the world.

CHAPTER I

The Creation and the Global Flood

In the beginning God created the heavens and the earth. (Genesis 1:1)

This is the story of the world, but it is really the story of the history of man. God created the world somewhere around 4174 BC.[1] We are not left to guess how the world came into being. Scripture tells us clearly that the world was made by the spoken Word of God, the second Person of the Trinity, the Lord Jesus Christ.

In the beginning was the Word, and the Word was with God, and the Word was God. He was in the beginning with God. All things were made through Him, and without Him nothing was made that was made. (John 1:1-3)

By the word of the Lord the heavens were made,
And all the host of them by the breath of His mouth.
He gathers the waters of the sea together as a heap;
He lays up the deep in storehouses.
Let all the earth fear the Lord;
Let all the inhabitants of the world stand in awe of Him.

For He spoke, and it was done;
He commanded, and it stood fast. (Psalm 33:6-9)

The Son of God was revealed to man at His birth in Bethlehem of Judea around AD 1, and we learn a great deal of His person and character from the Gospels. Indeed, the Son of God, the Creator of the world took on human flesh and lived thirty-three years with us. This glorious Person existed before the world was, and He made everything—all matter, the entire universe. He spoke and it came into being. His Word is a powerful word. When He spoke and instructed a dead man to come out of the tomb, Lazarus came out. When He told the winds and the waves to be still, they obeyed immediately. He needed only to speak a word, and bacteria or viruses would disappear from people's bodies and the cells in their bodies would repair at twenty miles' distance. This we read in Matthew 8:

Now when Jesus had entered Capernaum, a centurion came to Him, pleading with Him, saying, "Lord, my servant is lying at home paralyzed, dreadfully tormented." And Jesus said to him, "I will come and heal him." The centurion

answered and said, "Lord, I am not worthy that You should come under my roof. **But only speak a word, and my servant will be healed.** *For I also am a man under authority, having soldiers under me. And I say to this one, 'Go,' and he goes; and to another, 'Come,' and he comes; and to my servant, 'Do this,' and he does it." When Jesus heard it, He marveled, and said to those who followed, "Assuredly, I say to you, I have not found such great faith, not even in Israel!" (Matthew 8:5-10)*

At the beginning it was this person, the Son of God, who created the world by His Word. God decided to make the world and to make man, so the Lord spoke His will. He commanded what He willed when He said, "Let there be light." And He got what He wanted. This is the Power that created the world.

How Do We Know the Age of the Earth?

Unbelieving historians think the world is much older than God's Word teaches, but they have no good basis for this belief. Their theories are not substantiated by an eyewitness account or by reliable eyewitnesses who recorded the events as they played out. They rely heavily upon the carbon dating method for determining the age of the earth and particularly the history of man. Evolutionists and archaeologists measure the amount of Carbon 14 in organic matter and arrive at a conclusion as to the age of the material. Their studies assume that the Carbon 14 to Carbon 12 ratio in the atmosphere remained the same over thousands of years (and that the decay rates stay the same as well). Yet, there is no way to know for sure what the Carbon 14 to Carbon 12 ratio was 5,000 years ago, calling into question the reliability of the method itself.

The most accurate and the most reliable way to determine the age of the earth is to rely on God's revelation and the genealogies contained in Genesis and the rest of the Bible. Some have argued that the Genesis genealogies contain gaps of many generations. This is hard to believe because we find genealogies carefully recording the age of each father when his first son was born and the age at which each of the early patriarchs died.

The most reliable way to determine the earth's age using scientific observation is by counting tree rings. The oldest tree in the world, called "Methuselah" is located in the California White Mountains, and it is estimated to be 4,800 years

Methuselah Tree

old. It's not always easy to distinguish the rings, so there may be a 5% margin of error in the count. Assuming "Methuselah" began growing soon after the flood, this dating method would put the flood somewhere around 2720 BC. (Because the worldwide flood would have killed every tree in the world, counting tree rings would not help us identify the age of the earth prior to the flood.) Biblical creationists hold to God's promise that the regularity of the seasons from winter to summer have continued uninterrupted since the flood, and therefore conclude the accuracy of tree ring data (Gen. 8:21-22). In other words, we can hold to the fact that uniformitarian conditions have continued since the flood because of the promise of God clearly revealed in Genesis 8.

Conservative Christian scholars offer varying interpretations of both the date of the flood and the age of the earth. Some date the flood at 2304 BC, others at 2348 BC, and still others at 2518 BC.

The Creation of Man and the Fall of Man

Stained-Glass Representation of Adam and Eve

The Lord created mankind on the sixth day of creation. He made man out of the dust of the earth and breathed the breath of life into him. He made woman from the man, taking one of his ribs to form her body. Then the Lord God established marriage as a permanent institution for human society. Such a special unity exists within this human relationship that the Lord Jesus would later declare: "They are no longer two, but one flesh" (Matt. 19:6).

Adam was put in charge of the animals and was given a garden to cultivate. God gave him a single rule to obey. But an evil angel named Satan tempted the woman Eve, and consequently both Adam and his wife disobeyed God's rule. This brought sin into the world along with the curse of death, fear of death, bondage, tribal wars, despair, depression, disease, abuse, addictions, violence, murder, envy, divorce, sexual perversion, and broken relationships. Every evil that entered the world was a consequence of this original sin. A great darkness spread over the entire world and the prince of darkness, Satan himself, gained control of the sons of men.

> *We know that we are of God, and the whole world lies under the sway of the wicked one. (1 John 5:19)*

This was the condition of the world after the Fall of man into sin. Darkness was everywhere. All were without God and without hope in the world (Eph. 2:12), except for a few people who lived on a very small sliver of land on the eastern coast of the Mediterranean Sea.

The Promised Seed

Despite man's horrible sin, God had a plan in place to save the world. Even as He pronounced the curse of death upon Adam and Eve in Genesis 3, right away He left them with an encouraging and hopeful promise.

> *So the LORD God said to the serpent:*
> *"Because you have done this,*
> *You are cursed more than all cattle,*
> *And more than every beast of the field;*
> *On your belly you shall go,*
> *And you shall eat dust*
> *All the days of your life.*
> *And I will put enmity*
> *Between you and the woman,*
> *And between your seed and her Seed;*
> *He shall bruise your head,*
> *And you shall bruise His heel." (Genesis 3:14-15)*

Thus the Lord promised a Seed which would crush Satan's head while Satan would only wound His heel. And this Seed would come from the womb of the woman. God would put enmity between Satan and the righteous seed—and this enmity would continue throughout history. Satan does not want his head crushed, and he is constantly aware of the threat of the Seed of the woman.

Sometimes called the protoevangelium, this was the first revelation of the salvation of God and the Savior of God in the person of Jesus Christ.

The Devil's Enmity

> *Now Adam knew Eve his wife, and she conceived and bore Cain, and said, "I have acquired a man from the LORD." Then she bore again, this time his brother Abel. Now Abel was a keeper of sheep, but Cain was a tiller of the ground. And in the process of time it came to pass that Cain brought an offering of the fruit of the ground to the LORD. Abel also brought of the firstborn of his flock and of their fat. And the LORD respected Abel and his offering, but He did not respect Cain and his offering. And Cain was very angry, and his countenance fell. So the LORD said to Cain, "Why are you angry? And why has your countenance fallen? If you do well, will you not be accepted? And if you do not do well, sin lies at the door. And its desire is for you, but you should rule over it." (Genesis 4:1-7)*

The devil quickly began to wage war against the Seed of the woman. Adam and Eve's firstborn son, Cain, killed his younger brother (Gen. 4). Abel appeared to be the righteous seed because he brought an acceptable sacrifice to God while Cain did not. Although the Lord warned Cain that sin or the devil was "crouching at the door," Cain refused to heed this warning. Instead, he gave in to his envy and hatred of his brother, murdering him in cold blood. This did not put an end to the promise of the Seed as the devil had hoped. Rather, Eve bore another son and named him Seth. This initiated the line of the "sons of God" out of which would come the promised Seed many generations later.

Cain was not to be executed by his family for his horrible crime. At this time, the Lord would not permit the family to take the role of the civil government into its own hands. Instead God banished Cain to wander "east of Eden" like a vagabond in the earth.

The Line of Cain

> *Then Lamech said to his wives:*
> *"Adah and Zillah, hear my voice;*
> *Wives of Lamech, listen to my speech!*
> *For I have killed a man for wounding me,*
> *Even a young man for hurting me.*
> *If Cain shall be avenged sevenfold,*
> *Then Lamech seventy-sevenfold."*
> *(Genesis 4:23-24)*

The characteristics of the line of Cain are a picture of the world without God. First, man isolates himself from relationship with others. He kills his brother and wanders east of Eden. He builds a city where anonymity prevails, and he seeks to gain increasing degrees of power over the rest.

Cain's great-great-great-grandson Lamech became the world's first polygamist, taking to himself multiple wives. This is an aberration of God's plan for marriage—creating marital competition, coldness, and distance wherever it has been practiced. Polygamy is another example of human isolation and the destruction of true companionship. It was not God's original design for marriage, in which the two become one (Mark 10:8).

To make matters worse, Lamech killed another man in personal

vengeance. His threatening speech is the first recorded example of human tyranny. He positions himself as more severe than God by seventy-fold. The ungodly rule by severe threats, torture, and cruelty, and this is the record borne out by thousands of tribes, nations, and empires throughout the history of the world. Proud tyrants distinguish themselves like Lamech—severe, regulative, arbitrary, and controlling. In their futile attempts to compete with God, they abandon all moderation and reject the most excellent, wise, and just law of liberty laid down by God Himself.

The Nephilim

> *There were giants on the earth in those days, and also afterward, when the sons of God came in to the daughters of men and they bore children to them. Those were the mighty men who were of old, men of renown. (Genesis 6:4)*

Cain and Lamech's legacy was passed on to their sons and daughters. We read in Genesis chapter six that the earth became corrupted and filled with violence (Gen. 6:11-12). This was the work of the Nephilim, who were the offspring of mixed marriages between the sons of God and the daughters of men. These men may have been giants in physical size and strength, but certainly they were men of great power and renown, capable of exercising tremendous violence in the earth. Most likely, these powerful men formed empires or cruel dictatorships. Something similar to this occurred in the 20th century when dictators in the Soviet Union, Germany, China, and Cambodia killed hundreds of millions of people.

This horrible violence followed the intermarriage of the righteous line of Seth with the unrighteous line of Cain—men married women who did not worship the true and living God. This kind of synthesis or apostasy is always dangerous and brings unimaginable evil in later generations.

These men and their wicked violence was the cause for the judgment that came upon the earth by the worldwide flood of Noah's day. The antithesis between the godly line of Seth and the line of Cain no doubt continued with the Nephilim. Could Noah's father Lamech have been murdered by the Nephilim so that he died at an earlier age than the rest of the patriarchs? Scripture indicates that Lamech was a man of faith. He named his son "Noah" in hopes that the earth would one day enjoy rest from the strife and violence. Methuselah died at 969 years of age in the year of the flood, possibly

killed by the Nephilim as well. What we do know for certain is that there was only one man and his family left of the righteous line by the time of the flood.

Assuming that the extended longevity for those who lived prior to the flood meant an improvement in physical health and an improved ability for women to bear children, the birth rate would have been as high as 29 children per couple. That would equate to 33 billion people in the world by the time of the flood—all of whom would have perished in the floodwaters (minus eight persons). If the average woman bore twelve children (only twice the birth rate of the present world without birth control), there would have been about 140 million people in the world by the time of the flood.

Whatever the case, when the floodwaters covered the earth, the salvation of the world rested on one man and his family of eight. God promised that the seed of the woman would bring salvation to the world. As He brought about the destruction of the whole world by water, this promise hung on a very thin thread. From a human perspective, the odds of one family surviving a worldwide flood were slim indeed. Yet, God saved one family from a watery grave. But, more importantly, He was determined to save the promised Seed, who would come through Noah's son Shem. Thanks be to God, the Seed survived, and that Seed would save the world from sin and death by His death and resurrection in AD 33.

The Flood

There is no event more talked about in all of the ancient histories across the various cultures around the world than the global flood. It was an extremely memorable event. To be true to the ancient records, every history book should recognize this event as central to world history. Yet, modern histories taught in almost every public educational institution in the world today will ignore this major historical record. Modern men and all sinful men will always refuse to face the fact of God's judgment. They do not want to admit that God is paying careful attention to their lives and that He will bring judgment on the world in His time. In his final epistle, the Apostle Peter appropriately explained why these modern historians and scientists would reject all records concerning the worldwide flood of Noah's day.

> *Knowing this first: that scoffers will come in the last days, walking according to their own lusts, and saying, "Where is the promise of His coming? For since the fathers fell asleep, all things continue as they were from the beginning of creation." For this they willfully forget: that by the word of God the heavens were of old, and the earth standing out of water and in the water, by which the world that then existed perished, being flooded with water. But the heavens and the earth which are now preserved by the same word, are reserved for fire until the day of judgment and perdition of ungodly men.* (2 Peter 3:3-7)

God brought the flood upon the ungodly about the year 2518 BC, and He will bring a judgment of fire upon the ungodly once more at the end of history.

The Lord God revealed to Noah the coming flood 120 years before it happened. This gave the man of God ample time to build an ark to save his family and the land animals. Scientists estimate that there were about 16,000 animals needing shelter in the ark. Before the massive multiplication and diversification of animal species which has occurred over the last 4,500 years, there would have been far fewer distinct varieties of animals. Assuming that some if not most of the animals taken aboard were still immature, there would have been plenty of room to house them, with about half of the space in the ark unfilled according to scientific calculations.[2] Even the largest dinosaur, of the sauropod family, might have only weighed 500 pounds by the time he left the ark (fourteen months after embarking). That would be the size of a small horse.

The ark was about 510 feet long (155 m), 80 feet wide (24 m), and 50 feet high (15 m). In comparison, some freight trailer trucks can carry about 250 sheep. This huge vessel could have accommodated about 450 of these trailers or about 120,000 sheep.

Before the rains came, the Lord brought the animals to the ark, Noah and his family settled in, and then the Lord shut the door of the ark. For forty days and nights the rain fell. Waters broke out from under the earth's surface, and a water layer located in the atmosphere above emptied on the earth. Of most significant note, this major cataclysm was no accident—it came as a judgment upon man for his violence and wickedness. Millions of men, women, and children died in the deluge.

> *Now the flood was on the earth forty days. The waters increased and lifted up the ark, and it rose high above the earth. The waters prevailed and greatly increased on the earth, and the ark moved about on the surface of the waters. And the waters prevailed exceedingly on the earth, and all the high hills under the whole heaven were covered. The waters prevailed fifteen cubits upward, and the mountains were covered. And all flesh died that moved on the earth: birds and cattle and beasts and every creeping thing that creeps on the earth, and every man. All in whose nostrils was the breath of the spirit of life, all that was on the dry land, died. So He destroyed all living things which were on the face of the ground: both man and cattle, creeping thing and bird of the air. They were destroyed from the earth. Only Noah and those who were with him in the ark remained alive. And the waters prevailed on the earth one hundred and fifty days. (Genesis 7:17-24)*

Noah and his family stayed in the ark for about fourteen months. After eight months, mountaintops appeared in sight (perhaps as high as 14,000-18,000 feet, as in the case of the Ararat mountain range). Over the next several months, Noah released a dove three times. The second time, nine months after the flood began, the dove returned with an olive leaf in its mouth—a sign of renewed life in that vegetation was beginning to grow on the hills once more. This would be essential for feeding man and animals as they exited the ark.

Evidence of the Worldwide Flood

The most convincing argument for a worldwide flood comes from scriptural record in both Old and New Testaments. The worldwide extent of the flood is underscored by the explicit statement of Genesis 7: "The waters prevailed exceedingly upon the earth, and all the high hills that were under the whole heaven were covered" (Genesis 7:19-20). The wording could not have been made more clear—this was a flood that covered the entire globe.

The physical or geological evidence for a worldwide flood should be obvious—at least to those who accept God's authoritative revelation and interpret the evidence from a biblical worldview perspective. Fossils of sea creatures are found on mountaintops all over the earth. How did they get there?

In 1987 a team of unbelieving scientists discovered whale fossils high up in the Andes Mountains. How did whales climb 5,000 feet up these mountains? Even unbelieving, evolutionary scientists had to conclude that this "South American mountain chain rose very rapidly from the sea."[3] Fossils of cephalopods have been found high up in the Himalayas—a good distance from the Indian Ocean and miles above sea level. In 1998 a Japanese researcher chipped out a brachiopod shellfish fossil just six meters below the peak of Mount Everest, the highest point on earth—ultimate proof that Noah's flood covered the highest peak in the world—29,000 feet (8,880 m) above sea level.[4] There is only one reasonable explanation for all of this: there must have been a worldwide flood in which great reservoirs of water were released from below the earth's surface. To create these huge mountain ranges rapidly, with marine fossils embedded in each of them, some great watery catastrophe of biblical proportions must have been unleashed on the world.

Psalm 104 explains in detail how the mountains formed during the worldwide flood:

> *Bless the LORD, O my soul! O LORD my God, You are very great: You are clothed with honor and majesty, . . . You covered it with the deep as with a garment; The waters stood above the mountains. At Your rebuke they fled; at the voice of Your thunder they hastened away. They went up over the mountains; They went down into the valleys, to the place which You founded for them. (Psalm 104:1, 6-8)*

As the waters under the earth's crust gushed out (Gen. 7:11), no doubt molten rock also poured out into the ocean bed. This lava would have caused the sea level to rise and cover the earth. Creation scientists believe the waters would have risen about 3,500 feet (1,067 m), covering the highest mountains on earth at the time. As the volcanic rock began to cool, the floodwaters would have drained off the mountains, leaving behind billions of dead animals, fossilized into the strata.

Fossils usually form under extreme catastrophic conditions, such as a flood or volcanic eruption. However, the universal presence of fossils all over the world point to a large cataclysmic event that impacted the whole globe at one time. Even the tracks of some animals crawling along were rapidly encased in sediment and preserved for us to see today.

Within the fossil record scientists have never found a record of gradual change or evolution of one particular kind of animal to another. The fossil record is static; each animal is fully formed and no evidence of any creature changing into another kind of organism by millions of iterations are to be found. Each distinct animal kind either disappeared after the flood or the same organisms are present in our world today.

The billions of fossils buried in rock layers all over the earth are a constant reminder of the severe judgment that God brought upon the earth for man's sin. Men and women gave way to unrestrained violence, abortion, infanticide, the killing of the elderly, and other murderous tendencies. These fossils testify to the holy, almighty God's outlook and response towards such wicked behavior.

> *And God said to Noah, "The end of all flesh has come before Me, for the earth is filled with violence through them; and behold, I will destroy them with the earth. (Genesis 6:13)*

Day of the Dead

After the flood, the tribes of the earth generally refused to celebrate God's redemption and the salvation that He brought to Noah. Instead the world inaugurated an event called "The Day of the Dead."

In celebration of this day, Egyptians placed the coffin of Osiris (the god of death and the afterlife) into a boat and, according to Plutarch, the god was sent to float on the waters on the seventeenth day of the month Athyr (around November).[5] Similarly, the Japanese celebrate the "Bon" festival in mid-August, in which they send the "dead spirits" into the sea in little boats. The Hindus in India perform a ceremony called Shraddha during Pitru Paksha (in September) for the benefit of the souls of ancestors, and the ceremony takes place by a river or other body of water. The ancient Assyrians commemorated the dead during the month of Arahsamna (between mid-October and mid-November). The Aztecs and other native Americans celebrated the Day of the Dead in the fall of the year as far back as 1000 BC. It is still commemorated by Mexicans between October 31st and November 2nd. This pagan holiday honored the dead lost in the flood. Prior to the flood, relatively few people had died of natural causes since most lived over 900 years. The mass deaths of millions or even billions of people must have left a strong psychological impression upon the descendants of Shem, Ham, and Japheth.

Flood Stories

An event that literally shook the entire world would have been difficult to ignore for the eight survivors and their progeny. Undoubtedly stories would have been told for generations upon generations, especially since Noah and his sons lived for about 400 years after the flood. As it turns out, flood legends are found in almost every indigenous (native) culture in the world. Oral traditions are notorious for losing accuracy in the details, and most of these cultures relied on oral methods to communicate the stories until they developed their own written languages. However, the basic elements of the story have been preserved for thousands of years. In almost every account the flood was understood to have been a worldwide event.

Though flood legends from various cultures are helpful in providing secondary evidence of the flood, only the Bible can be trusted for its perfect accuracy because it is God's word. Nevertheless, it is still remarkable how many details were retained with a high degree of accuracy in various oral traditions. The following table illustrates the general agreement among these traditions.

Elements of the Flood Story	% of Stories Retaining the Element
A favored family saved	88%
Forewarning provided	66%
Cause of flood is man's wickedness	66%
Catastrophe is only a flood	95%
Flood of global proportions	95%
A boat is the means of survival	70%
Animals saved	67%
Animals play a part	73%
Survivors land on a mountain	57%
Birds sent out	35%
Rainbow mentioned	7%
Survivors offered a sacrifice	13%
Specifically eight persons saved	9%[6]

Tablet Containing the Epic of Gilgamesh

Not surprisingly, the earliest written mentions of the flood are found in the oldest human writings ever discovered—the Sumerian King's List and the *Instructions of Shuruppak* from Mesopotamia, both of which date to around 2300-2200 BC. Also, the oldest detailed flood story is found in the Eridu Genesis Cuneiform tablet (dated around 1600 BC). This ancient tablet explains the original creation and the names of the first pre-flood cities—Eridu, Bad-Tibira, Larak, Sippar, and Šuruppak. Although set in a polytheistic religious framework, the story presents the flood as lasting only seven days and "sweeping over the cities," destroying mankind. It was excessive noise produced by mankind which apparently irritated the (rather amoral) gods enough to destroy the earth. Noah is named Ziusudra, and he is commended for saving the "small animals and the seed of mankind."[7]

In 2010 the British Museum obtained an ancient Mesopotamian "Ark Tablet" which dates from about 1900 BC (about 500-600 years after the flood). Most intriguing about the cuneiform tablet were the instructions on how to make an ark! Described as a round coracle, the ark is dimensioned as 230 feet in diameter and 20 feet tall. A description is provided of how wild animals came into the ark two-by-two. This is one of the earliest written references to the worldwide flood on record.

Even more ancient than this tablet is the Epic of Gilgamesh. Fragments bearing parts of the story have been found dating back to around 2100 BC (about 300 years after the flood). The fullest known version was written by a Babylonian scribe somewhere around 1300 BC. The tale relates a horrible, tangled story of false gods, demigods (half gods), and sexual sin, like most of the ancient pagan myths that followed. The story's main protagonist, Gilgamesh, also shows up in the list of kings, and it is possible he was a real character in history, albeit the story that followed him is mythical.

In his travels, Gilgamesh meets the Noah character (Utnapishtim) and his wife. This could very well have been a true element of the story since Noah survived for 350 years after the flood. Assuming a birth rate of about six per family (for the first seven post-flood generations), Noah would have been alive to see 3,250,000 of his progeny. However, these peoples would have been largely distributed into small tribes and city states by the time of Noah's death around 2100-2000 BC. Noah would probably have been over 700 years old when Gilgamesh paid him the visit.

Although the flood story comes across garbled in the Epic, the Noah character offers Gilgamesh a thorough account of the worldwide flood. The reason given for the destruction of the world can only be described as lame—the god Enlil was tired out by all the "noise and confusion" on the earth. Ea, another god in the polytheist pantheon, warns Utnapishtim (Noah) of the coming flood. The rains descend and everything is killed except for Noah and the living things collected on the boat. As they come to rest on Mount Nisir, Noah releases three birds from the ark—a dove, a swallow, and a raven. Utnapishtim offers sacrifices which don't appease Enlil. However, the Ea god pacifies Enlil and the survivors are taken to the island of Dilmun.

Ancient Assyrian Statue in the Louvre, Thought to Represent Gilgamesh

At the end of the Gilgamesh flood account Noah is granted everlasting life on earth. It would undoubtedly have seemed to Gilgamesh that Noah had an eternal existence since people were living less than 200 years by the time that Noah was nearly wrapping up a 950-year life span.

The distant tribes of Siberia remember a flood that lasted seven days. The animals and a few people were saved by climbing on logs. The Eskimos of Orowingnatak, Alaska record that "a great inundation, together with an earthquake, swept the land so rapidly that only a few people escaped in their skin canoes to tops of the highest mountains."[8] Out in Tanzania, Africa, the tribes speak of two men who escaped from a flood which covered the mountaintops by using a ship. Specimens of each kind of animal were also saved.[9] The Tehuelche tribes of Patagonia, Argentina tell of a very wicked and violent people whom the sun-god chose to eliminate by sending a tremendous storm. Every person and land animal was killed in the deluge. Eventually, the sun-god sent out a dove which returned with several blades of grass in its beak. Then the sun-god made a man, a woman—and a dog to keep them company. Such stories have lost important details, but it is still remarkable how much of the 4,500-year-old true story was retained by a tribal people living in a remote corner of the world.

China has many flood legends in its lore, but it is the Miao tribe which presents the fullest picture for us. They speak of a pre-flood people, the first of whom was called "Dirt" because he was made out of the dirt, and a woman who was made out of the man. This ancient legend writes of creation:

> *On the day God created the heavens and earth. On that day He opened the gateway of light. In the earth then He made heaps of earth and of stone. In the sky He made bodies, the sun and the moon. In the earth He created the hawk and the kite.*[10]

Of the worldwide flood, the legend further explains:

> *These did not God's will nor returned His affection. But fought with each other defying the Godhead. Their leaders shook fists in the face of the Mighty. Then the earth was convulsed to the depth of three strata. Rending the air to the uttermost heaven. God's anger arose till His Being was changed; His wrath flaring up filled His eyes and His face. Until He must come and demolish humanity. Come and destroy a whole world full of people.*
>
> *So it poured forty days in sheets and in torrents. Then fifty-five days of misting and drizzle. The waters surmounted the mountains and ranges. The deluge ascending leapt valley and hollow. An earth with no earth upon which to take refuge! A world with no foothold where one might subsist! The people were baffled, impotent and ruined, despairing, horror stricken, diminished and finished. But the Patriarch Nuah was righteous. The Matriarch Gaw Bo-lu-en upright. Built a boat very wide. Made a ship very vast. Their household entire got aboard and were floated, The family complete rode the deluge in safety. The animals with him were female and male. The birds went along and were mated*

in pairs. When the time was fulfilled, God commanded the waters. The day had arrived, the flood waters receded. Then Nuah liberated a dove from their refuge, Sent a bird to go forth and bring again tidings. The flood had gone down into lake and to ocean; the mud was confined to the pools and the hollows.

There was land once again where a man might reside; there was a place in the earth now to rear habitations. Buffalo then were brought, an oblation to God, fatter cattle became sacrifice to the Mighty. The Divine One then gave them His blessing; their God then bestowed His good graces.

In their very ancient records, the Miao tribes trace their lineage to Japho and Gomen—most likely Japheth and Gomer, son and grandson of Noah. The genealogy that was retained by this tribe is remarkably similar to the biblical record.[11]

Several Chinese characters still in use today by both the Japanese and the Chinese recall the story of the worldwide flood. For example, the Chinese character for boat is composed of the pictograph for eight, the pictograph for mouth (or people), and the pictograph for vessel. Also, the character for flood includes the pictograph for water and the pictographs for together, earth, and eight. These characters were developed as early as 1,000 BC.

If there was one historical event in the ancient world of which all historians could be certain, primitive oral traditionalists, modern secularists, and Christians

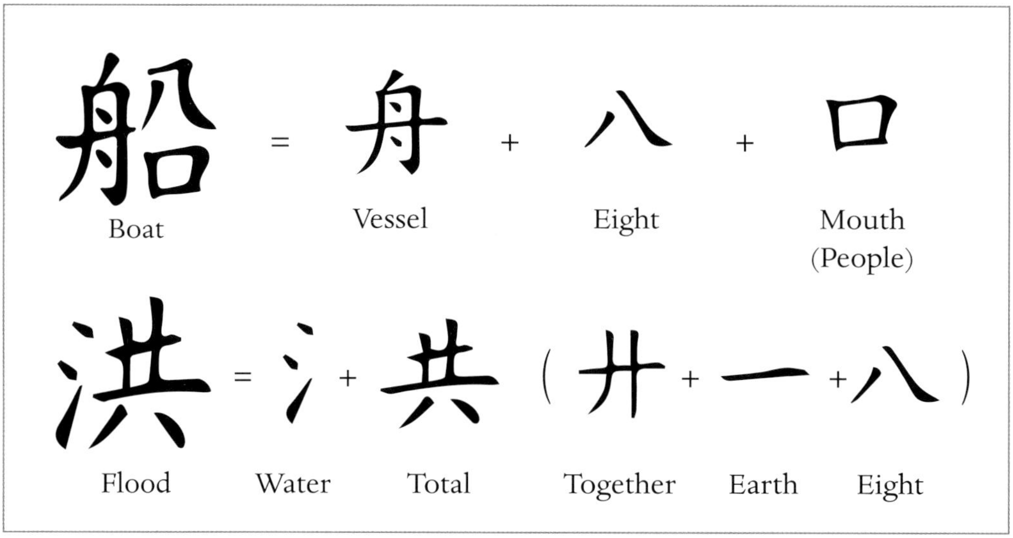

船 = 舟 + 八 + 口

Boat Vessel Eight Mouth (People)

洪 = 氵 + 共 (廾 + 一 + 八)

Flood Water Total Together Earth Eight

The Descent of the Miautso People of China

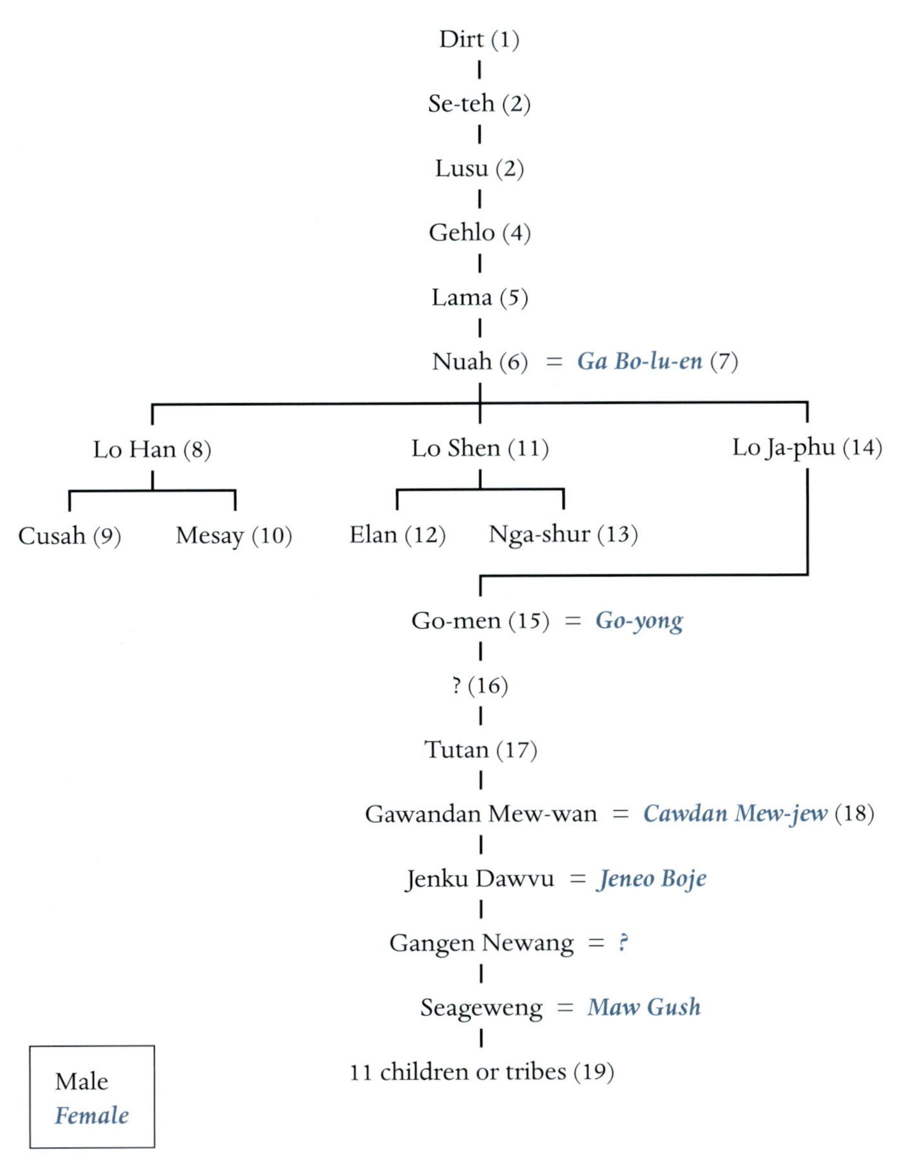

alike, it would have to be the worldwide flood. Other historical events do not receive universal coverage in the oral and written records. For example, we do not find every tribe in the world reporting on the Egyptian pyramids, the Akkadian empire, the discovery of silk in China, the destruction of Sodom, or the destruction of Pharaoh's army at the Red Sea. But, there is a remarkable unity in historical traditions from the far-flung tribes concerning this one event, only because all the peoples of the earth descend from one father and mother, and their three sons. All the peoples of the earth should testify to the salvation of Noah, Shem, Ham, and Japheth by the mercies of God. So quickly, ancient man would go on to forget the salvation of God and neglect to give him the glory for it. Then, modern man would work hard to purge out all remembrance of the judgment of God in the worldwide flood.

When the Son of God came the first time, He came on a mission to save the world. But His second coming will be for judgment, and it will come suddenly, as in the days of Noah.

> *But of that day and hour no one knows, not even the angels of heaven, but My Father only. But as the days of Noah were, so also will the coming of the Son of Man be. For as in the days before the flood, they were eating and drinking, marrying and giving in marriage, until the day that Noah entered the ark, and did not know until the flood came and took them all away, so also will the coming of the Son of Man be. (Matthew 24:36-39)*

Timeline Review

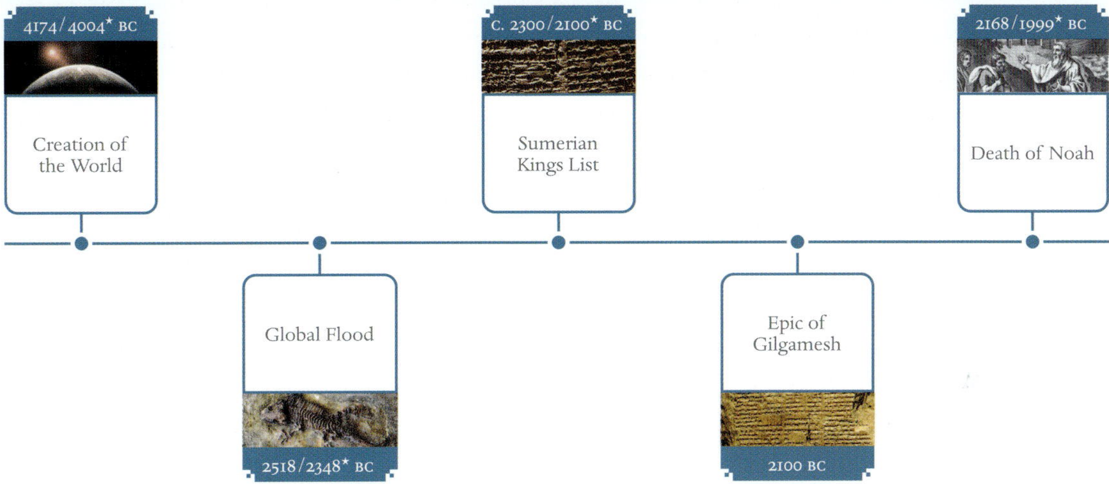

* Date according to Ussher's Chronology which assumes Israelites were in Egypt 215 years.

Chapter I Prayer

Almighty God, Holy Father,

As we look around us at the curse of sin, death in the world, and the fossils embedded in stone, we see your hand of judgment. What a tragedy our sin brought about the whole earth! What great devastation the worldwide flood brought upon the world! You are holy, holy, holy, Lord God almighty! Yet, your long suffering and mercy upon the earth is evident throughout all of our history. You have preserved the world for the coming of your Savior, that one day all will be made right and new again. We anticipate this with great longing and hope.

In the name of Jesus our Savior,
Amen.

CHAPTER II

The Whole Pagan World: Darkness Prevails (2518 BC - AD 33)

The people who walked in darkness
Have seen a great light;
Those who dwelt in the land of the shadow of death,
Upon them a light has shined. (Isaiah 9:2)

Arise, shine;
For your light has come!
And the glory of the LORD is risen upon you.
For behold, the darkness shall cover the earth,
And deep darkness the people;
But the LORD will arise over you,
And His glory will be seen upon you.
The Gentiles shall come to your light,
And kings to the brightness of your rising. (Isaiah 60:1-3)

The condition of the world before Jesus came in the flesh was one of darkness, despair, hopelessness, idolatry, and the fear of demons and death. For 4,000 years the world experienced an oppressive darkness until the

Light came. The great and crying need for a Redeemer was felt for thousands of years. Nothing else could satisfy man's deepest needs. All of man's false religions would prove futile and hopeless. All of his great kings and empires could never bring salvation to the world. Indeed, history would establish beyond any doubt that only the Messiah of God could address man's true needs.

When the Lord Jesus Christ came into the world, He came as the Truth to a world of deception and lies. He came as the Light to a world of darkness. He came to bring life where death reigned, and joy and hope where despair remained.

Any treatment of ancient history ignoring the darkness which utterly enveloped the pre-Christ world perpetuates the greatest lie of all. This was a time in which mankind lived in the very shadow of death. During the long millennia before the coming of Christ, a deep darkness had fallen upon the whole earth.

The Isolated Pagan World

> *Therefore remember that you, once Gentiles in the flesh—who are called Uncircumcision by what is called the Circumcision made in the flesh by hands—that at that time you were without Christ, being aliens from the commonwealth of Israel and strangers from the covenants of promise, having no hope and without God in the world. But now in Christ Jesus you who once were far off have been brought near by the blood of Christ. (Ephesians 2:11-13)*

During the Old Testament era, the Gentile world was very far away from the covenants of promise given by God to the Jews. Two things would contribute to the degradation and destruction of human society throughout the millennia before Christ.

1. The removal of some degree of God's common grace in a society that rejected God's most basic moral laws. Although God writes His law upon men's hearts, they will tend to suppress the truth in unrighteousness. When they reject those basic moral principles which would preserve human society relating to marriage and sexuality, honor of parents and authority, respect for private property, as well as the value of human life, that society is doomed.
2. The further away from the godly line of Noah, Shem, and Abraham the tribes wandered, the more human society would descend into a primitive

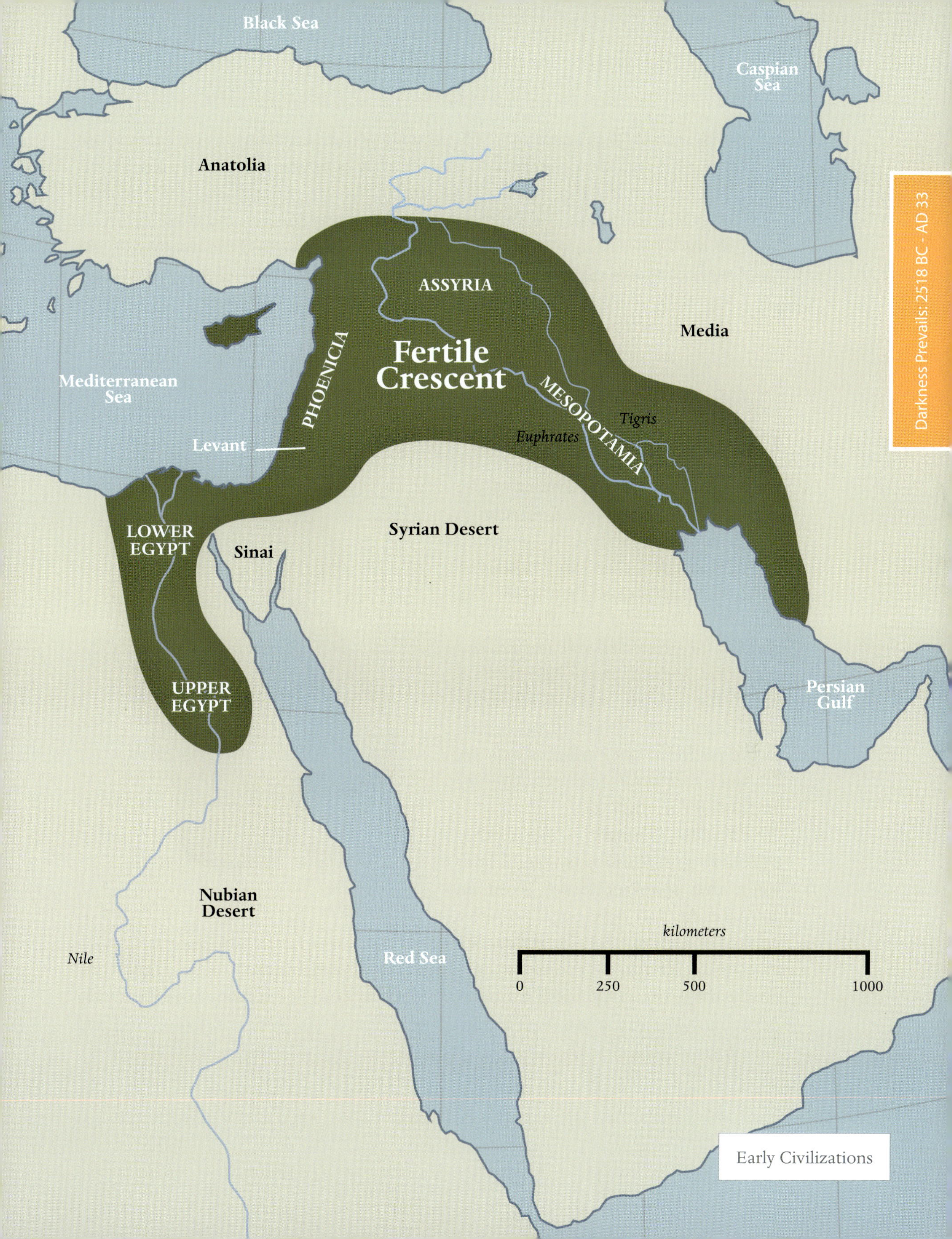

Early Civilizations

and morally degraded state. The first significant civilizations on earth arose in Egypt and Mesopotamia. Placed directly between these major kingdoms by God's ordination was the land of Canaan and the influence of one man of faith—Abraham. Throughout his life this one man would travel from Ur of the Chaldees into Egypt and thereby influence both these major cultures with the faith of the true and living God. Other civilizations would have less access to this trade route through Canaan and thus would have far less opportunity to come into contact with the oracles of Yahweh God.

Descending into Deep Darkness

No doubt, some little memory of the Creator, the all-powerful, sovereign God over heaven and earth continued to exist in the hearts and minds of Noah's descendants. Yet over the centuries the god of this world blinded the eyes of all cultures around the world. Indeed, as the Apostle Paul put it, the nations "walked according to the course of this world, according to the prince of the power of the air, the spirit that works in the children of disobedience" (Eph. 2:2).

Shang Dynasty Oracle Bone, c. AD 1200

Charles Darwin and other unbelieving evolutionists would later teach that mankind arose from an animal state and developed primitive polytheism. After that, he proceeded to a more "civilized" monotheism, until he realized himself to be a god, and finally arrived at a "superior" humanism. Nothing could be further from the truth. Actually, man started out with a right conception of the true and living God and then degenerated as he abandoned the revelation that had come to Adam and Noah.

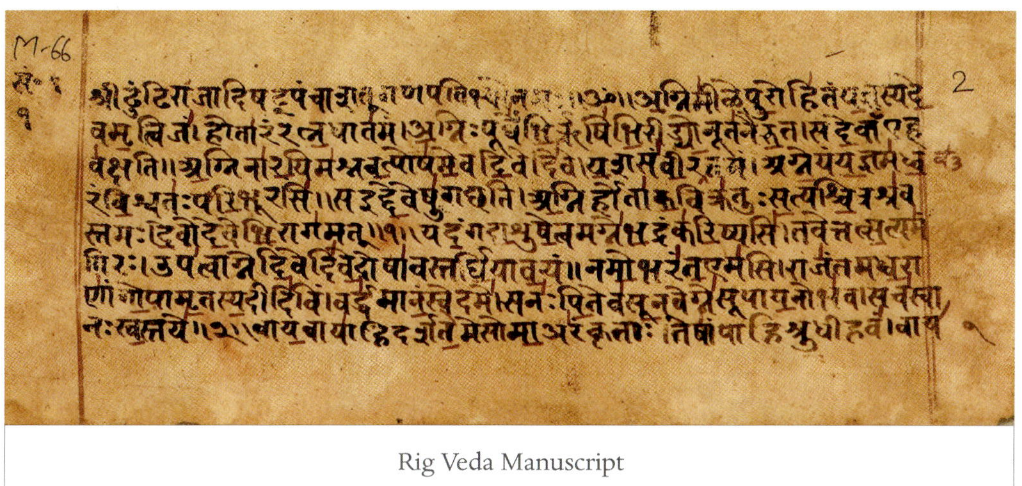

Rig Veda Manuscript

Some of the oldest Chinese writings available today come from the "Oracle Bones" dated around 1200 BC, during the Shang Dynasty. Here we find the first reference to God in pagan literature, and He is presented as One. The character used for "God," composed of several sub-pictographs, is translated: "The one above to whom the burning faggot of wood is offered" or "the one who is worshiped by sacrifice."[1] Another ancient Chinese inscription reads: "Inquire about God ordering rain; there will not be full harvest."[2]

Also, some have pointed out that the earliest Hindu writings, dating from 1500-1200 BC, present a monotheistic conception of God. From the Rig Veda, Book 1, we read, "They call him Indra, Mythra, Varunna, Agnis, that which is One, the Wise name by different terms."[3]

Numerous scholars believe that even the Egyptian nation began as a monotheistic society. Archaeologist Sir Flinders Petrie noted of Egypt and other ancient civilizations: "Wherever we can trace back polytheism to its earliest stages, we find that it results from combinations of monotheism."[4]

It wasn't long, however, before all nations descended into polytheism (the worship of many gods). Man degraded himself by worshiping the sun, moon, stars, earth, animals, humans, and make-believe gods that usually turned out to look more like demons than humans.

Karnak Temple in Egypt

Moreover, pagan peoples were often pantheists, who believed that god is in all. They did not distinguish between God, man, and other things. They attributed a soul to everything and claimed that a personality or life was in everything around them.

Sinful man looks around for something that has an appearance of permanence, such as a mountain, the sun, or the moon, and he worships that. The ancient Gauls (who lived in what is now France) worshiped trees and the Druid priests considered the mistletoe of the oak tree to be sacred. The pagans worshiped the earth itself as a goddess, giving it such names as Ishtar, Cybele, Ceres, Aphrodite, and Venus. Whenever the earth quaked, the Samoan islanders would gnaw the ground and plead with the god Mafuie to stop the shaking.

Man also began to worship himself, especially his kings, emperors, and governments. The Japanese emperor was regarded as a "descendant" of the gods. The Egyptian Pharaoh was considered the incarnation of a god named Horus who was supposed to have been the son of Osiris (the god of the afterlife).

Buddhist Temple

Beginning with the Zhou and Qin dynasties from 1046 BC through 206 BC, Chinese emperors referred to themselves as "the sons of heaven." The Qin dynasty would become the most despotic empire of the ancient world.

As already mentioned, the spirits of dead men were reverenced and worshiped as if they possessed some power over the earth. For the Egyptians, Greeks, Romans, Chinese, and Japanese, this institutionalized a respect for the social order—such that honor for the elders of the community helped to preserve their civilizations. Although God has hardwired a blessing to families and communities that honor parents and grandparents, these societies took the principle too far when they worshiped the dead spirits of departed relatives.

The pagan tribes of the world truly came under the absolute "control of the wicked one" (1 John 5:19). Throughout recorded history demons demonstrated supernatural activity through men such as tribal witchdoctors or the magicians of Egypt (Ex. 7:10-13). By inspiring awe among the populace, such demonic activity instilled a fearful respect for magic and the demon "gods." Among the Buddhists and Hindus, a little levitation or treading over a few coals is usually enough to keep the masses believing in demonic power (instead of fearing the true and living God who made heaven and earth). The witchdoctors would cast spells over people—or, more accurately, they would appeal to demons to injure or kill people. The Australian Aborigines thought these witchdoctors could kill a person at a hundred miles' distance. This kept native populations in abject fear of the evil, demonic world, instead of worshiping the true and living, sovereign God over all.

Writing his epistle to the Romans around AD 60, the Apostle Paul explains the horrible state of the pagan tribes as they turned against God:

> *. . . because, although they knew God, they did not glorify Him as God, nor were thankful, but became futile in their thoughts, and their foolish hearts were darkened. Professing to be wise, they became fools, and changed the glory of the incorruptible God into an image made like corruptible man—and birds and four-*

Fragment from the Temple of Inanna

footed animals and creeping things. Therefore God also gave them up to uncleanness, in the lusts of their hearts, to dishonor their bodies among themselves, who exchanged the truth of God for the lie, and worshiped and served the creature rather than the Creator, who is blessed forever. Amen. (Romans 1:21-25)

Pagan Worship

Human behavior reaches its lowest levels of sin and shame in pagan forms of worship practiced among primitive tribes. The demon gods worshiped by these peoples encouraged them to the most degrading activities imaginable. A missionary to Africa, H. Rowley, reported on the Bantu tribe's worship: "It is impossible to witness them without being ashamed. . . any visitor attending the festival is encouraged to indulge in licentiousness."[5] Babylonian pagan worship included temple prostitution until AD 325 when Constantine put an end to it. This same kind of demonically inspired "religious" practice continued until AD 1988 in southern India when the government banned it—although it still continues illegally in some parts of the country.[6]

Perverted forms of idolatrous worship began very early, dating to just 150 years after the flood. As early as 2360 BC, Sargon's mother was a priestess in the temple of Inanna, the goddess of sexual sin. The religious state would employ male priests who violated Deuteronomy 22:5 and 1 Corinthians 6:9 in their service in the temple.

Human sacrifice was extremely common in the pagan world—in the words of one historian, the practice "seems to have been honored at some time or another by almost every people."[7] The Phoenicians, the Canaanites, the Druids, the Etruscans, and the Carthaginians took part in it. In the Americas, the practice flourished among the North American Pawnee, Taensa, and Natchez tribes, and the South American Aztecs, Incas, and Mayans. When Julius Caesar fought the Gallic Wars around 58 BC, he encountered the Celt's sacrifice of "Wicker Man." The religious practice involved a gigantic wooden man filled with live humans which was set aflame as a sacrifice to the gods. Recently, archaeologists have uncovered evidence of child sacrifice among the Thracians (in modern-day Bulgaria) dating from the 9th century BC.

King Pomare of Tahiti

When missionaries finally arrived on the Pacific island of Tahiti in 1797, after Satan had ruled there for a millennium or more, they found human sacrifice to be a common occurrence. King Pomare boasted of offering some 2,000 of such sacrifices.[8] In almost all cases, the worshipers were seeking good crop yields and material prosperity. From the earliest times, sinful man has been quick to abandon natural affection and murder his own children if he thinks he can get more material prosperity for himself. Similarly, in the modern world, parents do not hesitate to kill their own children in the womb if they believe the children will be too expensive or inconvenient for them.

Believing they would receive the life force or the powers of whatever creature they ate, pagans were particularly drawn to consuming the blood and body of whatever was sacrificed to the gods. Scripture strictly rejected this pagan tendency. To eat the blood would desecrate the life God created.

> *Whatever man of the children of Israel, or of the strangers who dwell among you, who hunts and catches any animal or bird that may be eaten, he shall pour out its blood and cover it with dust; for it is the life of all flesh. Its blood sustains its life. Therefore I said to the children of Israel, "You shall not eat the blood of*

any flesh, for the life of all flesh is its blood. Whoever eats it shall be cut off." (Leviticus 17:13-14)

The idolatrous worship of pagan peoples inevitably tended towards bowing before images and revering inanimate statues and pictures. In Exodus 20 this bowing down before idols was strictly forbidden by the true and living God:

You shall not make for yourself a carved image—any likeness of anything that is in heaven above, or that is in the earth beneath, or that is in the water under the earth; you shall not bow down to them nor serve them. For I, the LORD your God, am a jealous God, visiting the iniquity of the fathers upon the children to the third and fourth generations of those who hate Me, but showing mercy to thousands, to those who love Me and keep My commandments. (Exodus 20:4-6)

Pagan man also turned to fetishes in hopes that these objects would themselves offer power, protection, or "good luck." Such beliefs attributed divine characteristics to that which is not God. All such superstition is part of man's revolt against the true God and is a blind, idolatrous, foolish acceptance of false deities. Forsaking the only true God, man invents gods for himself. Because these gods are constructed by his own imagination, they are by necessity of far less value than man himself.

O LORD, my strength and my fortress,
My refuge in the day of affliction,
The Gentiles shall come to You
From the ends of the earth and say,
"Surely our fathers have inherited lies,
Worthlessness and unprofitable things."
Will a man make gods for himself,
Which are not gods?
"Therefore behold, I will this once cause them to know,
I will cause them to know
My hand and My might;
And they shall know that My name is the LORD." (Jeremiah 16:19-21)

Man has also always sought ways to deal with his sense of guilt and contamination arising from sin. It is impossible for men and women who have sinned before God to deny their guilt. Thus, extreme standards for ceremonial cleanliness were established in many cultures around the world. Although Old Testament Israel was held to a certain standard of external, ceremonial cleanliness, Scripture clearly notes that these things were never sufficient to purify the heart (Proverbs 20:9; Hebrews 9:13-14). Polynesian peoples would forbid touching certain foods and things related to the dead, sometimes on pain of death. Women were treated as unclean by many cultures, particularly at certain times of the month. The Persians treated nail clippings and hair clippings as unclean. They would avoid eating or drinking anything on the street and would never blow their noses in public. The Zoroastrian holy book fills page after page with detailed requirements of various ceremonial cleansings. The Japanese Shinto religion requires purification with *temizu* (pure water), *haraigushi* (a purification wand waved by a priest), and *shubatsu* (salt).

To this day, Hindus place great importance on ritual baths, bathing in sacred (usually filthy) rivers, ritual cleansing with smoke (*dhupa*), light (*dipam*), and water (*achamanam*). They sprinkle with ritual water (*abhisheka*) and further purify to ward off the evil eye. They are fastidious about their sacraments (*Samskaras*), sacrificial ceremonies (*homas* and *yajnas*), expiation ceremonies (*prayascitta*), wearing of charms, amulets, and sacred objects, and abstaining from certain foods (*upavasa*).

These laws are external attempts to cleanse guilty consciences and befouled hearts—but it is all in vain. The Apostle Paul speaks of these futile systems of religion in Colossians 2:

> *Therefore, if you died with Christ from the basic principles of the world, why, as though living in the world, do you subject yourselves to regulations—"Do not touch, do not taste, do not handle," which all concern things which perish with the using—according to the commandments and doctrines of men? These things indeed have an appearance of wisdom in self-imposed religion, false humility, and neglect of the body, but are of no value against the indulgence of the flesh. (Colossians 2:20-23)*

Gross Immorality among the Nations

Marco Polo (1254-1324)

Before Jesus Christ came to redeem, to sanctify, and to restore, and to pour out His Spirit upon the nations, the moral flimsiness of mankind was readily apparent throughout the world. Divorce was provided for the Old Testament Jews because of the "hardness of their hearts" (Matt. 19:8). When Marco Polo encountered the Uyghur tribe in modern-day western China, he found a typical example of the state of marriage in the pagan world. He wrote that, "If a married man goes to a distance from home to be absent twenty days, his wife has a right, if she is so inclined, to take another husband. . ."[9] Fraternal polyandry was common in Tibet. Among the Baila tribe (in modern-day Zambia), young women in their early 20s frequently had "four or five husbands, all still living."[10] Polygamy marked most pagan nations. Young people were encouraged to commit sexual sin in tribes all over the world, including the Papuans of New Guinea, the Soyots of Siberia, the Igorots of the Philippines, the Kaffirs of Africa, the tribes of Uganda and Niger, and the Pacific Islanders. Cherokee men would in some cases exchange their wives three to four times a year. As the 19th century minister John Angell James once wrote: "Woman's virtue, dignity, honor, and happiness are nowhere safe but under the protection of the Word of God."[11]

Without the example and the Spirit of Christ, protection of the weak was never much of a value among the pagan tribes. Abortion and infanticide (the killing of a newborn child) was common almost everywhere. The Maori tribes in New Zealand used herbs to induce abortion. In many primitive tribes, infanticide was permitted for deformed children (or if the mother died giving birth). Strange superstitions also resulted in much child murder. For example, the Kamchadal tribe in Siberia would kill babies born in bad weather, and African tribes in Madagascar would put to death children born in March or April. Nomadic tribes were especially given to infanticide. Some of the Chaco Indian tribes would allow each family only one child every seven years. Half of the children born to the Bangarang tribe in northern Australia were killed.[12] Considered unlucky and dangerous to society, newborn twins were very often killed by the Bantu tribe in southern Africa and the Nuer tribe in southern Sudan.[13]

> *And even as they did not like to retain God in their knowledge, God gave them over to a debased mind, to do those things which are not fitting; being filled with all unrighteousness, sexual immorality, wickedness, covetousness, maliciousness; full of envy, murder, strife, deceit, evil-mindedness; they are whisperers, backbiters, haters of God, violent, proud, boasters, inventors of evil things, disobedient to parents, undiscerning, untrustworthy, unloving, unforgiving, unmerciful; who, knowing the righteous judgment of God, that those who practice such things are deserving of death, not only do the same but also approve of those who practice them. (Romans 1:28-32)*

Madagascar

Pagan tribes far separated from God's revelation and His people often reverted to cannibalism or the consumption of human flesh. Ancient remains of cannibalized humans have been discovered from extinct tribes once living in Spain, Belgium, and France.[14] The farthest distributed tribes in West and Central Africa, Melanesia (especially Fiji), Australia, New Zealand, New Guinea, Polynesia, Sumatra, and North and South America all practiced cannibalism. The Anasazi cliff dwellers (who lived in what is now the southwestern United States) were also cannibalistic. Judging from the reports of Christian missionaries who finally arrived with the Gospel of the Lord Jesus Christ in AD 1838, the Fijians might have been the worst example of this terrible practice. To the horror of the missionaries, cannibal sacrifices were made directly in front of the mission house. According to one estimate, two-thirds of all of the children born on Fiji were cannibalized, and the aged did not fare any better, often being killed and eaten by their own children.[15]

Such was the state of affairs in a world left to the devil's control. There seemed to be no respite from a continual state of sin and degradation. Sexual sin and child killing destroyed all trust and natural love in human relationships. The constant

Fiji

disintegration of family life undermined any possibility of the advancement of civilization. Without Christ, life on this earth continued year in and year out in a state of dread fear, violence, and instability, with a constant disregard for and destruction of human life and society.

Since the earliest days pagan tribes have also been committed to tattooing and body mutilation. In 1991 an ice-encased mummy was found in the Otztal Alps on the border of modern-day Italy and Austria. It was dated to the 31st century BC, more likely from the earliest days following the flood. Despite its age, the body was well preserved, and researchers found it covered with sixty-one tattoos. As explorers from Europe traveled into distant corners of the globe, they found tattooing common among Native Americans, indigenous Filipinos, and Pacific Islanders. With few exceptions, the more a society departed from the biblical heritage, the higher the frequency of this tattooing and body mutilation. The Abeokuta tribe (in modern-day Nigeria) would cut themselves to create scars that resembled lizards and alligators.

> *You shall not make any cuttings in your flesh for the dead, nor tattoo any marks on you: I am the LORD. Do not prostitute your daughter, to cause her to be a harlot, lest the land fall into harlotry, and the land become full of wickedness. (Leviticus 19:28-29)*

Tribes occasionally fell into the worst forms of sexuality, as enumerated in chapters 18 and 20 of Leviticus, as well as in Romans 1. The Central American Aztec priests (who sacrificed humans) also engaged in the practice of homosexuality, as did the Calusa Tribe in southern Florida. On rare occasions Pacific Islanders descended to these depths of destructive sexual perversion, as in the case of a Tahitian king in the early 19th century.[16] In the providence of God, both the Aztecs and the Calusa Tribe were quickly conquered by other nations. However, many of these degraded practices have returned to the post-Christian world of the 21st century.

> *For this reason God gave them up to vile passions. For even their women exchanged the natural use for what is against nature. Likewise also the men, leaving the natural use of the woman, burned in their lust for one another, men with men committing what is shameful, and receiving in themselves the penalty of their error which was due. (Romans 1:26-27)*

Moral Codes of the Larger Civilizations and Empires

Tablet Containing *Code of Hammurabi*

> *Do you not know that the unrighteous will not inherit the kingdom of God? Do not be deceived. Neither fornicators, nor idolaters, nor adulterers, nor homosexuals, nor sodomites, nor thieves, nor covetous, nor drunkards, nor revilers, nor extortioners will inherit the kingdom of God. And such were some of you. But you were washed, but you were sanctified, but you were justified in the name of the Lord Jesus and by the Spirit of our God. (1 Corinthians 6:9-11)*

Certainly, some civilizations lasted longer than others. Not all tribes were as morally degraded as others in various times and places throughout ancient history. By God's common grace, some societies were preserved because they maintained stricter moral codes and better social systems—especially respecting the integrity of marriage and the family. The more degraded tended to disappear more quickly. However, even the larger and more permanent civilizations would eventually degrade and then collapse. Inevitably, the time would always come when "a tribe would be wiped off its ice field, and the lights would go out in Rome."[17]

Although still a pagan nation, the Babylonians strictly forbade adultery. The famous *Code of Hammurabi* (1754 BC) required the death penalty for men and women caught in adultery. The Persians required the death penalty for the crimes of homosexuality, murder, and treason.[18] The sacred writings of the Zoroastrians, known as the *Avesta*, judged the sin of homosexuality to be so wicked that they called it "the deed for which there is no forgiveness."[19] The Avestan code also strictly forbade prostitution. Abortion was considered a worse crime than adultery by the Persians and was punishable by death.[20] Thankfully, the Word of the true God provides a way of forgiveness for these sins through Jesus Christ (1 Cor. 6:9-11).

Darius I (522-486 BC)

The Brutal World Before Christ

Before Jesus came, the great empires of antiquity were quite well-practiced in torture and brutality. Dictators ruled by fear, and senseless destruction of human life was common. Darius I boasted of his actions against a man named Fravartish, whom he mutilated and crucified.[21] The king's writings indicate that he was proud of his vile accomplishments. Like the Romans that came after them, the Assyrians were infamous for torturing captives, flaying men alive, and blinding children before the eyes of their parents.[22] King Ashurbanipal of Assyria (mentioned in Ezra 4:10) boasted of burning "three thousand captives with fire."[23] Reading these accounts, it appears the more torturous and brutal, the more the kings felt vindicated by the gods and the more they gained the right to rule. No concept of decency, mercy, or human rights appeared to exist in these men's minds. As the "great men" and tyrannical kings styled themselves as gods, they would take on the attitude of Lamech in Genesis 4:

> *Then Lamech said to his wives:*
> *"Adah and Zillah, hear my voice;*
> *Wives of Lamech, listen to my speech!*

For I have killed a man for wounding me,
Even a young man for hurting me.
If Cain shall be avenged sevenfold,
Then Lamech seventy-sevenfold." (Genesis 4:23-25)

Treatment of the Elderly

You shall not murder. (Exodus 20:13)

Before Christ came, the treatment of the elderly was similarly terrible. The Chinook Indians abandoned their elderly who could no longer hunt.[24] With the Inuit in northern Canada, the elderly were encouraged to commit suicide. These events were often advertised and celebrated. The Greeks were particularly enthusiastic about "euthanasia," from whom we borrow the word, directly translated "the good death." Aelius Theon, a Greek orator living around the time of the Apostle Paul, described the blessings of life as including: "education, friendship, respect, political position, richness, being blessed with children, and . . . *euthanasia.*"[25]

Suicide was regarded as honorable by the Inuit and the Japanese. In one famous historical account, three Japanese brothers—a 24-year-old, a 17-year-old, and an 8-year-old—are ordered to commit suicide by the tyrannical shogun Iyeyasu. The three obeyed and thus became folk heroes in Japan. That nation's suicide rate is still among the highest in the world.[26]

Treatment of Women in the Darkness Before Christ

Husbands, likewise, dwell with them with understanding, giving honor to the wife, as to the weaker vessel, and as being heirs together of the grace of life, that your prayers may not be hindered. (1 Peter 3:7)

One of the most distinguishing marks of a pre-Christ society is its treatment of women. When Meriwether Lewis encountered the Shoshone Indian tribe on the explorers' trek across America in 1805, he recorded that "the man is the sole

Widow-Burning (Sati)

proprietor of his wives and daughters, and can barter or dispose of either as he thinks proper."[27] Women were required to perform most of the work while "the man does little else except attend his horses, hunt, and fish."[28] Lewis noted that the men would rent out their wives for a night or two for financial gain. The Chinookan men would "prostitute their daughters for a fishing hook,"[29] in violation of Leviticus 19:29. One could hardly think of a more degraded manner of treating women.

The Code of Manu from India (dating from the 3rd century BC) states that "A faithful wife must serve . . . her lord as if he were a god."[30] To this day, women in some parts of India and Nepal are forbidden to eat until after the men have eaten.

The tradition of burning widows on the funeral pyre of their husbands dates back millennia. The ancient Scythians (in modern-day Ukraine) and Thracians (in modern-day Bulgaria) practiced this horrible rite. The pagan mind apparently considered that the husband would need a wife to care for him in the afterworld. The Indonesians in Bali and the Fijians were also known to have participated in this wicked practice. A missionary report from India counted 600 instances of widow-burning in one province each year through the 1820s. The British banned the practice in 1829 by Regulation XVII. Missionary William Carey was asked to translate the English legislation on a Sunday morning. His response came: "'No church for me to-day. . . .If I delay an hour to translate and publish this, many a widow's life may be sacrificed,' he said. By evening the task was finished."[31]

Therefore circumcise the foreskin of your heart, and be stiff-necked no longer. For the LORD your God is God of gods and Lord of lords, the great God, mighty and awesome, who shows no partiality nor takes a bribe. He administers justice for the fatherless and the widow, and loves the stranger, giving him food and clothing. (Deuteronomy 10:16-18)

In stark contrast with the pagan laws and traditions of the ancient world, God's law given to Israel provided a just standard to protect women and the weaker members of society, including the disabled, the widow, and the orphan (Leviticus 19:14; Deuteronomy 24:17; 27:19). When Jesus came, He modeled this standard by always treating women with compassion, mercy, and grace. A new day dawned with the coming of the Savior of the world.

> *When Jesus had raised Himself up and saw no one but the woman, He said to her, "Woman, where are those accusers of yours? Has no one condemned you?"*
>
> *She said, "No one, Lord."*
>
> *And Jesus said to her, "Neither do I condemn you; go and sin no more." (John 8:10-11)*

Postscript

After Jesus Christ came and died on the cross around AD 33, the world would never be the same. While not every person in the world would follow Christ, He came to change lives in the most fundamental way. He came to make a new creation, where the "old things would pass away and all things would become new" (2 Corinthians 5:17). He called his followers "the salt of the earth" and the "light of the world" because they would have a preserving and a transforming effect on the world (Matthew 5:13-16).

Transparency International conducts its Corruptions Perception Index annually, surveying over one hundred nations on matters concerning honesty and integrity in government and trade. Cross referencing the sixteen least corrupt nations on the list with the predominant religion of each country, the results show that religion or worldview truly matters. Of the sixteen least corrupt nations in the world, fourteen were predominantly Protestant nations and two were Buddhist nations with strong influence from the West. Of the twenty-one most corrupt nations in the world, seven were Roman Catholic, five were Muslim, five were Animist, and four were communist (or post-Christian and atheistic) or ex-communist nations.[32]

These are good indications as to the influence of God's people in the far off regions of the world, once terribly corrupted by sin and held in bondage by the devil.

The following table shows the improvement of prosperity for a nation as the corruption rating decreases. As the influence of Christianity penetrates the nation, there is also some indication of the improvement on corruption ratings, freedom ratings, and the blessing of prosperity upon the nation. This is especially evident in Africa and the South Pacific.

Nation	Corruption [33] Rating	Freedom [34] Rating	Prosperity [35] Rating	Percent [36] Christian
South America				
Uruguay	#23	#40	#47	10% Protestant
Chile	#27	#18	#51	15.5% Protestant
Costa Rica	#38	#61	#58	25% Protestant
Argentina	#85	#148	#59	10% Protestant
Colombia	#99	n/a	#85	10% Protestant
Brazil	#105	#150	#73	23% Protestant
Ecuador	#114	#170	#87	10% Protestant
Mexico	#138	#66	#72	10% Protestant
Venezuela	#168	#179	#122	10% Protestant
Africa				
Botswana	#34	#36	#76	66% Protestant
Namibia	#52	#99	#94	65% Protestant
South Africa	#73	#102	#91	68% Protestant
Uganda	#149	#95	#179	44% Protestant
Kenya	#144	#130	#141	47% Protestant
Sudan	#172	#166	#171	1.5% Christian
Somalia	#180	n/a	#177	0%
South Pacific				
Vanuatu	#64	#116	#126	70% Protestant
Solomon Islands	#70	#133	#142	73% Protestant
Indonesia	#89	#56	#118	7% Protestant
Philippines	#99	#70	#121	3% Protestant

Timeline Review

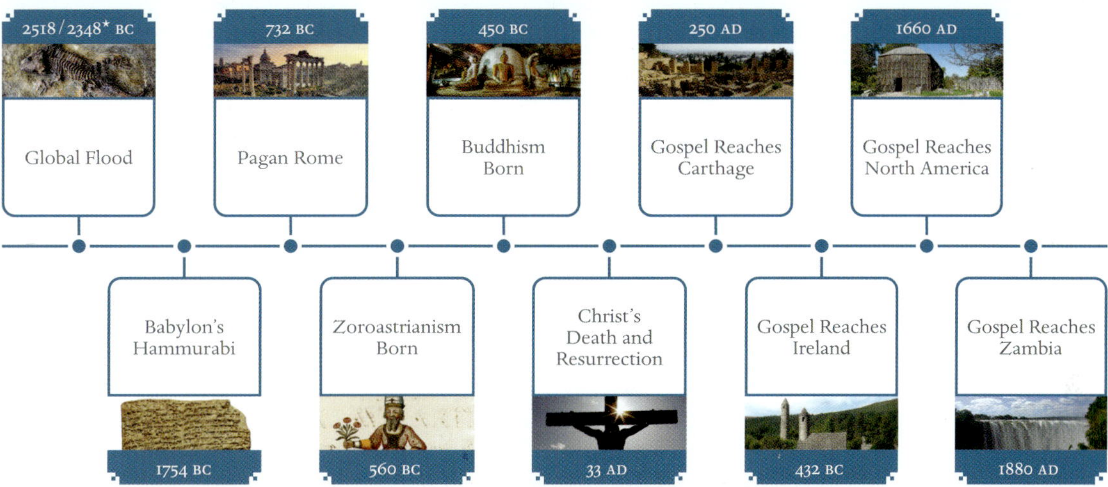

Chapter II Prayer

Our Father in Heaven,

Indeed, the lands that lay in darkness have seen a great light! We are thankful this day for the billions of lives that have been touched by the coming of our Lord and Savior Jesus Christ. What darkness dominated before the coming of your Son! There is no other Name by which we can be saved from our sin, from the captivity of the devil, and from the fear of death. What contrast we have seen between the lands that lay in darkness and this great Kingdom of light! May this kingdom of righteousness, truth, and life prevail today and forever.

Amen.

CHAPTER III

Babel and the Futility of the Kingdoms of Men

Cush begot Nimrod; he began to be a mighty one on the earth. He was a mighty hunter before the LORD; therefore it is said, "Like Nimrod the mighty hunter before the LORD." And the beginning of his kingdom was Babel, Erech, Accad, and Calneh, in the land of Shinar. (Genesis 10:8-10)

Genesis 10 presents Ham's grandson Nimrod as the powerful visionary behind the early empires formed in the Mesopotamian valley. These include Uruk, Babel, and Akkad, as mentioned in the text. Later in the Scriptural narrative we learn that Abraham came from Ur of the Chaldees, an indication that at least some of Shem's descendants started in the same place as Ham's descendants. Considering the longevities of Shem's line, Nimrod would probably have been born about seventy years after the flood (around 2448 BC) and he could have lived about 400 years. Nimrod launched the first major post-flood attempt to centralize power and build a totalitarian empire.

The Hebrew of Genesis 10:9 is better translated, "He [Nimrod] was a mighty hunter in the face of the LORD." Instead of humbling himself in the presence of the Lord, Nimrod lifted himself up against the Lord as if he were competing with

God. He was the first of the great tyrants of the post-flood world who followed in the footsteps of the pre-flood Nephilim.

The Tower of Babel (2418 BC)

Nimrod's greatest claim to fame was his construction of the Tower of Babel. Shem's great-grandson Peleg was born about 100 years after the flood, and Scripture points out that the dividing of the earth began around the time of his birth (Gen. 10:25). This puts the construction of the Tower of Babel around 2418 BC[1], well within the lifetime of Nimrod, who no doubt was the mastermind behind the city and the tower.

If the flood occurred in the year 2518 BC, the inhabitants of the world could have numbered about 32,000 by 2418 BC and 900,000 by 2318 BC. This assumes that each family had an average of 10.7 children (a number based on the biblical records for Shem, Ham, and Japheth) and that three additional generations would have appeared within 100 years. Such estimates for birth rate and population increase are reasonable considering that men and women continued to live 300-400-year lifespans for several generations after the flood. Suffice it to say that there would have been enough people to build a very large tower and a city by the year 2418 BC.

Some mystery surrounds the location of the original Tower of Babel. Most likely it was built somewhere between modern Syria in the north and the Persian Gulf in the south—along the Mesopotamian valley. There is no archaeological record of the tower, and it is likely that the dispersion of the peoples happened sometime before the reign of King Urukagina and the beginning of the Akkadian empire. It is also possible that the Tower of Babel was built in the far north towards Syria at the same time that the Akkadian empire was developing. This may be why there is no record of the Tower of Babel in Akkadian history. Regardless of where it happened, it is clear from the biblical text that man was building this tower out of a spirit of pride and rebellion against the Lord. This spirit continued in the hearts of countless empire builders for thousands of years of world history.

> *Now the whole earth had one language and one speech. And it came to pass, as they journeyed from the east, that they found a plain in the land of Shinar, and they dwelt there. Then they said to one another, "Come, let us make bricks and bake them thoroughly." They had brick for stone, and they had asphalt for mortar.*

> *And they said, "Come, let us build ourselves a city, and a tower whose top is in the heavens; let us make a name for ourselves, lest we be scattered abroad over the face of the whole earth." But the LORD came down to see the city and the tower which the sons of men had built. And the LORD said, "Indeed the people are one and they all have one language, and this is what they begin to do; now nothing that they propose to do will be withheld from them. Come, let Us go down and there confuse their language, that they may not understand one another's speech." So the LORD scattered them abroad from there over the face of all the earth, and they ceased building the city. Therefore its name is called Babel, because there the LORD confused the language of all the earth; and from there the LORD scattered them abroad over the face of all the earth.* (Genesis 11:1-9)

This desire to "make a name" for themselves forms the basis of the humanist religious worldview that continues to control many nations to this day. Natural man always seeks to glorify himself, largely by centralizing power, economic wealth, and opportunity for fame through a single city or an institution.

Modern-Day Syria (a Possible Location of the Tower of Babel)

This tower was representative of man's pride. Man in his sin has within himself that insatiable desire to become as god, and to displace God or the gods of his imagination. Such thinking is nothing less than arrogant rebellion, for natural man has no right to ascend to God or to displace God. The unholy cannot approach the holy, nor should the mortal and finite pretend to be otherwise. However, in Jesus Christ, God reverses this wrongheaded approach to life. Instead of man ascending to God, here God descended to man. Instead of taking His place at the highest position, Jesus was born in a stable and then He was crucified on a cross. More than that, He took upon Himself human nature in order that He would restore a right relationship between God and man.

> *Let this mind be in you which was also in Christ Jesus, who, being in the form of God, did not consider it robbery to be equal with God, but made Himself of no reputation, taking the form of a bondservant, and coming in the likeness of men. And being found in appearance as a man, He humbled Himself and became obedient to the point of death, even the death of the cross.* (Philippians 2:5-8)

Example of a Ziggurat

Chichen Itza
Mayan Temple in Mexico

Not surprisingly, for thousands of years after Babel, stepped ziggurats and pyramids were built in many empires around the world. Yet, this does demonstrate how man's quest for greatness should result in the dedication of so much time and resources placed in constructing something so impractical, so lacking in beauty, and wasteful. The Mayans, Aztecs, Incas, Egyptians, Sumerians, Elamites, Nubians, Chinese, Indians, Austronesians (Indonesia), and Babylonians all built pyramids and ziggurats from the 24th century BC until after the coming of Christ, when God descended to man.

Yet, these constructions were not simple to build. The design and technology used to assemble the structures must have been spread around the world after the diaspora of Babel. The tower began with Nimrod, and before long the Egyptians and Babylonians also began building these towers. The Egyptians built 135 of them, the tallest of which is 481 feet high. The Great Pyramid of Giza would remain the tallest structure in the world for over three millennia (until AD 1311). By the 14th century AD, man once again began his attempt to build big towers and large empires.

The pride of Nebuchadnezzar II is well documented in the Book of Daniel. In fact, the arrogance of this king was so great that God humbled him to eat grass like an ox for a time (Daniel 4). In 1917 an archaeologist named Robert Coldeway uncovered an ancient stele (stone slab) depicting the Etemenanki Ziggurat built to a height of about 300 feet. Next to a sketch of the seven-step tower is a picture of Nebuchadnezzar with an inscription proudly declaring that he made the tower "a wonder to the people of the world. . . . I raised its top to the heavens."[2] On a cylinder found under the tower in the 1880s was another inscription by Nebuchadnezzar's successor Nabopolassar that reads, "I made it an object fitting for wonder, just as it was in former times."[3] Biblical scholars find this to be a possible reference to the original Tower of Babel. Certainly, the spirit of the original Babel was carried on in the projects of this Babylonian king.

This biblical account of the Tower of Babel explains the reason for the 7,111 different spoken languages existing in the world today. It also explains the reason for varying cultures, civil governments, and people groups. The isolation of each people group and the development of unique languages inevitably produced varying cultures. This usually created cultural pride and national or tribal elitism as well as a strong desire to resist amalgamation and centralization of power. A people accustomed to a certain form of dress, food, language, and laws would not want to blend its traditions with those of other peoples.

By the division of the nations at Babel, our sovereign Creator God clearly showed that He does not want a centralized civil government among sinful humans. Why would He oppose such a concentration of power? What might sinful man do with such power? The Nephilim of the pre-diluvian world had already proven what sort of violence and destruction they could bring upon the world. So, to weaken the impulse for world government somewhat, God divided the languages and dispersed the people groups. If the tribes had stayed in close proximity, no doubt there would have been much civil war and mass killing. In general, the sons of Japheth scattered north and east into Europe and Asia. The sons of Ham moved into Africa and Canaan, and the sons of Shem settled in the Middle East.

As the descendants of Noah scattered, Scripture provides us with some idea of the nations they formed:

Name	Area Settled
Ham's Sons	
Mizraim	Egypt
Cush	Sudan, Ethiopia
Put	Libya, Mauritania
Canaan	Canaan (Hivites, Jebusites, Arvadites, Girgashites, Amorites, etc.)
Shem's Sons	
Elam	Arabia
Asshur	Assyria
Lud	Lydia (modern-day Turkey)
Aram	Armenia, Mesopotamia, Syria
Arphaxad	Mesopotamia, Syria, Canaan
Japheth's Sons	
Javan	Greece, France, Italy, Spain, Portugal
Magog	Scythia, Russia, Bulgaria, Bohemia, Poland, Slovakia, Croatia
Madai	India, Iran (Medes, Persians, Afghans, and Kurds)
Tubal	Georgia, North Turkey
Tiras	Thrace, Germany, Scandinavia, England
Meshech	Russia (Moscow was named after Meshech)
Gomer	China, East Asia

Evidence for the Distribution of Noah's Three Sons

Recently, scientists have studied the DNA of representative populations around the world, and they have grouped them by basic categories and traced their migrations. After analyzing the data, the researchers discover only three main mitochondrial DNA lineages existing in the world population. This is because every person on earth is descended from one of three women (the wives of Shem, Ham, and Japheth). Two of the women appear to be more closely related than the third in the computer analysis performed on human DNA in the present—meaning that one or two of Noah's three sons may have married into the line of Seth, while the other one or two married into the ungodly line.[4]

The True Unified People of God

There is no peace, says my God, for the wicked. (Isaiah 57:21)

Many attempts have been made to restore the unity of a humanist Babel, but all such labor is vain. Throughout history, the nations of the earth have constantly warred against one another. Kingdoms of men come and go. Men build their towers so tall that they fall, and this cycle is repeated again and again. Attempts are made to centralize power, build empires, and unify under a world government. But inevitably, decentralization always follows the centralizing trends. The Babel principle repeats itself throughout world history. Man cannot transcend his cultural differences. He cannot overcome his civil wars, coups, corruption, unfair trade tariffs, covetousness, murder, malice, slander, envy, and pride. His attempts at multiculturalism always result in more disunity and civil war. World unity is impossible with fallen mankind because sin stands in the way. But, more importantly, God stands in the way. God has ordained that mankind's hatred for one another will eventually trump his desire to unify himself under one world government against God Himself. In God's providence, this natural inclination within the heart of mankind works for the benefit of man by precluding a world unified in wickedness.

With the kingdom of Jesus Christ, comes a new Man and a restored unity. The temple He is building has no tower. It is His own body. His kingdom needs no geographical center, for wherever two or three are gathered, there He is in the midst of them (Matthew 18:20). His kingdom restores unity across cultural boundaries. In Christ the middle wall between Jew and Gentile comes crashing down (Ephesians 2:12). With the advent of the kingdom at Pentecost, the believers spoke of the mighty works of God in every foreign language represented by all of the people visiting Jerusalem in 33 AD. Pentecost was the reversal of Babel.

> *When the Day of Pentecost had fully come, they were all with one accord in one place. And suddenly there came a sound from heaven, as of a rushing mighty wind, and it filled the whole house where they were sitting. Then there appeared to them divided tongues, as of fire, and one sat upon each of them. And they were all filled with the Holy Spirit and began to speak with other tongues, as the Spirit gave them utterance. And there were dwelling in Jerusalem Jews, devout men, from every nation under heaven. And when this sound occurred, the multitude came together, and were confused, because everyone heard them speak in his own language. Then they were all amazed and marveled, saying to one another, "Look, are not all these who speak Galileans? And how is it that we hear, each in our own language in which we were born? Parthians and Medes and Elamites, those dwelling in Mesopotamia, Judea and Cappadocia, Pontus and Asia, Phrygia and Pamphylia, Egypt and the parts of Libya adjoining Cyrene, visitors from Rome, both Jews and proselytes, Cretans and Arabs—we hear them speaking in our own tongues the wonderful works of God." (Acts 2:1-11)*

Great Pyramid of Giza

Postscript: Göbekli Tepe (c. 2450 BC)

Exhibit of Göbekli Tepe in Instanbul Airport, Istanbul, Turkey

In 1996, archaeologists uncovered the earth's oldest known stone megaliths in southwestern Turkey near the Syrian border. The site known as Göbekli Tepe contained 200 large stone pillars, some as tall as twenty feet, weighing up to 20,000 pounds. These ancient "high places" for pagan worship would serve as the predecessor for Stonehenge found in Britain and Newgrange in Ireland—dating between 2300 BC and 2400 BC. Genetic testing indicates that early migrations into Britain originated in modern day Turkey, where these first megaliths were built.

Göbekli Tepe could very well have been the pre-Babel cradle of human civilization. Historians are calling this newly discovered archaeological site, the "earliest temple yet discovered." This being the earliest indication of a post-flood human civilization, the technological ability of ancient man to create something this massive has atheistic evolutionists stumped.

Could Göbekli Tepe have been the civilization that built the Tower of Babel? These were the first of Noah's progeny and they had the technology to do it.

Timeline Review

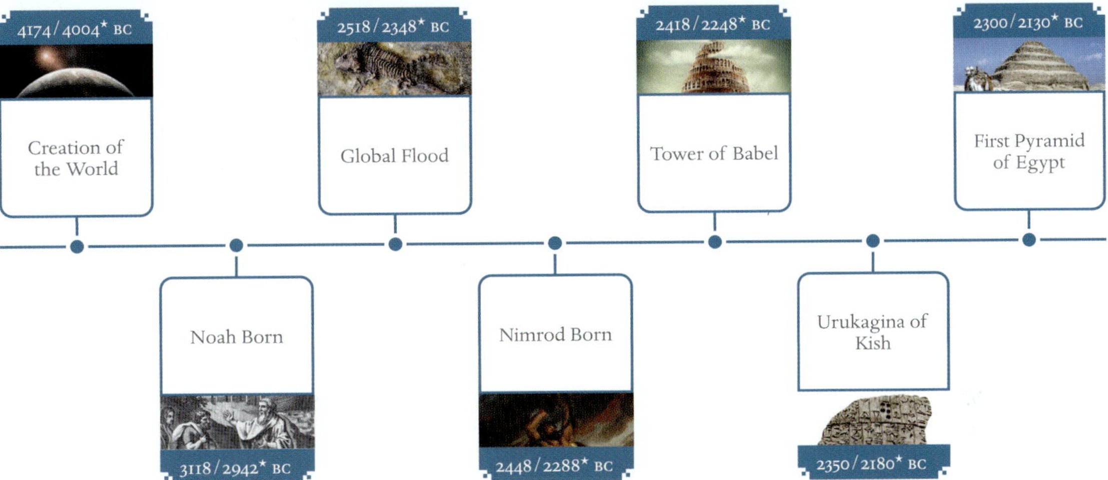

* Date according to Ussher's Chronology which assumes Israelites were in Egypt 215 years.

Chapter III Prayer

Almighty God, Sovereign Lord, and Heavenly Father,

Your works are very great, and we have studied them, and we take great pleasure in them, our God! The great empires of the world are accounted as less than the tiny flecks of dust on the balance in your eyes! Surely, the wrath of man will praise you, and if there is any part of man's evil works that will not give you the glory, you will restrain it. Nothing is out of your control, and we take great comfort in that this day. The proud kingdoms of men will fail, every time. But, today we delight in the kingdom of your Son—a kingdom of meekness, truth, and righteousness. It is a kingdom that serves one another and discovers ultimate peace through the fiercest war—the war on the cross. We delight in a kingdom without borders, a kingdom without towers, a kingdom to be found everywhere around the world today. We praise the Name of Jesus our Lord, and we commit ourselves to His kingdom's interests now. May this kingdom come on earth as it is in heaven.

In the Name of our King and Savior,
Amen.

Euphrates River

CHAPTER IV

First Empires in Mesopotamia (2360-1750 BC)

For thus has the Lord said to me: "Go, set a watchman, Let him declare what he sees." And he saw a chariot with a pair of horsemen, A chariot of donkeys, and a chariot of camels, and he listened earnestly with great care. Then he cried, "A lion, my Lord! I stand continually on the watchtower in the daytime; I have sat at my post every night. And look, here comes a chariot of men with a pair of horsemen!" Then he answered and said, "Babylon is fallen, is fallen! And all the carved images of her gods He has broken to the ground." (Isaiah 21:6-9)

The word that the LORD spoke against Babylon and against the land of the Chaldeans by Jeremiah the prophet. "Declare among the nations, proclaim, and set up a standard; proclaim—do not conceal it—Say, 'Babylon is taken, Bel is shamed. Merodach is broken in pieces; her idols are humiliated, her images are broken in pieces.'" (Jeremiah 50:1-2)

In the language of Scripture Babylon is the name used to best represent the proud city of man, even more so than Egypt, Assyria, or Rome. The declaration of the fall of Babylon comes in Isaiah 21:6-9, Jeremiah 50:1-2, and again in

Revelation 18:3. The fall of the powerful and proud empires of men is inevitable because such empires refuse to worship the true and living God. Or as with the Roman Caesars, they refuse to acknowledge the kingship of the Lord Christ.

The oldest known civilization in the world began in the Mesopotamian valley in modern-day Iraq. The Tigris and Euphrates rivers flow southward through the valley into the Persian Gulf. Importantly, both rivers rise near the mountains of Ararat, where Noah and his family disembarked from the ark. Starting with only eight persons on earth, this was the beginning of a new life for man and a new civilization. Noah's family and their descendants may very well have traveled down these rivers to start life anew in the fruitful Mesopotamian valley not long after the flood.

Three major nations formed in this river valley: the Akkadites to the north (including the city states of Eshnunna, Nippur, and Aggad), the Sumerians to the south (including Kish, Ur, Lagash, and Uruk), and the Elamites to the far southeast near the Persian Gulf (including Susa).

Unbelieving historians theorize that men lived as hunters and nomads prior to the establishment of these civilizations, but no evidence exists for this hypothesis. Smaller tribes who scattered around the world after Babel would certainly have hunted for a time before settling down in certain geographical locations. But these far-off tribes descending from Japheth (or even Shem and Ham) would have existed concurrently with the first civilizations developing in Egypt and Sumeria.

A list of Sumerian kings was produced around 2300-2200 BC (50-250 years after the flood), but the line between myth and history is a little murky in non-biblical ancient historical records. However, the list provides a clear delineation between the kingly dynasties after the worldwide flood and those that existed before the flood. If every king's reign and lifespan were taken into account, this King List would put the flood around 19,000 BC. Both secular and Christian historians find much of this early list unhistorical and mythical.

Nonetheless, Kings Urukagina of Lagash (c. 2350 BC) and Enmebaragesi of Kish (c. 2500 BC) are the first two kings on the list who seem to be substantiated by other records. Enmebaragesi must have been one of the sons or grandsons of Shem, Ham, or Japheth. Urukagina was overthrown by Sargon of Akkad somewhere around 2334 BC. Sargon founded a small Akkadian empire which survived until 2147 BC.

Prior to King Urukagina, the ancient tablet lists four dynasties of Kish, in which the average length of reign decreases quite abruptly following the flood:

First dynasty of Kish → 625-1,200-year rule

Second dynasty of Kish → 81-361-year rule

Third dynasty of Kish → 100-year rule

Fourth dynasty of Kish → 10-30-year rule

A similar pattern is seen in the kings listed in the city states of Ur and Uruk. The excessively long reigns can only be explained by a confusion of myth and history.

However, the sudden decrease of lifespans within this Sumerian King's List closely resembles the longevity decrease following the worldwide flood recorded in the Genesis account of the generations from Noah to Abraham. Also, the authors of this list clearly attempted to recall pre-flood civilizations. The length of these pre-flood kings' reigns are recorded in tens of thousands of years. Obviously, memory concerning the pre-flood world had clouded in the minds of those who wrote up the Sumerian King List.

The Akkadian Empire (c. 2334-2154 BC)

And Babylon, the glory of kingdoms,
The beauty of the Chaldeans' pride,
Will be as when God overthrew Sodom and Gomorrah.
It will never be inhabited,
Nor will it be settled from generation to generation;
Nor will the Arabian pitch tents there,
Nor will the shepherds make their sheepfolds there. (Isaiah 13:19-20)

By the year 2300 BC, the population of the post-flood earth would have totaled about one million (assuming the birth rate provided for Shem, Ham, and Japheth). Once dispersed into Egypt and Mesopotamia, these numbers would have given ample opportunity for the commencement of power struggles, wars, and rudimentary empire building.

Based on the size of the ancient cities discovered by modern archaeologists, Uruk had a population of 10,000 and Akkad a population of 36,000 by the year 2300 BC.[1] If the world population then totaled 1,000,000, it is likely that between 100,000 and 350,000 people then lived in the cradle of the Mesopotamian valley. According to extra-biblical histories, the world's second major empire was the Akkadian (mentioned in Genesis 10:10). Sargon ruled from 2334 BC to 2279 BC, and it is possible he was inspired by the proto-empire builder at Babel. If Nimrod was born in 2448 BC, he would have been 114 years old when Sargon I began his reign.

The connection between Sargon's Akkadian rule and Babel is made by the Chronicle of Early Kings Tablet A. Before the city of Babylon existed, reference

Victory Stele of Sargon

to a Babel appears in the following short excerpt. This portion is known as "the Curse of Akkad." The early Mesopotamians must have recognized the curse that would follow a man who wanted to replicate Nimrod's experiment. Here we read that Sargon took up dirt from the destruction of the first Babel and used it for a second attempt at an empire in the Mesopotamian Valley.

[Sargon] dug up the dirt of the pit of Babylon and
made a counterpart of Babylon next to Agade.
Because the wrong he had done the great lord Marduk became angry and wiped out his family by famine.
From east to west, the subjects rebelled against him
and Marduk afflicted him with insomnia.[2]

Sargon is believed to be a descendant of Shem. Born illegitimately of a temple priestess for Inanna, the goddess of sexual sin, this first of the mighty emperors comes from questionable beginnings. Sargon tells his story on a cuneiform tablet discovered in Nineveh in AD 1867:

My mother was a changeling, my father I knew not,
The brother of my father loved the hills,

My home was in the highlands,
where the herbs grow.
My mother conceived me in secret,
She gave birth to me in concealment.
She set me in a basket of rushes,
She sealed the lid with tar.
She cast me into the river, but it did not rise over me,
The water carried me to Akki, the drawer of water.
He lifted me out as he dipped his jar into the river,
He took me as his son, he raised me,
He made me his gardener.[3]

Image of Ishtar

The heathen goddess, Inanna (or Ishtar) legitimized sexual sin, especially for the women that worked in the temple like Sargon's mother. Often, children conceived outside of marriage as in the case of Sargon would have been aborted or killed on birth. Sargon went on to build temples for this goddess of sexuality in Uruk, Nippur, Lagash, Shuruppak, Zabalam, and Ur. This would institutionalize a perverted sexuality in the Mesopotamian Valley for 2,400 years (until Constantine abolished temple prostitution). Sargon's daughter Enheduanna is known to have written a number of hymns to this abominable idol. The Lord condemns this pagan idolatry involving these "harlots" in Micah 1.

Therefore I will make Samaria a heap of ruins in the field,
Places for planting a vineyard;
I will pour down her stones into the valley,
And I will uncover her foundations.
All her carved images shall be beaten to pieces,
And all her pay as a harlot shall be burned with the fire;

All her idols I will lay desolate,
For she gathered it from the pay of a harlot,
And they shall return to the pay of a harlot. (Micah 1:6-7)

Sadly, the Akkadian Empire engaged in cruel wars in which strong men jockeyed for control of land. Sargon himself fought thirty-four wars over fifty years with an army of 5,400 men, the world's first standing army after the flood. Sargon's empire included Syria and stretched to the Mediterranean Sea. His kingdom provides a breathtaking view of the pride of man. Sargon referred to himself as the "Lord of the Four Quarters (of the Earth)" or "Lord of the universe," ruling "the totality of lands under heaven." His grandson went further and called himself a "god." Fallen mankind often attempts to make himself or the state into a god on earth.

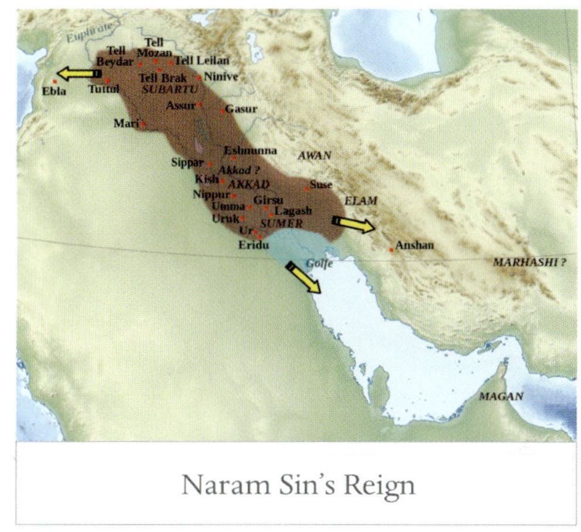

Naram Sin's Reign

Pride goes before destruction, and a haughty spirit before a fall. (Proverbs 16:18)

The Akkadian Empire flourished through the reign of Sargon's grandson Naram-Sin. But his great-grandson Shar-Kali-Sarri lost control of the empire because of constant battles with the Elamites (from the southeast), Amorites (in Syria), and the invading Gutians (from the hills east of Babylon).

Following the collapse of the Akkadian Empire, decentralized city states ruled Mesopotamia rather than a single empire. Secular historians call this a dark age, but it was actually God's way of checking man's sinful tendency to centralize power, create tyrannies, and wage massive wars with large armies. It was the unavoidable collapse that follows pride. Such ages should not be regarded as dark unless one's favored form of civilization is the powerful, tyrannical empire—the view of most secular historians.

Victory Stele of Naram Sin

Abraham was born into this age in Ur of the Chaldees in 2166 BC. At this time the Gutians, wild tribesmen of the Zagros Mountains, were attacking the Akkadians and the Chaldees, whose territories included the City of Ur. Sargon's grandson Naram-Sin lost 90,000 soldiers in battle with these warlike men from the east. The fighting may have led Abraham's father Terah and his family to leave Ur for Haran (Gen. 11:31).

The decentralization would not last. Sargon I would not be forgotten by later empire builders. Babylonian kings would appropriate the title "King of Akkad" for themselves and lord it over others as Sargon had.

> *Now there was also a dispute among [Jesus's disciples], as to which of them should be considered the greatest. And He said to them, "The kings of the Gentiles exercise lordship over them, and those who exercise authority over them are called 'benefactors.' But not so among you; on the contrary, he who is greatest among you, let him be as the younger, and he who governs as he who serves. For who is greater, he who sits at the table, or he who serves? Is it not he who sits at the table? Yet I am among you as the One who serves." (Luke 22:24-27)*

As the great men of the ancient Near East vigorously struggled to build their kingdoms and defend their lands, God chose one man to seed another kingdom which would never pass away.

First Law for Mankind at Creation

Then the LORD God took the man and put him in the garden of Eden to tend and keep it. And the LORD God commanded the man, saying, "Of every tree of the garden you may freely eat; but of the tree of the knowledge of good and evil you shall not eat, for in the day that you eat of it you shall surely die." (Genesis 2:15-17)

The first law code issued in history came in the Garden of Eden, though it was not intended for civil government. Law comes from God, and in this case the Lord told Adam not to eat of one specific tree in the Garden. Adam broke the covenant and disobeyed God by eating the forbidden fruit.

Directly after the flood, the Lord introduced a prohibition against murder and instituted capital punishment as the first and most fundamental law for every civil government. This would offer a protection from the terror, mass murder, and chaos that brought God's judgment upon the earth in the form of the flood. Those tribes and civilizations that would ignore this basic law code would quickly find themselves bound to complete ruin.

So God blessed Noah and his sons, and said to them: "Be fruitful and multiply, and fill the earth. And the fear of you and the dread of you shall be on every beast of the earth, on every bird of the air, on all that move on the earth, and on all the fish of the sea. They are given into your hand. Every moving thing that lives shall be food for you. I have given you all things, even as the green herbs. But you shall not eat flesh with its life, that is, its blood. Surely for your lifeblood I will demand a reckoning; from the hand of every beast I will require it, and from the hand of man. From the hand of every man's brother I will require the life of man.

Whoever sheds man's blood,
By man his blood shall be shed;
For in the image of God
He made man.
And as for you, be fruitful and multiply;
Bring forth abundantly in the earth
And multiply in it. (Genesis 9:1-7)

Mesopotamia: 2360-1750BC

Instructions of Shuruppak

Civilization is a blessing of God's common grace. We read in Colossians 1:17 that all things consist in the Lord Jesus Christ. He holds all things together "by the word of His power" (Heb. 1:3). Wherever man is willing to uphold something of God's moral law, civilization is enabled to continue, and even this can only happen by God's grace. Because the heart of fallen man is "deceitful above all things and desperately wicked" (Jer. 17:9, KJV), it is only by God's grace that nations can survive from generation to generation without their inhabitants annihilating each other.

DEFINITION

Common Grace: The favor God shows to unbelieving persons and societies. He sends rain on "the just and the unjust" (Matt. 5:45), helping their crops to grow. He gives them a conscience with a sense of right and wrong because the work of the law is written on it (Rom. 2:14-15). He keeps their wickedness from becoming too destructive and enables them to acquire scientific, medical, and technological knowledge.

Oldest Extant Human Writings: 2400 BC

Much ancient history written by post-Christians (those who have turned away from the true God in the modern age) is guesswork. It is not based on trustworthy recorded writings and must be taken with a grain of salt. In this brief history of the world before Christ, special attention will be given to only the most reliable ancient records.

The world's oldest extant writings come from Mesopotamia, primarily because the inhabitants of this region carved their hieroglyphics on tablets of stone and clay (wet clay tablets could be edited until the clay was dried). Since writing on these tablets and transporting them was quite laborious, the Egyptians developed a writing method using papyrus and ink. Although much more portable and easier to use, papyrus tends to disintegrate much more rapidly than tablets, so many early Egyptian writings have been lost.

The *Instructions of Shuruppak*, probably the oldest extant writing, dates from around 2400 BC, about 100 years after the flood. Discovered twelve miles from the ancient city of Nippur, the *Instructions* contain wisdom from a father to his son.

The *Instructions* were copied by scribes for hundreds of years, and some historians believe they formed part of a second grade curriculum in Sumerian schools.[4] Not surprisingly, they contain one reference to "the flood." Representative portions of the *Instructions* follow.

> *You should not locate a field on a road. You should not make a well in your field: people will cause damage on it for you. A loving heart maintains a family; a hateful heart destroys a family. You should not play around with a married young woman: the slander could be serious. My son, you should not sit alone in a chamber with a married woman. A thief is a lion, but after he has been caught, he will be a slave. My son, you should not commit robbery; you should not cut yourself with an ax. Do not pass judgment when you drink beer. You should not curse strongly. . . . You should not serve things; things should serve you. The artistic mouth recites words; the harsh mouth brings litigation documents; the sweet mouth gathers sweet herbs. You should not speak arrogantly to your mother; that causes hatred for you. You should not question the words of your mother and your personal god. The father is like a god: his words are reliable. The instructions of the father should be complied with.*[5]

Several important insights can be gleaned from these ancient writings. Shuruppak encouraged a fear of evil "gods." He tells his son: "On the unfamiliar way at the edge of the mountains, the gods of the mountains are man-eaters."[6] However, there is no hint that this man knew the true and living God. How quickly man can forget the Creator of heaven and earth and the righteous judgment He brought on the earth in the flood!

Also, the danger of drinking alcohol is mentioned several times in Shuruppak's instructions, possibly recalling the sins of Noah and Ham after the flood (Gen. 9:20ff).

These earliest records also indicate that ancient man was as intelligent, mature, and moralistic as modern man. His writings are not those of ape men. We find in them no trace of a primitive, lower form of mankind. Wherever there is civilization, there is always some standard of morality. Man is continually falling short of the laws he establishes for himself, but these rules are nevertheless vital for his existence.

Lucretius, a Roman philosopher who lived just before Christ, came up with an evolutionary concept of man's development. He rejected the idea of a round earth as ridiculous, and his theory of evolution is just as absurd as his theory of a flat earth. Two thousand years later, when the humanists were turning away from the Christian faith in the 1800s, evolutionists Christian Jurgensen Thomsen and John Lubbock popularized the terms "stone age," "bronze age," and "iron age" to describe man's supposed evolution. According to these modern "scientists," the Stone Age lasted for 3.4 million years, ending around 3000 BC and yielding to the Iron Age. This is sheer conjecture. There is no evidence of these ages in the earliest recorded writings available to us. Around 3400 BC, well before the flood, Tubal-Cain the son of Lamech was an expert in both iron and bronze (Genesis 4:22). Certainly, Adam's descendants had developed the use of iron and bronze before Tubal-Cain became an instructor at the "Academy of Metallurgy." These early humans were by no means primitive cavemen.

Bronze Helmet from 1st Dynasty

And as for Zillah, she also bore Tubal-Cain, an instructor of every craftsman in bronze and iron. And the sister of Tubal-Cain was Naamah. (Genesis 4:22)

Yet, it is true that many people groups have degraded in knowledge, morality, and civilization over time. Wherever some morality, law, and order survive, there is some opportunity to develop economically and scientifically. Yet, as these moral virtues decline and tribes resort to wars and gross evil, civilization will break down. This is familiar to any and every time and place in human existence. For example, a rich and successful businessman may become a drunkard and end up dying in a ditch in abject poverty. The same degradation occurs among people groups who have lost a moral compass and have had their consciences seared.

And even as they did not like to retain God in their knowledge, God gave them over to a debased mind, to do those things which are not fitting. (Romans 1:28)

When archaeologists discover a primitive tribe, they want to assign it to an "older age." They do not realize that these "primitives" have degenerated and lost the benefits of civilization. Those tribes that stayed closer to where Noah landed the ark probably retained a stronger memory of the true and living God and His moral law. They would certainly be more sensitive to the sin of shedding innocent blood which defiles the land. By His grace, the Lord gave the civil law forbidding murder to maintain social order in the tribes that would remember to keep it (Genesis 9:6).

I will praise You, O LORD, with my whole heart;
I will tell of all Your marvelous works. . . .
You have rebuked the nations.
You have destroyed the wicked.
You have blotted out their name forever and ever.
O enemy, destructions are finished forever!
And you have destroyed cities.
Even their memory has perished
But the LORD shall endure forever,
He has prepared His throne for judgment. (Psalm 9:1, 5-7)

First Legal Code on Record (c. 2360 BC)

Fragments of the first known legal code issued by a civil government date back to the reign of Urukagina of Lagash, somewhere around 2360 BC (about 150 years after the flood). This king arose fifty years after God scattered the builders of Babel. It seems that he was one of those rare, wise rulers who didn't care to build a power-hungry, cruel empire. Urukagina was concerned about the exploitation of the poor and about corruption among government officials. Evidently, according to the ancient "Cones of Urukagina," the chief of the boatmen had been confiscating people's boats, the fisheries inspector had been seizing the fish stores, and "donkeys by the head herdsman were seized."[7] Such corruption and tyranny is equally familiar today in nations around the world.

Urukagina decreed that a poor man could not be forced to sell his donkey to a superior:

When to a royal subordinate a fine donkey has been born, and his foreman: "I want to buy it!" has said to him, whether he lets him buy it from him and: "The

Fragment of the Urukagina Code

> *silver that will satisfy me pay me!" he has said to him, or whether he does not let him buy it from him, the foreman in anger must not strike him.*[8]

The King went on to exempt the poor from the temple tax and expanded liberties for his people. He was concerned with the debasing of money and therefore required the rich to pay in silver when buying something from the poor. In his law code he secured rights for the widow and orphan, protecting them from exploitation by the powerful.

His law code also assigned mutilation for thievery. Polyandry (the marriage of several men to one woman) was a crime punishable by death. A woman who spoke in a degrading manner to a man would have her teeth broken out. If a man and woman loved one another, Urukagina commanded that they must live together and that the man must share his house and field with the woman.[9]

These are indications of God's common grace poured out upon nations throughout history. Almost every civilization will have at least a few instances of sagacious, reasonable, and just kings and rulers through the centuries. While there is still room to critique Urukagina's conception of justice, his lawcode is still considered as more moderate and reasonable than most of what is found in the ancient world.

God stands in the congregation of the mighty;
He judges among the gods.
How long will you judge unjustly,
And show partiality to the wicked? Selah
Defend the poor and fatherless;
Do justice to the afflicted and needy.
Deliver the poor and needy;
Free them from the hand of the wicked. (Ps. 82:1-4)

The Second Legal Code (c. 2100 BC)

The second oldest extant legal code produced by human governors appears 200 years after Urukagina's code. It was issued by King Ur-Nammu, who ruled in Ur around 2112-2095 BC. As would be expected, the law of Genesis 9:6 shows up as the first on the list. Also included in the list is a sanction of capital punishment assigned to the male who commits adultery with a woman betrothed to another man. Restitution is required for breaking another's leg or knocking out another's tooth. Laws regulating slavery are also included in the thirty-two statutes. The first four of these are listed below:

1. If a man commits a murder, that man must be killed.
2. If a man commits a robbery, he will be killed.
3. If a man commits a kidnapping, he is to be imprisoned and pay 15 shekels of silver.
4. If a slave marries a slave, and that slave is set free, he does not leave the household.

Anyone coming upon these early writings for the first time would immediately take note of the high literacy of the Mesopotamian cultures, dating back to 2300 BC. Clearly, these people could read and write remarkably well, equal to scholars or political leaders in our day. Why then have no written documents been discovered prior to 2500 BC? The answer is simple: the earliest kings of whom we have records lived around 2400-2300 BC because they were the first kings to rule after the worldwide flood and the dispersion of Babel. The first complete law code available to us from Sumer includes the first civil law revealed to Noah after the flood. All of this points to some access to divine revelation, at least by oral tradition. Moreover, these are strong evidences that a major catastrophe must have occurred prior to 2400 BC which would have destroyed older records. Early cultural traditions handed down from people groups around the world point to a major deluge that took place prior to 2500 BC. But there are no written records available to us before 2400 BC except what God revealed to Moses in the book of Genesis. All pre-flood written records must have been lost in the deluge.

Brick Stamped with "Ur-Nammu"

Ur Nammu's son, Shulgi (ruling 2094 BC to 2047 BC), was also quite literate, and he is best known today for his boastful writings—one of the first of the kings to leave records of his exploits and accomplishments:

> *I have perfected my wisdom just as my heroism and my strength. Reliable words can reach me. I cherish righteousness but do not tolerate wickedness. I hate anyone who speaks wickedly. Because I am a powerful man who enjoys using his thighs, I, Culgi, the mighty king, superior to all, strengthened the roads, put in order the highways of the Land. I marked out the double-hour distances, built there lodging houses. I planted gardens by their side and established resting-places, and installed in those places experienced men. Whichever direction*

one comes from, one can refresh oneself at their cool sides; and the traveler who reaches nightfall on the road can seek haven there as in a well-built city. I am greatly expert in assigning work with the pickax and the brick-mould, in drawing plans, in laying foundations, and in writing cuneiform inscriptions on pedestals. . . When I was small, I was at the academy, where I learned the scribal art from the tablets of Sumer and Akkad. None of the nobles could write on clay as I could. There where people regularly went for tutelage in the scribal art, I qualified fully in subtraction, addition, reckoning and accounting. Let me boast of what I have done. The fame of my power is spread far and wide. My wisdom is full of subtlety. Do not my achievements surpass all qualifications? I stride forward in majesty, trampling endlessly through the esparto grass and thickets, capturing elephant after elephant, creatures of the plain; and I put an end to the heroic roaring in the plains of the savage lion, dragon of the plains, wherever it approaches from and wherever it is going. I do not go after them with a net, nor do I lie in wait for them in a hide; it comes to a confrontation of strength and weapons. I do not hurl a weapon; when I plunge a bitter-pointed lance in their throats, I do not flinch at their roar. I am not one to retreat to my hiding-place but, as when one warrior kills another warrior, I do everything swiftly on the open plain. In the desert where the paths peter out, I reduce the roar at the lair to silence. In the sheepfold and the cattle-pen, where heads are laid to rest, I put the shepherd tribesmen at ease.

I, Culgi, king of Urim, have also devoted myself to the art of music. Nothing is too complicated for me; I know the full extent of the tigi and the adab, the perfection of the art of music. When I fix the frets on the lute, which enraptures my heart, I never damage its neck . . .

Before Utu son of Ningal, I, Culgi, declare that in my long life in which I have achieved great things since the day that my kingly destiny was determined, in my life in which everything was richly provided in contentment, I have never lacked anything. . .

When I. . . like a torrent with the roar of a great storm, in the capture of a citadel in Elam. . . I can understand what their spokesman answers. By origin I am a son of Sumer; I am a warrior, a warrior of Sumer. Thirdly, I can conduct a conversation with a man from the black mountains. Fourthly, I can do service as a translator with an Amorite, a man of the mountains. . . I myself can correct his confused words in his own language. Fifthly, when a man of Subir yells . . . , I can even distinguish the words in his language, although I am not a fellow-citizen of his. When I provide justice in the legal cases of Sumer, I give answers in all five languages. In my palace no one in conversation switches to another language as quickly as I do.

While the words at their dining tables flow like a river, I tackle crime, so that the foundations are securely established for my wide dominions. I vanquish a city with words as weapons, and my wisdom keeps it subjected just as violence with burning torches would. I have taught them the meaning of the words "I have no mother"...

My words can be words smooth as the finest quality oil; I know how to cool hearts which are hot as fire, and I know how to extinguish a mouth set on fire like a reed-bed. I weigh my words against those of the braggart. I am a man of the very highest standards of value. The importance of the humble is of particular value to me, and they cannot be counter-productive to any of my activities.

Grand achievements that I have accomplished which bring joy to my heart I do not cast negligently aside; therefore I give pride of place to progress. I give no orders concerning the development of waste ground, but devote my energies to extensive building plots. I have planted trees in fields and in agricultural land; I devote my powers to dams,. . . ditches and canals. I try to ensure a surplus of oil and wool. Thanks to my efforts flax and barley are of the highest quality.[10]

Here we find clear indication of the advancing technology, education, and the musical and literary capabilities of ancient man, something very different from the typical narrative provided by modern evolutionary and anti-Christian historians. There was never a stone age or iron age. From the beginning, man retained the image of God as one created in knowledge, righteousness, and holiness. After the fall, it is true that man perverted this nature and rebelled against God. This inevitably resulted in cultural retrograde. Thick, undiluted arrogance drips from Shulgi's writings, and Babylonian history testifies to his "criminal tendencies," confiscating the properties of the villages around Ur. According to the ancient Babylonian *Chronicle of the Kings*, "Bel [god] consumed his body and killed him" for his great wickedness.[11]

Pride comes before destruction and a haughty spirit before a fall. (Proverbs 16:18)

Abram from Ur of the Chaldees: Born 2166 BC

Now the LORD had said to Abram:
"Get out of your country,
From your family
And from your father's house,
To a land that I will show you.
I will make you a great nation;
I will bless you
And make your name great;
And you shall be a blessing.
I will bless those who bless you,
And I will curse him who curses you;
And in you all the families of the earth shall be blessed."
So Abram departed as the LORD had spoken to him, and Lot went with him. And Abram was seventy-five years old when he departed from Haran.
(Genesis 12:1-4)

Abraham's Journey from Ur to Canaan

Sometime after Sargon's great Akkadian empire collapsed and shortly before Ur-Nammu founded the Sumerian Third Dynasty of Ur, Terah fathered Abram. He was the ninth generation from Shem, the son of Noah.

So quickly, the entire world had forgotten the one, true and living God, the Maker of heaven and earth. Abram grew up in Ur, and it is clear he was a product of Mesopotamian polytheism. The people of Ur worshiped some 4,000 gods, and at the center of the city stood a large ziggurat measuring 200 ft x 150 ft x 75 ft high (61 m x 46 m x 23 m). Joshua 24:2 tells how even Abraham and his fathers served the gods over the Euphrates River before God called this man to Himself (Joshua 24:2-3). While still in his father's house, the Lord called him to move into the land of Canaan, the dwelling place of the Amorites.

The Amorites were known to be the descendants of the Nephilim or the giants (Num. 13:29-32, Amos 2:9-10) and they probably gave impetus to the great Akkadian and Babylonian empires in the early days of empire building. They were descendants of Canaan, Ham's son who had been cursed by Noah after the flood. This tribe was infamous for black magic, witchcraft, and human sacrifice. In Scripture, they are usually mentioned as the prime example of a robust and wicked tribe whose lands reached into Syria and Canaan (1 Kings 21:26, 2 Kings 21:11). Concerning this wicked people, God told Abraham: "Now as for you, you shall go to your fathers in peace; you shall be buried at a good old age. But in the fourth generation they shall return here, for the iniquity of the Amorites is not yet complete" (Gen. 15:15-16).

Following Babel (2418 BC), the peoples of the earth had experienced the judgment of God upon their attempt to build a city in pride. Throughout the Scriptures, especially in the prophetic books, we find the great empires of men receiving God's curse and judgment. This includes Moab, Tyre and Sidon, Egypt, Babylon, Assyria, Greece, and Rome. Yet, God had other plans for the nations in the earth. For, immediately after the account of Babel in Genesis, He lays out this amazing promise for Abraham:

> *In you all the families of the earth shall be blessed. (Genesis 12:3)*

Later, in Genesis 22:18, the Lord God develops this promise, stating that "in your seed all the nations of the earth shall be blessed." From the very beginning of this call, God would choose to bless all the nations in Abraham's seed. It wasn't merely a promise and a blessing for a single national group. Isaiah speaks of this blessing falling upon the whole world through the promised Messiah:

> *Indeed He says, "It is too small a thing that You should be My Servant to raise up the tribes of Jacob, and to restore the preserved ones of Israel; I will also give You as a light to the Gentiles, that You should be My salvation to the ends of the earth." (Isaiah 49:6)*

In fact, the Seed of Abraham mentioned in the Genesis 12 promise was not referring to every natural descendant of Abraham. The blessing would actually come through one Seed—the Messiah of God. While the kingdoms of this earth would fail again and again at their attempts to produce righteousness, peace, and joy in the earth, God was planning another kingdom through His Son.

> *Now to Abraham and his Seed were the promises made. He does not say, "And to seeds," as of many, but as of one, "And to your Seed," who is Christ. (Galatians 3:16)*

So, Abraham was told he would bless all nations though Christ. This would occur by the outpouring of the Holy Spirit at Pentecost and the missionary work that ensued after the Lord ascended into heaven.

While empires were busy building gigantic pyramids and ziggurats to the glory of man and the glory of false gods, a lone man with his wife came wandering about the land of Canaan. This Abraham would build a small altar made of uncut stones and worship the true and living God at Bethel. As the Lord God communicates history to us in the Book of Genesis, He doesn't speak of the great pyramids or the impressive kingdoms of the Akkadians and Babylonians. He isn't interested in the great battles won by the kings of the earth. Yahweh God is establishing a covenant and forming a relationship with one man and his family. This is the history that matters.

> *Then the LORD appeared to Abram and said, "To your descendants I will give this land." And there he built an altar to the LORD, who had appeared to him. And he moved from there to the mountain east of Bethel, and he pitched his tent with Bethel on the west and Ai on the east; there he built an altar to the LORD and called on the name of the LORD. (Genesis 12:7-8)*

Archaeological Evidence for the Ancient World of Abraham

Over the last century, archaeologists have confirmed numerous biblical references surrounding the life of Abraham and early Israel. The 25,000 Mari Tablets were discovered in 1933, probably buried after the destruction of the city by Hammurabi in the 18th century BC. Mari is located in far south Syria (or northern

Mesopotamia). These ancient records, buried 350 years before Moses, refer to the biblical cities of Nahor and Haran. They also mention a name that is very close to Benjamin: "bini-yamina." The tablets reveal that the Mari people would make covenants or treaties by killing an ass foal, somewhat similar to the confirmation of God's covenant with Abraham in Genesis 15.

Over 20,000 cuneiform tablets were discovered in the ancient ruins of Ebla in 1974—the capital city of the Amorites. This was a very large and powerful city originally formed around 2400 BC (about 100 years after the flood). This may have been a city connected to the Tower of Babel, as the first great empire builders are typically linked to the Amorites.

The tablets found at Ebla are still being studied, but researchers are already finding references to the god Baal, the city of Haran (Hara-an), the city of Sodom (Si-da-dum), Abram (Ab-rum), and Israel (Is-ari).[12]

The four kings mentioned in Genesis 14:1 (Amraphel king of Shinar, Arioch king of Ellasar, Chedorlaomer king of Elam, and Tidal king of nations) are all familiar names or derivations among the Amorites and the ancient Nuzu and Mari peoples. Chedorlaomer is a derivative of two Elamite words referencing the "Servant of the Goddess Lagamar."

Amazingly, Abraham assembled his household staff of 314 men to war against these kings and won. He rescued his nephew Lot and the king of Sodom, along with the booty as recorded in Genesis 14.

God promised Abraham a seed and a son and fulfilled His promise with the birth of Isaac. He also promised Canaan's territory to Abram, which is a reference to the provision of the promised land for the nation of Israel and a further promise of a more permanent kingdom and homeland.

Speaking of Abraham, Hebrews 11 testifies:

> *These all died in faith, not having received the promises, but having seen them afar off were assured of them, embraced them and confessed that they were strangers and pilgrims on the earth. For those who say such things declare plainly that they seek a homeland. And truly if they had called to mind that country from which they had come out, they would have had opportunity to return. But now they desire a better, that is, a heavenly country. Therefore God is not ashamed to be called their God, for He has prepared a city for them. (Hebrews 11:13-16)*

The Destruction of Sodom and Gomorrah,
by John Martin

Sodom and Gomorrah: God's Temporal Judgment (c. 2066 BC)

> *The sun had risen upon the earth when Lot entered Zoar. Then the LORD rained brimstone and fire on Sodom and Gomorrah, from the LORD out of the heavens. So He overthrew those cities, all the plain, all the inhabitants of the cities, and what grew on the ground. (Genesis 19:23-25)*

Though the Lord had promised He would refrain from destroying the entire world again with water, He would continue to hold the nations in check when it came to grosser forms of evil. These included certain sexual sins, as detailed in Leviticus 18 and 20.

In 1973 researchers discovered what appeared to be the cities of Sodom and Gomorrah in an archaeological dig on the southeast corner of the Dead Sea. The two sites are known as Numeira and Bab edh-Dhra, the latter being a larger city with a population of 600-1,200 persons. The area must have been well irrigated, given that the archaeologists uncovered quite a diversity of crops grown in the area including barley, wheat, grapes, figs, lentils, flax, chickpeas, peas, and broad beans.[13] Incredibly, clusters of some 700 carbonized grapes were found in the burned city of Numeira.

Under the soil in both towns (separated by ten miles), archaeologists found 16 inches (0.40 m) of ashy debris, and under the ashes skeletons of humans who must have died in the fires. There was no evidence of a volcanic eruption in the area, although evidences of bitumen and petroleum were detected.[14] The caches of food provisions indicate that the destruction came in late spring, which is when God revealed to Abraham the destruction of Sodom and Gomorrah (Genesis 18:10, 14).

In future years, the city of Sodom would become the namesake for one of the most heinous sexual sins known to man, and that is sodomy. Until the end of the world, the story of Sodom and Gomorrah will remain a severe warning to cities and nations which degenerate into approving and practicing the worst sexual perversions.

Possible Remnants of Sodom or Gomorrah

God is intimately involved in human history. He appeared to Abraham in the form of a man and discussed the destruction of Sodom and Gomorrah with him (Genesis 18). The Lord God Himself destroyed these wicked cities of the plain. No matter what secular science or philosophy may speculate, the God who created the earth and mankind is still in absolute control of His creation, and He governs it according to His eternal standards and decrees. This is the only way to read human history.

> *But I want to remind you, though you once knew this, that the Lord, having saved the people out of the land of Egypt, afterward destroyed those who did not believe. And the angels who did not keep their proper domain, but left their own abode, He has reserved in everlasting chains under darkness for the judgment of the great day; as Sodom and Gomorrah, and the cities around them in a similar manner to these, having given themselves over to sexual immorality and gone after strange flesh, are set forth as an example, suffering the vengeance of eternal fire. (Jude 5-7)*

The Death of Joseph in Egypt (c. 1801 BC) and the First Babylonian Empire (c. 1728 BC)

The world's third major empire (after Babel and Sargon's Akkadian Empire) was the first Babylonian Empire of King Hammurabi.

The city of Babylon was located about ten miles northwest of Kish, the seat of the Akkadian Empire where Sargon began his rule in 2334 BC. Babylon grew into an empire under their first dynasty of kings. However, even at the height of the first Babylonian Empire with King Hammurabi, the city never exceeded 60,000 people—something near to the size of a small town in modern states.[15] Nonetheless, this city became the center of the Babylonian Empire and would retain its influence and power for over 1,000 years.

About 350 years after the dissolution of Sargon's empire, Hammurabi ascended the throne (around 1792 BC), and empire fever once more returned to the world. Technically, the Babylonian monarchy began in 1830 BC with an Amorite from Syria named Su-abu. Between 1830 and 1728 BC, six kings built the city of Babylon and gradually accumulated power and control over surrounding cities. By 1781 BC, the first wall was completed around the city of Babylon under the leadership of King Sumu-la-ilu.

The Babylonian Empire began forming shortly before the death of Joseph, Abraham's great-grandson (1801 BC.) Joseph's major concern was that his bones be carried back from Egypt to the promised land where God would eventually bring His people Israel. There also He would bring forth the Seed, His Son, for the salvation of the world 1,800 years later.

> *And Joseph said to his brethren, "I am dying; but God will surely visit you, and bring you out of this land to the land of which He swore to Abraham, to Isaac, and to Jacob." Then Joseph took an oath from the children of Israel, saying, "God will surely visit you, and you shall carry up my bones from here." So Joseph died, being one hundred and ten years old; and they embalmed him, and he was put in a coffin in Egypt. (Genesis 50:24-26)*

Relief of Hammurabi

Prior to Hammurabi's ascension to the throne of Babylon, a Hittite named Shamshi Adad I (c. 1809 BC – c. 1776 BC) had conquered Syria and northern Mesopotamia as far south as Eshnunna. But Shamshi's sons had lost his Hittite empire by the 1720s.

The Babylonian Empire already controlled an area of 40 by 100 miles (60 by 160 km) when Hammurabi ascended the throne upon the death of his father King Sin-Muballit in 1792 BC. This remarkable king proceeded to expand the empire across the Mesopotamian Valley. Over a 42-year career, Hammurabi conquered Eshnunna and Assyria (including Nineveh), some 300 miles to the north up the Tigris River, as well as Elam, located 430 miles to the southeast.

To this day, Hammurabi is best known for his comprehensive law code consisting of 282 laws. During an excavation at the Elamite capital of Susa in AD 1901, archaeologists found a large stele containing the law code, broken in three pieces. Most likely it had been dragged back to Susa as a war prize when the Elamites invaded Babylon around 1150 BC.

Code of Hammurabi

Hammurabi's code moderated the severity of civil punishment by employing what is known as the *lex talionis*. The same principle of justice is found in God's law revealed to Moses:

> *If men fight, and hurt a woman with child, so that she gives birth prematurely, yet no harm follows, he shall surely be punished accordingly as the woman's husband imposes on him; and he shall pay as the judges determine. But if any harm follows, then you shall give life for life, eye for eye, tooth for tooth, hand for hand, foot for foot, burn for burn, wound for wound, stripe for stripe. (Exodus 21:22-24)*

Somewhat like King Urukagina 600 years earlier, Hammurabi was concerned for the rights of the underdog. He considered the purpose of the civil government to be "to destroy the wicked and the evil-doers; so that the strong should not harm the weak."[16] Such wisdom forms the basis for liberty and enables society to flourish (as long as good and evil are rightly defined). This reasonable law and liberty can only exist in non-Christian societies by the common grace of God.

In the prologue to his code, Hammurabi referred to himself as one "who feared God" and who took upon himself a commitment "to bring about the rule of righteousness in the land."[17] He recognized many gods, but calls Anu the "great God" and the "father of the gods" in his prologue and postscript. Some elements of the Code of Hammurabi do align with justice as defined by God's revealed will in Scripture. Here are some of the key elements of the code:

1. Murder by conspiring would require the death penalty in accordance with the basic law given to Noah in 2518 BC (Code 153).
2. Abortion caused unintentionally when a pregnant woman is struck would result in a fine (Code 209).
3. Gross forms of incest would result in the death penalty, such as that mentioned in 1 Corinthians 5:1 (Codes 155 and 157).
4. The penalty for a son who hits his father was not as severe as what we find in the Mosaic Code (Code 195).
5. The penalty for adulterous rape was death (Code 130).
6. The penalty for kidnapping was death (Code 14).
7. The penalty for gross negligence which results in a person's death was a fine, which is less severe than that required in God's law given to Moses (Code 251).

8. The penalties for stealing appear arbitrary, sometimes requiring a biblically just restitution, sometimes the death penalty, and sometimes the severing of a hand.

To the extent that these laws aligned with the true definition of justice and the jurisdictional authority of the civil magistrate outlined in Scripture, the Babylonian civilization would have been blessed with some degree of stability and prosperity. Yet the code was unquestionably flawed. The institutions of prostitution, concubinage, and slavery were systems which King Hammurabi felt needed to be regulated. The unredeemed world has had to deal with these realities throughout history.

Hammurabi built Babylon into a great city. He constructed temples and forts, dug irrigation canals for agriculture, and built a bridge that spanned the Euphrates River. By the time of Hammurabi's death, historians consider Babylon to have been the largest city in the world. It ruled over the city states of Isin, Larsa, Ur, Uruk, Nippur, Lagash, Eridu, Kish, Adab, Eshnunna, Akshak, Akkad, Shuruppak, Bad-tibira, Sippar, and Girsu. The population of the empire by this time would have been about 1,000,000, out of a world population estimated at 27,000,000, with population centers in Egypt, Babylon, India, and China.

Hammurabi's Babylon fell, but it would rise again 1,000 years later under Nebuchadnezzar. But this second Babylonian empire would also fall. Babylon's eventual doom was predicted 200 years before the fact by the prophet Isaiah.

As for our Redeemer, the LORD of hosts is His name,
The Holy One of Israel.
"Sit in silence, and go into darkness,
O daughter of the Chaldeans;
For you shall no longer be called
The Lady of Kingdoms. . . .
And you said, 'I shall be a lady forever,'
So that you did not take these things to heart,
Nor remember the latter end of them.
Therefore hear this now, you who are given to pleasures,
Who dwell securely,
Who say in your heart, 'I am, and there is no one else besides me;
I shall not sit as a widow,
Nor shall I know the loss of children;
But these two things shall come to you

In a moment, in one day:
The loss of children, and widowhood.
They shall come upon you in their fullness
Because of the multitude of your sorceries,
For the great abundance of your enchantments.
For you have trusted in your wickedness;
You have said, 'No one sees me';
Your wisdom and your knowledge have warped you;
And you have said in your heart,
'I am, and there is no one else besides me.'
Therefore evil shall come upon you;
You shall not know from where it arises.
And trouble shall fall upon you;
You will not be able to put it off.
And desolation shall come upon you suddenly,
Which you shall not know. (Isaiah 47:4, 5, 7-11)

The City of Jesus

Babylon was a great city, and man has rebuilt this city over and over again throughout history, in many places around the world. The peoples of the earth flock into the city of man to be "made drunk with the wine of her fornication" (Revelation 17:2). Typically, these are the powers that persecute the people of God as well (Revelation 17:6). This Babylon's demise is always quick—"in one hour your judgment has come" (Revelation 18:10).

Yet, there is another city which has foundations, "whose builder and maker is God" (Heb. 11:10, 16). It is the city of the living God, the heavenly Jerusalem, and the church of the firstborn (Heb. 12:22-23). This church of the Lord Jesus Christ is seen all over the world. For Christ Himself is building this city. It is the city of righteousness and it will be perfected in heaven (Revelation 21:10-27).

I will restore your judges as at the first,
And your counselors as at the beginning.
Afterward you shall be called the city of righteousness, the faithful city.
Zion shall be redeemed with justice,
And her penitents with righteousness. (Isaiah 1:26-27)

When Jesus Came to Mesopotamia

Canaan and Syria were the first countries to receive the Gospel of the Lord Jesus Christ in the 1st century. Quickly after this the Gospel continued to spread down into the Mesopotamian Valley and into the east as far as Armenia and Persia.

Today, there are far more Christians in Kuwait and Saudi Arabia than there are in Iraq and Iran. Yet, the two fastest growing Christian churches in the world are found in Iran and Afghanistan, according to Operation World.[18] Kuwait rates at number nine in fastest growth. Islam was introduced to the Middle East in the 7th century, which slowed down Christian missionary work significantly in that area of the world. The worst nations in the world for morality, corruption, and political freedoms remain Muslim-controlled nations like Iran and Yemen. It has only been during the social unrest of the 19th, 20th, and 21st centuries that the Lord has opened doors for evangelism in these countries.

Nation	Corruptions Rating	Freedom Rating	Prosperity Rating	Percent Christian
Kuwait	78	90	8	18%
Saudi Arabia	58	91	13	6%
Iraq	168	n/a	76	2%
Iran	138	155	66	0.1%
Yemen	176	n/a	163	.00004%

To this day, the major industries for nations in the Middle East are as follows:

Nation	Major Resources / Exports
Kuwait	Petroleum, Acylic Alcohol
Saudi Arabia	Petroleum, Ethylene Polymers, Acylic Alcohol, Propylene Polymers
Iraq	Petroleum, Wheat, Barley, Corn, Rice, Vegetables, Dates, and Cotton, Cattle, and Sheep
Iran	Petroleum, Ethylene Polymers, Acylic Alcohol, Propylene Polymers, Iron Ore
Yemen	Petroleum, Fish, Nephthalene, Cigarettes, Fruits, Soap, Animal Hides

Much is still to be done to see the transformation of this part of the world. The corruption, tyranny, and poverty brought about by false religion are still very strong in these areas. Yet, the Gospel is making inroads, and nations like Kuwait are changing shape. The nation still most needing discipleship into the good news of Jesus Christ is Yemen.

Flock of Sheep on the Tigris River

Timeline Review

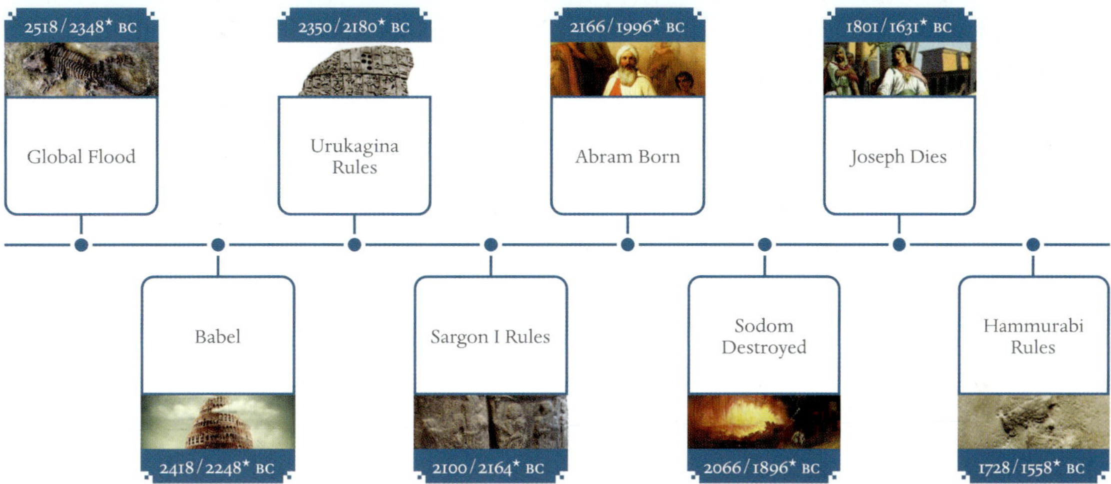

* Date according to Ussher's Chronology which assumes Israelites were in Egypt 215 years.

Chapter IV Prayer

Our Father in Heaven, Almighty God, Lord of All,

We are amazed by your mercy, your long suffering, and kindness to sinful man and his civilizations through the ages. We tremble in your presence, realizing your Hand is over all peoples and all nations. You personally visited Sodom and Gomorrah, bringing a thorough and complete judgment upon those wicked cities. Yet, you would still show mercy to the nations of the earth not through Hammurabi or Ur-Nammu or the other great kings of the earth. You would bless the nations through the Seed of Abraham, and that is our Lord Jesus Christ. And we have seen that great blessing come upon the world over these two thousand years. We praise you, gracious God, for these blessings in Jesus Christ our Lord.

Amen.

CHAPTER V

The Egyptian Empire (c. 2450-332 BC)

The wicked shall be turned into hell,
And all the nations that forget God.
For the needy shall not always be forgotten;
The expectation of the poor shall not perish forever.
Arise, O LORD!
Do not let man prevail;
Let the nations be judged in Your sight.
Put them in fear, O LORD,
That the nations may know themselves to be but men. (Psalm 9:17-20)

The Christian approach to history is radically different than that of the secularist. What is primarily to be seen in history are the mighty works of God. We are far less impressed with the works of men than we are with the sovereign hand of God. For it is God who raised Egypt up, only to bring the nation down in a crushing judgment. Thus, history is a humbling exercise. Most certainly, man never prevails against God, and one thing must be learned in all of these accounts—the fear of God.

When examining the records of ancient history, the humble student must also be especially cautious in handling the data available to him. Prideful academics are overconfident of their own interpretations of the data. Where no written records for an era exist, we cannot draw too much from fragments of pottery and broken-down buildings. Much of what is presented in ancient history textbooks is mere guesswork. For this study, we will rely on the Bible first, and then secondarily take into account the oldest recorded writings available in the civilizations considered.

Although historians who do not accept biblical revelation attempt to date the history of Egypt back to 3200 BC, there is little consensus among ancient Egyptian histories that would produce a clear picture of the distant past. Egyptologist Sir Alan Gardiner admitted that:

> *Even when full use has been made of the king lists and of such subsidiary sources as have survived, the indispensable dynastic framework of Egyptian history shows lamentable gaps and many a doubtful attribution. . . . What is proudly advertised as Egyptian history is merely a collection of rags and tatters.*[1]

Thus, it would be far better to organize a timeline of ancient Egypt's history around the inerrant record Scripture provides rather than the conflicting reports of later historians. There is more consensus with Christian historians, despite the slight differences of interpretation regarding scriptural genealogies and the length of Israel's sojourn in Egypt.[2]

Abram Born in Ur of the Chaldees (c. 2166 BC) and Pyramid-Building Optimized (c. 2308-2258 BC)

The Abydos King List includes twenty kings before Cheops (the builder of the Great Pyramid), and begins with Narmer (sometimes called Menes) as the first Pharaoh of Egypt on the list. Before Cheops, it appears that there were five Pharaohs who built pyramids, beginning with Djoser about fifty years before Cheops ascended the throne of Egypt. Djoser's vizier Imhotep is famous in Egyptian history for his work in architecture and medicine. This early scientist designed the Step Pyramid, which stands 204 feet high on temple grounds and originally covered about forty acres. Both Imhotep and Djoser's names were inscribed on the pyramid so future generations would know the source of this new attempt to resurrect Babel.

Pyramid-building continued to develop with Cheops' father Seneferu, who began his rule somewhere around 2282 BC. His "Bent Pyramid" appears a little lopsided, and it is thought the architects changed the design in the middle of the construction project. The angle begins at 55° and ends at 43° towards the upper levels.

The rapid development of pyramid-building technology is the most remarkable element of ancient Egyptian history. Such historical monuments completely dispel any ideas of primitive man as unintelligent. By the time that Seneferu's son Cheops took the throne of Egypt, the empire was well equipped to construct the largest pyramid in the world: the Great Pyramid of Giza. The builders used 2.3 million blocks weighing an average of seven tons each. At 450 ft. (137 m) in total height, this was one more attempt at making a tower to "reach the heavens." This was one more human attempt to "be as God." Not only was this the largest, it was also considered the most architecturally sound construction of Egypt's great pyramids, completed only seventy-five years after the development of the science.

Djoser's Step Pyramid

Seneferu's Bent Pyramid

An estimated 40,000 men worked full time to construct the Great Pyramid. For such a project to be funded by the civil government would have required an overall population of 500,000 men and another 1,500,000 women and children. That would put the population of Egypt somewhere around 2,000,000 at the time. The world population following the flood would have achieved about 4,000,000 by the year 2258 BC. Thus it is possible that the Great Pyramid was built around 2258 BC, about 160 years after the Tower of Babel. Djoser, Imhotep, Seneferu, and his son Cheops most likely borrowed the concept and technology for a tower "that would reach to the heavens" from Nimrod's project.

Ham's son, Mizraim, would have been born around 2478 BC, and it is quite possible that he began to settle what would become the country of Egypt around 2450 BC. This would leave about 200 years to work through the nineteen kings on the Abydos King List.

The oldest piece of writing found in Egypt dates from almost the same era as the oldest piece of writing found in Mesopotamia. In AD 2013, archaeologists unearthed an ancient papyrus in a cave at the Red Sea port of Wadi el-Jarf. What is extraordinary about this document is really the ordinariness of its contents. This oldest written record for mankind was actually just a logbook or diary kept by a project manager responsible for the transportation of huge limestone blocks down the Nile for assembly at the Great Pyramid of Giza. It is part ledger, including payments for food and labor. The author of the document, a fellow named Merer, references the Pharaoh Cheop's half-brother Ankhhaef who was, in his words, "chief for all the works of the king."

This record teaches several things. First, ancient man was as developed in intelligence, writing, accounting, and technology as modern man. British scholar George Rawlinson noted:

> *[I]n Egypt, it is notorious that there is no indication of any early period of savagery or barbarism. All the authorities agree that, however far we go back, we find in Egypt no rude or uncivilized time out of which civilization developed.*[3]

Great Pyramid of Giza

The Great Sphinx of Giza

Map of Ancient Egypt

Mediterranean Sea
Jerusalem
Dead Sea
Gaza
Rafah
Rosetta
Damietta
Alexandria
Buto
Nile Delta
Sais
Naukratis
Busiris
Tanis
Avaris
Pelusium
Wadi Natrun
Bubastis
Great Bitter Lake
Merimda
Heliopolis
Giza
Cairo
Saqqara
Memphis
Dashur
Helwan
miles
0
50
100
Sinai
Timna
Lake Moeris
Faiyum
Meydum
Lahun
Herakleopolis
Serabit al-Khadim
LOWER EGYPT
Nile
Bahariya Oasis
Beni Hasan
Hermopolis
Amarna
Eastern Desert
Asyut
Badari
Qau
Western Desert
Akhim
Thinis
Abydos
Nile
Dendera
Wadi Hammamat
Quseir
Red Sea
Naqada
Koptos
Dakhla Oasis
Kharga Oasis
Thebes
Luxor & Karnak
Tod
Hierakonpolis
Edfu
UPPER EGYPT
Kom Ombo
Aswan
First Cataract
Bernike
Dunqul Oasis
Nile
Nabta Playa
CUSH

This destroys the notion that man began unintelligent or with an inability to communicate through written language. There should be no doubt in our minds that Adam and Eve were able to communicate by written language. Since the oldest writings known to man date from the 23rd century in Egypt and Mesopotamia, the worldwide flood must have occurred only shortly before this time. Otherwise many more writings from previous centuries should have been discovered by now.

Pharaoh Cheop's sons Djedefre and Khafre followed in his footsteps, with Khafre building the tremendous Sphinx and the Pyramid of Khafre. With the end of the 4th Dynasty came the end of the grandest pyramid-building period in history, which took place around Giza (about 15-25 miles southwest of modern-day Cairo at the head of the Nile Delta). Based on our timeline, the 4th Dynasty would have ended about 2150 BC, around the time Abram was born in Ur of Mesopotamia. In God's providence, Egypt would pass through a period of internal strife and disintegration for the next 200 years. Divisions between the Upper Kingdom and Lower Kingdom and divisions between the priestly class and the political bureaucracy would inhibit any further progress or civil advancement.

Abram Visits Egypt (c. 2076 BC)

While Egypt was passing through this period of brokenness, God ordained to bring the man of the covenant into this land. The presence of Abram seemed to strike the fear of the true and living God into the heart of the Pharaoh. Wherever they go, God's people always bring common grace to the nations they visit and this was no exception to the rule. This influence serves as a restraint on the wickedness of unbelieving peoples. In the Genesis 12 account, Abram was forced to move to Egypt for a time because of a famine that struck the land of Canaan. While he was there, Pharaoh noticed Sarai, Abram's wife, and prepared to add the woman to his harem, but the Lord sent "great plagues" on his house (Gen. 12:17). He then sent Abram away from Egypt, but in the process this man of God received gifts of oxen, donkeys, camels, and servants. It was most likely these Egyptian servants who helped Abram fight the battle against the four kings of Mesopotamia in his effort to rescue his nephew Lot.

Shortly thereafter, Abram met another important figure in the history of the world. As he returned from the battle with the kings, he encountered

Melchizedek, king of Salem. This man was also a priest, to whom Abram gave a tithe. Melchizedek blessed Abram with these words:

> *Blessed be Abram of God Most High, Possessor of heaven and earth,*
> *And blessed be God Most High,*
> *Who has delivered your enemies into your hand.* (Genesis 14:19-20)

Thus, in a world of perpetual warfare, a symbol of peace arises from the King of Salem (Peace). In a world of evil kings, a glimmer of hope promises that a good King will arise. In a world of sin, a priest is very much required, a perfect Priest who would atone for the sins of the world. Though a prophet represents God to

Abraham Meets Melchizedek

man by bringing God's message to man, yet sinful man also needs a priest—one who will stand before God and represent man to God.

Who was this mysterious Melchizedek? Some believe him to be an angel. Others believe that he was Shem due to the fact that Shem outlived Abraham. The Book of Hebrews speaks of Melchizedek as having no beginning, at least in this world, and Shem had his beginning in the pre-flood world. Suffice it to say that we do not know where Melchizedek came from, when he died, or if he died. But we do know he was a type of the Christ who was to come, as referenced in the Book of Hebrews. The similarities are striking:

1. Both Melchizedek and Jesus are the King of Salem since Jesus Christ was declared to be the King of the Jews and He is the King that rules from the New Jerusalem.

   But you have come to Mount Zion and to the city of the living God, the heavenly Jerusalem, to an innumerable company of angels, to the general assembly and church of the firstborn who are registered in heaven, to God the Judge of all, to the spirits of just men made perfect, to Jesus the Mediator of the new covenant, and to the blood of sprinkling that speaks better things than that of Abel. (Hebrews 12:22-24)

2. Both Melchizedek and Jesus were kings and priests, and neither were of the tribe of Levi. It would have been impossible for a Levite to be both a priest and a king since the kingly line came from the tribe of Judah.
3. Both Melchizedek and Jesus were appointed to be priests by God Himself.
4. Both Melchizedek and Jesus come from a second line of priests. Neither of them came from the line of Levi but rather from the mysterious line having "no beginning."
5. Both Melchizedek and Jesus had a higher authority than Abram. Hebrews chapter 7 points out that Abram paid tithes to Melchizedek thus admitting his subservience to that priest's authority. Since Levi was Abram's great-grandson, the priesthood of Levi was of far lesser honor than the priestly line of Melchizedek.

   For this Melchizedek, king of Salem, priest of the Most High God, who met Abraham returning from the slaughter of the kings and blessed him, to whom also Abraham gave a tenth part of all, first being translated "king of righteousness," and then also king of Salem, meaning "king of peace," without father, without mother, without genealogy, having neither beginning of days nor end of life, but made like the Son of God, remains a priest continually. Now consider how great this man was, to whom even the patriarch Abraham gave a tenth of the spoils. And indeed those who are of the sons of Levi, who receive the priesthood, have a commandment to receive tithes from the people according to the law, that is, from their brethren, though they have come from the loins of Abraham; but he whose genealogy is not derived from them received tithes from Abraham and blessed him who had the promises. Now beyond all contradiction the lesser is blessed by the better. Here mortal men receive tithes, but there he receives them, of whom it is witnessed that he lives. Even Levi, who receives tithes, paid tithes through Abraham, so to speak, for he was still in the loins of his father when Melchizedek met him. (Hebrews 7:1-10)

Wrong-Headed Civilization

Why do the nations rage,
And the people plot a vain thing?
The kings of the earth set themselves,
And the rulers take counsel together,
Against the LORD and against His Anointed, saying,
"Let us break Their bonds in pieces
And cast away Their cords from us."
He who sits in the heavens shall laugh;
The LORD shall hold them in derision. (Psalm 2:1-4)

As fallen man became increasingly "civilized," we still find him in rebellion against God. The pyramids themselves are testaments to man's vain imaginations and unmitigated pride. These were useless buildings—nobody lived in them, worked in them, or shopped in them. They were built on a faulty worldview—the foolish notion that the Pharaohs would become gods in the afterlife. The Egyptians mistakenly believed that all the things they buried with the corpses would sustain the dead in the next life. Instead of leaving their resources to others in the

Entrance of the Great Pyramid

present life, they wasted them on building worthless pyramids, and they buried their treasures with the dead. It wasn't long before thieves realized they could rob the pyramids, dump the mummies on the ground, and make off with the golden caskets. By the time of the death of Pharaoh Tutankhamen in 1325 BC, the Egyptians were hiding the graves of their pharaohs in less conspicuous locations. It wasn't until AD 1922 that Howard Carter discovered King Tut's grave tucked away in the Valley of the Kings.

King Tut's Golden Mask

Life in Ancient Egypt

Egypt was the first of the empires to perfect the art of bureaucracy. The dynasties assembled very big governments with many employees, usually tasked with ridiculous projects. Managing huge projects like pyramid building required a host of accountants, taxmen, and census clerks as well. The vizier (or prime minister) was put in charge of the government—the treasury and the bureaucracy. The means of exchange for the Egyptians was typically grain, yeast, cattle, or beer.

Slavery was a way of life in Egypt. Huge numbers of slaves were required for the building projects. During his reign, Ramses III sent 113,000 slaves to work in the temples. As one example, transporting large obelisks down the Nile required 800 slave rowers in twenty-seven boats pulling a barge behind. Slaves were also killed and buried with the Pharaohs in their tombs.

The Pharaoh was treated like a god and possessed a staff of twenty who were in charge of his hair, makeup, and dress. One might be assigned to be "sandal-bearer to the king" and another "overseer of the cosmetic box." This usually contributed to the degeneracy of the Pharaoh. Incest was common among these rulers. Written on the walls of the tomb of a vizier were these words: "What is the king of Upper and Lower Egypt? He is a god by whose dealings one lives, the father and mother of all men, alone by himself without an equal."[4]

Egyptians were quite studied in medicine. Some doctors would specialize in childbirth, gastric disorders, or eye problems. A 1600 BC medical papyri outlines forty-eight forms of surgery, including treating skull fractures, spinal injuries, and other serious problems. The first medical manual, the Kahun Gynaecological Papyrus, comes from ancient Egypt (c. 1825 BC). This early medical science text presents methods to prevent pregnancy—employing crocodile dung, carbonate salt, and honey.[5]

Egyptian Art Depicting Slaves

The Egyptian Worldview

The Lord God warned His people Israel:

> *When you come into the land which the LORD your God is giving you, you shall not learn to follow the abominations of those nations. There shall not be found among you anyone who makes his son or his daughter pass through the fire, or one who practices witchcraft, or a soothsayer, or one who interprets omens, or a sorcerer, or one who conjures spells, or a medium, or a spiritist, or one who calls up the dead. For all who do these things are an abomination to the LORD, and because of these abominations the LORD your God drives them out from before you. You shall be blameless before the LORD your God. For these nations which you will dispossess listened to soothsayers and diviners; but as for you, the LORD your God has not appointed such for you. (Deuteronomy 18:9-14)*

The warning was apropos. These abominable activities were very common among all the ancient peoples, including the Egyptians, who were enslaved to the devil through the use of witchcraft. The priests and the people operated under the assumption they could control the spiritual realm. Incantations were scrawled in hieroglyphics on the walls of the pharaohs' tombs. In later centuries the *Book of the Dead* was assembled (somewhere around the 16th century BC), which included 192 spells. This magic was supposed to help the dead navigate their way into the afterlife. Ridiculous though it may sound, the Egyptians believed that if the dead knew the mystical names of certain gods or demons, they could somehow control them.

The *Book of the Dead* was intended to provide a "way" in the afterlife. There must have been in the Egyptian mind still a premonition of a final judgment. Perhaps there was still some faint memory of the horrifying judgment God unleashed on the world in the flood still extant in the conscience. Just in case one might forget what to say to the gods (or "God"), this manual was filled with defenses and flimsy excuses that the Egyptians hoped would help them in the judgment. Chapter 125 of this book offers a self-justification and a fatal lie:

> *I have not committed evil against men.*
> *I have not mistreated cattle.*
> *I have not committed sin in the place of truth. . . .*
> *I have not seen evil....*

Ritual Illustration from the *Book of the Dead*

I have not killed...
I have not caused anyone suffering.[6]

With this futile hope that the document might preserve their souls on the day of judgment, Egyptians of every class wanted to be buried with some portion of the *Book of the Dead*. When the 13th century BC Papyrus of Ani was unrolled, it stretched to eighty feet in length. Considered as one of the more complete, ancient copies of *The Book of the Dead*, the document defends the hapless dead man to the gods:

> *His heart is good: it has been weighed in the scale and no sin against god or goddess has been found. Thoth has weighed it as decreed by the gods, and it has been found to be true and just. Allow him to be given food and drink and permit him to make his appearance in the presence of Osiris and let him be as one of the followers of Horus for the rest of eternity.*[7]

Sadly, such vain and false testimonies would do no good for any who would stand before the great Judge of the earth on judgment day because all have sinned and come short of the glory of God. But the good news is that the gift of God is eternal life through Jesus Christ our Lord (Rom. 6:23).

Since the 1800s, the post-Christian western world has become somewhat enamored by these ancient mystery religions. Yet, biblical Christians still recognize these religions as demonic, perverse, deceptive, and enslaving. These religious ideas were just another way for the devil to deceive the nations and distract them from the knowledge of the true and living God. Men would find these religions as another convenient means of "suppressing the truth" of God in unrighteousness (Rom. 1:19).

The quest for super-human powers, a godlike status, and secret knowledge is insatiable in the mind of natural man. Such a desire fuels an interest in demonism, spiritism, occultism, and secret societies. Any supernatural magic that arises from a demonic source is especially exciting for those who have set themselves against the one supreme Sovereign. Fallen mankind is captivated by it, and witchdoctors who cast spells or perform wonders are therefore held in high esteem.

Painting Depicting Egyptian Gods and Pharaoh

Thus the magicians of Egypt who clashed with Moses before the Pharaoh (as recorded in Exodus 8), were fully aware of what was at stake. Their very position was being threatened by the true and living God. Certainly, the all-sovereign Lord permitted them a measure of power through the demonic realm. Copying Moses, these magicians successfully transformed their rods into serpents, but then Moses's serpent consumed theirs. The Egyptian witchdoctors followed up with repeating two of the plagues, but finally they had to admit defeat. The supernatural powers of Egypt were useless when faced with the almighty power of God, the Creator of heaven and earth.

> *Now the magicians so worked with their enchantments to bring forth lice, but they could not. So there were lice on man and beast. Then the magicians said to Pharaoh, "This is the finger of God." But Pharaoh's heart grew hard, and he did not heed them, just as the LORD had said. (Exodus 8:18-19)*

Religion in Ancient Egypt

Two aspects of the basic worldview of the Egyptians correlate with the way sinful man still thinks today. First, the Egyptians believed in evolution, that human life had formed out of lower, less complex material life forms. Secondly, they did not believe in a supreme and omnipotent God who is altogether separate from His creation. Instead, their religion was a mass of competing gods—a polytheism.

The god Neb-er-tcher is quoted in Egyptian religious texts as declaring: "I evolved the evolving of evolutions. I evolved myself under the form of the evolutions of the god Khepera, which were evolved at the beginning of all time. . . . I developed myself out of the primeval matter. My name is Ausares (Osiris), the germ of primeval matter."[8]

For the Egyptians, men and gods were composed of the same nature; the gods were merely located a little further up the pyramid of being. Since the priests were considered to be of the same nature as the gods, they were supposed to be able to manipulate the gods. The miracles that Moses performed were enabled by the command of God, but the miracles that the demons produced for the Egyptians were thought to have been manufactured by the command of the priests. The *Book of the Dead* offered a collection of incantations by which man thought he could manipulate the gods. This, of course, is the type of god that sinful mankind prefers. He doesn't want to believe that he is subject to an all-powerful, sovereign God, particularly when he realizes that he has sinned against this God. Man's pride will not allow him to submit to the concept of a God who is truly God above all and sovereign over all.

The belief in evolution and the refusal to acknowledge the one, true, and sovereign God usually leads to an infatuation with death. For a short time man pretends to turn himself into a god. He admires his great works of architecture and powerful empires. Soon however, he begins to realize the meaninglessness and futility of everything he has accomplished.

The Egyptian sage Ipuwer, writing in the 1800s BC, cries out in his papyrus: "Would that there might be an end of man, that there might be no conception, no birth!"[9] Another Egyptian philosopher writes: "Death is before me today like the recovery of a sick man, like going forth into a garden after sickness. Death is before me today like the odor of myrrh, like sitting under the sail on a windy day."[10] The Word of God explains the reason for this infatuation with death:

For whoever finds me [true Wisdom] finds life,
And obtains favor from the LORD;
But he who sins against me wrongs his own soul;
All those who hate me love death. (Proverbs 8:35-36)

Upper and Lower Egypt

Part of the problem encountered when trying to solve the mysteries of Egyptian chronology is that multiple pharaohs sometimes ruled at the same time. Fathers and sons would rule simultaneously, and some pharaohs ruled in northern Egypt (near modern-day Cairo) at the same time that other pharaohs were ruling in the south near Thebes. For example, the Fifth Dynasty pharaohs ruled from Thebes. Then the Twelfth Dynasty most likely moved further north, about seventy-five miles south of modern-day Cairo; these are probably the pharaohs who ruled during the life of Joseph (of Genesis). So much confusion in the timing of the pharaohs exists in the historical records that it is difficult to reconstruct a timeline. However, there are several clues to be found in Egyptian history that align with the infallible, inerrant historical writings of Scripture.[11] This history will attempt to piece it together.

Around 1990 BC Egypt began its first major imperialistic campaign in an effort to form a stronger empire under a military leader named Amenemhet. Although he may not have been a pharaoh himself, Amenemhet had a vision for greatness and a more powerful state. This Egyptian empire-builder waged war against the Nubians, a flourishing civilization further up the Nile River (in modern-day Sudan). After fighting many imperialistic battles, the Egyptians finally took control of the region and changed the name of the land to Cush. The Nubians served Egypt for the next 700 years.

Joseph Sold into Egyptian Slavery (c. 1911-1930 BC)

> *So it came to pass, when Joseph had come to his brothers, that they stripped Joseph of his tunic, the tunic of many colors that was on him. Then they took him and cast him into a pit. And the pit was empty; there was no water in it.*
>
> *And they sat down to eat a meal. Then they lifted their eyes and looked, and there was a company of Ishmaelites, coming from Gilead with their camels, bearing spices, balm, and myrrh, on their way to carry them down to Egypt. So Judah said to his brothers, "What profit is there if we kill our brother and conceal his blood? Come and let us sell him to the Ishmaelites, and let not our hand be upon him, for he is our brother and our flesh." And his brothers listened. Then Midianite traders passed by; so the brothers pulled Joseph up and lifted him out of the pit, and sold him to the Ishmaelites for twenty shekels of silver. And they took Joseph to Egypt. (Genesis 37:23-28)*

Egypt's troubles were those of every kingdom and tribe in the world. Man needed a solution for death, but it was not found in the pyramids. He needed deliverance from famine, slavery, and war, but the pharaohs could not bring it. Yet God had another plan working through the seed of Abraham.

At the time of Joseph's birth (around 1911 BC), the proud empire of Egypt comprised both Upper and Lower Egypt as well as Nubia to the south. Joseph was Abraham's great-grandson, born to Jacob, the son of Isaac.

Joseph was Jacob's favorite son, but out of hatred and jealousy his brothers sold him into slavery in Egypt. As God's providential plan played out, Joseph was made vizier over the land of Egypt. This was a standard official position in Egypt dating from the time of the Old Kingdom.

> *Then Pharaoh said to Joseph, "Inasmuch as God has shown you all this, there is no one as discerning and wise as you. You shall be over my house, and all my people shall be ruled according to your word; only in regard to the throne will I be greater than you." And Pharaoh said to Joseph, "See, I have set you over all the land of Egypt."*

Joseph Sold into Slavery

> *Then Pharaoh took his signet ring off his hand and put it on Joseph's hand; and he clothed him in garments of fine linen and put a gold chain around his neck. And he had him ride in the second chariot which he had; and they cried out before him, "Bow the knee!" So he set him over all the land of Egypt. Pharaoh also said to Joseph, "I am Pharaoh, and without your consent no man may lift his hand or foot in all the land of Egypt." And Pharaoh called Joseph's name Zaphnath-Paaneah. And he gave him as a wife Asenath, the daughter of Poti-Pherah priest of On. So Joseph went out over all the land of Egypt. (Genesis 41:39-45)*

Records indicate that Sesostris (of the 12th Dynasty) appointed a powerful vizier over the land by the name of Mentuhotep, whose very word was "like the declaration of the king's power."[12] We also read from the ancient records that this Mentuhotep "appears as the alter ego of the king. When he arrived, the great personages bowed down before him at the outer door of the royal palace."[13] Considering that the Scriptures describe an identical scenario, this Mentuhotep could have been the biblical Joseph (Gen. 41:43).

Joseph was appointed to administer the food supply during the seven years of plenty and seven years of famine that followed. Ancient records indicate that a severe famine occurred during the reign of the Pharaoh Senusret. A man named Hekanakhte, writing to his mother and another relative, described the situation as so severe that some had resorted to cannibalism:

> *How are you two? Are you alive, prosperous and healthy? . . . Do not be anxious about me, for I am healthy and alive. Behold, you are like the one who eats his fill, having once been so hungry that his eyes sank in, although the entire land is dead from hunger. . . . So it may be said that to be held alive is better than death outright. . . . they have begun eating people here.*[14]

When the Lord ordained a famine in the land of Egypt which extended up into Canaan where Jacob and his sons were living, they were forced to come to Egypt for food. They did not recognize Joseph at first, and it was only on their second visit, after Joseph had tested his brothers, that he revealed himself to them.

The Genesis account of Joseph provides still another revelation of man's problem and God's solution to that problem. Man needs a deliverer, one who will deliver him from the threat of death as well as death itself. To Adam and Eve

God promised that the Seed of the woman would crush the evil serpent—thus destroying the "bad guy" or the source of evil. But man still needs to be saved from the consequences of sin and the curse of death. To better understand this, the Lord put together a very elaborate object lesson for us in this record from Genesis (and Exodus). The parallels between Joseph in this account and Jesus, the Savior who is to come, are amazing.

Both Joseph and Jesus:

- Were beloved of their fathers (Gen. 37:3a; Matt. 3:17b)
- Were envied and hated without a cause (Gen. 37:4; Mark 15:10; John 15:25b)
- Prophesied of a day in which they would rule (Gen. 37:7; Matt. 26:64b)
- Were sent by the father to seek out their brothers' condition (Gen. 37:14a; Luke 20:13b)
- Were rejected and condemned to die (Gen. 37:18b; Luke 23:21)
- Were stripped of their clothing (Gen. 37:23b; Matt. 27:28a)
- Were thrown into a pit, alone and forsaken (Gen. 37:24a; Matt. 12:40b)
- Were sold for silver into the hands of Gentiles, Joseph for twenty pieces of silver and Jesus for thirty pieces of silver (Gen. 37:28b; Matt. 26:15b)
- Were raised out of the pit (Gen. 37:28a; 1 Cor. 15:4b)
- Became slaves (Gen. 39:1-2; Luke 22:27b; Phil. 2:7b)
- Prospered in what they did (Gen. 39:3b; Isa. 53:10b)
- Resisted temptation (Gen. 39:7-12; Heb. 7:26; 4:15b)
- Were falsely accused (Gen. 39:17-18; Matt. 26:60-61)
- Were numbered with prisoners or transgressors (Gen. 39:20a; Luke 23:33)
- Were promised deliverance after three days (Gen. 40:13; Luke 23:43b)
- Proved to be good counselors (Gen. 41:39; Isa. 9:6b)
- Were promoted to honor and glory and given a new name (Gen. 41:41; Phil. 2:9)
- Had people bow before them (Gen. 41:43b; Phil. 2:10a)

- Provided bread for those in need (Gen. 41:57a; John 6:35a)
- Were not recognized by their brothers (Gen. 42:8; 2 Cor. 3:14a; John 14:9a)
- Were unjustly dealt with, as determined by God's purpose. In both cases, the greater good was to bring about a great salvation (Acts 2:23; Gen. 50:19-20)
- The story ends in both cases with an announcement of peace and reconciliation (Gen. 45:3-8; John 20:9-10)

Hebrew Slaves in Egypt

Most importantly, Joseph provided a wonderful picture of the ultimate salvation which God would bring about for His people. Surely, it was the Lord God who sent Joseph into Egypt. It was the same sovereign God who sent a famine into the land that devastated the peoples in the surrounding area for seven consecutive years. It was God who sent the brothers to Egypt and who kept the people of Israel in Egypt for succeeding generations. All this was done because the Lord desired to demonstrate a great salvation from death in Joseph and another great salvation with Moses four hundred years later.

> *Then Joseph said to his brothers, "I am Joseph; does my father still live?" But his brothers could not answer him, for they were dismayed in his presence. And Joseph said to his brothers, "Please come near to me." So they came near. Then he said: "I am Joseph your brother, whom you sold into Egypt. But now, do not therefore be grieved or angry with yourselves because you sold me here; for God sent me before you to preserve life. For these two years the famine has been in the land, and there are still five years in which there will be neither plowing nor harvesting. And God sent me before you to preserve a posterity for you in the earth, and to save your lives by a great deliverance. So now it was not you who sent me here, but God; and He has made me a father to Pharaoh, and lord of all his house, and a ruler throughout all the land of Egypt." (Genesis 45:3-8)*

So, Joseph became that "great deliverer" for his brothers, the one who would save the entire family from starvation and death. All of this points to the coming Messiah—who would be known best by His birth name "Jesus," which is translated "Savior" or "Deliverer." "You shall call His name Jesus, for He shall save His people from their sins." (Matthew 1:21)

All of us are born spiritually famished. We stand in need of salvation from spiritual starvation and death. We are by nature in bondage to sin, death, and the devil. We are in need of salvation from the bondage of these tyrants. This would be depicted in the spectacular deliverance that would come at the Red Sea—and would be fulfilled in Jesus Christ by His death and resurrection.

The Birth of Moses (c. 1526 BC)

The children of Israel multiplied greatly in Egypt. The original seventy who came down to Egypt with Jacob had expanded to a great nation of 2,000,000 people by the time of the Exodus. The Pharaoh, concerned that the Hebrews were "more and mightier than we" (Ex. 1:9), enslaved and oppressed the Israelites. Suggesting that they would "join our enemies and fight against us" (Ex. 1:10), he set taskmasters over them to "afflict them." To control the Israelite population then, he commanded the Hebrew midwives to kill the male babies born to the Hebrew mothers (Ex. 1:16). Nevertheless, the midwives Shiphrah and Puah refused to obey the king because they feared God.

The Israelites were assigned to build bricks of mud and straw, as recorded in Exodus 5:10-14. By the time of the reign of Sesostris III (around 1800 BC), the Egyptians had ceased using stones for their buildings (as conventionally employed for their large pyramids in 2200 BC). Cities in the Delta such as Bubastis, Qantir, and Ramses were constructed out of bricks composed of mud and straw.

The village of Kahun consisted of a large Semitic slave population which very well could have been the Israelites, who served as slaves c. 1846-1446 BC. The Brooklyn Papyrus (discovered in 1933) lists 100 domestic servants, including at least forty-eight names of Semitic origin, including Shiphrah (the Hebrew midwife referenced in Exodus 1:15), Issachar, and Ashar. An extraordinary number of infants have also been discovered in cemeteries in Kahun and Tel ed-Daba. Wooden boxes hidden under homes in Kahun contained the bodies of babies, in some cases "buried two or three to a box, and aged only a few months at death."

Archaeologists also found that 65% of the dead at the cemetery in ed-Daba were infants, possibly Israelite children killed at the dictate of the Pharaoh.

Saving the Babies

> *By faith Moses, when he was born, was hidden three months by his parents, because they saw he was a beautiful child; and they were not afraid of the king's command. (Hebrews 11:23)*

Sphinx Statue of Amenemhet III

When the Lord God cursed the serpent in the garden, right there He determined there would be enmity between the seed of the serpent and the seed of the woman. Based on God's declaration, the devil was sure that a baby born of the woman would eventually crush his head, and he did not want these babies to survive. If he could kill all the male babies in Egypt, perhaps he could prevent the Messiah's line from continuing and would thereby save his skull. For this reason among others, the devil strongly advocates abortion and infanticide, especially for God's people. Wicked rulers like the Egyptian Pharaoh played into Satan's hands. Yet always, opposing the purposes of God is futile.

Women of faith, like Moses's mother, are adamantly pro-life, and they will do their utmost to save the lives of their babies. By faith, Moses's mother hid her baby in a little ark in the Nile River amidst the bulrushes. His sister Miriam watched out for him until the child was discovered by Pharaoh's daughter.

This may have occurred around the time of the reign of Amenemhet III. This king had only two daughters, and according to the 1st century historian Josephus, the daughter who found Moses was herself childless. Josephus quotes the woman, "As I have received him [Moses] from the bounty of the river, in a wonderful manner, I thought proper to adopt him for my son and the heir of thy kingdom."[15] It turns out that Amenemhet III's daughter Sobekneferu was childless for a brief time and took the throne when her father died. This is possible, given the fact that Moses was exiled after he killed the Egyptian for beating an Israelite slave.

Sunrise Over the Nile River

The Exodus from Egypt (c. 1446 BC)

> *And God spoke to Moses and said to him: "I am the LORD. I appeared to Abraham, to Isaac, and to Jacob, as God Almighty, but by My name LORD I was not known to them. I have also established My covenant with them, to give them the land of Canaan, the land of their pilgrimage, in which they were strangers. And I have also heard the groaning of the children of Israel whom the Egyptians keep in bondage, and I have remembered My covenant. Therefore say to the children of Israel: 'I am the LORD; I will bring you out from under the burdens of the Egyptians, I will rescue you from their bondage, and I will redeem you with an outstretched arm and with great judgments.'" (Exodus 6:2-6)*

Subsequently Moses left Egypt for forty years, escaping to the land of Midian, where he married and fathered two sons. While tending his sheep, Moses came upon a burning bush and there encountered the Lord God of his fathers—Abraham, Isaac, and Jacob. God revealed His Name "Yahweh" to Moses and explained His Name as "I am who I am." God is always ever existent, the very source of all life and all existence.

Furthermore, the Lord revealed to Moses His intention to deliver His people from Egyptian slavery and His commitment to fulfill the covenant promise He had made to Abraham. Then He commissioned Moses to lead the people of Israel out of Egypt. Moses was at first hesitant to take up the task, but his faith grew to meet the challenge in the days and weeks that followed.

It is clear at this point in human history that God has a higher and more important purpose for the stage set in Egypt. His purpose for Egypt, for Israel, and for the slavery of God's people was to lay out a powerful object lesson that would never be forgotten as long as this world continues. Man needs redemption. Every person born into this world by natural generation is a slave to sin. Because slaves cannot purchase their own freedom, they must be redeemed by the grace of someone else. Thus God allowed Israel to become enslaved in Egypt in order that He might purchase their freedom.

The price with which the Israelites were redeemed (according to Exodus 6:6) was extremely high—the judgments of God upon Egypt. Ultimately, God paid for their freedom by taking the lives of every firstborn in Egypt—as many as 100,000 dead sons. Yet, this judgment against sinful Egypt and the redemption price for

Israel served primarily as an illustration, a type, or an object lesson for the real redemption that was yet to come. The price of the redemption of God's people from the slavery of sin would turn out to be the priceless life of God's Firstborn, His only begotten Son—Jesus Christ. It was a high price to pay.

For the following 1,400 years, the Israelites would redeem the firstborn males of their children, sheep, and goats (Ex. 13:11-14). The families of Israel were assigned to pay the temple a certain fixed price at the birth of their firstborns. This redemption would serve as a constant reminder that a firstborn Son would finally redeem God's people with His own life in AD 33.

> *And it shall be, when the LORD brings you into the land of the Canaanites, as He swore to you and your fathers, and gives it to you, that you shall set apart to the LORD all that open the womb, that is, every firstborn that comes from an animal which you have; the males shall be the LORD's. But every firstborn of a donkey you shall redeem with a lamb; and if you will not redeem it, then you shall break its neck. And all the firstborn of man among your sons you shall redeem. So it shall be, when your son asks you in time to come, saying, "What is this?" that you shall say to him, "By strength of hand the LORD brought us out of Egypt, out of the house of bondage." (Exodus 13:11-14)*

The Passover Lamb

> *Knowing that you were not redeemed with corruptible things, like silver or gold, from your aimless conduct received by tradition from your fathers, but with the precious blood of Christ, as of a Lamb without blemish and without spot. (1 Peter 1:18-19)*

Ten plagues were unleashed upon the land of Egypt, the last of which was the worst—the slaughter of the firstborn sons. Each of the plagues targeted one of the key gods worshiped by the Egyptians.

Throughout the ordeal, the Egyptian Pharaoh refused to let the people of Israel go. Repeatedly we read that the king hardened his heart and that God hardened his heart. Ten times Pharaoh's heart is said to be hardened. This is in line with Egyptian theology regarding their treatment of the dead. The *Book of the Dead* was supposed to prepare the dead to justify themselves before the gods on the day of judgment. The idea was to "fake it 'til you make it" at the judgment. However, those pharaohs who were burdened with a heavy conscience at death would need a hardening of the heart to prevent any acknowledgment of guilt on the final day. What if they admitted to having sinned and thereby contradicted the forty-two statements of innocence? In Spell 30B in the *Book of the Coming Forth by Day*, the heart is instructed not to contradict the testimony before the god Osiris: "Do not act against me with the gods. . . . Do not make my name stink to the gods who made mankind."[16] A scarab beetle was used as a sacramental or symbolic means for hardening the heart against the gods. According to the Exodus record, the true and living God who rules over heaven and earth saw to it that the Pharaoh's heart became hardened, not for the purpose of escaping judgment, but instead to set him up for a more devastating judgment and to demonstrate the power and glory of God.

> *And the LORD said to Moses, "When you go back to Egypt, see that you do all those wonders before Pharaoh which I have put in your hand. But I will harden his heart, so that he will not let the people go." (Exodus 4:21)*

Plague	Egyptian god targeted
Plague 1—Water turns to blood	**Hapi**—The god of the Nile
Plague 2—Frogs appear out of the water	**Heket**—The goddess bearing the head of a frog
Plague 3—Dust of earth turns into gnats	**Geb**—The god of the earth
Plague 4—Swarms of flies	**Khepri**—The god of insects
Plague 5—Livestock die	**Hathor**—The goddess with the head of a cow
Plague 6—Boils and sores on man	**Sekhmet**—The god of disease
Plague 7—Hail and firestorms from sky	**Nut**—The goddess of the sky
Plague 8—Locust clouds destroy crops	**Seth**—The god of crops
Plague 9—Sky is darkened	**Ra**—The god of the sun
Plague 10—Firstborn dies	**Pharaoh**—The god of the state, man

Several times in his exchanges with Moses, the Pharaoh momentarily softened and confessed, "I have sinned against the LORD your God and against you" (Ex. 10:16). Yet each time the scarab beetle returned, and he hardened his heart once more.

The Lord exempted the Israelites from the plague of the firstborn by instituting the Passover. A lamb was chosen on a Sunday and slaughtered on the following Thursday. The blood was placed on the lintel of the door and on the two side posts. When the avenging angel passed by the Israelite houses, he would see the blood and pass over, exempting their sons from the slaughter. The children of Israel then roasted and ate the Passover Lamb, thus identifying themselves with the sacrifice.

This Passover was later perfectly fulfilled in the Lord Jesus Christ, for He flawlessly met every condition required for the lamb. The instructions were

Institution of the Passover

clear—the lamb was to be without blemish (Ex. 12:5); none of the lamb's bones were to be broken (Ex. 12:46). The lamb was to be selected four days before it was slaughtered. It was to be roasted with fire and was to be killed on an annual basis in Jerusalem. After 1,400 years of the Passover institution, Christ became the Passover Lamb for us, as testified to in 1 Corinthians 5:7. He was a Lamb, holy, harmless, and undefiled. He was selected to be killed upon His entry into Jerusalem four days earlier. Not one of His bones was broken. He was set out in the sun on the cross, pierced by a sword and left to bake in the sun. And He was sacrificed in Jerusalem.

This great living, historical illustration ordained by God was intended to demonstrate a mighty redemption from slavery.

Israel Leaves Egypt

Salvation from Egypt

The sheer magnitude of the miraculous deliverance from Egypt is bigger than any other illustration or sign found throughout the entirety of human history. It was the epochal event of the Old Testament narrative. It was a spectacular salvation—serving as the most wonderful visual illustration of God's salvation of His people.

After allowing the people of Israel to leave his dominion, Pharaoh decided to pursue them. As God directed, Pharaoh's heart was hardened repeatedly throughout the whole ordeal of the ten plagues. Egypt was at the height of its power. By this time the Egyptians had developed horse-drawn chariots, and the Israelites had no such weapons. They had been reduced to the slave class for generations and they were not trained soldiers. The Red Sea stood before them with a mountain on the left and a mountain on the right—and no means of escape. They were helpless. Such was the spectacular scenario ordained by God in which He was to visually demonstrate His grand redemption. We read in Exodus 14:

> *And when Pharaoh drew near, the children of Israel lifted their eyes, and behold, the Egyptians marched after them. So they were very afraid, and the children of Israel cried out to the LORD. Then they said to Moses, "Because there were no graves in Egypt, have you taken us away to die in the wilderness? Why have you so dealt with us, to bring us up out of Egypt? Is this not the word that we told you in Egypt, saying, 'Let us alone that we may serve the Egyptians'? For it would have been better for us to serve the Egyptians than that we should die in the wilderness."*
>
> *And Moses said to the people, "Do not be afraid. Stand still, and see the salvation of the LORD, which He will accomplish for you today. For the Egyptians whom you see today, you shall see again no more forever. The LORD will fight for you, and you shall hold your peace." (Exodus 14:10-14)*

Moses then raised his rod—and the seas parted. Two million people strung out over 4-5 miles crossed over the sea on dry land. Somehow the Lord maintained a wall of water on the right and a wall of water on the left as His people escaped through the Red Sea. The Egyptians pursued the Israelites into the dry seabed. But when all the Israelites were safely on the other side, the waters returned, and the Egyptian army was washed away to the grave.

This is the spectacular object lesson by which we can better understand the magnitude, power, and awe-inspiring nature of God's salvation. We cannot save

Israel at the Red Sea

ourselves. We are quite helpless against the enemies of sin, death, and the devil. All we can do is stand still and see the salvation of the Lord. This Old Testament event illustrates the salvation God has provided through the death and resurrection of Jesus Christ. In the providence of God, Israel was oppressed by the mightiest empire on earth. He took an empire to the zenith of its power, and hardened Pharaoh's heart to demonstrate His glory and to illustrate the sheer power of His redemption. By this real-life, living-color, historical enactment, the Lord would teach His people something of the metaphysical nature of His powerful redemption and incomparable glory. There is a violence to it. Man's redemption must come by the violent destruction of the enemy. At the cross, the Lord Jesus simultaneously crushed principalities and powers and set His people free from the bondage of sin, death, and Satan—the greatest tyrant of all. Our Christ was then raised from death by the power of God, proving once for all that death would not have dominion over Him or us. Here is seen a living picture of Jesus, the mighty Savior holding back the waters of the Red Sea as His people escape—and then

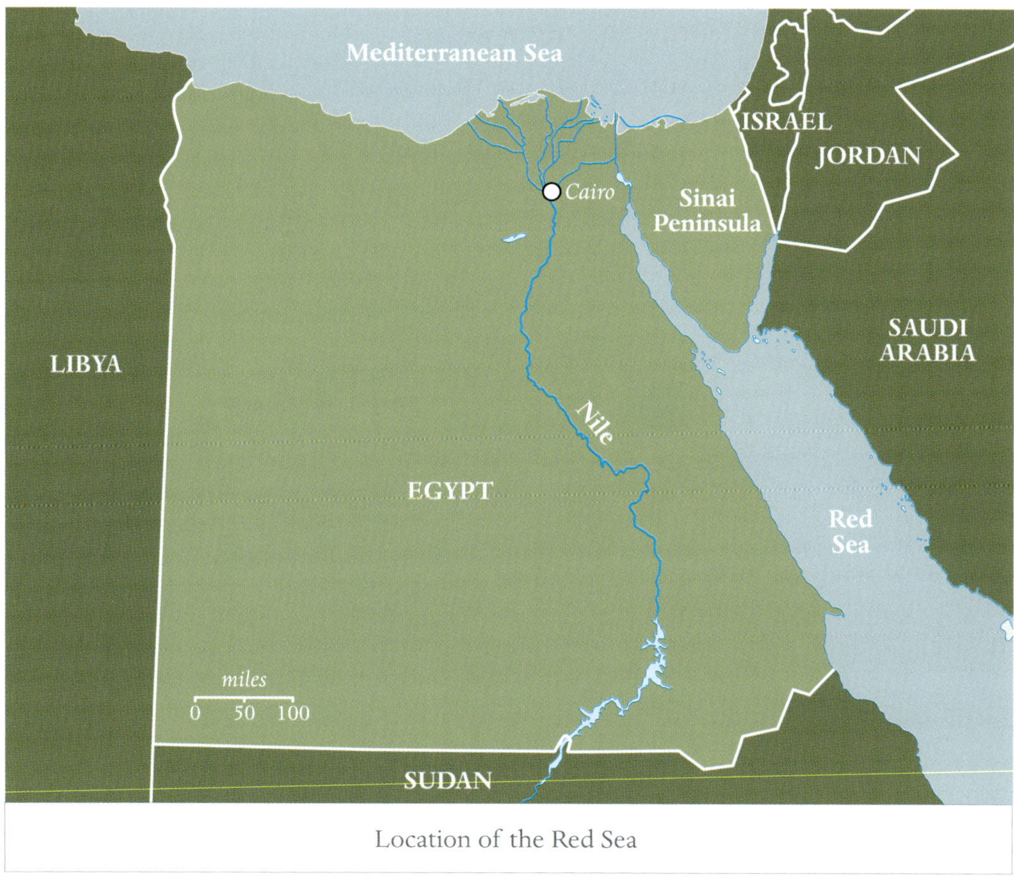

Location of the Red Sea

letting the waters break over the armies of the evil one. It was nothing less than a complete rout of the enemy and a total deliverance of His people from the bondage of the tyrant.

Such a salvation calls for song and dancing, which is how Moses and Miriam respond in Exodus 15.

> *I will sing to the LORD, for He has triumphed gloriously! The horse and its rider He has thrown into the sea! The LORD is my strength and song, and He has become my salvation; He is my God, and I will praise Him; my father's God, and I will exalt Him. The LORD is a man of war; the LORD is His name. Pharaoh's chariots and his army He has cast into the sea; His chosen captains also are drowned in the Red Sea. (Exodus 15:1-4)*

The Devastation of Egypt

History is filled with dramatic and clear demonstrations of God's sovereign power over the nations. He judges empires, bringing the proud low and raising up the humble. While the kings of the earth may believe they are working their own agendas, God is working a more ultimate purpose through them.

> *Then the LORD said to Moses, "Rise early in the morning and stand before Pharaoh, and say to him, 'Thus says the LORD God of the Hebrews: "Let My people go, that they may serve Me, or at this time I will send all My plagues to your very heart, and on your servants and on your people, that you may know that there is none like Me in all the earth.... But indeed for this purpose I have raised you up, that I may show My power in you, and that My name may be declared in all the earth."'" (Exodus 9:13-14, 16)*

In fact, it appears that a few Egyptians recorded some of the trauma they experienced under the hand of God's judgment in the words of a sage in the Ipuwer Papyrus, first translated into English in 1909. It speaks of the miseries of Egypt during the time of the plagues:

> *The river is blood. If you drink of it, you lose your humanity. (Ipuwer 2:10)*
>
> *Gone is the barley of abundance . . . Food supplies are running short. The nobles hunger and suffer. (Ipuwer 6:3, 3:3, 7:13)*
>
> *What shall we do about it? All is ruin! (Ipuwer 3:13)*
>
> *Behold, plague sweeps the land, blood is everywhere, with no shortage of the dead. . . . He who buries his brother in the ground is everywhere. . . . Woe is me for the grief of this time. (Ipuwer 2:5, 6, 13, 4:3)*
>
> *Wailing is throughout the land, mingled with lamentations. (Ipuwer 3:14)*[17]

The destruction of Egypt's firstborn was a devastating blow to the proud empire. God broke the back of the nation by removing the firstborn sons—who would have been the heirs to provide the energy to carry on the legacy of Egypt.

Archaeologists have learned that during the reign of Neferhotep I a sudden departure occurred from the slave-inhabited cities of Tel ed-Daba and Kahun. The remains of the city give impression that the slaves left their tools and possessions in a hasty departure.

Mass shallow graves populated with large numbers of bodies quickly buried appear at this same time. This would indicate that a terrible plague had killed a multitude of people all at one time. Despite the fact that Neferhotep's pyramid is easily identifiable today, his mummy has not been found—probably because he drowned in the Red Sea. There is also no record of his son reigning—his brother took his place on the throne of Egypt.

Egypt Goes into Decline After the Exodus (1446-1246 BC)

Some time after the Exodus, Egypt's Middle Kingdom entered a period of decline. The nation was overrun by an invading tribe from the north, known as the Hyksos. Egyptian chronicler Manetho records that the Hyksos occupied Egypt without fighting a single battle.[18] Could the Egyptian army have been lying at the bottom of the Red Sea? Devastated by God's judgment, Egypt would have been easy prey for invaders.

The Hyksos may have been the Amalekites. Scripture records that the Amalekites attacked the Israelites just after they left Egypt (Exod. 17). They could have learned from Israelite stragglers (Deut. 25:18) about the destruction of Egypt's army and seized the opportunity to invade Egypt. Forty years after the Exodus, when Israel was about to enter Canaan, Amalek is called "first among the nations" (Num. 24:20), a fitting description for the new rulers of Egypt.

The Hyksos ruled Egypt for a few centuries. They were eventually expelled by Ahmose I of Thebes, who founded the New Kingdom and the 18th Dynasty. The Amalekites oppressed Israel during the time of the Judges. But about 400 years after the Exodus, King Saul annihilated most of the Amalekites and destroyed their city (1 Sam. 15). The brief topographical description of the city of Amalek which Saul attacked seems consistent with the Hyksos capital of Avaris in the Eastern Nile Delta (1 Sam. 15:5).

Saul was succeeded as king by David and then by David's son Solomon. During Solomon's reign, the Queen of Sheba visited Jerusalem (1 Ki. 10). Jesus calls this woman the "Queen of the South" (Matt. 12:42), a term that can refer to

The Queen of Sheba Visits King Solomon

Egypt (Dan. 11). The Jewish historian, Josephus identifies her as queen of both Egypt and Ethiopia.[19] Ahmose's I granddaughter (or great-granddaughter) was Hatshepsut. After the death of her husband, Hatshepsut ruled Egypt as pharaoh, with her young step-son Thutmose III, as co-regent. The most famous event from Hatshepsut's reign is her expedition to "Punt" or "God's land," recorded on the walls of her mortuary temple at Deir al-Bahari. While the location of Punt is uncertain, a strong case can be made from other Egyptian records that this included the land of Palestine. The goods she brought back from this journey—ivory, incense, precious stones, and thirty-one live myrrh trees—were the type of valuables that Solomon regularly imported or received as tribute (1 Ki. 10:22, 25).

Five years after Solomon's death, God judged his son Rehoboam and the tribe of Judah for abandoning His law by bringing Pharaoh Shishak against them. Shishak took the treasures of the Temple and the King's house, including the golden shields that Solomon had made (1 Ki. 14; 2 Chr. 12).

In his records carved in the temple complex of Karnak, Thutmose III depicts the loot of a rich temple captured during his first military campaign in Palestine. The treasures he brought back include furniture with rings and poles for carrying 300 gold shields (2 Chr. 9:15-16), one bronze altar, one gold altar, 95 golden basins, 30 doors of copper (2 Chr. 4:9), and many ornate vessels, but none of the grotesque elements that might be expected from a pagan temple.

God had decreed that the people of Judah would be Shishak's servants so they could experience the contrast between serving foreigners and serving Him (2 Chr. 12:8).

Relief Depicting Pharaoh Shishak

Ruins of Karnak Temple

Thutmose III continued to collect tribute in Palestine and areas further north each year, until old age forced him to taper off his military campaigns.

Thutmose III's successor, Amenhotep II, may have been trying to renew Egyptian dominance of Judah when he sent an army under his commander Usertatet. The Bible records that God destroyed a million-man army under Zerah the Ethiopian during the reign of King Asa of Judah (2 Chr. 14). Although Egyptian sources do not record their defeats, the meager booty from Amenhotep II's ninth-year campaign may indicate one: "[H]e could boast of returning with only two horses, one chariot, and some bows and arrows."[20]

Egypt declined during the period of the divided Israelite kingdom and fell to Assyria around 650 BC. Egypt regained its independence and power for a time, however.

Ironically, in their weakest and most compromised moments, the remnant of Israel would look back to Egypt for salvation and protection from the Babylonians (Jer. 42-44). Despite continual warnings not to resort to Egypt, the Israelites persisted, in their stiff-necked opposition to God and faithless rejection of His amazing salvation at the Red Sea. The Babylonians took Jerusalem in 586 BC, destroying the temple and taking Judah captive to Babylon. Around this time, Pharaoh Merneptah mentions Israel, and no doubt refers to this event on the Israel Stele:[21]

> *Canaan weeps in her captivity; Ashkelon has been taken and Gezer seized. Yanoam no longer endures; Israel lies devastated, bereft of its seed.*[22]

But the Lord would bring His judgment down upon Egypt as well. He announced through His prophet Jeremiah the destruction of Egypt at the hands of Nebuchadnezzar:

> *The word that the LORD spoke to Jeremiah the prophet, how Nebuchadnezzar king of Babylon would come and strike the land of Egypt. . . . "The daughter of Egypt shall be ashamed; she shall be delivered into the hand of the people of the North." The LORD of hosts, the God of Israel, says, "Behold I will bring punishment on Amon of No [the sun god] and Pharaoh and Egypt, with their gods and their kings—Pharaoh and those who trust in him. And I will deliver them into the hand of those who seek their lives, into the hand of Nebuchadnezzar king of Babylon and the hand of his servants." (Jeremiah 46:13, 24-26).*

This prophecy occurred around 580 BC, and its fulfillment followed soon afterward. Egypt was later conquered by the Persians as well. Then, in 332 BC, Alexander the Great took Egypt in his conquests, and this once-proud nation was subjugated to the Greeks for 300 years, but that is the subject of another chapter. Egypt became a Roman province in 30 BC and remained under Roman rule until it was conquered by the Muslim Arabs in AD 642.

And so, proud Egypt fell from its prominence, but slowly. The painfully slow and steady decline of Egypt is a testimony to the power of God. This nation played an important part on the stage of redemptive history, bearing the brunt of God's judgment for their severe treatment of His people. The Red Sea event was the greatest living illustration of God's redemption, finally fulfilled at the cross of Calvary.

The Kingdom of Cush

Because of Your temple at Jerusalem,
Kings will bring presents to You. . . .
Envoys will come out of Egypt;
Ethiopia will quickly stretch out her hands to God. (Psalm 68:29, 31)

And in that day there shall be a Root of Jesse,
Who shall stand as a banner to the people;
For the Gentiles shall seek Him,
And His resting place shall be glorious.
It shall come to pass in that day
That the Lord shall set His hand again the second time
To recover the remnant of His people who are left,
From Assyria and Egypt,
From Pathros and Cush,
From Elam and Shinar,
From Hamath and the islands of the sea. (Isaiah 11:10-11)

There are many references to "Cush" and "Ethiopia" in the Old Testament Scriptures, all of which refer to the kingdoms south of Egypt on the Nile River in modern-day Sudan. Moses married a woman from the land of Cush—a woman of darker color and a descendant of Ham.

Nile River

With Egyptian dominance of Cush including all territory to the Fourth Cataract of the Nile, this land was tributary to the Pharaoh, and the local chiefs were made servants in the king's court. The Egyptian language was adopted by the Cushites, who also began worshiping Egyptian gods until Christ came over a thousand years later.

Eventually, Egyptian control over Cush ceased and these peoples probably dissolved into locally-controlled tribal groups. A powerful king from Napata (in the land of Cush) arose around 750 BC and conquered Upper Egypt. King Kashta ruled from Thebes until 740 BC. His successor conquered Egypt, and the dynasty

Pyramids of Nuri in Ancient Cush

continued for about 100 years. The last of these Cushite kings was defeated not by Egyptians but by a new powerful empire—the Assyrians—around 674 BC. This Pharaoh, Taharqa, managed to regain control of Thebes until 665 BC, at which time the Assyrians returned and expelled him from Egypt. Thebes never recovered from the devastation it took at the hands of the Assyrians. The city was finally completely destroyed in a three-year siege by the Greek Ptolemy Lathyrus. This was the end of the glory days of Egypt and Ethiopia.

The destruction of Egypt during the rise of the Assyrian Empire was announced by the prophet Isaiah in chapter 19.

The burden against Egypt.
Behold, the LORD rides on a swift cloud,
And will come into Egypt;
The idols of Egypt will totter at His presence,
And the heart of Egypt will melt in its midst.
"I will set Egyptians against Egyptians;
Everyone will fight against his brother,
And everyone against his neighbor,
City against city, kingdom against kingdom.
The spirit of Egypt will fail in its midst;
I will destroy their counsel,
And they will consult the idols and the charmers,
The mediums and the sorcerers.
And the Egyptians I will give
Into the hand of a cruel master,
And a fierce king will rule over them,"
Says the LORD, the LORD of hosts. (Isaiah 19:1-4)

Despite these initial sobering words concerning Egypt's destruction, Isaiah's prophecy continues on a much more positive note when referring to "that day" in which the Messiah would come. Africa would most certainly receive the blessing of Christ, the Messiah of God.

In that day five cities in the land of Egypt will speak the language of Canaan and swear by the LORD of hosts; one will be called the City of Destruction. In that day there will be an altar to the LORD in the midst of the land of Egypt, and a

> *pillar to the LORD at its border. And it will be for a sign and for a witness to the LORD of hosts in the land of Egypt; for they will cry to the LORD because of the oppressors, and He will send them a Savior and a Mighty One, and He will deliver them. Then the LORD will be known to Egypt, and the Egyptians will know the LORD in that day, and will make sacrifice and offering; yes, they will make a vow to the LORD and perform it. And the LORD will strike Egypt, He will strike and heal it; they will return to the LORD, and He will be entreated by them and heal them. In that day there will be a highway from Egypt to Assyria, and the Assyrian will come into Egypt and the Egyptian into Assyria, and the Egyptians will serve with the Assyrians. In that day Israel will be one of three with Egypt and Assyria—a blessing in the midst of the land, whom the LORD of hosts shall bless, saying, "Blessed is Egypt My people, and Assyria the work of My hands, and Israel My inheritance." (Isaiah 19:18-25)*

Fourteen hundred years before Christ, Egypt was the epitome of tyranny and the primary antagonist opposing the people of God. After eight hundred years of decline, and six hundred years before the coming of the Messiah, Africa's salvation was clearly revealed as part of the purposes and plans of God. This wonderful prophecy of Isaiah goes so far as to say that the Gospel of Christ would penetrate further into the heart of Africa to reach Cush (or Sudan and Ethiopia) in the south. These are the nations that will come to bow before Jesus and acknowledge the true and living God.

> *Thus says the Lord:*
> *"The labor of Egypt and merchandise of Cush*
> *And of the Sabeans, men of stature,*
> *Shall come over to you, and they shall be yours;*
> *They shall walk behind you,*
> *They shall come over in chains;*
> *And they shall bow down to you.*
> *They will make supplication to you, saying, 'Surely God is in you,*
> *And there is no other;*
> *There is no other God.' " (Isaiah 45:14)*

When Jesus Came to North Africa

Athanasius of Alexandria (AD 296-373)

The early church leader Mark (associate of the Apostle Peter) carried the Gospel message into Egypt in the mid 1st century AD, and the Egyptian church he founded would stand strong through waves of Roman persecution. North African men like Athanasius and Augustine were mightily used by God to define orthodoxy and defend the faith against heresies. Indeed, these African men have provided rock-solid foundations for Western Christianity. Augustine grew up in modern-day Algeria (near Carthage), and Athanasius was a pastor/bishop of the church in Alexandria. The oldest extant Christian document in the world was discovered in Egypt, dating to the 230s AD. It is penned by a Christian brother to a man named Paulus, and the letter closes with a greeting, "I pray that you will fare well in the Lord." The letter indicates that Christians were already active in local politics at the time.[23]

Egypt was conquered by Arab Muslims in AD 642 and has been ruled by Muslims ever since. Although the Christian population of Egypt has declined over the centuries, a remnant has remained faithful to Christ through many years of discrimination and persecution. Today Egypt is 10-15% Christian, but only 1-2% Protestant. Located further south along the Nile, Ethiopia is 43% Oriental Orthodox and 18% Protestant Christian by profession, and the Christian population is growing. Much still remains to be done to see the transformation of this part of the world. The corruption, tyranny, and poverty brought about by bad worldviews (especially under Muslim influence) are still very strong in this area of the world.

All these nations stand in dire need of further discipleship in the good news of Jesus Christ. Economically, these nations—which were the richest and most prosperous in previous eras—are now among the most oppressed and most impoverished, especially

Augustine of Hippo (AD 354-430)

Sudan, Ethiopia, and Libya. This is largely due to Islam, which has severely curtailed the Christian faith in North Africa since the 7th century AD.

North African Nation	Corruption Rating [24]	Freedom Rating [25]	Prosperity Rating [26]	Percent Christian
Egypt	105	144	94	10%
Sudan (Cush)	177	166	138	4%
Ethiopia	114	137	164	62%
Algeria	105	171	82	1%
Libya	170	125	102	1%
Tunisia	73	125	97	1%
Morocco	73	75	113	1%

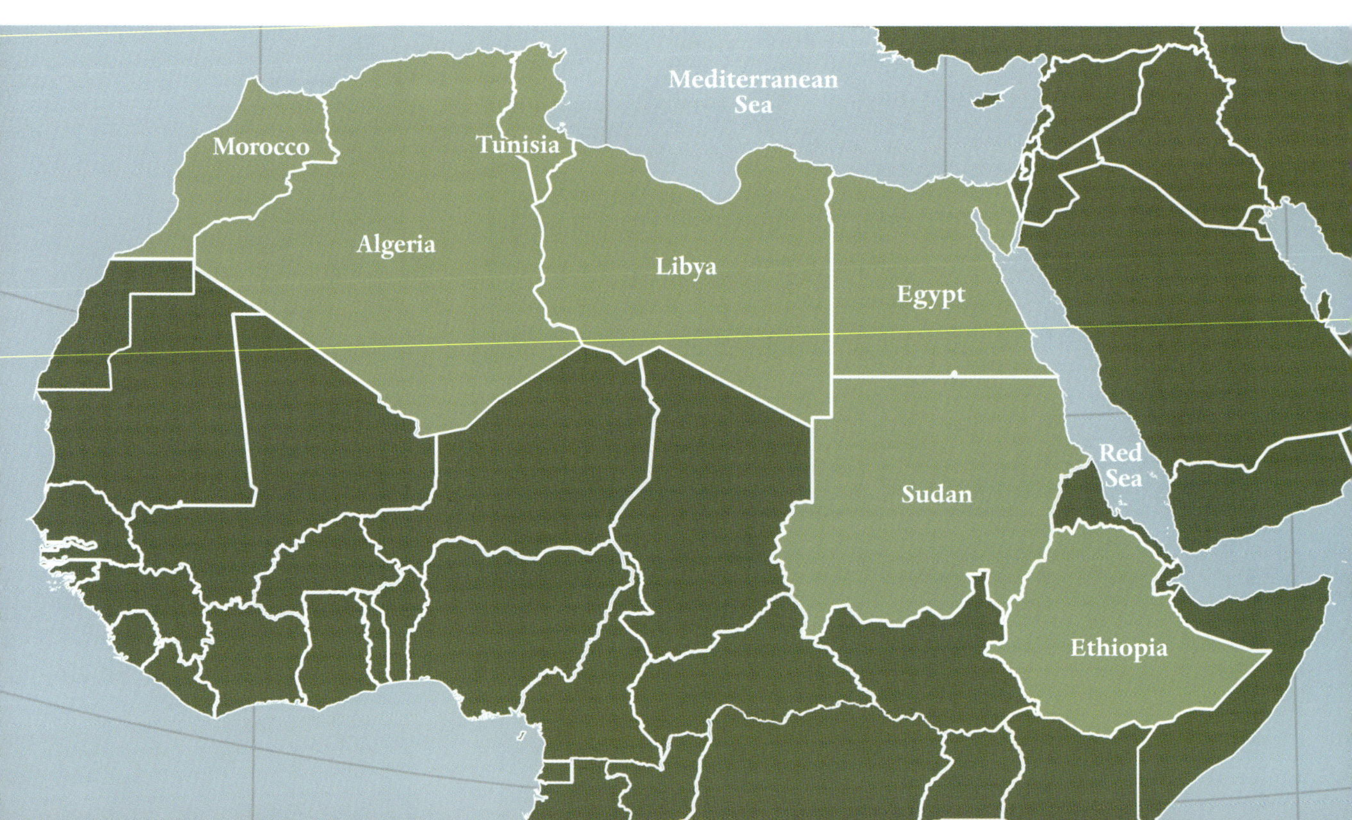

Economically, God has blessed the nations of North Africa with the following major resources and exports.

Country	Major Resources / Exports
Egypt	Oil, Cotton, Dates, Figs, Onions, Strawberries, and Watermelon
Sudan (Cush)	Oil, Cotton, Peanuts, Sesame Seeds, Sugar, and Gold
Ethiopia	Coffee, Gold, Leather, Live Animals
Libya	Oil, Natural Gas, Chemicals
Algeria	Oil, Natural Gas
Tunisia	Oil, Car Parts, Textiles, Electrical Equipment, Olives, Dates, Almonds, Grains
Morocco	Wheat, Chicken, Olives, Tomatoes, Cattle, Sheep, Almonds, Oranges, Phosphate Minerals, Clothing, and Seafood

Ram Sphinxes

Sand Dunes in Egypt

Timeline Review

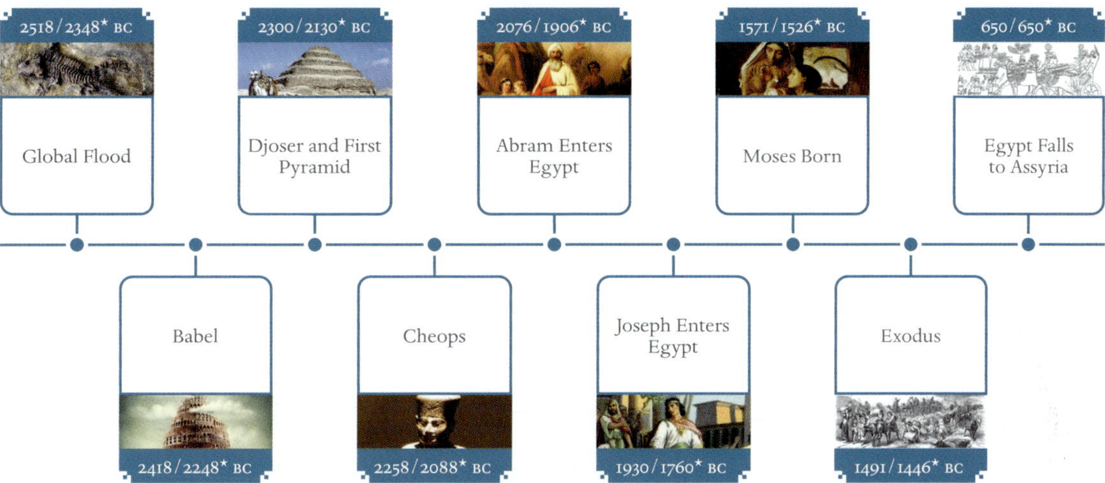

* Date according to Ussher's Chronology which assumes Israelites were in Egypt 215 years.

Chapter V Prayer

Our great God and Father, Redeemer, and Judge of all,

We stand amazed at the other side of the Red Sea as we consider your judgment and mercy—a people saved and an army destroyed! You are to be feared, oh God, and trusted and worshiped and loved for your mercy upon your covenant people. All of the empires of men and all of the great leaders of nations are at your command. They may set themselves against you, but they cannot thwart your purposes. You will accomplish all of your sovereign purposes through these great powers. Through it all, your kingdom will never fail. Your church will never perish. But, all things will work out for the good of your church through the ages. We are thankful for the picture of redemption provided at the Red Sea. Now, we better understand the mighty salvation our Lord Jesus Christ accomplished against our greatest enemies, that tyrant the devil, and our sin. We praise the Name of Jesus, our mighty Redeemer!

Amen.

View from Arbel Cliff, Galilee, Israel

CHAPTER VI

The Special People of God

What advantage then has the Jew, or what is the profit of circumcision? Much in every way! Chiefly because to them were committed the oracles of God. (Romans 3:1-2)

By God's mercies, He did not leave the world without a revelation concerning His truth, His law, and His plan of redemption. His revelation was committed to Moses first, and His prophets continued passing along the oracles of God to Israel until the coming of Christ. The land given to the people of God was strategically laid out directly between the first great human civilizations on earth. The land of Canaan was exactly in the center of the action, with direct access to Egypt, the Hittites, the Assyrians, the Babylonians, the Persians, and the Greeks—all of the important civilizations in the west and the east. No trade routes were more critical to human civilization for 2,000 years than these routes coming through the land of Canaan.

The Nations that Populated Canaan Before 1400 BC

After the city states of Sodom and Gomorrah were destroyed, Abraham's nephew Lot remained in the area to the east of the Dead Sea. The two sons born to him by his daughters were given the names Moab and Ammon. The Moabites remained in the approximate area where Lot settled. They did not worship and serve the true and living God, but made themselves a scourge to the people of God for many centuries. Lot's other son, Ammon, was the father of the Ammonites, also antagonistic to God's people. The earliest reference to the Moabites outside of Scripture is found in a sarcophagus in Luxor (Egypt) which details how the Pharaoh Ramses II conquered these peoples in the 1100s BC, while Israel was ruled by the Judges.

Abraham's son, Isaac had two sons—the eldest Esau and the younger Jacob. While Jacob became the father of the twelve tribes of Israel, Esau rejected his birthright and lost his father's blessing. His descendants were the Edomites and they settled south of Moab on the southeast corner of the Dead Sea.

Esau rejects his birthright

While the Israelites were wandering in the wilderness, they came to the borders of the land of the Moabites, where the king of Moab sent a prophet, Balaam the son of Beor, to curse them. The story is told in Numbers 22-23.

> *Then the children of Israel moved, and camped in the plains of Moab on the side of the Jordan across from Jericho. Now Balak the son of Zippor saw all that Israel had done to the Amorites. And Moab was exceedingly afraid of the people because they were many, and Moab was sick with dread because of the children of Israel. So Moab said to the elders of Midian, "Now this company will lick up everything around us, as an ox licks up the grass of the field." And Balak the son of Zippor was king of the Moabites at that time. Then he sent messengers to Balaam the son of Beor at Pethor, which is near the River in the land of the sons of his people, to call him, saying: "Look, a people has come from Egypt. See, they cover the face of the earth, and are settling next to me! Therefore please come at once, curse this people for me, for they are too mighty for me. Perhaps I shall be able to defeat them and drive them out of the land, for I know that he whom you bless is blessed, and he whom you curse is cursed."* (Numbers 22:1-6)

Found on a wall of a destroyed building only thirty miles north of Moab in the Jordan Valley in 1967 was an inscription containing the "sayings" of one Balaam the son of Beor. Four references are made to Balaam, who was apparently seeking help from the goddesses Ashtar and Shegard. These were gods who were sought after using fertility rites (which usually involved grotesque sexual sin). This was the very sin into which the children of Israel were drawn by Balaam (Num. 25). The inscription dates back to 900 BC, and it is the oldest extant writing in the Aramaic language. It begins, "The sayings of Balaam, son of Beor, the man who was a seer of the gods. Lo! Gods came to him in the night and spoke to him."[1]

The Ammonites, Moabites, and Edomites are all referred to in Sennacherib's Prism uncovered in AD 1919. This prism mentions the Israelite King Hezekiah as well as other kings from which the Assyrian king received tribute. What follows is a direct translation from the Prism, which was probably written in 689 BC.

> *From Menachem, the Shamsimurunite, Tuba'lu the Sidonite, Abdi-liti the Arvadite, Uru-milki the Gublite, Mitinti the Ashdodite, Budu-ilu the Beth Ammonite, Kammusu-nadbi the Moabite, Malik-rammu the Edomite, kings of Amurru, all of them, numerous presents as their heavy tribute, they brought before me for the fourth time, and kissed my feet.*[2]

Location of Edom and Moab
kilometers
0
20
Beirut
Sidon
Tyre
PHOENICIAN STATES
Acre
Damascus
ASSYRIAN EMPIRE
KINGDOM OF ARAM DAMASCUS
Umomium
Mediterranean Sea
KINGDOM OF ISRAEL
Samaria
Shechem
Jerash
KINGDOM OF AMMON
Jaffa
Jericho
Rabbath-Ammon
Jerusalem
Ashdod
Lachish
ARAMEAN TRIBES
Ashkelon
Dibon
Hebron
PHILIS-TINE STATES
KINGDOM OF JUDAH
Gaza
KINGDOM OF MOAB
Beersheba
ARABU TRIBES
KINGDOM OF EDOM
NABATU TRIBES
Petra

A hundred years after this historical record was made, around 580 BC, the prophet Jeremiah brought the Word of the Lord against Moab. For many years, the Moabites had been antagonists to God's people. In the end, Jeremiah said the nation would be utterly destroyed "because he exalted himself against the LORD" (Jer. 48:26).

No more praise of Moab.
In Heshbon they have devised evil against her:
"Come, and let us cut her off as a nation."
You also shall be cut down, O Madmen!
The sword shall pursue you;
A voice of crying shall be from Horonaim:
"Plundering and great destruction!"
Moab is destroyed;
Her little ones have caused a cry to be heard;
For in the Ascent of Luhith they ascend with continual weeping;
For in the descent of Horonaim the enemies have heard a cry of destruction."
(Jeremiah 48:2-5)

This prophecy was fulfilled around the time of the Persian conquest about a century later. All existing descendants of Moab were scattered, and the nation was no more. The Ammonites also seem to have disappeared around this time.

The Edomites, or Idumeans, continued as a nation much longer. Around 110 BC, Jewish Hasmonean King John Hyrcanus conquered Idumea and forced all the Idumeans to convert to Judaism. King Herod was an Idumean who seized control of Palestine with the help of the Romans, ruling from 37-4 BC. However, the Idumeans joined forces with the Jews in rebelling against Rome in the 1st century AD. Consequently, the Edomites were completely destroyed even as the Jews were decimated in AD 70 and over the years that followed. Ironically, it was Edom's hostility to God's people centuries earlier that precipitated the prophecy of their destruction by Ezekiel in 550 BC.

Thus says the Lord GOD: "The whole earth will rejoice when I make you desolate. As you rejoiced because the inheritance of the house of Israel was desolate, so I will do to you; you shall be desolate, O Mount Seir, as well as all of Edom—all of it! Then they shall know that I am the LORD." (Ezekiel 35:14-15)

The Exceedingly Wicked Amorites

Thus says the LORD . . .
"It was I who destroyed the Amorite before them,
Whose height was like the height of the cedars,
And he was as strong as the oaks;
Yet I destroyed his fruit above
And his roots beneath.
Also it was I who brought you up from the land of Egypt,
And led you forty years through the wilderness,
To possess the land of the Amorite."
(Amos 2:6, 9-10)

Of all the tribes of the ancient world, the Amorites left the longest lasting and most wicked legacy. They were a powerful people, probably dating back to the days of the Tower of Babel. Amorite blood ran in the veins of Hammurabi and the first great dynasty of Babylon. In the earliest writings of Sumer we read of the Amorites who controlled the northern and western lands (which would include modern-day Syria and Israel). Naram Sin, the grandson of Sargon I, battled with the Amorites in 2240 BC. The Amorites captured Ebla in 2000 BC and built for themselves a temple and a palace. Around this time they proliferated in Canaan and gained a reputation for evil practices. According to the Hebrew Book of Jubilees written sometime in the 1st or 2nd century BC, "the former terrible

Terracotta Image of Amorite couple

giants, the Rephaim, gave way to the Amorites, an evil and sinful people whose wickedness surpasses that of any other, and whose life will be cut short on earth."[3] However, the most reliable account of the Amorites is given in Scripture itself.

The Old Testament record lumps the Amorites with the Kenites, Kenizzites, Kadmonites, Hittites, Perizzites, Rephaim, Canaanites, Girgashites, and Jebusites (Gen. 15:19-21). These all lived in the land of Canaan and derived their genetic roots from the man Canaan, the son of Ham who was cursed by Noah for his indecent behavior (Gen. 9:25-27).

Although not a great deal is known about the Amorites, the most egregious sins for which God destroyed these tribes were the sexual perversions listed in Leviticus 18 and 20. Clearly, Sodom and Gomorrah were representative of the sinful cities of Canaan before Israel settled the land. After listing various sexual perversions, including homosexuality, the Lord instructs Israel:

> *Do not defile yourselves with any of these things; for by all these the nations are defiled, which I am casting out before you. For the land is defiled; therefore I visit the punishment of its iniquity upon it, and the land vomits out its inhabitants. You shall therefore keep My statutes and My judgments, and shall not commit any of these abominations, either any of your own nation or any stranger who dwells among you (for all these abominations the men of the land have done, who were before you, and thus the land is defiled), lest the land vomit you out also when you defile it, as it vomited out the nations that were before you. For whoever commits any of these abominations, the persons who commit them shall be cut off from among their people. (Leviticus 18:24-29)*

Through the centuries, many nations and empires have been consumed by war, idolatry, witchcraft, human sacrifice, cruelty, and sexual perversion. For many hundreds of years, God was patient with the Canaanite nations. With the entrance of Israel into the land around 1400 BC, the judgment of God finally descended upon these wicked peoples.

Since AD 2000, most of the Western world of Europe and North America has been returning to the sins of Canaan and Sodom and Gomorrah, inviting the judgment of God upon them as well. For a time, people celebrate their sin with pride marches and the symbol of the rainbow. Ironically, the rainbow is a symbol of God's preserving hand and common grace upon the world in the

Noahic Covenant. Yet Westerners today use the symbol to celebrate their sexual perversion and, with it, the removal of God's common grace from them.

When the Apostle Paul addressed the pagan Greeks on Mars Hill around AD 50, he rebuked them for their idolatry and called them to repentance. He warned them against testing the patience of God, as they had been doing for centuries.

> *Truly, these times of ignorance God overlooked, but now commands all men everywhere to repent, because He has appointed a day on which He will judge the world in righteousness by the Man whom He has ordained. He has given assurance of this to all by raising Him from the dead. (Acts 17:30-31)*

Forty Years in the Wilderness (1446-1406 BC)

After crossing the Red Sea, God gave Moses the law at Mount Sinai, a most gracious and wise provision for His people. He engraved the Ten Commandments on stone tablets, which were placed in the Ark of the Covenant and kept in the Holy of Holies, which was part of the tabernacle or temple.

The words of this law are straightforward and fundamental. They communicate God's will for man and God's covenant with man. He redeems His people from bondage and then He asks for their faith, love, and obedience to His commandments.

Mt. Sinai

The Ten Commandments

I am the LORD your God who brought you out of the land of Egypt, out of the house of bondage.

I. You shall have no other gods before Me.

II. You shall not make for yourself a carved image—any likeness of anything that is in heaven above, or that is in the earth beneath, or that is in the water under the earth; you shall not bow down to them nor serve them. For I, the LORD your God, am a jealous God, visiting the iniquity of the fathers upon the children to the third and fourth generations of those who hate Me, but showing mercy to thousands, to those who love Me and keep My commandments.

III. You shall not take the name of the LORD your God in vain, for the LORD will not hold him guiltless who takes His name in vain.

IV. Observe the Sabbath day, to keep it holy, as the LORD your God commanded you. Six days you shall labor and do all your work, but the seventh day is the Sabbath of the LORD your God. In it you shall do no work: you, nor your son, nor your daughter, nor your male servant, nor your female servant, nor your ox, nor your donkey, nor any of your cattle, nor your stranger who is within your gates, that your male servant and your female servant may rest as well as you. And remember that you were a slave in the land of Egypt, and the LORD your God brought you out from there by a mighty hand and by an outstretched arm; therefore the LORD your God commanded you to keep the Sabbath day.

V. Honor your father and your mother, as the LORD your God has commanded you, that your days may be long, and that it may be well with you in the land which the LORD your God is giving you.

VI. You shall not murder.

VII. You shall not commit adultery.

VIII. You shall not steal.

IX. You shall not bear false witness against your neighbor.

X. You shall not covet your neighbor's wife; and you shall not desire your neighbor's house, his field, his male servant, his female servant, his ox, his donkey, or anything that is your neighbor's. (Deuteronomy 5:6-21)

These words constitute the basic moral law of God. For those who have a change of heart, and those who by faith realize God as Savior, these rules provide insight into the will of God for life. All other ethical systems concocted by man over the ages are wrong. Only the moral laws of God summarized here and expanded upon in Exodus, Leviticus, Numbers, and Deuteronomy (and by the revelation of the Lord Jesus Christ) should be used to define right and wrong. To the extent that nations would keep these laws, they would find temporal blessings and flourish. These laws would be a blessing to every nation, whether in covenant with God like Israel or otherwise. Moses elaborates on the law throughout the book of Deuteronomy and remarks:

Moses with the Ten Commandments

Surely I have taught you statutes and judgments, just as the LORD my God commanded me, that you should act according to them in the land which you go to possess. Therefore be careful to observe them; for this is your wisdom and your understanding in the sight of the peoples who will hear all these statutes, and say, "Surely this great nation is a wise and understanding people." For what great nation is there that has God so near to it, as the LORD our God is to us, for whatever reason we may call upon Him? And what great nation is there that has such statutes and righteous judgments as are in all this law which I set before you this day?" (Deuteronomy 4:5-8)

Laws for the Civil Government

God's law also laid out the bounds of jurisdiction and the rules of justice for the civil magistrate. This law was careful, first and foremost, to address the crime of murder.

He who strikes a man so that he dies shall surely be put to death. However, if he did not lie in wait, but God delivered him into his hand, then I will appoint for you a place where he may flee. (Exodus 21:12-13)

But if anyone hates his neighbor, lies in wait for him, rises against him and strikes him mortally, so that he dies, and he flees to one of these cities, then the elders of his city shall send and bring him from there, and deliver him over to the hand of the avenger of blood, that he may die. Your eye shall not pity him, but you shall put away the guilt of innocent blood from Israel, that it may go well with you. (Deuteronomy 19:11-13)

Instead of resorting to torture and imprisonment as a means of punishment, God's law wisely ordained a system of restitution to victims in cases of theft. Crimes are not committed against the state. They are committed against the victims and, above all, against God.

If a man steals an ox or a sheep, and slaughters it or sells it, he shall restore five oxen for an ox and four sheep for a sheep. . . If the theft is certainly found alive in his hand, whether it is an ox or donkey or sheep, he shall restore double. (Exodus 22:1, 4)

Instead of the regulatory police state, God's law required heavy penalties in cases of gross negligence (which would affect modern crimes like drunk driving).

> *"If an ox gores a man or a woman to death, then the ox shall surely be stoned, and its flesh shall not be eaten; but the owner of the ox shall be acquitted. But if the ox tended to thrust with its horn in times past, and it has been made known to his owner, and he has not kept it confined, so that it has killed a man or a woman, the ox shall be stoned and its owner also shall be put to death." (Exodus 22:28-29)*

God's law also gave death as a maximum penalty for more severe crimes like homosexuality, adultery, certain forms of incest, witchcraft, and human sacrifice to false gods.

The Ceremonial Law

Since the days of Cain and Abel, man has seen the need to approach God by sacrifice. Even the polytheists, blinded by the devil in their gross paganism, recognized their guilt and usually offered sacrifices.

In His revelation to Moses, God laid out the terms of sacrifice and religious worship. However, these practices were intended for a pattern, as symbols or shadows of what was to come with the Lord Jesus Christ.

The Lord God of Israel assigned for them a tabernacle or a temple for the place of meeting, and laid out very specific requirements for its construction and its accoutrements. This would be the place where God would meet with His people. Sinful man is faced with the question: "How does a holy God meet with an unholy people?" With His people under the Old Testament, the Lord would meet in the tabernacle equipped with the Holiest of Holies, in which was found the Ark

Ark of the Covenant

of the Covenant, on top of which was the Mercy Seat. With the coming of Christ, His body, the church, becomes the new Temple or Tabernacle.

> *Do you not know that you are the temple of God and that the Spirit of God dwells in you? If anyone defiles the temple of God, God will destroy him. For the temple of God is holy, which temple you are. (1 Corinthians 3:16-17)*

At the center of the tabernacle was the Holy of Holies into which the High Priest would enter only once a year on the Day of Atonement (Leviticus 16). The priest would enter through the curtains and sprinkle blood seven times over the Mercy Seat—the cover on the Ark of the Covenant. All others would be killed instantly if they entered this holy place. With the coming of Christ however, we may all enter the holiest place "by the blood of Jesus" in prayer. We walk into the holiest through the curtain of Christ.

> *Therefore, brethren, having boldness to enter the Holiest by the blood of Jesus, by a new and living way which He consecrated for us, through the veil, that is, His flesh, and having a High Priest over the house of God, let us draw near with a true heart in full assurance of faith, having our hearts sprinkled from an evil conscience and our bodies washed with pure water. (Hebrews 10:19-22)*

Inside the Holy of Holies sat the Ark of the Covenant, and inside the Ark were to be found Aaron's rod that budded, the Ten Commandments of Exodus 20:1-17 written on stone, and a container of manna (collected in the wilderness). These signified new life from death, the Word of God, and sustenance for our life here on this side of glory. All of this is provided in Christ upon His coming. "For all the promises of God in Him are Yes, and in Him Amen, to the glory of God through us." (2 Corinthians 1:20)

Covering the Ark of the Covenant was a Mercy Seat made of pure gold. This is where He would meet with His people. The cover was called a *kapporeth* in the Hebrew or *hilasterion* in the Greek—translated as a "ransom" or "reconciliation" (Hebrews 9:4-5). This speaks to the need for placating or reconciling with God who is wrathful towards man for sin and rebellion. Thus, it was blood that covered the mercy seat—and this is the covering that Christ brought for us.

> *For all have sinned and fall short of the glory of God, being justified freely by His grace through the redemption that is in Christ Jesus, whom God set forth as a propitiation [hilasterion] by His blood, through faith, to demonstrate His righteousness, because in His forbearance God had passed over the sins that were previously committed, to demonstrate at the present time His righteousness, that He might be just and the justifier of the one who has faith in Jesus. (Romans 3:23-26)*

Thus, the Old Testament tabernacle, the Holy of Holies, the Ark of the Covenant, and the Mercy Seat all pointed to the coming of Christ. Also, five different sacrifices were instituted for Old Testament Israel and each of these prefigured Christ's single sacrifice.

1. Christ would become our "whole burnt sacrifice" or the *olah*. (Reference Leviticus 1 and Genesis 22:2, Isaiah 53:12.)
2. Christ would become our meal offering (Leviticus 2:1-3, John 6:35).
3. Christ would be our peace offering (Leviticus 3, 7:11-34, Colossians. 1:20, 1 Corinthians 10:14-22)
4. Christ would be our sin offering (Leviticus 4:1-5:13, Hebrews 10:14, Romans 8:3, 1 Peter. 8:13
5. Christ would be our trespass offering (Leviticus 5:14-6:7, 7:1-6, Romans 6:23)

Now, 2,000 years after the coming of Jesus the Christ, the majority of religions and cultures have ceased offering sacrifices of animals and humans. This was due mostly to the influence of Christ upon the world. Although the majority of the world would not receive Christ by faith in the modern age, still there was a universal sense that human and animal sacrifice was no longer needed for sins.

Israel's Lapse in Faith

Moses led the Israelites up from the south through the Wilderness of Zin. From there he sent twelve spies into the land of Canaan, who searched out the area as far north as Hebron (thirty miles south of Jerusalem). They came upon the descendants of Anak, or the Rephaim (Num. 13:22). These people were giants, perhaps after the order of Og, king of Bashan. This man had a bed thirteen feet long, which means he could have been eleven to twelve feet tall. These giants

would continue to plague the Israelites for the next 400 years. David faced Goliath of the Philistines, reported to have been 9 feet, 9 inches tall (2.97 m). This race of giants were intimidating to ten of the spies, and their faithless report discouraged the people of Israel from taking the land. Two spies, Joshua and Caleb, were the exception.

Sadly, the children of Israel did not trust that God could save them from their troubles and deliver them safely to the promised land of Canaan. They did not have faith, so He consigned them to wander in the wilderness for forty years.

This is the simple message concerning salvation—trust in God to save you. Over a thousand years later, He would save the world by His Savior-Son. But those who still do not trust in His Son as Savior will never be saved. They will perish in the wilderness of their sin just like the Israelites who would not trust in His salvation when crossing over into the Promised Land (Heb 3:12-4:1).

Moving into the Promised Land (1406 BC)

> *For you are a holy people to the LORD your God; the LORD your God has chosen you to be a people for Himself, a special treasure above all the peoples on the face of the earth. The LORD did not set His love on you nor choose you because you were more in number than any other people, for you were the least of all peoples; but because the LORD loves you, and because He would keep the oath which He swore to your fathers, the LORD has brought you out with a mighty hand, and redeemed you from the house of bondage, from the hand of Pharaoh king of Egypt. (Deuteronomy 7:6-8)*

As Egypt began a slow and steady decline, and as Assyria was just developing its Middle Empire and the Chinese Shang Dynasty was gathering strength, the true and living God was forming a covenant with an ethnic group called the Israelites in the land of Canaan. Of all the peoples of the earth, they were the least impressive and most insignificant. The Lord God's intent was to show His special blessing on this people by revealing His truth, providing temporal earthly prosperity, and saving them from the enemies surrounding them.

Israel Crosses the Jordan River

This was an era in which tribal groups were constantly wiping each other out by warfare. No tribe or nation was ever safe. Thus Yahweh God offered a picture of His eternal salvation for His people by providing them with temporal salvation from enemies like the Philistines, Amorites, Moabites, Syrians, Assyrians, and Babylonians. The real enemies, the basic enemies of God's people, are the world, the flesh, and the devil. Israel's national enemies served as a constant reminder that they had more deadly spiritual enemies.

The Lord was testing Israel. Would they trust Him to save them from their enemies? Would they trust Him to give them the Promised Land? Would they trust Him to give them heaven? This is the story of Old Testament Israel.

After forty years of leading God's people through the wilderness, Moses died on the eastern side of the Jordan River. He failed to obey at a key point in his leadership, and the Lord directed him to turn the leadership over to Joshua. Moses would not enter Canaan, but the Lord allowed him to view the Promised Land from Mount Nebo.

And they tested God in their heart
By asking for the food of their fancy.
Yes, they spoke against God:
They said, "Can God prepare a table in the wilderness?
Behold, He struck the rock,
So that the waters gushed out,
And the streams overflowed.
Can He give bread also?
Can He provide meat for His people?"
Therefore the LORD heard this and was furious;
So a fire was kindled against Jacob,
And anger also came up against Israel,
Because they did not believe in God,
And did not trust in His salvation. (Psalm 78:18-22)

Another Battle for Another Day

And it came to pass, when Joshua was by Jericho, that he lifted his eyes and looked, and behold, a Man stood opposite him with His sword drawn in His hand. And Joshua went to Him and said to Him, "Are You for us or for our adversaries?"

So He said, "No, but as Commander of the army of the LORD I have now come."

And Joshua fell on his face to the earth and worshiped, and said to Him, "What does my Lord say to His servant?"

Then the Commander of the LORD's army said to Joshua, "Take your sandal off your foot, for the place where you stand is holy." And Joshua did so. (Joshua 5:13-15)

Just before initiating the campaign against Canaan, Joshua was visited by the Commander of the army of the Lord. When asked if he was for Israel or their adversaries, this Commander answered with a simple "No." This highly significant and intriguing response points to another battle that would be fought by the Captain of our salvation 1,400 years later. Another Joshua was still to come—the Greek rendering of His name is "Jesus." Indeed, this Savior would come to fight a much greater war, and He would make a public spectacle of principalities and powers, triumphing over them at the cross of Calvary (Col. 2:15). The conquest of Canaan was a sign of something much greater to come.

The Siege of Jericho

The Fall of Jericho

At the beginning of the conquest of Canaan, the Israelites used an unconventional military strategy. On their first assault, the people marched around the walls of Jericho for seven days. At the end of this week of marching around the city, we learn how the city fell:

> *So the people shouted when the priests blew the trumpets. And it happened when the people heard the sound of the trumpet, and the people shouted with a great shout, that the wall fell down flat. Then the people went up into the city, every man straight before him, and they took the city. And they utterly destroyed all that was in the city, both man and woman, young and old, ox and sheep and donkey, with the edge of the sword. (Joshua 6:20-21)*

Archaeologists identified ancient Jericho in AD 1867. The destruction of the city is dated around 1400 BC, which is about when Joshua and the Israelites destroyed it. Jericho was one of the earliest cities to be built after the flood, and it remained a citadel in Canaan for 900 years, from 2300-1405 BC. Located on the western side of the Jordan Valley, the city possessed a wonderful water supply and a fruitful agricultural enterprise. Archaeologists discovered that the outer walls of Jericho had crumbled; some have suggested this occurred by an earthquake. The town was burned, but archaeologists have found "many store jars full of grain."[4] One researcher uncovered six bushels of grain. This means that the town was not

Israel: 1400-450 BC

plundered by soldiers, as is ordinarily the case in wars among nations. Not a single person was left alive, and the city must have been entirely abandoned after the burning. The research at Tell es-Sultan (the ruins of Jericho) to date has confirmed:

- The city was surrounded by a great wall (Josh. 2:5, 7, 15; 6:5, 20).
- The attack occurred just after the first harvest in the spring (Josh. 2:6; 3:15; 5:10).
- The inhabitants had no opportunity to flee with their foodstuffs (Josh. 6:1).
- The siege must have been short, because the grain was not consumed (Josh. 6:15).
- The mud-brick walls were completely flattened to the ground, perhaps by an earthquake (Josh. 6:20).
- The grain and pottery found in the city indicated that no plundering occurred (Josh. 6:17-18).
- The city was burned. Archaeologist Kathleen Kenyon reports that "walls and floors were blackened or reddened by fire. . . . In most rooms the fallen debris was heavily burnt. . . . A layer of burnt ash and debris about one meter thick" was found on the east side of the city. (Josh. 6:20).[5]

The city covered an area of about eight acres and was surrounded by two walls separated by an embankment. The outer wall stood 46 feet (14 m) above the ground, and the inner wall was about 12-15 feet high. It was a seemingly impregnable city until it came down around 1400 BC.

Over a 38-year career, Joshua made significant progress with the military conquest of Canaan. A fair percentage of the land of Canaan was settled, and distributed to the twelve tribes. The tribe of Levi received its inheritance in cities and pasture lands distributed throughout Israel. However, Israel abandoned the mandate to continue its conquest of Canaan and exterminate the remaining tribes living there.

In obedience to the Lord's command, Joshua built an altar on Mount Ebal after initial victories in the war on Canaan. The altar was uncovered by Israeli archaeologists in 1980, presumably dating back to 1400 BC. Made of large unhewn stone, the altar measured 30 ft x 46 ft (9 m x 14 m). Connected to the altar were the remains of a typical Israeli house with four rooms, probably used for the priest or the persons administering the sacrifices.

Dwellings Unearthed at Tell-es-Sultan

> *Now Joshua built an altar to the LORD God of Israel in Mount Ebal, as Moses the servant of the LORD had commanded the children of Israel, as it is written in the Book of the Law of Moses: And there, in the presence of the children of Israel, he wrote on the stones a copy of the law of Moses, which he had written. (Joshua 8:30-32)*

The invasion of the Israelites into Canaan did not escape notice in the ancient pagan records. During the period of the Exodus and Joshua's incursion into the promised land, the Israelites referred to themselves by the Hebrew word "Ha-ibri." In fact, there are 34 references to the "Hebrews" found in the Pentateuch (Genesis through Deuteronomy). References to a tribe called the "Habiru" have been found on what is known as "the Amarna tablets" in Upper Egypt (dating from 1350s-1330s BC). This would have been about the time of Joshua's conquests. These are letters on clay tablets sent to the Pharaohs, written mostly in Akkadian (the trade language of the day in and around Canaan).

Multiple references to the "Habiru," found on these "letters" written from various sources to the Pharaohs almost certainly indicate an Israelite invasion. Egypt being the largest kingdom close by, kings were interested in communicating their concerns with the Hebrews to the Pharaoh. For example, the king of Gezer writes that "there is war against me from the mountains."[6] He pleads with the Pharaoh that he would "save my land from the power of the Habiru." He adds that "the Habiru are stronger than we."[7] Although, Joshua never conquered the city of Gezer, as indicated in Joshua 10:33, it seems that this king had serious reasons to be concerned.

Then Horam king of Gezer came up to help Lachish; and Joshua struck him and his people, until he left him none remaining. (Joshua 10:33)

In Amarna Letter 273, the city of Zorah is mentioned as a city captured by the "Habiru"—this was where the Hebrew leader Samson was born about 300 years afterwards. Letter 274 contains another cry for help to the Egyptian Pharaoh in these words, "May the king, my lord, save his land from the 'Habiru'. Let it not perish. The city of Sapuma is pillaged."[8]

Although Jerusalem was never conquered until King David laid siege in 1000 BC, the ruler of the city registered his concerns with the Pharaoh on another of the Amarna tablets, quoted as follows:

I am situated like a ship in the midst of the sea. The strong arm of the king [of Egypt] took the land of Naharaim [northern Mesopotamia] and the land of Cush [south of Egypt], but now the Habiru have taken the very cities of the [Egyptian] king. Not a single mayor remains to the king, my lord; all are lost.[9]

Most interesting, however, is the Jerusalem king's reference to Labayu, the king of Shechem. He asks the Pharaoh if he should want Egypt's governors to give away control of their cities in the same way as Labayu "who gave Shechem to the Habiru?"[10]

Interestingly, biblical records do not indicate that the Israelites ever laid siege on the key city of Shechem. Yet, Shechem becomes the center of religious compromise with Baal worship in the period of the Judges. Amarna Tablet 289 provides a key to how this happened. Evidently, something of a concession, a covenant, or an agreement to cooperate was made with these Canaanites, and this must have been the beginning of the religious compromise that came to mark Shechem in later years.

One of the Amarna Tablets

The same thing must have happened with Gezer, as we read in Judges 1:29: "Nor did Ephraim drive out the Canaanites who dwelt in Gezer; so the Canaanites dwelt in Gezer among them."

This was the accusation brought against them by the Angel of the Lord in Judges 2:

> *Then the Angel of the Lord came up from Gilgal to Bochim, and said: "I led you up from Egypt and brought you to the land of which I swore to your fathers; and I said, 'I will never break My covenant with you. And you shall make no covenant with the inhabitants of this land; you shall tear down their altars.' But you have not obeyed My voice. Why have you done this? Therefore I also said, 'I will not drive them out before you; but they shall be thorns in your side, and their gods shall be a snare to you.'"*

The Period of the Judges (1400-1095 BC)

During the period of the Judges, Israel was perpetually giving in to idolatry, serving the gods of the Canaanites. They failed to remember the works of God and His mighty deliverance from Egypt. Hence, they lapsed in faith and did not trust the Lord. This pattern of disobedience and idolatry was usually followed by subservience to enemies and oppression. Then the Israelites would repent briefly, cry out to Yahweh God for deliverance, and He would send them a deliverer in the form of a judge. For a time, they would enjoy a period of peace and freedom and then once more fall back into idolatry, and the pattern would repeat.

The period of the Judges and the era of the early kings is typically regarded by historians as a dark age for the Near Eastern lands of Egypt, Greece, and Assyria.

The Conquest of Ai

Judge	Rule	Approximate Date	Scripture Reference
1. Othniel	40 years	1400 - 1360 BC	Judges 3:9-11
2. Ehud	80 years	1360 - 1280 BC	Judges 3:15-30
3. Shamgar	Unknown	1260 BC	Judges 3:31; 5:6
4. Deborah and Barak	40 years	1280 - 1240 BC	Judges 4:4-5:31
5. Gideon	40 years	1240 - 1200 BC	Judges 6:11-8:32
6. Abimelech	3 years	1200 - 1197 BC	Judges 9:1-57; 2 Samuel 11:21
7. Tola	23 years	1197 - 1174 BC	Judges 10:1-2
8. Jair	22 years	1174 - 1152 BC	Judges 10:3-5
9. Jephthah	6 years	1152 - 1146 BC	Judges 11:1-12:7
10. Ibzan	7 years	1146 - 1139 BC	Judges 12:8-10
11. Elon	10 years	1139 - 1129 BC	Judges 12:11-12
12. Abdon	8 years	1129 - 1121 BC	Judges 12:13-15
13. Samson	20 years	1121 - 1101 BC	Judges 13:1-16:31
14. Samuel	6 years	1101 - 1095 BC	1 Samuel 2:18-4:1

Under the rule of the Hyksos, Egypt declined in power. In the providential ordinance of God, the great empires largely left the small nation states alone. This was a period of tribal wars between smaller city states and nomadic groups.

Gideon and His Wicked Son

The Midianites (from modern-day Saudi Arabia) subjugated the children of Israel in the 13th century BC, employing a scorched-earth, militaristic mode of operation. This tribe had their beginning as descendants of Abraham by his second wife, Keturah.

God raised up a deliverer named Gideon to fight the Midianites, in the famous battle of the 300 against the 140,000. While the Lord wanted Israel to rely upon Him for the victory, the nation always reverted back to resting in their own powers. Gideon took many wives to himself, following the customs of the powerful pagan kings of the day. His son, conceived by a concubine from Shechem, killed almost all of his 70 sons and took on the typical name of a king in

Gideon Invades the Midianite camp

Canaan, Abimelech (translated "father of kings"). Not much of a father of kings himself, Abimelech ruled for only three years over the city of Shechem, which is located between Mount Ebal and Mount Gerizim in the Tribe of Manasseh. This was the de facto capital of Israel for a time, and also the location of the largest pagan temple in Canaan—the temple of "Baal-Berith." Translated as the "covenant god of Baal," this was a veiled allusion to the covenant which Yahweh God, the true God, made with Abraham, Isaac, and Jacob. It is a clear example of the pagan synthesis that broke down the faith in Israel during the period of the judges. Uncovered by archaeologists in the 1960s, this pagan temple was a large multi-storied building about 70 feet by 86 feet (21.2 m x 26.3 m) at its base, with foundations 17 feet (5.2 m) thick. Such foundations would have been adequate to hold a 100 foot tall building.[11]

Evidently, Gideon's son Abimelech grew up with this pagan worship in Shechem, and rather unsuccessfully tried to establish Israel's first kingly dynasty. By God's wise providences, relationships between Abimelech and the Israelites living in Shechem broke down badly. Eventually, he stormed the city with a small army of men and utterly annihilated it.

A thousand of the city's residents rushed into the temple of Baal-Berith as their last defense. Abimelech and his men created a gigantic bonfire around the tower, and burned up the pagan temple and all of the Israelites who were hiding in it. Not too many days later, Abimelech himself was killed when besieging another Israelite city. God's retribution upon the false Baal god, the compromised people of God, and the man who would be king is carefully chronicled in Judges 9. The largest tower and strongest pagan temple in Canaan was not strong enough or high enough to protect the people crowding into it. The Baal god could not protect the people from the wrath of Abimelech and the judgment of the true and living God.

ITALY
GREECE
CRETE
Mediterranean Sea
miles
0
200

The Philistines

The Philistines, populating the cities of Gaza, Ashdod, Ashkelon, Ekron, and Gath, were also a persistent irritant to the children of Israel. According to Deuteronomy 2:23 and Amos 9:7, the Philistines were not indigenous to Canaan. They were descendants of Mizraim, and evidently God brought them to Canaan from an island known as Caphtor, most likely Crete or Cyprus. Recently an archaeogeneticist named Michal Feldman traced the genetics of the Philistines across the Mediterranean Sea to Europe (most likely Greece, Italy, Cyprus, or Crete). They immigrated to the coastland of Canaan in the 12th century BC.[12] This correlates with the timeframe in which the Philistines became a problem for Israel in Scripture. Beginning in the days of Samson (1081 BC) and continuing until the days of Hezekiah (700 BC), wars proliferated between Israel and this tribe. Controlling the land from the Mediterranean Sea as far south as Gaza and as far north as Jerusalem, as well as half the distance from the sea to Jerusalem to the east, they were the nearest enemy to the tribes of Judah, Simeon, and Dan.

Location of Philistia

Illustration of Dagon

During the period of the Judges, Israel's greatest victory against the Philistines occurred when Samson brought the Philistine temple of Dagon down upon 3,000 people. A recent excavation at Tell Qasile and Tel Miqne (where the city of Ekron once stood) unearthed an ancient temple. Significantly, two pillars located about 6 1/2 feet (2 m) apart had been used to support the entire temple. A very strong, tall man could have destroyed the temple by pushing these pillars off their bases.

Dagon was a fish god, with very ancient roots dating as far back as 2300 BC, most likely originating in Syria. Given that Philistia borders the sea, this god would have been of special interest to these pagans. He was also supposed to have been the father of Hadad or Baal. Nonetheless, this god did not do very well when pitted against Yahweh, almighty God of Israel.

Now the lords of the Philistines gathered together to offer a great sacrifice to Dagon their god, and to rejoice. And they said:

"Our god has delivered into our hands Samson our enemy!"

When the people saw him, they praised their god; for they said:

"Our god has delivered into our hands our enemy,
The destroyer of our land,
And the one who multiplied our dead."

So it happened, when their hearts were merry, that they said, "Call for Samson, that he may perform for us." So they called for Samson from the prison, and he performed for them. And they stationed him between the pillars. Then Samson said to the lad who held him by the hand, "Let me feel the pillars which support the temple, so that I can lean on them." Now the temple was full of men and women. All the lords of the Philistines were there—about three thousand men and women on the roof watching while Samson performed.

Then Samson called to the LORD, saying, "O Lord GOD, remember me, I pray! Strengthen me, I pray, just this once, O God, that I may with one blow take vengeance on the Philistines for my two eyes!" And Samson took hold of the two middle pillars which supported the temple, and he braced himself against them, one on his right and the other on his left. Then Samson said, "Let me die with the Philistines!" And he pushed with all his might, and the temple fell on the lords and all the people who were in it. So the dead that he killed at his death were more than he had killed in his life. (Judges 16:23-30)

It was about 480 BC when the prophet Zechariah prophesied an end to the Philistines and a final destruction of Tyre.

For Tyre built herself a tower,
Heaped up silver like the dust,
And gold like the mire of the streets.

Behold, the Lord will cast her out;
He will destroy her power in the sea,
And she will be devoured by fire.

Ashkelon shall see it and fear;

Gaza also shall be very sorrowful;
And Ekron, for He dried up her expectation.
The king shall perish from Gaza,
And Ashkelon shall not be inhabited.

A mixed race shall settle in Ashdod,
And I will cut off the pride of the Philistines. (Zechariah 9:3-6)

The Philistines were finally decimated when Alexander the Great conquered Gaza

Samson Destroys the Temple of the Philistines

in 332 BC.

Israel's Monarchy (1095-586 BC)

Following 400 years under the rule of judges, the Israelites demanded a king of the prophet/judge Samuel and, with the Lord's approval, Samuel relented. Saul became Israel's first king, but the Lord shifted the ruling dynasty to David around 1055 BC. This would become the longest dynasty in world history. In AD 33 God established the rule of His Son and David's son, the Lord Jesus Christ. He was anointed King of kings and Lord of lords, and though some of the rulers of the earth ignore Him, they do so to their peril.

The Old Testament Scriptures are filled with the history of the nation of Israel. Yet what we find in them is strikingly different from ancient pagan histories, which focus on the military accomplishments of their rulers and almost never record military defeats. Rather, biblical history is concerned with the sins and failings of the people of God and their leaders. Its testimony is painfully realistic. Judah, the father of the Jews (and Jesus), commits incest with his daughter-in-law. Moses strikes the rock contrary to the command of God, and is forbidden entrance into the Promised Land. David commits adultery with the wife of one of his military commanders, and has him murdered. Many of the kings of Israel encourage the people to idolatry, child sacrifice, and other horrible sins. The Old Testament is mainly a record of Israel's failures—not its successes.

A military man known for his faith in God and valor in battle, King David solidified the kingdom and enlarged the borders of the nation. He conquered the Jebusites and gained control of the city of Jerusalem, where he established the capital city of Israel. Though he gave in to sin, he was also a humble, repentant man. He is known for writing many of the psalms, and his love for God is evident throughout them.

During the reign of David's son Solomon, the first temple was built in Jerusalem. Remnants of this temple were discovered by excavators in AD 2006—an ancient wall of what appears to have served as a chamber to store oil for temple worship. Inscriptions on various implements found in the dig reference "YHWH," the Hebrew name for Jehovah God, as well as the name "Azaryahu son of Hilkiyahu" (referenced in 1 Chron. 9:10). These significant finds date back to 800-700 BC, evidence that there were active building programs and worship going on during this period.

Samuel Anoints David

Interestingly, there are also "ritual buildings" or temples dating from around the same timeframe which have been excavated around Jerusalem. These temples were dedicated to pagan gods, as for example the pagan temple found in Tel Motza, dating to the 800s BC. Idol figurines of animals were also discovered, along with sacred vessels used for sacrifice.

For centuries Israel was caught in a horrible synthesis between the worship of Yahweh and devotion to the gods of the nations around them. Solomon was the first king to introduce this syncretism into Israel:

For it was so, when Solomon was old, that his wives turned his heart after other

Dedication of the Temple

> *gods; and his heart was not loyal to the LORD his God, as was the heart of his father David. For Solomon went after Ashtoreth the goddess of the Sidonians, and after Milcom the abomination of the Ammonites. Solomon did evil in the sight of the LORD, and did not fully follow the LORD, as did his father David. Then Solomon built a high place for Chemosh the abomination of Moab, on the hill that is east of Jerusalem, and for Molech the abomination of the people of Ammon. And he did likewise for all his foreign wives, who burned incense and sacrificed to their gods. (1 Kings 11:4-8)*

During the reign of Solomon's son Rehoboam, the nation of Israel divided into two parts. Rehoboam reigned in Judah to the south while the northern tribes of Israel followed King Jeroboam. The northern tribes engaged in near-constant war with Syria for many years. Because of their idolatry, the Lord did not allow much rest from warfare for Israel. King Ahab married into the family of the king of Tyre and Sidon when he took Jezebel as wife. She proved to be a major influence for evil in the north, persecuting the prophets of God and promoting Baal worship in the land. Yet the Lord sent the prophets Elijah and Elisha to this disobedient nation as a witness against them.

Elijah Confronts Ahab

The Syrians had made a successful incursion into Israel under Ahab's father Omri. Emboldened by this victory, the Syrian king Ben-Hadad launched two invasions of Israel around 905 BC. As prophesied, Israel was successful in its defensive war, and the Syrians sustained over 127,000 casualties (1 Kings 20). Ben-Hadad escaped with his life and ended up returning the Israelite cities his father had taken from Omri. But Ben-Hadad did not return Ramoth-Gilead to Israel and Ahab sought an alliance with King Jehoshaphat of Judah to retake the city.

Though a cadre of false prophets lined up to prophesy that Ahab and Jehoshaphat would be victorious, Ahab was killed in the conflict, as Micaiah, God's true prophet had predicted. Ahab's elder son Ahaziah died after an unsuccessful two-year reign. During the reign of Ahab's younger son Joram, Ben-Hadad again attempted several campaigns against Israel. Each time, however, he was thwarted as Elisha the prophet communicated the enemy's movements to Joram. When Ben-Hadad learned it was Elisha who was thwarting his military efforts, he sent an army to apprehend the prophet. However, by the power of

The Prophet Michaiah Before Ahab

God, the entire army was struck with blindness.

Eventually, Elisha visited Damascus, the capital of Syria, where Ben-Hadad lay sick. The prophet was visited by Hazael. Elisha informed Hazael that he would become the next king of Syria. In tears Elisha told the young man that he would bring terrible destruction upon the people of Israel. Hazael smothered Ben-Hadad and assumed the Syrian throne. Under Hazael, Syria invaded Israel several times, conquering many Israelite towns and wounding Israel's king Joram. As Joram lay recuperating from his wounds at Jezreel, Elisha anointed Jehu as king of Israel. Jehu swiftly dispatched Joram, the entire house of Ahab, and all the prophets of Baal. Later, Syria continued its attacks on Israel well into the years of Jehu's son Jehoahaz. It would keep up these assaults upon Israel until the reign of Jehoash when the Lord would extend mercy to Israel and deliver them from the dominion of Syria. All of this occurred according to the word of the Lord spoken to Elijah the prophet thirty years earlier:

> *Then the LORD said to him: "Go, return on your way to the Wilderness of Damascus; and when you arrive, anoint Hazael as king over Syria. Also you shall anoint Jehu the son of Nimshi as king over Israel. And Elisha the son of Shaphat of Abel Meholah you shall anoint as prophet in your place. It shall be that whoever escapes the sword of Hazael, Jehu will kill; and whoever escapes the sword of Jehu, Elisha will kill." (1 Kings 19:15-17)*

Tel Dan Inscription

One of the most important ancient records referring to the events of the period of the kings of Israel is the Tel Dan Inscription. It appears to be the writing of King Hazael. However, this Syrian king wrongly claimed to have killed King Joram and King Ahaziah. Actually, Jehu was the one who put an end to these kings. Other than this detail, the inscription seems to be accurate. Although badly damaged, the following includes what we can still read from this ancient record:

> *. . .my father went up. . .fighting against [Ahab]. And my father lay down; he went to his fathers. And the king of Israel penetrated into my father's land. And Hadad made me—myself—King. And Hadad went in front of me, and I departed from. . . of my kings. And I killed two powerful kings who harnessed two thousand chariots and two thousand horsemen. I killed Joram King of Israel, and I killed Achazyahu son of Joram King of the House of David. And I set their land. . .other. . .and Jehu ruled over Israel. . .siege upon. . .*[13]

Unfaithful, Idolatrous Israel

For the most part, Israel exhibited a pattern of idolatry through the period of the kings while the southern tribes were slightly more faithful to Yahweh God. This idolatry and compromise with the worldviews of foreign nations would lead to the destruction of both the northern and southern kingdoms of Israel. Although the Lord was very patient with the Israelites, and provided them with many warnings through His prophets, He finally brought the armies of the great empires against His people to chasten them for their sins. In 722 BC the Assyrians decimated the northern tribes, and in 586 BC the Babylonians took Jerusalem in the south. God raised up these world powers for this very purpose and exiled His people into foreign lands. Only the tribe of Judah would return in significant numbers to rebuild the temple and resettle the land. (A remnant of Levites and a few representatives of other tribes would survive as well.)

Occasionally a righteous king such as Hezekiah or Josiah would attempt a national reformation. Around 630 BC, twenty-six-year-old Josiah, King of Judah, uncovered the lost book of the law (probably the book of Deuteronomy). He tore his clothes in grief and penitence and then launched an unprecedented national reformation. We read in 2 Kings 23:

> *[Josiah] removed the idolatrous priests whom the kings of Judah had ordained to burn incense on the high places in the cities of Judah and in the places all around Jerusalem, and those who burned incense to Baal, to the sun, to the moon, to the constellations, and to all the host of heaven. And he brought out the wooden image from the house of the LORD, to the Brook Kidron outside Jerusalem, burned it at the Brook Kidron and ground it to ashes, and threw its ashes on the graves of the common people. . . . The altars that were on the roof, the upper chamber of Ahaz,*

David Tower in Jerusalem

which the kings of Judah had made, and the altars which Manasseh had made in the two courts of the house of the LORD, the king broke down and pulverized there, and threw their dust into the Brook Kidron. Then the king defiled the high places that were east of Jerusalem, which were on the south of the Mount of Corruption, which Solomon king of Israel had built for Ashtoreth the abomination of the Sidonians, for Chemosh the abomination of the Moabites, and for Milcom the abomination of the people of Ammon. And he broke in pieces the sacred pillars and cut down the wooden images, and filled their places with the bones of men. Moreover the altar that was at Bethel, and the high place which Jeroboam the son of Nebat, who made Israel sin, had made, both that altar and the high place he broke down; and he burned the high place and crushed it to powder, and burned the wooden image.

The king also exiled the witches and spiritists and destroyed the houses of the

Baal Worship

Stele Depicting Baal

Baal worship was common in Syria, probably inspired by the Phoenicians. A grand temple grounds was constructed at Baal-bek, and to this day the largest monolith in the world is found there. The 64' x 20' x 18' rock, weighing about 1,650 tons, was quarried a kilometer away. No one knows the technology the ancients employed to move the rock. (The heaviest object moved across land in the modern world was an evaporator for a desalination plant in Saudi Arabia. It weighed about 5,000 tons and was transported by a truck outfitted with 172 axles and 688 double-wide tires.)

This temple city, renamed Heliopolis by Alexander the Great, clung to its pagan roots as Christianity expanded into Syria in the 3rd century. However, the Emperor Constantine put an end to temple prostitution and polygamy within the city after AD 325. During the reign of Julian the Apostate, the Christian deacon Cyril was killed and cannibalized by angry pagans when he tried to tear down the pagan idols.

temple prostitutes. This reforming work shows how extensively Israel had corrupted herself with foreign gods. The above account covers 350 years of religious compromise for this people. Nonetheless, King Josiah's top-down, government-initiated reformation did nothing to change the hearts of the people. They reverted to their old ways almost immediately under Josiah's sons Jehoahaz and Jehoiakim.

King Josiah Cleanses Judah

For over a thousand years the Israelites proved that no human king could save them from sin and its destructive effects. Even though they had access to the laws of God, they could not live up to them. They proved themselves dead in sin, incapable of saving themselves. The world would have to wait for another King and another Savior who would deliver His people from the great enemy of the human soul. This was the major point of Old Testament prophecy, which the prophets of God drove home over and over again.

The people who walked in darkness
Have seen a great light;
Those who dwelt in the land of the shadow of death,
Upon them a light has shined.
You have multiplied the nation
And increased its joy;
They rejoice before You
According to the joy of harvest,
As men rejoice when they divide the spoil.
For You have broken the yoke of his burden

And the staff of his shoulder,
The rod of his oppressor,
As in the day of Midian.
For every warrior's sandal from the noisy battle,
And garments rolled in blood,
Will be used for burning and fuel of fire.
For unto us a Child is born,
Unto us a Son is given;
And the government will be upon His shoulder.
And His name will be called
Wonderful, Counselor, Mighty God,
Everlasting Father, Prince of Peace.
Of the increase of His government and peace
There will be no end,
Upon the throne of David and over His kingdom,
To order it and establish it with judgment and justice
From that time forward, even forever.
The zeal of the LORD of hosts will perform this. (Isaiah 9:2-7)

The Kings of Israel

Note: There were several co-regencies and interregnums during Israel's Divided Kingdom period.

Kings of United Israel			
Name	**Approximate Dates**	**Years Ruled**	**Rating**
1095-1055 BC	Saul	40	Evil
1055-1015 BC	David	40	Good
1015-975 BC	Solomon	40	Good/Compromised

Kings of the Northern Tribes			
Name	**Approximate Dates**	**Years Ruled**	**Rating**
975-954 BC	Jeroboam I	22	Evil
954-953 BC	Nadab	2	Evil
953-930 BC	Baasha	24	Evil
930-929 BC	Elah	2	Evil
929 BC	Zimri	7 days	Evil
929-925 BC	Tibni	5	Evil
929-918 BC	Omri	12	Evil
918-897 BC	Ahab	22	Evil
898-897 BC	Ahaziah	2	Evil
897-886 BC	Joram	12	Evil
886-857 BC	Jehu	28	Mostly Evil
857-840 BC	Jehoahaz	17	Evil
840-825 BC	Jehoash	16	Mostly Evil
825-784 BC	Jeroboam II	41	Evil
773 BC	Zechariah	6 months	Evil
772 BC	Shallum	1 month	Evil
771-761 BC	Menahem	10	Evil
761-759 BC	Pekahiah	20	Evil
759-739 BC	Pekah	20	Evil
730-721 BC	Hoshea	9	Mostly Evil

Kings of the Southern Tribe of Judah			
Name	**Approximate Dates**	**Years Ruled**	**Rating**
975-958 BC	Rehoboam	17	Mostly Evil
958-955 BC	Abijah	2	Mostly Evil
955-914 BC	Asa	41	Mostly Good
914-889 BC	Jehoshaphat	25	Good
893-886 BC	Jehoram	8	Evil
886 BC	Ahaziah	1	Evil
886-879 BC	Queen Athaliah	7	Evil
879-839 BC	Joash	40	Mostly Good
839-810 BC	Amaziah	29	Mostly Good
810-758 BC	Azariah (Uzziah)	52	Mostly Good
758-742 BC	Jotham	16	Good
742-726 BC	Ahaz	16	Evil
726-697 BC	Hezekiah	29	Good
697-642 BC	Manasseh	55	Mostly Evil
642-640 BC	Amon	2	Evil
640-609 BC	Josiah	31	Good
609 BC	Jehoahaz	3 months	Evil
609-598 BC	Jehoiakim	11	Evil
598-597 BC	Jehoiachin	3 months	Evil
597-586 BC	Zedekiah	11	Evil

The United Kingdom of Israel
Around the Time of Saul and David
•••••• = Vassals & Defeated Peoples

Sidon
ARAMEANS
Tyre
Dan
miles
0
60
Mediterranean Sea
Ashtoroth
Megiddo
Jezreel
Ramoth Gilead
KINGDOM OF ISRAEL
Jaffa
Shiloh
AMON
Jericho
Ashdod
Jerusalem
Gath
Bethlehem
Mount Nebo
Ashkelon
Gaza
PHILISTIA
MOAB
Beersheba
Kir-Haraseth
AMALEK
Zoar
EDOM
Kadesh

Timeline Review

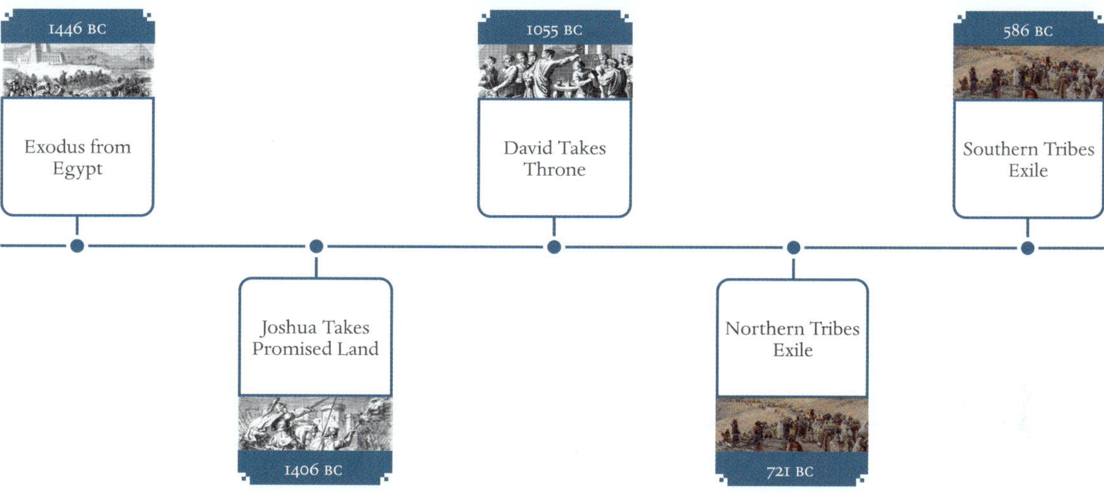

Chapter VI Prayer

Our heavenly Father and covenant-keeping, merciful God,

We glory in your faithfulness, that you were true to your promise over 2,000 years. You preserved the seed of Abraham through the ages, because you would be sure that Jesus, our Savior would come though Jacob, Judah, and David. Despite Israel's unfaithfulness, you were always faithful. Egypt, Assyria, Babylon, and all the enemies of your people were always reined in by your almighty power, through all those many years. You proved yourself a mighty Savior over and over again, and we trust you to save us from all of our enemies too. We glory in your salvation, in all the many ways it is manifested in our lives and throughout the centuries of your church.

In the Name of Jesus, our Savior,
Amen.

Bavaria, Germany

CHAPTER VII

Western and Eastern Europe After the Flood (2518 BC - AD 33)

Listen, O coastlands, to Me,
And take heed, you peoples from afar!
The LORD has called Me from the womb;
From the matrix of My mother He has made mention of My name.
And He has made My mouth like a sharp sword;
In the shadow of His hand He has hidden Me,
And made Me a polished shaft;
In His quiver He has hidden Me.
And He said to me,
"You are My servant, O Israel,
In whom I will be glorified."
Then I said, "I have labored in vain,
I have spent my strength for nothing and in vain;
Yet surely my just reward is with the LORD,
And my work with my God."
And now the LORD says,
Who formed Me from the womb to be His Servant,

To bring Jacob back to Him,
So that Israel is gathered to Him
(For I shall be glorious in the eyes of the LORD,
And My God shall be My strength),
Indeed He says,
"It is too small a thing that You should be My Servant
To raise up the tribes of Jacob,
And to restore the preserved ones of Israel;
I will also give You as a light to the Gentiles,
That You should be My salvation to the ends of the earth." (Isaiah 49:1-6)

What Scripture would refer to as "the Gentile World" was composed largely of the sons and daughters of Japheth who moved out to populate Western Europe, Eastern Europe, Scandinavia, and Russia. For most of the period before the coming of Christ, these peoples were not typically referred to as "civilizations" because they had sunk into primitive paganism and decentralized tribalism. They had little connection with the trade routes that passed through Israel where the oracles of God had been revealed to the descendants of Abraham. These Gentile peoples were regarded as "barbarians" mainly because they did not communicate through writings and they did not build lasting cities.

Unbelieving historians confuse the dating of the Neanderthals and other pagan tribes throughout Europe because they reject the historical worldwide flood. The Neanderthals of Europe were probably descendants of Japheth. Instead of cultivating the land as the civilizations did along the Nile, Mesopotamian, and Indus river valleys, these tribes tried to survive by hunting and gathering. This proved to be a poor way to take dominion of the land. It is not sustainable. Until man is willing to cultivate the land and domesticate animals, he fails to follow through on the dominion task that God gave to Adam and Noah. Man simply cannot live solely by hunting wild animals. Moreover, this lifestyle almost inevitably gives way to infanticide, the killing of the elderly, cannibalism, and illiteracy.

The Neanderthals were a tough, stocky, and short people, and their graves have been discovered in modern-day France, Spain, and even Israel or Palestine. They carried long, heavy spears and most likely hunted large animals like mammoths and dinosaurs not long after the flood. These people were found to have owned jewelry, they would set broken bones, and they conducted formal burials. From

Palace of Knossos, Crete

genetic studies recently conducted, there is evidence that they intermarried with Semites—which means that they lived at the same time as other descendants of Noah. This places the Neanderthals in the era following the Babel dispersion—between 2418 BC and 1800 BC.

Sinful man is usually left with two options in a sinful world. Either powerful or tyrannical kings will develop strong empires to tightly regulate the behavior of sinful, natural man by coercive force, or small tribes will engage in continual war, killing each other off in fruitless fighting. Anarchy, highway robbery, and piracy are therefore common where there are no powerful kings to maintain control.

More often than not, piracy was the rule of the day on the Mediterranean Sea before the coming of Christ. On the island of Crete, however, a small civilization called the "Minoans" developed. Trade was difficult due to piracy, but the king of the Minoans built larger ships and began policing the waters with a rudimentary navy. The Minoans became the most skilled shipbuilders of the ancient world. They were also known for an early circus event called "bull jumping." Daring acrobats would leap onto the backs of raging bulls in arenas. Children were trained from an early age in this dangerous sporting event, which was also considered as a way to honor false gods. While they lived, the bull jumpers were honored with status and wealth, but not many survived their twentieth year. Minoans worshiped the god Zeus, whose son Minos was supposed to have been confined to the island of Crete. One of the first of the upper Mediterranean civilizations, the Minoans flourished from 2200 BC to about 1700 BC. Theirs was an advanced culture, evidenced by the fact that the king's palace at Knossos stood four stories tall. In the providential purposes of God, the civilization disappeared, probably as a result of a gigantic volcanic eruption occurring somewhere near the island.

The Phoenicians and the Colonization of Italy, Spain, and Africa

> *Then Hiram king of Tyre sent messengers to David, and cedar trees, and carpenters and masons. And they built David a house. So David knew that the LORD had established him as king over Israel, and that He had exalted His kingdom for the sake of His people Israel. (2 Samuel 5:11-12)*

The great kings of the earth must eventually come to serve the King of kings, the Lord Jesus Christ, who is the rightful heir of David's throne. The glory days of Israel appear during the reigns of King David and King Solomon around 1000 BC, and it is highly significant that the king of Tyre was willing to serve both David and Solomon at this time.

> *Now Hiram king of Tyre sent his servants to Solomon, because he heard that they had anointed him king in place of his father, for Hiram had always loved David. Then Solomon sent to Hiram, saying:*
>
> *"You know how my father David could not build a house for the name of the LORD his God because of the wars which were fought against him on every side, until the LORD put his foes under the soles of his feet.*
>
> *"But now the LORD my God has given me rest on every side; there is neither adversary nor evil occurrence.*

"And behold, I propose to build a house for the name of the LORD my God, as the LORD spoke to my father David, saying, 'Your son, whom I will set on your throne in your place, he shall build the house for My name.'

"Now therefore, command that they cut down cedars for me from Lebanon; and my servants will be with your servants, and I will pay you wages for your servants according to whatever you say. For you know there is none among us who has skill to cut timber like the Sidonians."

So it was, when Hiram heard the words of Solomon, that he rejoiced greatly and said, "Blessed be the LORD this day, for He has given David a wise son over this great people!"

Then Hiram sent to Solomon, saying: "I have considered the message which you sent me, and I will do all you desire concerning the cedar and cypress logs. My servants shall bring them down from Lebanon to the sea; I will float them in rafts by sea to the place you indicate to me, and will have them broken apart there; then you can take them away. And you shall fulfill my desire by giving food for my household." Then Hiram gave Solomon cedar and cypress logs according to all his desire. And Solomon gave Hiram twenty thousand kors of wheat as food for his

Map of Phoenicia

household, and twenty kors of pressed oil. Thus Solomon gave to Hiram year by year." (1 Kings 5:1-11)

Some civilizations developed through military might. Others were founded on trade, which introduced tremendous wealth to the nations. The latter was the case with the Phoenicians. It was only after the Minoan and Mycenaean cultures had faded that the city states of Tyre and Sidon began to flourish. Developing around the 1300s BC, the Phoenicians were known for their cedar forests and purple dye obtained from a certain type of seashell. In a day when there wasn't much variety in fabric colors, the Phoenicians introduced a product that caught the eye of the wealthy, the vanity shoppers, and those seeking status symbols. The Phoenicians sailed around the Mediterranean, planting colonies in southern Spain, northern Africa, and Cyprus. They also founded colonies in Sicily, Sardinia, and Corsica and claimed the city states of Carthage, Ugarit, Arwad, Beirut, Symira, Byblos, and Acco. In North Africa the cities of Hippo, Tunis, Leptis, and Hadrumetum all had their origins as Phoenician trading colonies. The influence, wealth, and learning of the Phoenicians dominated in the Mediterranean world for a thousand years, until the Lord brought them down by the hands of the Babylonians and Greeks.

Perhaps motivated by their focus on financial wealth, the Phoenicians quickly developed a written language, no doubt to facilitate contracts for buying and selling. It would have been difficult to record written agreements without a universal language understood by all parties involved. Around 1050 BC, the Phoenicians were using an alphabet of twenty-two consonants. Unbelieving historians insist that the old Hebrew script was derived from the Phoenicians. However, it was actually the Phoenicians who derived their alphabet from the Hebrews. This civilization was the closest in proximity to the Israelites, who had received the writings of Moses in 1400 BC, well before any Phoenician writings appear. Later, the Aramaic, Arabic, and Greek alphabets would borrow from the Phoenician alphabet. The Greek alphabet would contribute to the Latin, Cyrillic, and Coptic alphabets.

The earliest use of the Phoenician alphabet is found in King Hiram's tomb in Byblos, dating from around 1000 BC. The sarcophagus contains a curse upon any king who should attempt to attack the city of Byblos. Following this curse is an exhortation carved into the passageway entering the tomb that reads: "Concerning knowledge: here and now be humble (you yourself!)" Sadly, Phoenicia did not submit itself to this admonition as is well documented in biblical prophecies.

Phoenician Alphabet

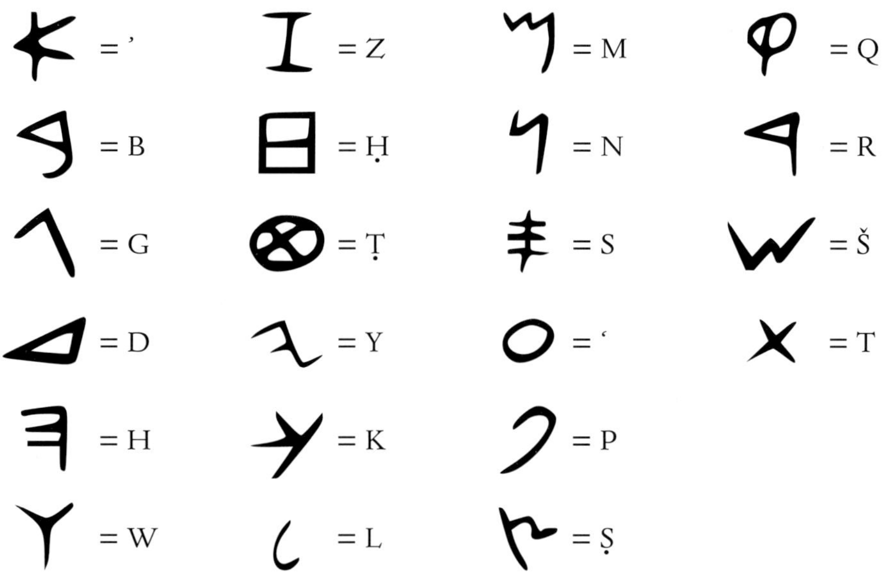

𐤀 = ’	𐤆 = Z	𐤌 = M	𐤒 = Q
𐤁 = B	𐤇 = Ḥ	𐤍 = N	𐤓 = R
𐤂 = G	𐤈 = Ṭ	𐤎 = S	𐤔 = Š
𐤃 = D	𐤉 = Y	𐤏 = ‘	𐤕 = T
𐤄 = H	𐤊 = K	𐤐 = P	
𐤅 = W	𐤋 = L	𐤑 = Ṣ	

Rich nations are often composed of proud and self-reliant peoples, and this was the reason the Lord gave for the destruction of Tyre and Sidon at the hands of the Babylonians in 573 BC. Evidently, Tyre and Sidon were delighted at the destruction of Jerusalem in 589 BC, and, according to Ezekiel 26:1-2, they were singing, "Aha! She is broken who was the gateway of the peoples; now she is turned over to me; I shall be filled; she is laid waste." The following three chapters of Ezekiel are dedicated to the proclamation and lament concerning the destruction of Phoenicia. The root cause of this destruction is laid out in Ezekiel 28:5: "your heart is lifted up because of your riches." These riches caused the kings and rulers of Tyre and Sidon to believe themselves to be gods:

Therefore thus says the Lord GOD:
"Because you have set your heart as the heart of a god,
Behold, therefore, I will bring strangers against you,

The most terrible of the nations;
And they shall draw their swords against the beauty of your wisdom,
And defile your splendor.
They shall throw you down into the Pit,
And you shall die the death of the slain
In the midst of the seas.
Will you still say before him who slays you,
'I am a god'?
But you shall be a man, and not a god,
In the hand of him who slays you."
(Ezekiel 28:6-9)

The richest and proudest nations in the world in all eras of history would do well to heed such warnings. A recent study of national pride (released in 2002 AD) determined that the United States was the proudest nation in the world in six out of the ten categories considered (science, economic strength, history, democracy, political strength, and fair treatment).[1] The Phoenicians paid no attention to these

Ruins in Tyre

Ruins of Phoenician Temple in Sidon

warnings issued by the God of Israel, and they paid dearly for it.

The Babylonian siege of Tyre was a tough war. After a thirteen-year assault, King Nebuchadnezzar took Tyre—probably destroying the mainland city. The island city continued until it was destroyed by Alexander the Great 200 years later.

Ancient Ruins in Carthage

With the fall of Phoenicia, however, the sovereign God who rules over all nations would enable another world power to rise. Once a product of the Phoenician colonies, Carthage soon spread its influence over the rest of the North African colonies. It was a small empire that would present the greatest military threat to Rome between 346 and 146 BC.

First Settlements in Ireland and Britain

> *They joined themselves unto Baalpeor, and ate the sacrifices of the dead. Thus they provoked [the LORD] to anger with their inventions; and the plague brake in upon them. (Psalm 106:28-29 KJV)*

Evidence of early civilizations in Northern Europe dates back thousands of years before Christ. However, it is impossible to determine when Irish civilization began because there is no evidence of written language among the Celts until the 6th century BC. Both the Celts in Britain and those in Ireland communicated in a similar language—the Brittonic and Gaelic dialects, respectively. The first known Celtic writings (dating from around the time of Christ) are referred to as "the Curse Tablets," in which curses are pronounced upon another person in the name of a god or goddess.

The early Irish began mining copper very early in their history. Among the first settlements in Ireland after Babel, between 2400 BC and 500 BC, researchers estimate a total of 370 tons of copper were excavated from mines in Cork and Kerry. These mines would have supplied plentiful material for spear tips, axes, daggers, picks, drinking cups, bronze trumpets, and jewelry through the centuries.

The very ancient Gaelic people were much concerned with honoring the dead and perhaps the worship of the dead (like their Egyptian counterparts and others) by building large monoliths to serve as burial locations. At least 1,200 of these pillars have been identified throughout Ireland. The most elaborate is the Newgrange "grand passage tomb" discovered in County Meath, Ireland. This very early structure predates Stonehenge in England and the Great Pyramid of Giza and could very well have been the largest structure in the world when it was constructed, assuming it was built before 2400 BC, as some dating estimates indicate. Taking up the space of 1.1 acres, Newgrange was built out of 200,000 tons of rock. Conservatively, it would have taken 1,000 men at least a year to build. The monument includes a 60-foot (19 m) passageway lined with large rock entering into the 39-foot-high (10 m) mound. This inner sanctuary contains three chambers in which no doubt the dead bodies of important people were interred, though now long disintegrated. The walls are decorated with familiar Celtic spiral and arc patterns etched into the rock.

Newgrange Tomb

Already, the winter solstice must have been an important holiday for these early Irish. For the monument is positioned facing the rising of the sun so that at Winter Solstice (December 21st) the sun beam shines directly into the inner chamber and illuminates the triple spiral carved on the front wall. The light enters through what is known as a "roofbox" located above the main entrance. At the present day, the light appears four minutes after sunrise. However, scientists estimate that 4,500 years ago the light would have appeared through the roofbox keyhole precisely at sunrise.

Blinded by sin and rebellion against God after the flood, the pagan mind could only celebrate death and deify the dead. There was no hope for a bodily resurrection, no purpose in life, and little motivation to develop civilization. Only with the Lord Jesus Christ would come true wisdom and a hope for eternal life. Until then, the world would retain an infatuation with death.

All those who hate me love death. (Proverbs 8:36)

Stonehenge in Britain (2200 BC)

Stonehenge remains the most famous stone-structured burial ground in the world, located in Wiltshire in southern England. Although evolutionists had theorized Stonehenge's existence dating back 5,000-8,000 years, recent dating of the first stone circle laid down by this human civilization puts it between 2200 and 2300 BC.[2] This would have been about 100-200 years after the Tower of Babel dispersed the tribal groups—exactly corresponding to the biblical narrative of human civilization.

The blue stones in the ancient circle were thought to have healing properties because the bodies of people buried there appeared to have wandered in from all around Britain to visit the place.

At the completion of the construction, the monument would have been about 108 feet in diameter, with some 60 huge stones standing upright, connected by 30 lintel stones all around. Within the circle there were even larger stones forming a horseshoe shape, each of which weighed about 50 tons. The lintel stones were 10 feet (3.2 m) long, 3.3 feet (1 m) wide, and 2.6 feet (0.8 m) thick. The topside of the lintels would have stood about 16 feet (4.9 m) high. To lift such heavy stones to form the lintels would have required some significant engineering work.

Recent DNA analysis of the remains of cremated bodies that were buried under the ground at Stonehenge and other burial areas has provided some insight into the early migrations of human civilization into Britain. These first settlers in Britain came via two routes, through the Iberian peninsula (modern-day Spain) and Gaul/Germany—all of which originated from Anatolia (modern-day Turkey).

Stonehenge

The British Isles

SCOTLAND
Inverness
Aberdeen
Glasgow
Edinburgh
North Sea
North Atlantic Ocean
NORTHERN IRELAND
Belfast
IRELAND
Dublin
Cork
Irish Sea
St. George's Channel
ENGLAND
York
Liverpool
London
Stonehenge
Plymouth
WALES
Cardiff
English Channel
FRANCE
Calais

No doubt, these were the Hittites, the Assyrians, or the Hattians, which were living there when Sargon I invaded somewhere around 2300 BC. Typically, the wars of the nations would have sent small tribal groups wandering further into Spain, and then on into Britain. It is safe to conclude therefore, that these first settlements in Britain occurred somewhere between 2300-2000 BC. Tracing the DNA of the settlers in Britain has shed light on the dispersions from the Tower of Babel. The gradual migration began at the Tower of Babel in Syria or Mesopotamia to the south, settling first in Anatolia. From there these groups migrated through Germany or Spain and eventually ended up in Britain.[3]

> *So the LORD scattered them abroad from there over the face of all the earth, and they ceased building the city. Therefore its name is called Babel, because there the LORD confused the language of all the earth; and from there the LORD scattered them abroad over the face of all the earth. (Genesis 11:8-9)*

Further to the northwest in Greenland, the pagan world was well known for its practice of infanticide. Recent excavations have found well-preserved mummies of a young child who appears to have been buried alive with its mother. The mummies were also decorated with tattoos on the chin and forehead.[4]

Druid Worship in Gaul

> *Hear the word which the LORD speaks to you, O house of Israel.*
> *Thus says the LORD:*
> *"Do not learn the way of the Gentiles;*
> *Do not be dismayed at the signs of heaven,*
> *For the Gentiles are dismayed at them.*
> *For the customs of the peoples are futile;*
> *For one cuts a tree from the forest,*
> *The work of the hands of the workman, with the ax.*
> *They decorate it with silver and gold;*
> *They fasten it with nails and hammers*
> *So that it will not topple.*
> *They are upright, like a palm tree,*
> *And they cannot speak;*

They must be carried,
Because they cannot go by themselves.
Do not be afraid of them,
For they cannot do evil,
Nor can they do any good."

Inasmuch as there is none like You, O LORD
(You are great, and Your name is great in might),
Who would not fear You, O King of the nations?
For this is Your rightful due.
For among all the wise men of the nations,
And in all their kingdoms,
There is none like You.
But they are altogether dull-hearted and foolish;
A wooden idol is a worthless doctrine.
Silver is beaten into plates;
It is brought from Tarshish,
And gold from Uphaz,
The work of the craftsman
And of the hands of the metalsmith;
Blue and purple are their clothing;
They are all the work of skillful men.
But the LORD is the true God;
He is the living God and the everlasting King.
At His wrath the earth will tremble,
And the nations will not be able to endure His indignation.
(Jeremiah 10:1-10)

Information concerning the religious practices of the Gaelic tribes in northern Gaul, Britain, and Ireland comes from records shortly before the coming of Christ. It turns out that human sacrifice was common with the Celtic druids. When the Roman soldiers came upon the sacred groves, they found altars covered with human remains.[5] It was a frightful, horrible religion. Apparently, certain Celtic gods, such as Teutates, Esus, and Taranis, were especially desirous of human sacrifice. The Druid religion held to the doctrine of reincarnation and the eternality of the

Druidic Human Sacrifice

human soul, but there was no hope of resurrection and glorification among these blinded peoples. While Satan reigned over the dark world of the Gauls, before Christ came, the witchdoctors were notoriously effective with their dark magic. The "mnas brictom" women were known for casting spells and the Druid priests were feared for their lethal magic.

The first eyewitness reports of primitive Druid worship come from Julius Caesar around 54 BC. He reports human sacrifice on a massive scale, which involved the horrible rite of burning people in a gigantic wooden structure known as the "wicker man."

> *The Druids are in charge of all religious matters, superintending public and private sacrifices, and explaining superstitions. A large crowd of young men, who flock to them for schooling, hold the Druids in great respect. For they have opinions to give on almost all disputes involving tribes or individuals, and if any crime is committed, any murder done, or if there is contention about a will or the boundaries of some property, they are the people who investigate the matter and establish rewards and punishments. Any individual or community that refuses to abide by their decision is excluded from the sacrifices, which is held to be the most serious punishment possible. Those thus excommunicated are viewed as impious criminals, they are deserted by their friends and no one will visit them or talk to them to avoid the risk of contagion from them. They are deprived of all rights in court, and they forfeit all claim to honors.*
>
> *There is one arch-druid of supreme power. On his death, he is succeeded either by someone outstanding among his fellows, or, if there are several of equal caliber, the decision is reached by a vote of all the Druids, and the election is sometimes managed by force. At a fixed time of year they assemble at a holy place in the territory of the Carnutes, which is thought to be the center of Gaul. Anyone with a grievance attends and obeys the decisions and judgments which the Druids give. The general view is that this religion originated in Britain and was imported into Gaul, which means that any keen student of Druidism now goes to Britain for information. . . .*
>
> *The whole Gallic nation is virtually a prey to superstition, and this makes the serious invalids or those engaged in battle or dangerous exploits sacrifice men instead of animals. They even vow to immolate themselves, using the Druids as their ministers for this purpose. They feel that the spirit of the gods cannot be*

appeased unless a man's life is given for a life. Public sacrifices of the same sort are common. Another practice is to make images of enormous size, with the limbs woven from osiers [willows]. Living human beings are fitted into these, and, when they are set on fire, the men are engulfed in the flames and perish. The general feeling is that the immortal gods are better pleased with the sacrifice of those caught in theft, robbery or some other crime. But if a supply of such criminals is lacking, then they resort to the sacrifice of completely innocent victims.[6]

This burning man ritual and other forms of human sacrifice were done away with after Constantine in AD 325. Nevertheless, several pagan organizations in the United States have attempted to resurrect the practice in Utah and Nevada since AD 2000. Human sacrifice like this was soundly condemned by holy Scripture. Such sacrifices to false gods were nothing more than murder and a waste of human life.

"For the children of Judah have done evil in My sight," says the LORD. "They have set their abominations in the house which is called by My name, to pollute it. And they have built the high places of Tophet, which is in the Valley of the Son of Hinnom, to burn their sons and their daughters in the fire, which I did not command, nor did it come into My heart." (Jeremiah 7:30-31)

To Julius Caesar, the Druids were barbarous and despicable with a predilection for human sacrifice. The idea of burning oneself to death was horrible even to the mind of a "more civilized" pagan, although Julius Caesar would eventually sponsor human sacrifice himself. Human life was cheap to the far-off tribes, and this prevented their civilizations from developing. No less than the modern, the pagan had to confront the perennial problem of guilt. While the modern world would attempt to deal with guilt by drugs and psychiatry, the ancient pagan worked hard to pacify the gods by his human and animal sacrifices. Guilt for sin runs deep in the human heart, and all of man's attempts to solve this problem would prove fruitless. Only the holy, harmless, and undefiled Lamb of God would offer a sufficient sacrifice for this guilt. And this was a sacrifice that only God Himself could provide by giving His only begotten Son.

For God so loved the world that He gave His only begotten Son, that whoever believes in Him should not perish but have everlasting life. (John 3:16)

The Barbarian World of Blonde-Haired Germanic Peoples (1300 BC - AD 33)

Moving east, the Lusatian culture developed in the area of modern-day Poland, Czech Republic, and the Ukraine somewhere between 1300 BC and 500 BC. Not much is known of them except that they preferred cremation over burial and used horses and chariots. There is some evidence of human sacrifice as part of their religious rites.

Sometime between 745 BC and 525 BC, another tribe called the Biskupin settled in central Poland. Archaeologists have uncovered a village of one hundred pine and oak-constructed log cabins, each of which could accommodate eight to ten people, located on three streets. The village was located on a marsh and was defended using a 1,480 foot (450 m) rampart. The Biskupin tribe raised cattle and pigs, as well as sheep and goats. They were most likely wiped out by a Scythian raid around the 6th century BC.

The Scythians are said to have spread from Persia north of the Black Sea into Ukraine, Bulgaria, and Poland. They were a warlike tribe, known to have mastered

Reconstruction of a Lusatian Settlement

warfare on horseback—and their women fought alongside the men in battle. They are referred to in Colossians 3:11.

> *And [you] have put on the new man who is renewed in knowledge according to the image of Him who created him, where there is neither Greek nor Jew, circumcised nor uncircumcised, barbarian, Scythian, slave nor free, but Christ is all and in all. (Colossians 3:10-11)*

The Greek historian Herodotus described the inhabitants of the large city of the Scythians known as Gelonus located in modern-day Ukraine:

> *The Budini are a large and powerful nation: they have all deep blue eyes, and bright red hair. There is a city in their territory, called Gelonus, which is surrounded with a lofty wall, thirty furlongs (*τριήκοντα σταδίων *= c. 5.5 km) each way,*

built entirely of wood. All the houses in the place and all the temples are of the same material. Here are temples built in honor of the Grecian gods, and adorned after the Greek fashion with images, altars, and shrines, all in wood. There is even a festival, held every third year in honor of Bacchus, at which the natives fall into the Bacchic fury. For the fact is that the Geloni were anciently Greeks, who, being driven out of the factories along the coast, fled to the Budini and took up their abode with them. They still speak a language half Greek, half Scythian.[7]

Herodotus (c. 484-425 BC)

These eastern European tribes may be the roots of the blonde-haired, blue-eyed Germanic peoples who would populate Northern Europe.

Further south were the beginnings of Greece—the tribes of Arcadians, Ionians, Boeotians, Dorians, Illyrians, and Thracians. These were the makings of an empire that would only appear briefly on the world stage and would prepare the way for the Roman Empire—the zenith of all world empires to date.

The Germanic peoples appear to have had their roots either in Scythia to the southeast or Scandinavia to the north. In the 4th century BC a Greek explorer named Pytheas of Massalia journeyed north to Britain, where he came upon the Picts (or the "painted ones"). These pagans would paint or tattoo themselves. To the west, Pytheas came upon Norway, which he referred to as "Thule," and then across the sea to the Baltics. This was the home of the Goths. They were described as blonde-haired giants with blue eyes. They were known to be treacherous and cruel, but chaste.

From the 1st century forward, the Romans would feed their slave trade in the empire from Gaul, the Germanic tribes, and the Dacians (modern eastern Europe) by enslaving the blonde-haired, blue-eyed barbarians. These were considered to be the lowest of the tribes of the earth when compared to the sophisticated civilizations of North Africa, the Middle East, Italy, and Greece. Nonetheless, the Gospel came to these humble, despised peoples. With the Christian faith came political liberties, economic prosperity, and a vast improvement in public morality throughout northern, eastern, and western Europe. Sadly, however, arrogance and pride would follow hard on the heels of these blessings from God. And in the 20th and 21st centuries these Europeans, who now also lived in North America and Oceania, are reverting back to the paganism of child sacrifice (abortion), sexual perversion, and idolatry.

The Apostle Paul warned these Gentile peoples of the danger of such pride in Romans 11.

> *You will say then, "Branches were broken off that I might be grafted in." Well said. Because of unbelief they were broken off, and you stand by faith. Do not be haughty, but fear. For if God did not spare the natural branches, He may not spare you either. Therefore consider the goodness and severity of God: on those who fell, severity; but toward you, goodness, if you continue in His goodness. Otherwise you also will be cut off. (Romans 11:19-22)*

Postscript: When Jesus Came to the Europeans in the North, the West, and the East

The terribly degraded and primitive tribes of Europe were some of the first to receive the Gospel with unparalleled enthusiasm after the fall of Rome. This part of the Gentile world received the mission work of men like St. Patrick, Germanus, Columbanus, Augustine of Canterbury, Boniface, and others. The story of these men is told in the next volume of this history.

By 1910, 80% of professing Christians in the world lived in Europe and North America. This was the result of an effective missionary movement that started in the first centuries after Christ. However, by 2010 only 42% of professing Christian lived in Europe and North America. This shift occurred because of rising atheism and apostasy in these areas and a massive expansion of the church in Asia, Africa, and Latin America.

The nations most impacted by the Christian faith (and especially the nations most affected by the Protestant Reformation) have enjoyed higher levels of morality, political liberty, and prosperity. Those nations influenced by the Protestant Reformation are most likely to rank high in honest trade and political liberties. World prosperity rating by gross domestic product also tends to be very high among the peoples.

Western Nation	Corruptions Rating [8]	Freedom Rating [9]	Prosperity Rating [10]	Percent Christian [11]	Protestant or Catholic
New Zealand	2	3	22	48%	P
Sweden	3	19	11	65%	P
Switzerland	3	4	2	70%	P
Norway	7	26	3	77%	P
Netherlands	8	13	12	34%	P
Canada	9	8	18	67%	P
UK	11	7	20	59%	P
Germany	11	24	16	56%	P
Australia	13	5	10	52%	P
Austria	14	31	13	65%	C
Belgium	17	48	17	67%	C
Ireland	18	6	4	84%	C
France	21	71	19	53%	C
United States	22	12	8	71%	P
Portugal	30	62	36	84%	C
Poland	36	46	54	94%	C
Czech	38	23	38	34%	C
Spain	41	57	31	71%	C

The Economy of the West

God blessed the western world with the most thorough application of science in world history. Western Christians have done much to develop science and technology. The technological revolution of the last few centuries served to advance the economies of the Christian West. This was the means by which most of these nations became rich and dominated the world economy.

Western Nation	Major Resources/Exports
New Zealand	Concentrated milk, sheep & goat meat, butter, rough wood, bovine meat
Sweden	Cars, refined petroleum, medicaments, delivery trucks
Switzerland	Gold, packaged medicaments, human or animal blood, base metal, watches
Norway	Petroleum & petroleum products, machinery & equipment, metals, chemicals, ships, fish
Netherlands	Machinery, computers, mineral fuels, pharmaceuticals, optical and medical equipment, cars, plastics, iron, steel
Canada	Crude petroleum, cars, coal, wheat, fertilizers, aluminum
UK	Cars, refined petroleum, pharmaceuticals, gas turbines, diamonds
Germany	Cars, pharmaceuticals, aircraft, machinery, petroleum, ,medical instruments
Australia	Iron ore, coal, tourism, gold, natural gas, beef, aluminum ores, wheat
Austria	Pharmaceuticals, vehicle parts, cars, human or animal blood
Belgium	Chemicals, machinery & equipment, finished diamonds, metals & metal products
Ireland	Malt extract, bovine meat, butter, pig/sheep/goat meat
France	Aircraft, pharmaceuticals, cars, petroleum, gas turbines, wine, beauty products
United States	Planes, cars, integrated circuits, refined petroleum, pharmaceuticals, soybeans
Portugal	Refined petroleum, cars, leather footwear, uncoated paper
Poland	Vehicle parts, cars, furniture, video displays
Czech	Cars, computers, broadcasting equipment, office machine parts
Spain	Cars, Refined Petroleum, Pharmaceuticals, and Delivery Trucks

Timeline Review

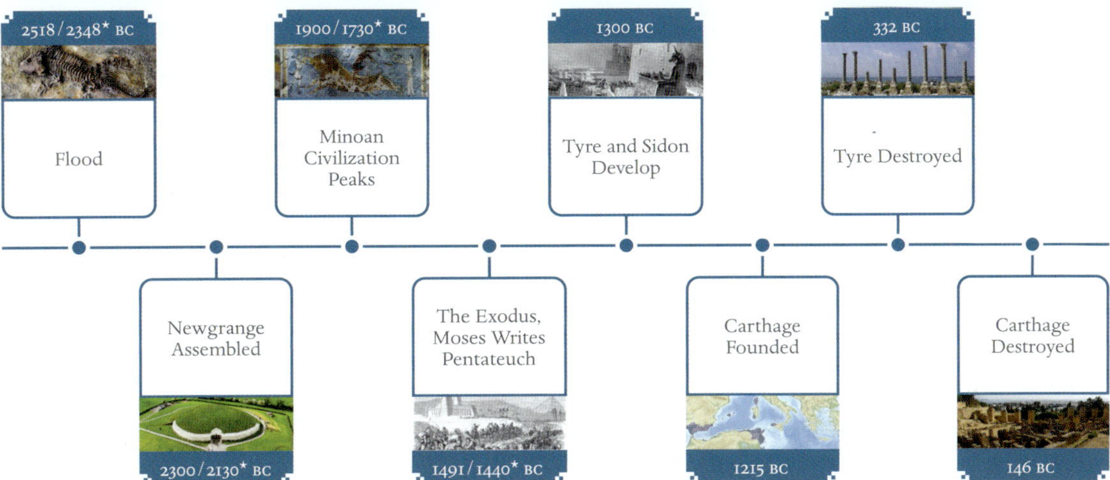

* Date according to Ussher's Chronology which assumes Israelites were in Egypt 215 years.

Chapter VII Prayer

Our Father, Almighty God, Creator, Provider, and Savior,

You are perfectly righteous, holy, and just, and we are a sinful people. We have all sinned against you, and our sin and guilt would completely overwhelm us, but for the sacrifice that you provided in your Son. We thank you, heavenly Father, for sending the Light into our darkness. We praise you for coming to the most degraded, the most shameful, the most sin-darkened, and the most hopeless peoples in the world. Missionaries came with the Gospel of the Lord Jesus Christ, and a great light shined into the darkness of our world. Please forgive us for our pride, self-confidence, and ungratefulness. There is nothing to be proud of in our own heritage. But, we will boast in Christ, and His powerful salvation He brings. We would always be humble and grateful that you brought the Gospel to the depraved Gentile world, and given us a heritage with the saints!

Amen.

CHAPTER VIII

India Waits for the Coming of Christ (2200 BC - AD 33)

God, who made the world and everything in it, since He is Lord of heaven and earth, does not dwell in temples made with hands. Nor is He worshiped with men's hands, as though He needed anything, since He gives to all life, breath, and all things. And He has made from one blood every nation of men to dwell on all the face of the earth, and has determined their preappointed times and the boundaries of their dwellings. (Acts 17:24-26)

Paul's sermon at Mars Hill, given sometime around AD 55, introduced the true God to the Greeks, in contrast to the pantheon of false gods they had collected for themselves. This truth concerning God was revealed to the Greeks at the very center of their society in Athens. Most significantly, the apostle describes Him as absolutely sovereign over all peoples in every place around the world. There were no accidents in the distribution of the tribes and nations in the earth. The Lord God, Creator of all things, is omnipresent. He is not limited to one location. He created all men and women on the earth, and He placed them in various geographical locations.

The second largest civilization in the world today is found in India—second only to China. As already covered in previous chapters, the first two major civilizations grew up around rivers—the Nile and the twin rivers, Euphrates and Tigris. At a time when roads were few and cost-prohibitive to build, human societies quickly realized that rivers were the best way to move materials to markets. Also, rivers provided regular irrigation for fields as God's rainwater poured off the mountains into fertile valleys.

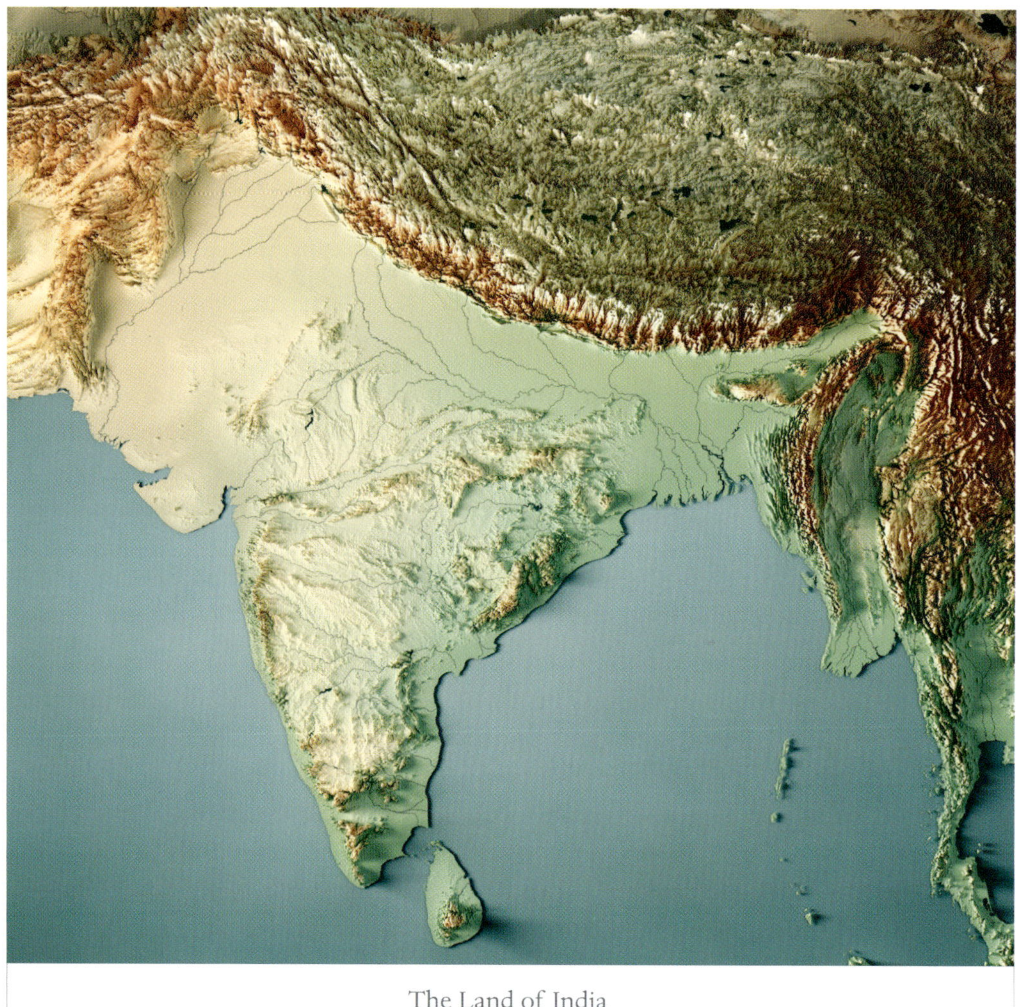

The Land of India

First Settlements (2200-1750 BC)

The breakdown of empires (like Babel and the Akkadian Empire) is usually followed by periods of anarchy and unrest. When anarchical, nomadic tribes begin to attack nearby towns and villages, families leave to protect their lives. Most likely, Terah and his family left Ur in the Mesopotamian valley for Haran soon after the breakdown of Sargon's first major empire in Akkad. At the same time, other family groups would have left the Mesopotamian river valley, but instead, they went southeast either by land or by sea. The next major river valley to the east would have been the Indus River on the west side of modern-day India. Beginning as early as 2200 BC, an entire civilization called "the Harappan" formed along the enormous Indus River. And then, mysteriously, it disappeared around 1750 BC.

When modern archaeologists discovered the ancient city of Mohenjo Daro, they learned something about the maturity of this civilization. At least 40,000 people had inhabited the city. At the center of each of the cities in the Indus Valley were large walled citadels where families could find protection from attacks from lawless bands or armies belonging to other city states.

Ruins of Mohenjo Daro

Washroom and Drainage System at Lothal

The Harappan went on to domesticate elephants and water buffalo for plowing fields and other tasks. They used toilets in their homes and plumbing systems that would drain the wastewater into gutters on the streets. Once again, these early civilizations provide clear evidence that ancient man was not lacking in intelligence. The only reason that these societies did not have 21st century technology was that human knowledge and science could only develop over multiple generations. Each generation grows off of the technological know-how of the previous generation.

Nonetheless, the Harappan civilization did not survive. There are several reasons for the disappearance of civilizations—tribal warfare, famine and droughts, and natural disasters brought about by the hand of God. Upon the excavation of this old city of the Mohenjo Daro, researchers were surprised to find a quick and sudden demise of the once flourishing city. They discovered multiple skeletons of people lying in the streets and in homes, but there was no indication of violent deaths (or a military attack). Strangely enough, one of the dead bodies was emitting a very high level of radioactivity. Theories abound as to the cause of the demise, but we can be sure of one thing. God brought an end to this society by some sudden, violent, and deadly manner. A similar pattern was seen with the cities of Sodom and Gomorrah. Here could have been a replication of the destruction of the cities of the plain as witnessed by Lot. The destruction of these cities is the work of God, as stated in Ezekiel 26.

> *For thus says the Lord GOD: "When I make you a desolate city, like cities that are not inhabited, when I bring the deep upon you and great waters cover you, then I will bring you down with those who descend to the Pit, to the people of old, and I will make you dwell in the lowest part of the earth, in places desolate from antiquity, with those who go down to the Pit, so that you may never be inhabited; and I shall establish glory in the land of the living." (Ezekiel 26:19-20)*

The Aryan Religion and the Caste System (1500 BC)

> *And the word of the LORD came to me, saying, "Son of man, these men have set up their idols in their hearts, and put before them that which causes them to stumble into iniquity. Should I let Myself be inquired of at all by them?. . . Therefore say to the house of Israel, 'Thus says the Lord GOD: "Repent, turn away from your idols, and turn your faces away from all your abominations." (Ezekiel 14:2,3,6)*

Modern India was formed out of three people groups: early hunter-gatherers who still make up some of the genetic heritage of the Andaman Islands, Persian farmers who immigrated into the Indus Valley, and an Aryan population who migrated down from the steppes of the Ukraine in the north.[1]

The Hindu religion was developed primarily by Aryans who make up the priestly class of the Brahmins (according to modern genetic studies). The term "Arya" is used among Indians for addressing another as "respected sir."

The Aryans probably settled the lands along the Ganges River somewhere around 1500 BC. By this time, any remembrance of the true and living God had been well suppressed, and these sons of Japheth invented the god Shiva and the river goddess Ganga. As the legend goes, Ganga created the Ganges River in a fit of anger—not out of any feeling of benevolence or compassion for men.

The Aryans introduced the first written material in the Indian language in the form of four "vedas"—the Rig Veda, the Yajur Veda, the Sama Veda, and the Atharva Veda. The Rig Veda dates back to the 16th century BC and consists of some 1,028 hymns of praise dedicated to the worship of various false gods. Hundreds of pages are taken up with heathen sacrifices, and Book 30 of the Yajur Veda explains in detail the rules for human sacrifice to various gods. The Atharva Veda lays out magical spells, charms, and incantations. Through the ages, millions of pages were added to the sacred writings, much of which is filled with confusing contradictions and incomprehensible ramblings. Sexual immorality and racial discrimination are apparent throughout. Prejudice against those of darker skin is marked, complete with instructions to "give protection to the Aryan color."[2]

Ganges River

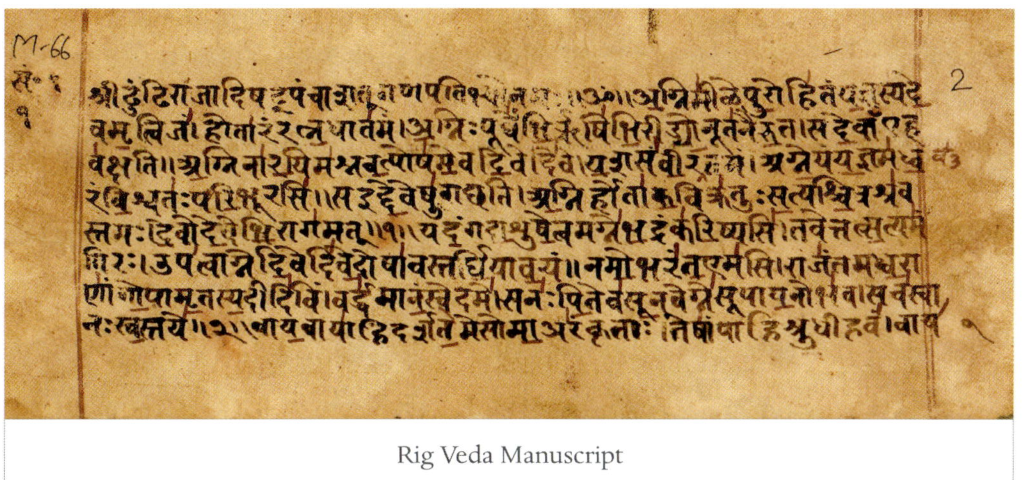

Rig Veda Manuscript

The basis for this racism is found in a historical account in which, "the mighty Thunderer [Indra] with his fair-complexioned friends won the land, the sunlight, and the waters."[3] This fixation on skin color and historical cultural roots would result in a perpetual caste system within Indian culture and go on to plague the world for thousands of years. In the 20th century, Adolf Hitler would borrow these ideas to glorify his conception of a light-skinned, Aryan race and bring untold sorrows upon the world.

Later Hindu Vedas would describe, command, or condone the most perverse and degraded forms of sexuality. These ancient religious writings speak of Brahma assaulting his own daughter; Shiva and Vishna are described as committing shameful sexual sin as well.

These early religious beginnings left a sad immoral heritage, which would sentence elements of Indian society to a degraded state for millennia to come.[4] What a tragedy that the first written communications from this civilization were inspired by the irrational ramblings, confused polytheism, and immoral influences of the demonic realm!

Brahma

The original source of the Indian caste system is found in the early Vedas. Placing the Aryans mostly in the Brahmin (or highest) caste would guarantee an advanced social placement for those who authored the Vedas. Five different levels of castes exist in India, originally defined by their position and occupation in society:

Brahmins → priests and scholars
Kshatriyas → political rulers and soldiers
Vaishyas → merchants
Shudras → laborers, peasants, artisans, and servants
Untouchables → trash collectors, taxidermists (those who skin dead animals)

The caste system was canonized in the Bhagavad Gita, dating between 200 BC and AD 200. The duties and rights of each caste were carefully enumerated, as for example, marriage across caste lines was forbidden. While a lower caste member could receive food from a Brahmin, the Brahmin would be contaminated if he were to receive food from a member of the lower caste. An untouchable would contaminate a well for the upper castes if he drew water from it. The untouchables were not permitted within the temples at all, and the Shudras were prohibited from offering sacrifices to the gods.

Man's Religions—Two Ways to Deal with Guilt

Not one but two influential world religions developed out of India (and modern-day Nepal) before Jesus came—Hinduism and Buddhism. The devil is always actively working to present new ways to deceive mankind. World religions can be boiled down into two different alternatives. Either men will attempt to placate the gods by sacrifice and ritual cleanses, or they will attempt to placate their own consciences by a set of moral rules and disciplines. Buddhism and Islam are of the latter sort, and Hinduism and animism represent the former. The root problem for man is the guilt of sin. Man sets out on his own to deal with the reality of his guilt and the contamination that sin introduces into his heart and life. He wants to salve his guilty conscience on his own terms. This is quite different from the Christian faith, which honestly confesses that all sin is against God. Reconciliation and atonement can only come on His terms. If we will be saved, if the condemnation and contamination of sin will be taken care of, it can only

Hindu Temple in New Delhi, India

happen by God's salvation. God must save us, and His salvation comes by the death and resurrection of His Son, the Lord Jesus Christ. Only by His work in us are we enabled to love Him and keep His commandments. True saving faith centers on God and His powerful work to bring about our salvation from sin.

Hinduism introduced another idea called "Maya," a doctrine very similar to the teachings produced by western Christian apostates known as "transcendentalism" and "existentialism." For the Hindus, all that happens in the physical world is nothing but an illusion. Such teachings are just another weak attempt to pacify the guilty conscience. For, if one can pretend he does not exist, then he may be able to avoid guilty feelings for the sin committed against God. Like the monkeys who see nothing, hear nothing, and say nothing in the famous picture, men will pretend they are unaware of their sin and guilt. If for just a moment, they could assume their nonexistence, perhaps this might serve to relieve a guilty conscience. It was a futile and absurd attempt to avoid the reality of the true and living God.

Buddha Statue in Phuket, Thailand

The Rise of Buddhism (450-185 BC)

For the LORD is great and greatly to be praised;
He is to be feared above all gods.
For all the gods of the peoples are idols,
But the LORD made the heavens. (Psalm 96:4-5)

A man named Siddhartha Gautama was born in the 5th century BC in what is modern Nepal, and he became a teacher of a new religion called Buddhism. As a young man raised in a wealthy, privileged family, Siddhartha was overcome by all the poverty, the beggars, and the suffering he witnessed all around him. He could not see that this was the result of sin in the world, rebellion against God, and the curse that came with the fall of man. So, the young man rejected his own inherited wealth and took on the lifestyle of a beggar for a time. Eventually Siddhartha received enlightenment from a demonic spirit named "Brahma" who claimed to be the head over 3,000 worlds. He explained that man's problem is not a broken relationship with his Creator, nor is it pain or poverty. The problem (according to Brahma) is the suffering which is brought about by desire—that is, wishing the world was something which it is not. This demonic lie rejects the fall of man, sin, the reality of evil, and God's judgment on the world. Siddhartha (the Buddha) died a sad death, some say poisoned by his own people. He did not rise from the dead.

The teachings of the Buddha, written down later by monks whom he discipled, fill 35-45 large volumes. Above all, Buddhism is moralistic. Tens of thousands of pages are consumed with moralistic lessons—things to do and things not to do. Such religious writings contrast sharply with God's single-volume revelation—which is primarily concerned with the story of God's work of redemption, reconciling us to God, and enabling us to love Him and keep His commandments.

> *For by grace you have been saved through faith, and that not of yourselves; it is the gift of God, not of works, lest anyone should boast. For we are His workmanship, created in Christ Jesus for good works, which God prepared beforehand that we should walk in them. (Ephesians 2:8-10)*

Mahabodhi Temple, the Site Where the Buddha Claimed to Attain "Nirvana" or Enlightenment

Although hamstrung by bad worldviews, India became an important trade center as early as 2000 BC. The Mohenjo had developed cotton, although it was Arab traders who gave it the name "quttan." These were also the first people to mine gold, using an animal something like an anteater or pangolin to sniff it out. The Roman Empire traded freely with India for silk, muslins, and gold, and Indian cheetahs, tigers, and elephants showed up in the great colosseums. Historians record that the Parthian wars between Rome and Persia (from 54 BC to AD 217) were fought largely to keep the trade routes to India open.

Prior to the 5th century BC, India was a mass of tribal groups, some stronger than others—the most notable of which was the Magadha Kingdom with its origins in the northeast (around modern-day Nepal). Between 420 BC and 320 BC, three successive dynasties expanded the Indian empire—the Shishunaga, the Nanda, and the Maurya dynasties. It was a king named Chandragupta Maurya, however, who carried India to the zenith of its power. By 320 BC the Maurya empire extended around almost the entire Indian peninsula and well into modern-day Pakistan and Afghanistan.

The Buddhist religion did not take hold in India immediately. By the onset of the third century BC, Aryans from the north were gaining political power, and in the year 260 BC an Aryan king named Asoka unified the nation by force. Thousands died in his bloody conflicts. After uniting the tribes in the largest Indian empire ever, Asoka turned to Buddhism. He became a vegetarian and built monasteries, spreading this new doctrine as far as Greece and Sri Lanka. Pacifism usually doesn't hold empires together, so Asoka's dynasty faded by 185 BC, and the kings of the Shunga Dynasty (185-73 BC) did their best to rid India of the new religion.

The coastlands of India would continue in darkness, awaiting the arrival of God's Law-Word, until after the coming of the Messiah. One day the name of the true God would be great even among the tribes of India. These far-off peoples were most surely included in the Messianic prophecies of Isaiah 42 and Malachi 1:

Behold! My Servant whom I uphold,
My Elect One in whom My soul delights!
I have put My Spirit upon Him;
He will bring forth justice to the Gentiles.

He will not cry out, nor raise His voice,
Nor cause His voice to be heard in the street.
A bruised reed He will not break,
And smoking flax He will not quench;
He will bring forth justice for truth.
He will not fail nor be discouraged,
Till He has established justice in the earth;
And the coastlands shall wait for His law. (Isaiah 42:1-4)

For from the rising of the sun, even to its going down,
My name shall be great among the Gentiles. . . (Malachi 1:11)

Athirapally Falls in India

Kerala, India

Timeline Review

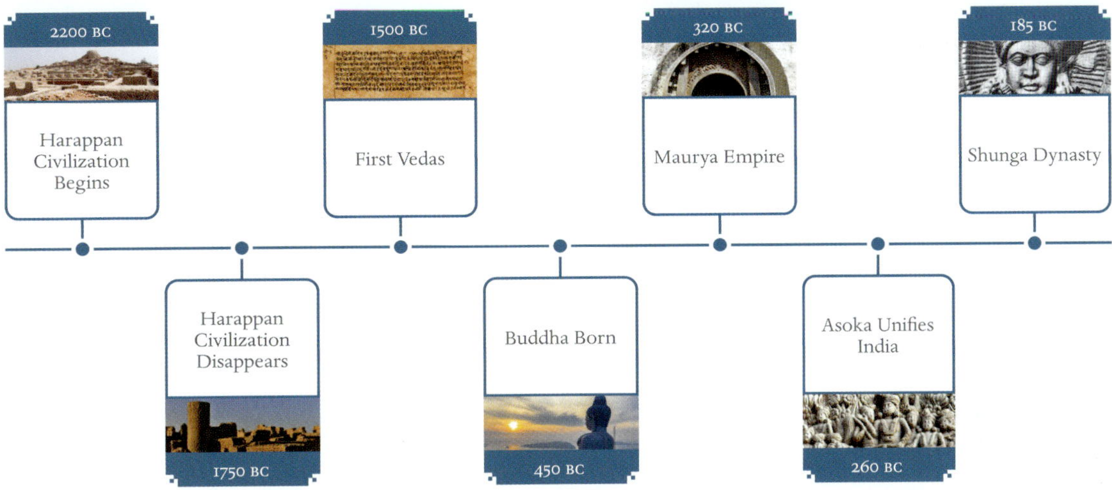

Chapter VIII Prayer

Our Father in Heaven, Almighty God,

You are the Judge of all the earth. How many ancient civilizations have you destroyed through the centuries? While the world is ultimately foolish and refuses to fear you, oh God, we will fear your Holy Name. You have destroyed nations that continue in rebellion, and you will destroy our nations as well if they cast off the rule of your Son, the King of kings and Lord of lords. You have made man upright, but man has sought out many schemes, many religions, and many false ideas. We confess that we have sinned against you. We have broken your law. We reject all false religions, all of man's schemes, and we seek for our salvation in your provision alone. We cannot atone for our own sins, but we rely fully on the sacrifice of your Son, Jesus Christ. Mighty God and Father, we praise you for the great resurrection of Christ from the dead. Where the pagan religions fail at every point, you have raised us all to newness of life, and you will bless us with eternal life in a world free of all evil, suffering, and death. We praise you, our God! Gracious Savior, may your Gospel reach into the furthest corners of India, that all the tribes of the earth may see your glory and rejoice in your salvation!

Amen.

Great Wall of China

CHAPTER IX

The Far East Before the Coming of Christ (2300 BC - AD 33)

Thus says the LORD:
"In an acceptable time I have heard You,
And in the day of salvation I have helped You;
I will reserve You and give You
As a covenant to the people,
To restore the earth,
To cause them to inherit the desolate heritages;
That You may say to the prisoners, 'Go forth,'
To those who are in darkness, 'Show yourselves.'
They shall feed along the roads,
And their pastures shall be on all desolate heights.
They shall neither hunger nor thirst,
Neither heat nor sun shall strike them;
For He who has mercy on them will lead them,
Even by the springs of water He will guide them.
I will make each of My mountains a road,
And My highways shall be elevated.

Surely these shall come from afar;
Look! Those from the north and the west,
And these from the land of Sinim." (Isaiah 49:8-12)

The Isaiah passage contains the strongest possible reference to China in biblical revelation. It is a promise that the wonderful Messiah of God will restore the earth and cause His people to dwell in once-desolate places. The Christ would come to be a light to the Gentiles "to the ends of the earth," which must include the land of Sinim. Indeed, these people would also come to the new Jerusalem, the church of the Firstborn, the church of the living Christ. To this day, the Hebrew rendering of China is "Sin." Also, the Latin prefix for China is "Sino."

The History of China: 2418-212 BC

Similar to Egypt, Mesopotamia, and India, ancient Chinese civilization formed along the Yellow River valley, between the Yangtze and Yellow Rivers.

As previously mentioned, the Miao tribe claimed its lineage from Japheth and his son Gomer. Chinese history must have gotten its start as early as 2418 BC, following the Babel dispersion, as Gomer and his progeny migrated into the area.

Huang Di was the first Chinese emperor on record, and he is credited with uniting the tribes along the Yellow River. He is admired for his discovery of medicinal treatments, and his wife Lei Zu is said to have discovered the fiber produced by the silkworm. The Lord of creation was gracious to the early Chinese, providing them with scientific and agricultural know-how early on. The Huang dynasty is thought to have lasted from 2350 BC to 1800 BC.

The term "Huang Di" provides key insight into the worldview of the earliest Chinese civilizations. "Di" is the Chinese word for God, and therefore the first king would have been referred to as the Huang god. From the outset, Chinese kings equated themselves to a godlike being, and the second emperor in the line, Ku Di, assumed the same term for himself. Ku's son Yao lived for 118 years—longevity seems to be characteristic of the post-flood era (even for these early Chinese). Then Ku's son Shun took up the throne and produced the first legal code—"the canon of Shun." This legislation lends important insight into the authoritarian cruelty which would characterize Chinese rule over the following 4,000 years. Punishments in the Shun law code included cutting off the nose, feet, and other

body parts, branding the face, and death. Shun instructed his prosecuting judges as follows:

> *The barbarous tribes disturb our beautiful land, and there are also among our own people robbers, murderers, insurgents, and traitors. It is your duty, as a criminal officer, to apply the five corporeal punishments.*[1]

Nonetheless, this king was careful to distinguish between inadvertent mistakes and what he called "intentional offenses," and if he had to err between condemning an innocent person and shedding innocent blood or releasing a guilty person, he recommended "choosing the latter."[2]

Another ancient Chinese law code appears during the reign of the emperor Muh (956-918 BC). This legislation was created after the villages had gone through a period of anarchy in which "the whole population . . . became robbers, murderers, oppressors of the righteous, adulterers, conspirators, and traitors."[3]

Although Muh resisted the "five corporeal punishments" as cruel, he did not modify them. His main concern was that the rulers of Meaou had not properly judged their cases, and guilty persons escaped scot-free while the innocent were condemned. He permitted the exchange of a fine for bodily mutilation if the condemned "offered excuses." To save one's feet, for example, the condemned party was required to pay 5,000 ounces of copper. With Muh's communique to his judges, he placed special emphasis on judging justly and in the fear of "God":

> *When you have any doubts as to the existence of the crime, then you should not inflict either corporeal punishment or fine, but should acquit the prisoner. Even when you have closely examined the evidence and have taken testimony, so as to remove any reasonable doubt, yet you must not make a hasty conclusion, but form a judgment from studying the appearance of the criminal. Any prosecution which is not substantiated by evidence should be dismissed immediately. In everything stand in awe of the dread majesty of God. . . . Stand always in awe of the punishment of God. God deals with men impartially, but men ruin themselves by evildoing.*[4]

Similar to the Egyptian monarch Amenhotep IV, this Chinese emperor appears to have been a monotheist. There also seems to be a measure of the fear of God in the king's language, though the nature of God and His law was obviously clouded in his mind. Nonetheless, to preserve civil order, Emperor Muh promulgated a law code with a commitment to equitableness and truth. And, by God's common grace, Chinese civilization was enabled to continue through the centuries. This testimony of a Chinese emperor corresponds with the revelation of David in 2 Samuel 23.

> *Now these are the last words of David.*
> *Thus says David the son of Jesse;*
> *Thus says the man raised up on high,*
> *The anointed of the God of Jacob,*
> *And the sweet psalmist of Israel:*
> *"The Spirit of the LORD spoke by me,*
> *And His word was on my tongue.*
> *The God of Israel said,*
> *The Rock of Israel spoke to me:*
> *'He who rules over men must be just,*
> *Ruling in the fear of God.' " (2 Samuel 23:1-3)*

Ancient Chinese Writings

Chinese writings discovered in the area of modern Shanghai in AD 2003 date back to somewhere around 2300-2200 BC.[5] Although other ancient markings appear as pictures and random designs, these writings place six characters on the same line indicating a sentence. This is a strong evidence that this early Chinese civilization was communicating in written form at the same time that the Mesopotamian and Egyptian descendants of Noah were communicating by cuneiform and papyri. (Of course no written language would be available prior to 2518 BC because the worldwide flood would have destroyed all previously-existing records of human civilizations.) These early writings have been found on hundreds of fragments of ceramic, stone, ivory, bone, and wood. A character that appears to be the Chinese symbol for "man" is visible on one of these ancient artifacts.

China's Second Dynasty (1766-1122 BC)

Shang Dynasty

China's second dynasty began with the emperor T'ang Shang, who commenced his rule in 1766 BC. The Shang Dynasty continued until 1122 BC and brought significant developments in writing and technology. The earliest complete Chinese writings are found near the end of the Shang dynasty (dating from 1200 BC) on what was known as the "oracle bones"—animal bones upon which messages were written. Sadly, these writings consist of divinations communicated via witchdoctors to include inquiries from kings concerning the will of their dead ancestors or the highest deity who is named "Di." For example, we read the text from one of the oracle bones as follows: "The Fang [enemy] are harming and attacking; it is Di who orders [them] to make disaster for us."[6] Divination was a near-universal practice in pagan lands, a practice which the Lord God continually warned His people against in the Old Testament:

O house of Jacob, come and let us
walk
In the light of the LORD.
For You have forsaken Your people,
the house of Jacob,
Because they are filled with eastern
ways;
They are soothsayers like the
Philistines,
And they are pleased with the
children of foreigners. (Isaiah 2:5-6)

And the LORD said to me, "The prophets prophesy lies in My name. I have not sent them, commanded them, nor spoken to them; they prophesy to you a false vision, divination, a worthless thing, and the deceit of their heart." (Jeremiah 14:14)

Bronze Vessel from the Shang Dynasty

The Legacy of Hegemony

Why do you boast yourself in mischief, O mighty man? The goodness of God endures continually. Your tongue devises mischiefs; like a sharp razor, working deceitfully. You love evil more than good; and lying rather than to speak righteousness." (Psalm 52:1-3)

From the reign of the legendary Huang Di onward, the god state developed in China and a spirit of hegemony prevailed more and more. Chinese government was dominating, authoritative, and predominantly tyrannical for almost its entire history. The Shang Dynasty (1766-1122 BC) accepted the Canon of Shun with all its enforced body mutilations and developed a bureaucracy that far exceeded that of Egypt and Mesopotamia.

Emperor T'ang's first official words (offered by later historians) from 1766 BC refer to himself as "the One Man" four times in his speech. T'ang declares, "It is given to me, the One man, to secure the harmony and tranquility of your states and clans."[7]

Thereby considering himself "the man" to bring peace to the world, he set his people up for another disappointment in a long history of disappointments. Only the Son of Man, the true Messiah of God, the coming Prince of Peace could warrant the call by Pilate to "Behold the Man" in John 19. The man, the one man worth speaking of in this way would appear on the scene 1,766 years later.

The Chinese kings used language concerning themselves only fitting for Jesus. With the Zhou Dynasty (1027-249 BC) came a Book of Odes to the kings.

> *King Wen ascends and descends,*
> *On the left and the right of God . . .*
> *His fame is without end . . .*[8]

The emperor's intent to rule the world and claim ownership of the land comes in another hymn:

> *All land under heaven belongs to the king,*
> *And all people on all shores are subject to this king.*[9]

Under this dynasty the king would come to be described as the "Son of heaven," another none-too-subtle reference to the Son of God who was to come.

Feudalism continued in some 172 districts through the Zhou Dynasty—with titles given to the local lords somewhat similar to the western titles of duke, marquis, earl, viscount, and baron (gong, hou, bo, zi, and nan.) Although some kings used

Fittings from the Zhou Dynasty

this absolutist power wisely, others like King Li of Zhou (877 BC -841 BC) gave way to corruption and decadence. He increased taxes on his citizens and instituted the death penalty on those who spoke against him. Consequently, this king was exiled by his nobles, leading to a weakening of the house of Zhou. So then, Duke Zhuang, the feudal lord of the most powerful state of Zheng, went to war against the King of Zhou and conquered him by 707 BC. National unity collapsed and civil war broke out among the feudal states, lasting about 250 years. Bloodshed was unrelenting, with some 483 wars fought throughout the Chinese districts.

The Chinese totalitarian hegemony would take further shape under a man by the name of Duke Huan, who ruled in the state of Qi from 685 BC to 643 BC. If China was to be unified, it became clear to Huan and others that it could only happen under a tight-fisted, centralized, bureaucratic state. In his first experiment with statist rule, Duke Huan and his prime minister Guan Zhong created a state centered around military force. Well before Karl Marx, Josef Stalin, and Franklin D. Roosevelt, these early Chinese power-hungry tyrants were imposing regulation on the marketplace. They initiated a state monopoly on money and instituted state control of salt production and iron ore.

Duke Huan's government was the first to advocate the Chinese philosophy of Legalism, largely masterminded by the prime minister. Guan Zhong recorded his precepts in a book called "The Book of Master Guan." Simply stated, from this point on, the king would be the very source of law. Look no further than the whims of the existing ruler or civil government for the source of civil law. The logic was simple. If the king or ruler was god on earth, then by definition, he had to be the source of law as long as he lived. Quoting Master Guan from his book:

"The sovereign is the creator of law. The officials are the followers of the law, and the people are subjects of the law."[10]

Absolute power is therefore endowed upon whoever happens to be king at the moment, and no Bill of Rights, Constitution, Law of God, or any other law would control the ruler's policies and actions. Guan went on to state in his Book:

> *The wise sovereign holds six powers: to grant life and to kill; to enrich and to impoverish; to promote and to demote.*[11]

At first only local states accepted this philosophy of hegemonic power, which resulted in an expansion of the military within these states. But then, the more powerful states (Qi, Jin, and Chu, for example) seized control of the smaller districts in a dog-eat-dog survival of the fittest contest. Survival depended on who could incorporate Legalist philosophy, maintain standing armies, and incorporate the "Machiavellian" strategies of deceit and deception at the fastest rate. Military generals like Sun Tzu and Wáng Jinx were particularly admired for developing these strategies and waging aggressive war with the intent of building power bases. The goal was crystal clear—enrich the state and strengthen the military (fuguo qiangbing).

Statue of Sun Tzu

Sometimes viewed as the Machiavelli of China, Han Fei (280-233 BC) was the great systematizer of the Legalist theory. He cut the theory down to its bare root: "He who has the most power wins." The goal for the state is always the accumulation of money and power: "He who has great power will be paid tribute by others, he who has less power will pay tribute to others, therefore the wise ruler cultivates power."[12] Han Fei wrote, "The ruler occupies the position of power; [he] dominates the people and commands the wealth of the state."[13]

Early writings from these Legalists laid out the foundations of the first tyrannical state, a recipe which would be replayed by the communists and socialists in Russia, Germany, Eastern Europe, Sweden, the United States, and the whole developed world in the 20th and 21st centuries. The Legalists recommended:

1. The largest group of people possible to rule over. The ruler of men desires to have more people for his own use.[14]
2. The elimination of associations of people not connected to the state—which would include private schools, etc. The early kings always made certain that the interests of their subjects diverged. Thus under perfect governance, spouses, and friends, however close to one another, can neither refuse to

report another's crimes nor cover up for them.[15]

3. The encouragement of informers who will report on those people who have violated state rules. The wise ruler forces the whole world to hear and to watch for him. . . . No one in the world can hide from him or scheme against him.[16]

4. A government based more on fear and punishment than on rewarding and blessing its citizens. Mass executions of citizenry usually produce this fear. A well-governed state . . . employs nine punishments to one reward.[17] If crimes are punished by execution then the law wins over the people and the army is strong.[18]

5. A very well-organized surveillance program and a complete removal of all rights of privacy. The people were commanded to be organized into groups of fives and tens. They must be under mutual surveillance and punished for crimes committed by other members of the group. Those who failed to inform against a crime were to be cut in half at the waist.[19]

The plans of the Legalists and the new tyrants were finally brought to consummation with the great Qin Empire, beginning in 231 BC. The kingdom of Qin was thoroughly dedicated to the Legalist theory of eliminating local ownership of land, turning it over to the kingdom, centralizing political power, and militarizing society.

In 273 BC the armies of Qi led by General Bai Qi won the battle of Huayang. No mercy was shown to the surrendering army—130,000 men lost their heads. Finally, in 262 BC, Qin faced the Zhao king at Changping. The Zhaos surrendered and 400,000 men were buried alive in what would come to symbolize the cruelty of Chinese hegemony for the next 2,200 years.

Once the empire was consolidated, the Legalists went to work to create the first massive socialist state in history. Ownership of weapons was banned, and all swords and arrows were collected at the capital. Wandering minstrels were replaced with official state-sanctioned entertainers. Rich landowners and their families were moved to the capital to remain under the watchful eye of the central government. If someone violated a major law, his entire family was executed. Work camps were created for those violating minor state regulations, and millions populated these "gulags." There was plenty of work to do, with 700,000 workers enslaved and employed for the construction of Emperor Qin Shi Huang's palace. Others were used to build 4,000 miles of highways and thousands of miles of canals—not to mention the 1,500 miles of the Great Wall in the north.

The emperor was endowed with godlike qualities, and a state cult worship developed. Most essential for this state was the eradication of any opposition to the Legalist ideology. His closest advisor, the ruthless Legalist Li Si, told the king, "Your Majesty . . . has firmly established for yourself a position of sole supremacy. . . . And yet these independent schools [Confucianists and others], joining with each other, criticize the codes of laws and instructions. Hearing of the promulgation of a decree, they criticize it, each from the standpoint of his own school. . . . If such license is not prohibited the sovereign power will decline above and partisan factions will form below. It would be well to prohibit this. Your servant suggests that all books in the imperial archives, save the memoirs of Qin, be burned."[20]

Terracotta Warriors from the Period of Qin Shi Huang

Emperor Qin Shi Huang

The imperial edict that followed became the prototype for all future tyrannies the world over:

Memorial on the Burning of Books—Li Si

Anyone owning classical books or treatises on philosophy must hand them in within thirty days. After thirty days anyone found in possession of such writings will be branded on the cheek and sent

Great Wall of China

to work as a laborer on the northern wall or some other government project. The only exceptions are books on medicine, drugs, astrology, and agronomy.

Private schools will be forbidden. Those who wish to study law will do so under government officials.

Anyone indulging in political or philosophical discussion will be put to death, and his body exposed in public.

Scholars who use examples from antiquity to criticize the present, or who praise early dynasties in order to throw doubt on the policies of our own, most enlightened sovereign, will be executed, they and all their families.

Government officials who turn a blind eye to the above-mentioned crimes will be deemed guilty by virtue of the principle of collective responsibility, and will incur the same punishment as that inflicted for the offense itself.

What followed this edict was not to be soon forgotten in the annals of history. Emperor Qin Shi Huang personally tried the case of 463 Confucian scholars. They were assigned to five different horrible tortures, buried up to their necks in dirt, and their heads were crushed by chariot wheels. The actions of Qin would maintain a special significance and authoritative precedent for the future of Chinese governance. For the succeeding 2,200 years, any and all dissent would be crushed by powerful governments in China (and later, North Korea) in a similar manner.

Large power-oriented empires need powerful systems to keep them together, especially when there are competing forces fighting for power—or where there are portions of the empire which would prefer to be self-governed. If the goal of human life was to control large empires or to rule the world (at the hands of one person or small group of persons), then hegemony was the only way to do it. Violence and war would be the only way to achieve these power centers. And terrifying, torturing penal systems and omnipresent, iron-handed, tough-fisted bureaucracy would be the only way to maintain it. This was all based on the assumption that man's chief goal is to empower himself or his governments, which he hoped would achieve the greatest good. Of course, this is all based on a demonic lie. The greatest good comes only when man loves God and obeys His commandments, and this can only happen through the preaching of the Gospel and the work of the Lord Jesus Christ. Peace on earth and righteousness in the world can never come by merely increasing the power and control of centralized governments. This blessing results from the outpouring of the Holy Spirit of God.

Until the Spirit is poured upon us from on high,
And the wilderness becomes a fruitful field,
And the fruitful field is counted as a forest.
Then justice will dwell in the wilderness,
And righteousness remain in the fruitful field.
The work of righteousness will be peace,
And the effect of righteousness, quietness and assurance forever.
My people will dwell in a peaceful habitation,
In secure dwellings, and in quiet resting places. (Isaiah 32:15-18)

Confucianism— The Other Humanist Philosophy of the East

Heavy-handed Legalism was not the only philosophy attempted for the betterment of mankind by Chinese philosophers and political leaders. With the development of human civilization comes man's optimistic attempts to better himself by a higher or greater knowledge. With increasing knowledge, man believes he will become less dependent on the gods for wisdom and blessing and more dependent on himself. However, this always turns into one more mistaken approach that inevitably leads to ruin.

Man knows that something is wrong with him, and at first he seeks salvation and blessing from the gods. He tries to atone for his sins by sacrifice, but that is never seen as enough. Then come the philosophers who propose that man is perfectible on his own and that he can salve his conscience by espousing the worldview of atheism and humanism—turning himself into a god. The end goal for these philosophers seems to be the collection of wealth and power for man, even if it is only for a short season.

Confucius was one such philosopher, born in 551 BC and raised mostly by a single mother, his father having died when the boy was three years old. Confucius took a position in the government of the state of Lu, ended up on the wrong side of a political battle, and exiled himself. For most of his life he traveled about the decentralized Chinese states, explaining his philosophical and political ideas without gaining much ground. Yet his ideas would have a strong influence on Chinese civilization for the next 1,500 years. Confucius is best known for the aphorism:

What you do not wish for yourself, do not do for others.

Statue of Confucius

His was another moralistic worldview. Confucius rightly saw that sheer coercive, tyrannical force probably would not improve the world. He understood that the family falls apart and civil society collapses when men do not "first rectify their hearts."[21] Then he explained that a change of heart could not happen unless people were thinking correctly—and this he felt could come about by careful investigation and education. Right thinking then would result in self-cleansing of the heart and self-improvement, and families would be regulated well and states rightly governed. He felt that seeking impartial knowledge would produce sincere thinking, which would cleanse the heart of wrong desires.

Politically, Confucius would be associated with modern socialists. He argued for the redistribution of wealth. He wanted the government to provide "a competent portion" for the aged, employment for the middle-aged, and education for children. He believed that in a socialist nation people would avoid idleness and would be less concerned for their own advantage. "Selfish schemings are repressed and find no way to rise. Robbers, filchers, and rebellious traitors do not exist."[22]

Confucius founded his philosophy on the wrong view of human nature and the human heart, which is by nature "deceitful above all things and desperately wicked." (Jer. 17:9) He didn't realize the inherent selfishness, slothfulness, dishonesty, and covetousness that governs the hearts of men. His over optimism

Confucian Temple in Beijing, China

concerning human nature produced socialist theories that would do as much damage or more than the Legalists. Confucius didn't realize that heart change could only happen by regeneration, and that a change of mind could only come through repentance, which would only occur by the work of God in the life of the soul (2 Tim. 2:24-26). More fundamental than a need for more knowledge or a change of perspective, what man really needed was a change of heart. The words of Jesus Christ, the Word of God, must correct the thinking of this great philosopher. His words pierce through the darkness, as he speaks: "You must be born again" (John 3:7). The true prophets of God had to conclude that self-improvement is impossible for the natural man:

Tomb of Confucius,
Shandong Province, China

Can the Ethiopian change his skin or the leopard its spots?
Then may you also do good who are accustomed to do evil. (Jeremiah 13:23)

Only by the power of God can men and women be set free from their sinful tendencies. The character of men cannot change in any substantial way without a heart change and a release from the control of sin and the devil. Without the coming of Christ, man is left with anarchy, self-destruction, and more coercion and enslavement to powerful governments over and over again. But, thanks be to God, the Savior did come to set the captives free!

Jesus answered them, "Most assuredly, I say to you, whoever commits sin is a slave of sin. And a slave does not abide in the house forever, but a son abides forever. Therefore if the Son makes you free, you shall be free indeed." (John 8:34-36)

Such humanist thinking would greatly influence the world in the 19th and 20th centuries. The United States and many other countries came to believe that right education would bring about a change of the minds and hearts of people and produce strong families and nations. When the collapse of education, the family, and the socio-economic systems followed a century of socialism in the 20th century, once again man came to realize that humanism, socialism, and Confucianism are complete failures.

Quick Power Shift—Han Dynasty: 206 BC - AD 220

The government of Qin Shih Huang-Ti ended with the tyrant's death. He was buried with one hundred maidens entombed with him in his grave. Mechanical devices were placed in his tomb which would automatically fire projectiles at intruders, and the workmen who placed the coffin in the tomb were buried alive to prevent them from revealing the secret passage to the body of the dead emperor.

Shih Huang's twenty-one-year-old son assumed the throne but he was unable to quell the revolts cropping up around the empire. After losing a key battle, the young ruler was forced by his own prime minister to commit suicide at 22-23 years of age. China quickly splintered into eighteen kingdoms, and two of the more powerful rulers (Xiang Yu and Liu Bang) fought for control of the empire.

Liu Bang would afterward become Emperor Han Kau Chou and reign from 202 BC to 195 BC. This ruler introduced a more moderate tyranny, relaxing the Legalist philosophy of the Qin Dynasty. He issued a document somewhat resembling a shortened Magna Charta, the contents of which read:

> *In your presence, I do solemnly make the tripartite compact with all my people, to-wit:*
>
> 1. *that the death penalty shall be imposed for murder,*
> 2. *that appropriate punishments shall be imposed for injuries to the person, and*
> 3. *that appropriate punishments shall be imposed for theft and robbery. The laws of the Ch'in Dynasty are hereby revoked.*[23]

These sensible laws much better reflected God's law recorded in Genesis 9:6 and Exodus 21. It is the law of the true and living God that provides the basis for appropriate human rights as well as good and just law.

Also, Emperor Wen (reign 179-157 BC) produced his own legal reforms, which included:

1. Removing all the mandates requiring family members to be punished for crimes committed by another individual in the family
2. Abolishing punishment by mutilation, for the first time in 2,000 years
3. Restoring the right to free speech and inquiry, and abolishing thought-crimes.

Emperor Wen's proclamation reads:

> *In the good old times, the rulers used to plant in each public market a flag, called "the flag of remonstrances," and they also hung up a board of wood, called "the board of criticisms." These proved very serviceable in helping to attain a proper method of government, and in removing the bar between the king and his subjects. Now, our law punishes persons for criticizing policies of our government and for spreading heresies. This causes the ministers and the people to refrain from pouring out their whole hearts to us. And now, how can we know our faults and mistakes, being deprived of such a valuable source of instruction? For the above reasons, we hereby repeal the said statute.*[24]

Ceramic Cavalryman from the Han Dynasty

However, since each new emperor was still treated as the source of law and endowed with a god-like status and authority in the Chinese mind, these reforms never lasted long. Until the people acknowledged a sovereign God and a transcendent law with authority over all kings and governments, lasting liberties could never exist. Such an acknowledgment would not appear until it was encoded in constitutional law in the Christianized West in the 13th century.

Early Experiments with Socialism

Ancient China formed its largest empire and widest rule under the governance of Wu Ti, the greatest of the Han emperors (ruling 140-87 BC). During his reign, Chinese boundaries extended to the east and west over modern-day Korea, Mongolia, and Uzbekistan. However, Emperor Wu Ti is best remembered for experimenting with socialism. He claimed state ownership of natural resources, hoping to prevent private persons from "reserving to their sole use the riches of the mountains and the sea in order to gain a fortune and from putting the lower classes into subjection to themselves."[25] The state also seized control of production of iron and alcoholic beverages. Through buying up huge inventories, the Wu Ti government found ways to undercut the market for goods and to fix prices. Their goal was to prevent rich merchants from making "big profits." An annual income tax was incorporated at 5%, extremely low in comparison with modern socialist tyrannies. Nonetheless, China became the first nation in the world to experiment with big government socialism.

China was at the height of its power (as was the Roman Empire) by the time of the birth of our Lord Jesus Christ. Salvation by government and the enforcement of a system of equality was the only hope and dream of the Han Empire during these years.

While Christ was growing up in Nazareth of Galilee, an official named Wang Mang took control of the Han empire, ruling from AD 9 to AD 23. It was this man who attempted a complete incorporation of Confucian philosophy into Chinese life. He abolished slavery and tried to equalize wealth in the nation. He stopped all private purchasing of land, seized ownership of mines, and controlled the sale of wine.

Stone Carved Pillar from Han Dynasty

This extensive government intervention only served to break down the character of the nation, and it wasn't long afterwards that the Han Empire met its demise. The great empire—once at its zenith when Christ was born—collapsed in AD 220, only two centuries before the fall of that other great empire, Rome. So then, China entered a dark age as the Tatars poured over the Great Wall en masse, and man's empire-building efforts once again proved futile.

> *And in the days of these kings the God of heaven will set up a kingdom which shall never be destroyed; and the kingdom shall not be left to other people; it shall break in pieces and consume all these kingdoms, and it shall stand forever. (Daniel 2:44)*

First Historical Record of Korea (194 BC)

The Korean Peninsula

Historical records for the land of Korea begin in 194 BC, when a Chinese military leader (from the Han Empire) appeared in Gojosean in northwestern Korea and wrested the throne from the ruling king Gijun. Known as Wiman, this military captain established his rule in what would be modern-day Pyongyang. His dynasty lasted until 108 BC. When the Han armies appeared, the city of Gojosean attempted resistance but fell quickly, and the king (the grandson of Wiman) was assassinated. Chinese Emperor Wu Ti left four "Commanderies" to govern Korea—basically all the land north of the Han River (the territory which makes up North Korea today). China's control of Korea continued until the waning of the Han Dynasty in the 3rd century AD.

Proud Japan (700 BC - AD 33)

> *Surely oppression destroys a wise man's reason, and a bribe debases the heart. The end of a thing is better than its beginning; The patient in spirit is better than the proud in spirit. (Ecclesiastes 7:7-8)*

Japan is a proud and independent nation, and its people have never been subjugated to any other power. Its one and only attempt to create an empire took place in the 20th century before and during World War II. For a short while after the war, Japan had the second most prosperous economy in the world. However, birth implosions and massive debt spending throttled the nation's economy, and Japan would assume a humbler position in the world.

Japan's isolation is first due to its geographical situation—the country's four main islands are entirely surrounded by oceans. This has made it more difficult for enemies to invade, and by God's common grace the nation was enabled to

develop and prosper through the ages. Since Japan is mainly mountainous—only about 13% of the land is farmable—the Japanese have been quite innovative and efficient in farming hillsides and mountain areas by cultivating rice fields in ascending steps. Japan's economy was based on fishing and agriculture until the 20th century, at which point the country became one of the most technologically advanced on earth—producing a large percentage of the world's automobiles and electronic gadgets.

As long as tribal conflicts were kept at a minimum, the Japanese economy developed and the population increased. A decentralized, feudal approach to economy and government also enabled some prosperity for the island nation. Like Europe, Japan empowered local feudal lords who provided adequate defenses by building castles in various parts of the country. China disposed of this sort of economy when the Legalists took over in the 3rd century BC.

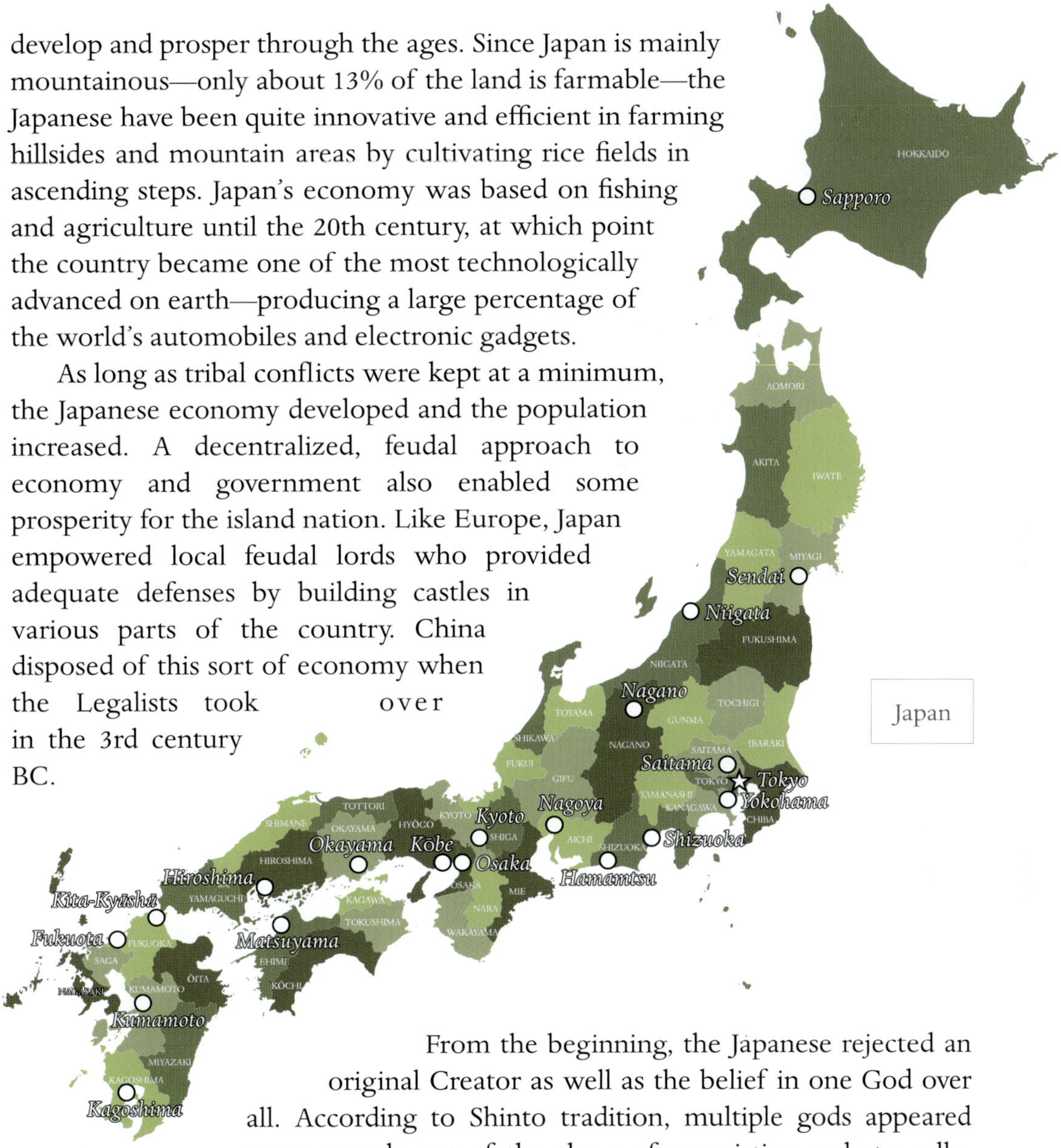

Japan

From the beginning, the Japanese rejected an original Creator as well as the belief in one God over all. According to Shinto tradition, multiple gods appeared spontaneously out of the chaos of preexisting and eternally-existing matter. These gods gave birth to more gods, thus making the gods appear very similar to the humans who invented them. From its inception, Japan was crippled morally by its commitment to infanticide and abortion. According to ancient Shinto legend, the first two humans

Shinto Shrine in Hiroshima, Japan

created by the kami (gods) were brother and sister, named Izanami and Izanagi. Their first child, Hiruko, was born deformed and was therefore "legitimately" abandoned by her parents. The two produced other gods (or "kami" in Japanese) as well as the islands of Japan—the first land to be created on earth.

> *LORD, how long will the wicked, How long will the wicked triumph? They utter speech, and speak insolent things; All the workers of iniquity boast in themselves. . . They slay the widow and the stranger, and murder the fatherless.*
>
> *Yet they say, "The LORD does not see, Nor does the God of Jacob understand."*
>
> *Understand, you senseless among the people; and you fools, when will you be wise? He who planted the ear, shall He not hear? He who formed the eye, shall He not see? . . .The LORD knows the thoughts of man, that they are futile. (Psalm 94:3-9,11)*

Due to this harsh view of human life, Japan would come to be known for its cruel utilitarianism especially in regard to war and childbirth. The Japanese "perfected" methods of torture to be used on Christians during the 17th century persecutions. Japanese cruelty with the Chinese during World War II was practically unprecedented in modern warfare, and the military leadership did not stop short of cannibalism in their treatment of the enemy. Japan would also be one of the first nations to enthusiastically embrace Margaret Sanger, the world's foremost leader in birth control. During the early part of the 21st century, Japan turned up at the front of the pack in the worldwide birth implosions caused by the widespread use of abortifacients and abortion. After Japan legalized abortion in 1948 with their Eugenic Protection Law, Japanese women resorted to this form of child killing as the preferred method of birth control for fifty years. By 1955 Japan's abortion rate reached an internationally unprecedented 55%.[26] Fifty years later, it is estimated that 2/3 of Japanese women had participated in this terrible moral travesty. For the first time in hundreds if not thousands of years, Japan's population began decreasing in AD 2010. At current birth rates, the Japanese population will reduce from 128,000,000 to 85,000,000 in 90 years.

The Japanese embraced Buddhist moralisms and Shinto religious ceremonies—both of which bear a faint resemblance to the faith of Old Testament Israel. Comparing Japan's religion, economy, and life with more primitive forms in Africa or South America, the Japanese worldview appears as something of an improvement. Nevertheless, these manmade religious ideas and rituals could only suppress and conceal the sinfulness of the human heart. On the surface, Japanese society might appear quite honorable, moral, and clean, but sin persists within. After World War II, Japan would enthusiastically embrace western atheism, post-Christian humanism, evolution, and materialism. This would hasten the destruction of Japanese traditional morality, family integrity, and the social-economic system that had been preserved by God's common grace through the centuries. The bankruptcy of Japan's religion and social morality would manifest itself with a sharper clarity in the 21st century.

All faithless, Christless, moralistic religions are described by the Apostle Paul in 2 Timothy 3:5 as "having a form of godliness but lacking the power thereof." The religions "have an appearance of wisdom in self-imposed religion, false humility, and neglect of the body, but are of no value against the indulgence of the flesh." (Col. 2:23).

Shinto Purification Basin at Shrine

A Faint Heritage from Judaism

> *Now it came to pass after these things that God tested Abraham, and said to him, "Abraham!"*
>
> *And he said, "Here I am."*
>
> *Then He said, "Take now your son, your only son Isaac, whom you love, and go to the land of Moriah, and offer him there as a burnt offering on one of the mountains of which I shall tell you." (Genesis 22:1-2)*

Whatever morality and society is preserved by these far off cultures before Christ came is cause for wonder and praise. Certainly, we should be thankful for God's common grace that enables societies to continue despite their rebellion and sinfulness. Yet, Japan, China, India, Persia, Greece, and Egypt had access to the revelation of God through the exiles of Israel and Judah, as well as by the trade routes that passed through Canaan in Old Testament times. Perhaps it was this revelation that sustained some moral conscience for the nation of Japan through the centuries.

To this day, Japanese celebrate the Ontohsai festival at Mt. Moriya (1650 m) on the main island of Honshu. The mountain bears a name strikingly similar to Mount Moriah referred to in Genesis 22. As the Japanese tradition goes, a young boy is tied to a wooden pillar and placed on a bamboo mat. A Shinto priest approaches him with a knife but the priest is prevented by another priest from killing the lad, and the boy is removed from the makeshift altar. Traditionally, seventy-five deer were sacrificed at the festival—a completely unique element to the Shinto tradition. This event is referred to as "the festival of the Mi-isakuchi-god." "Mi" is an honorific title meaning "great and honorable," and "isaku" may be a reference to Isaac.

Honshu

By the time of the Meiji era (19th century) the inclusion of the young boy was regarded as too pagan, and only stuffed animals are included in the ceremony at the present. Historical records contained in a museum near Suwa-Taisha indicate that the Moriya ceremony has continued for seventy-eight generations—which would amount to 2,184 years.

Some have pointed out the similarities between the Shinto temple and the Jewish temple. The Shinto temple is made of cedar wood, as was the Old Testament temple built by Solomon (2 Samuel 5, 7). The famed Meiji Shrine was constructed from 5,500 cypress logs.

Other references to Old Testament Israel are also apparent within the Shinto religion. The ancient star of David is located on the Ise-jingu Shinto Shrine. The emperor's line is also referred to as Mikado, and some believe that Kado is a reference to the Israelite tribe of Gad. Could some of the Israelites in the dispersion of the Northern tribes have wandered into Japan around the 600s BC? Or perhaps, indigenous tribes settling Japan may have been influenced by the dispersion of the Israelites around that time. The early beginnings of the Japanese nation coincide with the first exile.

Also, in Japanese tradition the secret regalia held by the emperor included a staff and a jar. The early contents of the ark of the covenant were a staff, a jar of manna, and the Ten Commandments. Those who have attended Japanese festivals witness Shinto priests carrying a sacred shrine held up by poles through the city. The sight is quite reminiscent of the Israelite priests carrying the ark of the covenant. Shinto priests also wear fringes on their garments (see Deut. 22:12), and the Shinto shrine is typically composed of a courtyard with a laver for purification, a holy place, and the holy of holies (separated by steps).

As with most of the far-flung ancient tribes who lived under the dominion of the devil, the Japanese held to animism. That is, they worshiped many spirits, they thought of inanimate objects as having spirits, they feared the spirits of dead relatives, and they would attempt to speak to the spirit world using shamans. Communication with the demon world and respect for their advice is among the most degraded and depraved activities of fallen man, and is soundly condemned by God in Scripture.

> *There shall not be found among you . . . one who conjures spells, or a medium, or a spiritist, or one who calls up the dead, for all these things are an abomination to the LORD, and because of these abominations, the LORD your God drives them out from before you. (Deuteronomy 18:10-12)*

Out of this animism Shintoism arose somewhere around the 5th century BC. Shintoism is a polytheistic religion, and to this day some 80,000 shrines exist in Japan, each honoring one or more gods invented by the imaginations of men. Shintoism is concerned with purification rites, honoring dead relatives, balance and harmony, and getting on the good side of the gods (especially those gods who happen to be in charge of wealth).

Ancient Japanese History

Not much is known of ancient Japanese history because a written language did not appear until well after Christ came to earth. Archaeologists find evidence of early settlements in Japan in Sannai-Maruyama as far back as 2300-2000 BC, with populations running around 100,000. The early indigenous peoples were planting rice around 800 BC. Although there are no written records, the early Japanese left pottery designs that indicate a people gifted in artistry, beauty, and innovation.

Ancient Chinese writings reveal that the Japanese were known for internal conflicts and civil wars in these early centuries before Christ. Man is continually plagued with malice, envy, hatred, competitions, strife, and every work of the flesh (Gal. 5:19-21). It would take a religious emperor cult to unify the country.

About AD 220, Chinese emissaries traveled to Kyushu (the southern island of Japan), and their report constitutes the first historical record of these peoples. The embassy visited several areas, recording populations of 1,000, 3,000, 4,000, 20,000, 50,000, and 70,000 households in respective cities. Other than the eight or so tribes he visited, the author lists twenty-one other "countries" or tribes he was unable to see at the time. This would put the population of Japan

Ancient Japanese Vase (c. 2000 BC)

somewhere around 500,000 to 600,000 households, or roughly 2,000,000 people. The Chinese traveler reported that "all men tattoo their faces and decorate their bodies."[27] Apparently, at the time the Chinese emissaries made contact, as much as one third of Japan had united under a single female shaman queen, a very odd and wicked woman who controlled people by "magic and sorcery" and who kept 1,000 female attendants in her court. Similar to other pagan peoples in ancient times, the Japanese attempted to tell the future by throwing tortoise shells into the fire and examining the cracks to "tell what will happen."[28]

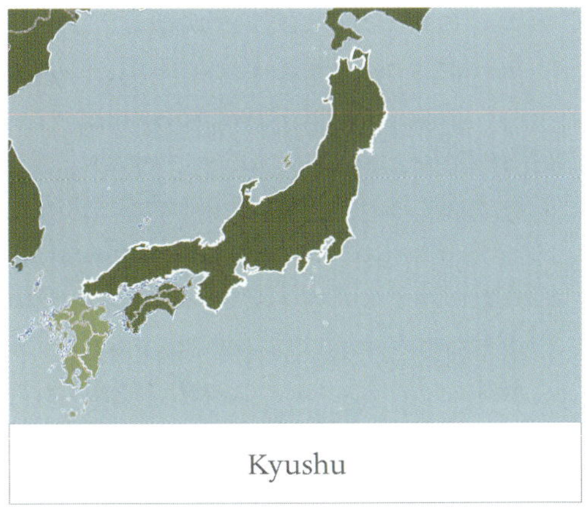
Kyushu

As far as social customs and civil law was concerned, the Chinese historian recorded:

> *In public meetings all sit together and there is no difference between father and son or man and woman. They are fond of liquor. In their worship, men of importance simply clap their hands instead of kneeling or bowing. The people live long, some to one hundred, others to 80 or 90 years. Ordinarily, men of importance have four or five wives, the lesser ones two or three. Women are not loose in morals or jealous. There is no theft and litigation is infrequent. When there is a violation of the law, the wives and children of a lesser offender are enslaved, a great offender is killed along with his entire household and other kinsmen. There are class distinctions and some men are subordinate to others. Taxes are collected. There are granaries as well as markets in each province where necessities are exchanged under the supervision of an official.*[29]

The Chinese visitors noted the primitiveness of Japanese society, along with their politeness, severity, high value for cleanliness, and fine craftsmanship.

> *The social customs are not lewd. The men wear a band of cloth around their heads, exposing the top. Their clothing is fastened around the body with little sewing. The women wear their hair in loops. Their clothing is like an unlined bed cover and is worn by slipping the head through an opening in the center. They cultivate grains,*

> *rice, hemp, and mulberry trees. They spin and weave and produce fine linen and silk fabrics. There are no cattle, horses, tigers, leopards, sheep, or magpies. Their weapons are spears, shields, and wooden bows made with a short lower part and long upper part [the pattern of later bows also]. The arrows are bamboo, tipped with either iron or bone. In their material culture they are like the people of Hainan Island.*
>
> *The land of Wa is warm and mild. In winter as in summer people can eat vegetables and go barefooted. Their houses have rooms and father and mother and older and younger sleep separately. They smear their bodies with pink and scarlet as the Chinese use powder. They serve food on bamboo and wooden trays, helping themselves with their fingers. When a person dies they prepare a single coffin, without an outer one. They cover the graves with sand to make a mound. When death occurs mourning is observed for at least 10 days, during which time they do not eat meat. The head mourners wail and lament, while friends sing, dance, and drink liquor. When the funeral is over, all members of the family go into the water to bathe, to purify themselves.*
>
> *When they cross the sea to visit China, they always choose a man who does not arrange his hair, does not rid himself of fleas, lets his clothing get as dirty as it will, does not eat meat, and does not approach women. This man behaves as a mourner and is known as the fortune keeper. If the voyage ends successfully, they lavish on him slaves and other valuables. In case there is disease or other mishap, they kill him, saying that he must not have been scrupulous in his duties.*[30]

Thus it is clear that superstition, witchcraft, polygamy, and slavery dominated the land of Japan before the coming of the Messiah and the Savior of mankind. Instability, tribal warfare, and extermination of villages was the inevitable consequence where no central government existed—though the tyranny caused by centralizing power failed to produce anything better, as is witnessed by the history of China to the west.

Moralistic religions, cultural hegemony, or rigidly-imposed traditions may salvage a nation for awhile. But, these things can't do any thing to fundamentally change a selfish, proud, and lust-filled heart. They can't do anything to save a nation from the judgment of God, and they cannot save a soul from hell. Salvation for the Japanese, the Chinese, the Koreans, and everybody else in the world could only come by God's Savior, the Lord Jesus Christ. No one else and no system invented by man could save us from our sins and cleanse us from all unrighteousness.

Giving thanks to the Father who has qualified us to be partakers of the inheritance of the saints in the light. He has delivered us from the power of darkness and conveyed us into the kingdom of the Son of His love. (Colossians 1:12-13)

A Nation Ruled by Emperors

The kingdom of Japan is the oldest dynasty in the world—with the exception of King David's dynasty. Early Japanese history is lost in myth largely because of the worldview of those who wrote the history in AD 712. These court historians desired to amalgamate the line of the human emperors into a line of the gods, so they fashioned a sun goddess named Amaterasu who produced a son, and a grandson named Nininu. This Nininu is commissioned to rule Japan—he descends to the earth and lands on Kyushu, where he gets into a political struggle with a ruler already located there named Okuninushi. They arrive at an amenable agreement—Okuninushi would head up the priestly class while Nininu would take on the political rule of the nation. Okuninushi is also a polygamist, and one of his wives abandons a newborn child in the branches of a tree.

Jimmu Tennō

As the story recounts, Nininu's grandson is Jimmu Tennō, who becomes the first emperor of Japan—ruling from 660 to 585 BC. The reference "Tennō" is translated "from heaven." This marks one of the world's most successful attempts at turning man into a god and making room for an authoritarian ruler with godlike qualities. If the sun goddess gives birth to the emperor, then he ought to be treated as the son of god, as the story goes. Here is a perversion of the truth. Indeed, Christ is the only begotten Son of God, but He does not bear children with the goal of holding authoritarian rule over people. Natural man sees a need for a connection with God (or the gods), but this relationship cannot come about by natural birth. It happens only by spiritual rebirth and by the Son of God taking upon Himself human flesh.

The pride of the Japanese nation is bound up in tracing their emperor's line back to the 7th century BC. This earthly line of kings appears as a surrogate and futile competitor to the true King, the true Son of God, and the eternal dynasty purposed by God.

The Lord's Covenant with King David (1000 BC)

Now therefore, thus shall you say to My servant David, "Thus says the LORD of hosts: 'I took you from the sheepfold, from following the sheep, to be ruler over My people, over Israel. And I have been with you wherever you have gone, and have cut off all your enemies from before you, and have made you a great name, like the name of the great men who are on the earth. Moreover I will appoint a place for My people Israel, and will plant them, that they may dwell in a place of their own and move no more; nor shall the sons of wickedness oppress them anymore, as previously, since the time that I commanded judges to be over My people Israel, and have caused you to rest from all your enemies. Also the LORD tells you that He will make you a house. When your days are fulfilled and you rest with your fathers, I will set up your seed after you, who will come from your body, and I will establish his kingdom. He shall build a house for My name, and I will establish the throne of his kingdom forever. I will be his Father, and he shall be My son. If he commits

David Commissions Solomon

iniquity, I will chasten him with the rod of men and with the blows of the sons of men. But My mercy shall not depart from him, as I took it from Saul, whom I removed from before you. And your house and your kingdom shall be established forever before you. Your throne shall be established forever.' " (2 Samuel 7:8-16)

From the beginning, man has been in search of an eternal, peaceful, stable, and blessed kingdom on earth. About 400 years before Jimmu assumed the Japanese throne, the true and living God established His covenant with David, the King of Israel, promising an eternal kingdom and an everlasting throne in his generations. Man's kingdoms rise and fall. The Japanese kingdom has lasted a very long time. But there is only one kingdom that will last forever. That kingdom was inaugurated at the resurrection of the Lord Jesus Christ, the Son of David and the Son of God. The Apostle Peter stood in Jerusalem on the day of Pentecost, forty days after the Lord rose from the dead, and reported to the tribes and nations assembled there:

This Jesus God has raised up, of which we are all witnesses. Therefore being exalted to the right hand of God, and having received from the Father the promise of the Holy Spirit, He poured out that which you now see and hear.

For David did not ascend into the heavens, but he says himself:

"The Lord said to my Lord,
'Sit at My right hand
Till I make Your enemies Your footstool.'"

Therefore let all the house of Israel know assuredly, that God has made this Jesus whom you have crucified, both Lord and Christ. (Acts 2:32-36)

When Jesus Came to Asia

The coming of Christ into Asia has been steady and gradual through the centuries. Beginning with the Apostle Thomas in the 1st century AD, the Gospel message broke into India. China received fragments of the Gospel through the ages, finally culminating in a massive reception over the last century.

Through the last five centuries, Japan has proven itself to be the hardest nation in the world to reach with the Gospel of the Lord Jesus Christ. The pride of the nation is almost impenetrable. When the first small piece of the Christian message came in the 17th century, a massive persecution squelched it. Finally, in the 20th century, some inroads were made for the discipleship of this isolated, dark, despairing, and hardened nation.

Meanwhile, South Korea and China would claim the fastest-growing churches in the world throughout the late 20th and early 21st centuries. Hong Kong retained even more of the Christian faith due to the steady work of Christian missionaries over a period of 156 years (especially while the country remained a British colony).

Asian Nation	Corruptions Rating[31]	Freedom Rating[32]	Prosperity Rating[33]	Percent Christian[34]
Hong Kong	#12	#1	#10	11.6%
Japan	#14	#30	#28	1.0%
South Korea	#45	#29	#29	27.7%
India	#78	#129	#119	2.3
China	#87	#100	#73	2.5%
Indonesia	#89	#56	#96	9.9%
Philippines	#99	#70	#112	11% Protestant
Thailand	#99	#43	#86	1.2%
Vietnam	#117	#128	#130	1.5% Protestant
Nepal	#124	#136	#155	1.4%
Myanmar	#132	#139	#153	6.2%
North Korea	#176	#180	#179	1.7%
Pakistan	#117	#131	#133	1.6%

To this day, God has blessed the nations in Asia with the following major resources and exports.

Country	Major Resources/Exports
China	Electronics and computers, furniture, bedding, lighting, signs, prefab buildings, plastic articles, cars, clothing, medical equipment
Hong Kong	Electronics, computers, gems, precious metals, medical equipment, plastics, clocks, watches, toys, games, clothing, leather and animal products
South Korea	Integrated circuits, electronics, cars, ships, vehicle parts, petroleum, photo equipment, coal briquettes
North Korea	Coal briquettes, men's and women's coats, mollusks
Japan	Vehicles, computers, electronics, medical equipment, iron, steel, plastics, organic chemicals, mineral fuels, ships, gems, precious metals
Nepal	Fibers, yarn, carpets, flavored water, fruit juice, nutmeg
India	Mineral fuels, oil, gems, precious metals, computers, vehicles, organic chemicals, pharmaceuticals, electronics, iron, steel, cotton, clothing
Pakistan	Textiles, clothing, cotton, cereals, leather, sugar, mineral fuels, beverages, vinegar, salt, sulfur, cement
Indonesia	Mineral fuels, oil, animal and vegetable fats, electronic equipment, vehicles, rubber, computers, iron, steel, gems, precious metals, ores, footwear
Philippines	Electrical equipment, computers, medical equipment, fruits, nuts, gems, precious metals, copper, ores, ships, animal and vegetable fats, waxes, and mineral fuels
Myanmar	Mineral fuels, oil, clothing, ores, copper, vegetables, footwear, gems, precious metals, fish, cereals
Vietnam	Electrical machinery, equipment, footwear, computers, clothing, furniture, bedding, lighting, prefab buildings, medical equipment, fish, coffee, tea, spices, leather
Thailand	Computers, electrical machinery, equipment, vehicles, rubber, plastics, gems, precious metals, mineral fuels, seafood, organic chemicals

Mt. Fuji in Japan

Timeline Review

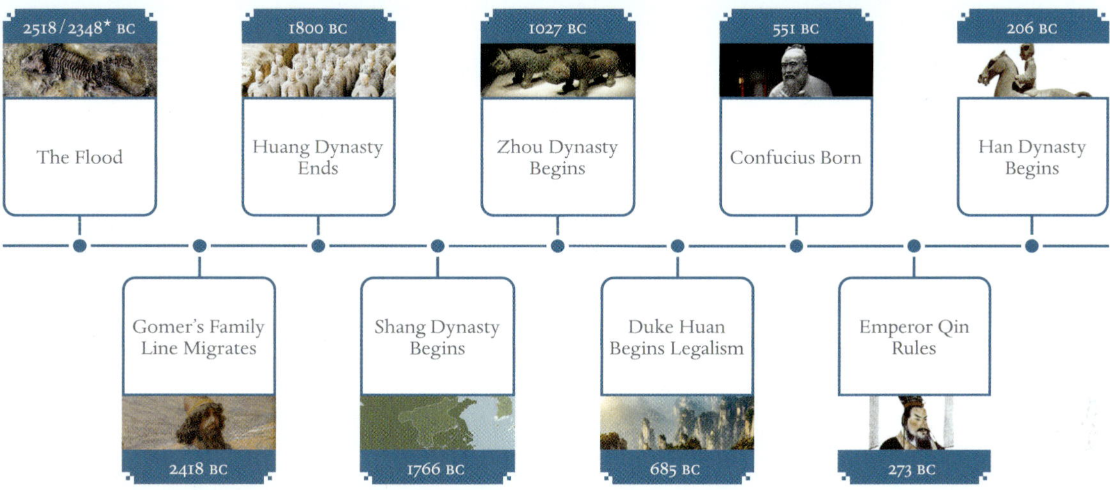

* Date according to Ussher's Chronology which assumes Israelites were in Egypt 215 years.

Chapter IX Prayer

Our Father, Creator God, and Almighty Savior,

We thank you for your common grace that blesses nations even when they do not bless you. We thank you for the influence of those who uphold your revelation, and bring your Word to the nations. We praise you for your goodness, your preserving grace, and your longsuffering shown to China, Japan, Korea, and other nations throughout the east and the far east through the centuries. Father, bring your salvation to these nations. We ask for your mercy upon Japan, Korea, and China. The governments of these nations have long ignored your Son, who reigns on your right hand. May they kiss the Son, lest they perish from the way. May they turn from their idolatry, their cruelty, their murders and thefts, and their insistence upon turning themselves into a god. Bring repentance and true faith to these lands. Where the Gospel has yet to penetrate, send your Holy Spirit to regenerate hearts and bring your beautiful kingdom of righteousness, peace, and joy into these lands.

In the glorious Name of your Son, Jesus Christ,
Amen.

Mountains of Kurdistan, Iraq
(Once Part of the Assyrian Empire)

CHAPTER X

The Assyrian Empire: Power by Cruelty (1200-612 BC)

The lofty looks of man shall be humbled,
The haughtiness of men shall be bowed down,
And the LORD alone shall be exalted in that day.
For the day of the LORD of hosts
Shall come upon everything proud and lofty,
Upon everything lifted up—
And it shall be brought low—
Upon all the cedars of Lebanon that are high and lifted up,
And upon all the oaks of Bashan;
Upon all the high mountains,
And upon all the hills that are lifted up;
Upon every high tower,
And upon every fortified wall;
Upon all the ships of Tarshish,
And upon all the beautiful sloops. (Isaiah 2:11-16)

Upon the decline of the Egyptian Empire following the Red Sea incident in 1440 BC, the land of Mesopotamia (to the south and east) would rise to produce the world's next great empires. God will raise up these powers for His own purposes, sometimes to teach His people object lessons, to discipline them in their disobedience, or to demonstrate His power and glory. Through all of human history, He greatly humbles man's greatest empires and demonstrates the utter futility of human pride. By His severe judgments, He impresses upon all who witness these things the critical need for the fear of almighty God.

The Rise and Fall of the Hittites

> *You are your mother's daughter, loathing husband and children; and you are the sister of your sisters, who loathed their husbands and children; your mother was a Hittite and your father an Amorite. Your elder sister is Samaria, who dwells with her daughters to the north of you; and your younger sister, who dwells to the south of you, is Sodom and her daughters. You did not walk in their ways nor act according to their abominations; but, as if that were too little, you became more corrupt than they in all your ways. (Ezekiel 16:45-47)*

Through the years, Israel came to look a lot like the nations around them—the Hittites, Amorites, Syrians, and Sodomites. Yahweh God had called His people away from these idolatrous, pagan nations, but the Israelites embraced the sins of the surrounding nations instead of trusting and obeying Him. So then, He would use these nations to punish His people in later years.

Between 1700 BC and 1280 BC, the Egyptians and the Hittites remained the dominant powers in the Mediterranean world. Although not much was known about the Hittites until archaeological evidence surfaced in Turkey at the beginning of the 20th century AD, the Old Testament Scriptures helpfully and accurately referenced this tribe and traced them back as far as 2066 BC. While wandering through Canaan, Abraham purchased the cave of Machpelah from Ephron the Hittite (Gen. 23). Then, about 100 years later, Esau married a Hittite woman (Gen. 26:34). The Hittites were among the tribes recorded as dwelling in the land of Canaan in 1400 BC (Ex. 13:5; Num. 13:29; Josh. 11:3), and King David tragically gave into the sin of adultery with the wife of Uriah the Hittite (2 Sam. 11) around 1050 BC.

Sphinx Gate in Hattusa

The Hittite kingdom covered a large part of modern-day Turkey and eventually expanded as far south as Syria. This small empire developed around the city state of Hattusa (located in modern-day central Turkey). Forming a settlement not long after Babel, sometime around 2300 BC the city was able to ward off an attack from the first great empire-builder after Nimrod, Sargon the Great of Akkad. The city was destroyed by another local tribe but was afterward rebuilt by a visionary king, Hattusili I (reigned 1586-1556 BC). It was the beginning of the Hittite Empire. An ancient account of Hattusili's reign dates from the 16th century BC and speaks of the instability of an empire run by sinful, envious, conniving men:

Hittite Gods of the Underworld in Hattusa

Afterwards, Hattusili was king, and his sons, brothers, in-laws, family members, and troops were all united. Wherever he went on campaign he controlled the enemy land with force. He destroyed the lands one after the other, took away their power, and made them the borders of the sea. When he came back from campaign, however, each of his sons went somewhere to a country, and in his hand the great cities prospered. But, when later the princes' servants became corrupt, they began to devour the properties, conspired constantly against their masters, and began to shed their blood.[1]

Hittite Law

Ancient Hittite law has been uncovered on cuneiform tablets, revealing a law code which at points was terribly unjust (especially as compared to God's revealed law found in Scripture). For instance, the crime of murder required the forfeiture of four lives of those belonging to the murderer's family.

If someone kills a man or a woman in a quarrel, he (the killer) produces the body (lit. 'that one') and gives (in recompense) four people (lit. 'heads')—whether (he kills) a man or a woman—he shall look to his house for it.

If someone kills a male slave or a female slave in a quarrel, he (the killer) produces the body (lit. 'that one') and gives (in recompense) four people (lit. 'heads')—whether (he kills) a man or a woman—he shall look to his house for it.[2]

At other points though, the Hittites came closer to replicating the biblical standard. The following may be compared with Exodus 21:18-19.

If someone injures a person and makes him ill, he performs sick maintenance for him. In his place, he provides a person to work his estate while he recovers. When he recovers, [the assailant] will give him six shekels of silver, and he will also pay the doctor's fee himself.[3]

The Hittite mini-empire reached the apex of its power during the biblical period of the Judges, under the reigns of King Suppiluliuma I (c. 1344-1321 BC) and his son Mursilli II (c. 1321-1295 BC). With the weakening of Egypt after the judgments which the Lord God, the sovereign Ruler, brought upon them, the Hittite King Suppiluliuma took full advantage of the enfeebled nation. Upon the death of the young Pharaoh Tutankhamen in 1323 BC, Suppiluliuma offered his son to the Egyptian widow queen. When the young man died on his trip to Egypt, a further breakdown of relations between the two empires resulted. Suppililiuma then turned his armies on the Egyptian vassal states in Canaan and Syria, taking much territory and solidifying the Hittite position as a world power.

Peace Treaty Between Egypt and Hittites

However, in the providence of almighty God, these conflicts would weaken Hittite control over Canaan. The Lord did not intend for any empire to achieve any real ascendance until later on in Israel's history. As the Hittites were gaining the upper hand over Egypt, the Egyptian prisoners of war were afflicted by some strange plague which spread through the land of the Hittites. The disease ended up taking the life of King Suppiluliuma I and his successor, Arnuwanda II.

For two hundred years (beginning around 1500 BC) the Hittites and the Egyptians engaged in a series of tug-of-war contests over control of Syria. Finally, in 1279 BC, Ramses II conquered the Hittite kingdom, ending with the first significant peace treaty preserved in writing. The agreement stipulated that, "There shall be no hostilities between them, forever. The great chief of Kheta shall not pass over into the land of Egypt, forever, to take anything therefrom. Ramses-Meriamon, the great ruler of Egypt, shall not pass over into the land of Kheta, to take anything therefrom, forever."[4] Interestingly, the wives of the Egyptian Pharaoh and the Hittite king also communicated with each other in hopes of maintaining peaceful relations during this time. Within this short excerpt we discover that queens from these powerful and competing empires would refer to themselves as "sisters," and the kings as "brothers." Queen Nefertari of Egypt writes to the queen of the Hittites:

Queen Nefertari

> *The great Queen Naptera (Nefertari) of the land of Egypt speaks thus: "Speak to my sister Puduhepa, the Great Queen of the Hatti land. I, your sister, (also) be well!! May your country be well. Now, I have learned that you, my sister, have written to me asking after my health. You have written to me because of the good friendship and brotherly relationship between your brother, the king of Egypt. The Great and the Storm God will bring about peace, and he will make the brotherly relationship between the Egyptian king, the Great King, and his brother, the Hatti King, the Great King, last for ever . . . See, I have sent you a gift, in order to greet you, my sister . . . for your neck (a necklace) of pure gold, composed of 12 bands and weighing 88 shekels, colored linen maklalu-material, for one royal dress for the king . . . A total of 12 linen garments."*[5]

In the end, the Egyptians would not hold on to their victory for long, and the Hittites did not survive the century. Another great world power was just developing. Four years after Ramses' historical victory the Assyrians would make their mark, and the Hittite kingdom was done. This also ended the Hittite and Egyptian conflict over Canaan. In God's providence, Israel His people would be left unmolested from 1274 BC until the Assyrians entered the picture in the 8th century. This would allow plenty of time for King David and the rising kingdom of Israel to develop.

The Rising Assyrian Power

Then the runners went throughout all Israel and Judah with the letters from the king and his leaders, and spoke according to the command of the king: "Children of Israel, return to the LORD God of Abraham, Isaac, and Israel; then He will return to the remnant of you who have escaped from the hand of the kings of Assyria. And do not be like your fathers and your brethren, who trespassed against the LORD God of their fathers, so that He gave them up to desolation, as you see. Now do not be stiff-necked, as your fathers were, but yield yourselves to the LORD; and enter His sanctuary, which He has sanctified forever, and serve the LORD your God, that the fierceness of His wrath may turn away from you. For if you return to the LORD, your brethren and your children will be treated with compassion by those who lead them captive, so that they may come back to this land; for the LORD your God is gracious and merciful, and will not turn His face from you if you return to Him." (2 Chronicles 30:6-9)

Between 1200 BC and 539 BC, the world power center moved to Assyria and Babylon. These historical exigencies would play an important part in the life of Israel, that incorrigible, disobedient people of God who had settled in the land of Canaan. The letter from King Hezekiah to Israel as contained above explains clearly the challenge that was ever facing the nation. If the Israelites were obedient and trusted in God, He would deliver them from this great military threat. If not, He would give them over to their Assyrian captors.

Although secular sources like to place the establishment of Nineveh as far back as 3000 BC, the Scriptures clearly provide for us the origins of this city. According to Genesis 10:11, Nimrod built Nineveh, presumably after the fall of the tower of Babel somewhere around 2418 BC.

Ancient Assyrian Relief

Incredibly, the capital cities of the two great empires of Babylon and Assyria lay only about 200 miles (280 kilometers) apart in the Mesopotamian Valley. The Assyrians

Reconstructed Mashki Gate in Ancient Nineveh

gained economic strength first by establishing a colony north of Syria called Ebla (located in modern-day Turkey). The region was called Anatolia, and a prosperous trade between the colony and the city of Ashur in Assyria continued from 1960 BC to 1760 BC. The militaristic and power-hungry Amorites maintained control over Ashur for a while, but an Assyrian king named Shamashi Adad I (1813-1791 BC) successfully drove the parasitic rulers out of his country and delineated Assyria's borders to the north and south.

Babylon did not want this upstart nation gaining ascendance however, and it wasn't long before Hammurabi from Babylon (reigned 1792-1750 BC), had subjugated Assyria. Another half century later, Assyria regained its independence under King Adasi (ruled 1726-1691 BC).

In God's timing, Assyria was not ready to become a world power as of yet.

Between 1500 BC and 1240 BC, another obscure tribe from Anatolia gained control of what is now southern Turkey and Syria. Over time their rule extended as far south as Ashur and the Assyrian peoples. This people known as the Mitanni were particularly skilled at training horses and fighting with chariots. At first a competing power with the Hittites to the northwest, they were soon absorbed into the Hittite kingdom. However, the Mitanni had already gained control of Ashur to the southeast by 1475 BC, and the Hittite-Mitanni kingdom dominated the Assyrians until 1392 BC. Eriba-Adad I successfully resisted Mitanni influence over Assyria, and his son Ashur-uballit I defeated the Mitanni king Shuttarna II, beginning a series of wars between the two nations. This Assyrian king reigned around 1353-1318 BC and gained dominance over Babylon to the south. These were the crude beginnings of what would become the Assyrian Empire.

After Egypt had severely weakened the Hittites in 1297 BC, the Assyrian king Adad-Nirari invaded Hittite-Mitanni territory. During his reign from roughly 1295 BC to 1264 BC, Adad-Nirari once again conquered Babylon to the south (the Kassites) and tribes to the east (pushing into modern-day Iran). In 1275 BC, Adad-Nirari invaded Syria (the Mitanni), which was then governed by a Hittite king. Apparently the Hittite kingdom was too weak to defend its territories, having been beaten back by the Egyptians, and so refused to help the Mitanni. Adad-Nirari established the Hittite king as his vassal and assigned tribute to the Mitanni—marking the beginning of the Assyrians as a world power. Interestingly, Adad-Nirari wrote a letter to the Hittite king in which he referred to him as a "brother," in the common parlance used at the time by the various kings. However, the Hittite king rebuffed him, which did not bode well for relations with Adad Nirari, who at the time was referring to himself as "the king of the universe."

By this time kings were summarizing their accomplishments on stone steles lavishly adorned with a good bit of pride and sometimes exaggeration. Adad-Nirari's was no exception:

> *Adad Nirari, illustrious prince, honored of the gods, lord, viceroy of the gods, city-founder, destroyer of the mighty hosts of Kassites, Kuti, Lulumi, Shubari, who destroys all foes north and south, who tramples down their lands from Lubdu and Rapiku to Eluhat, who conquers the whole Kashiaeri region.*[6]

The kingdom was further developed under King Shalmaneser I (ruled 1264-1234 BC). For a brief time the Mitanni rebelled against Assyria, hoping to resist their forces with a little help from the nomadic Amorites. King Shattuara and the Mitanni

Statue of the God Kidudu, Guardian of the Wall of the City of Ashur

forces tried to prevent Shalmaneser's army from gaining access to water by occupying the mountain passes. None of this worked, however, and Shalmaneser quickly crushed the rebel armies. The fallout was terrible for the Mitanni people as this king set out to earn the Assyrian reputation of conquest and subjugation by cruelty. Shalmaneser blinded all the prisoners of war and turned 180 Hittite and Mitanni cities into "rubble mounds." From that point forward, Assyria would be known for its domination by fear, torture, and unspeakable cruelties.

This marked the end of the Hittite kingdom and the beginning of the Assyrian Empire. A century later, Tiglath-Pileser (ruled 1114-1076 BC) turned out to be the Alexander the Great or Julius Caesar of Assyria. This king listed his military exploits on a large octagonal prism—one of the first of its kind in history. He summarized the first five years of his reign in this way:

> *Altogether I conquered 42 lands and their rulers from the other side of the Lower Zab in distant mountainous regions to the other side of the Euphrates, people of Hatti, and the Upper Sea in the west—from my accession year to my fifth regnal year.*[7]

This powerful warrior defeated the Phrygians in Asia Minor (Turkey), the wild Gutians in the Zagros Mountains, the tribes of Anatolia, as well as the city states of Byblos, Tyre, Sidon, Simyra, Berytus (Beirut), Aradus, and Arvad. However, in the providence of Almighty God, he stopped short of subjugating the land of Canaan. For the moment, Israel would be preserved.

Map of Assyria (Judah Exempted from Assyrian Control)

As the kingdom of Israel formed under Saul and David, the Lord enfeebled Assyria by civil war in 1055 BC. All kingdoms of the Middle East were weakened during the rise of the kingdom of David and Solomon until 900 BC. The Lord was clearly protecting His people from the ravages of the large empires at these key moments in history.

Then, as the northern tribes of Israel rejected God and refused to worship in Jerusalem (around 950 BC), once again the Assyrian power collected strength.

> *In the seventeenth year of Pekah the son of Remaliah, Ahaz the son of Jotham, king of Judah, began to reign. Ahaz was twenty years old when he became king, and he reigned sixteen years in Jerusalem; and he did not do what was right in the sight of the LORD his God, as his father David had done. But he walked in the way of the kings of Israel; indeed he made his son pass through the fire, according to the abominations of the nations whom the LORD had cast out from before the*

> *children of Israel. And he sacrificed and burned incense on the high places, on the hills, and under every green tree.*
>
> *Then Rezin king of Syria and Pekah the son of Remaliah, king of Israel, came up to Jerusalem to make war; and they besieged Ahaz but could not overcome him. At that time Rezin king of Syria captured Elath for Syria, and drove the men of Judah from Elath. Then the Edomites went to Elath, and dwell there to this day.*
>
> *So Ahaz sent messengers to Tiglath-Pileser king of Assyria, saying, "I am your servant and your son. Come up and save me from the hand of the king of Syria and from the hand of the king of Israel, who rise up against me." And Ahaz took the silver and gold that was found in the house of the LORD, and in the treasuries of the king's house, and sent it as a present to the king of Assyria. (2 Kings 16:1-8)*

The Assyrian kings Adad-Nirari II, Ashurnarsirpal II, and Shalmaneser III (who ruled from 904-869 BC), quickly expanded the Assyrian empire to include Babylon to the south all the way up through Damascus (Syria) to the west.

As early as 898 BC, Assyria began invasions into Israel and Syria. King Hadadezer of Syria organized eleven kings, including King Ahab of Israel, to fight against Shalmaneser III at the Battle of Qarqar. Ahab contributed 2,000 chariots and 10,000 soldiers to the war effort, which ended in something of a draw. In 886 BC, Shalmaneser made another run at Syria, but was unable to capture Damascus in the ensuing siege.

Finally, in 740 BC, Tiglath-Pileser II invaded Israel and the country of the Philistines to the southwest. Shamefully, King Pekah of Israel and the king of Syria had united themselves against Judah, so King Ahaz appealed for help to the king of Assyria. Tiglath-Pileser gladly cooperated. In what was probably the lowest point in the history of the people of God, both the northern and southern tribes of Israel were allied with pagan nations with the intent of bringing about each other's destruction. Such was the treachery against God and His covenant. The Assyrians conquered Damascus, killed King Resin, and destroyed much of northern Israel.

Finally, during the reign of the Israelite King Hoshea in 721 BC, Assyria invaded once more and put a final end to the northern kingdom, exiling some 27,000 persons. The explanation for the total destruction of the nation and the resulting diaspora is found in 2 Kings 17:

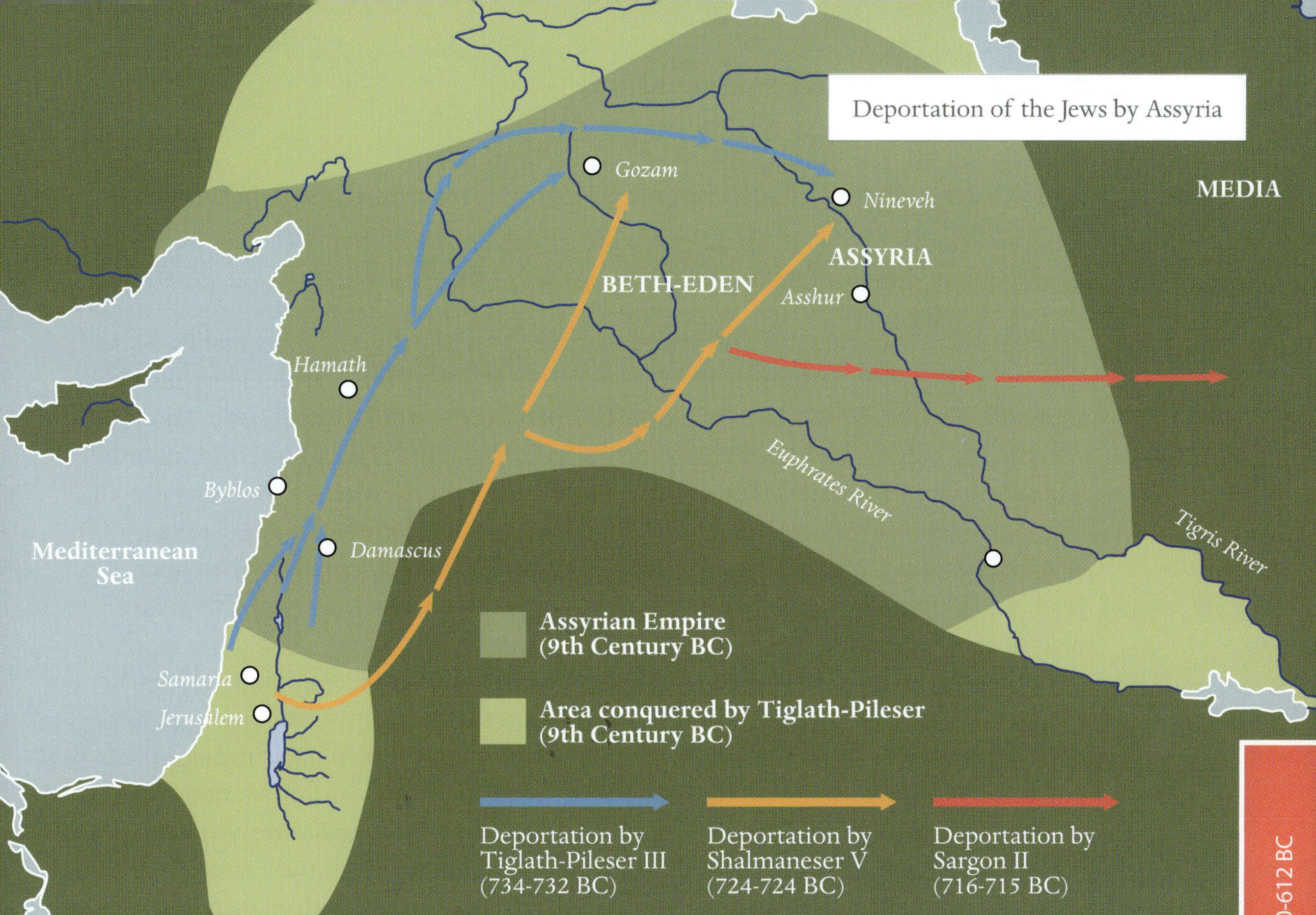

Now the king of Assyria went throughout all the land, and went up to Samaria and besieged it for three years. In the ninth year of Hoshea, the king of Assyria took Samaria and carried Israel away to Assyria, and placed them in Halah and by the Habor, the River of Gozan, and in the cities of the Medes.

For so it was that the children of Israel had sinned against the LORD their God, who had brought them up out of the land of Egypt, from under the hand of Pharaoh king of Egypt; and they had feared other gods, and had walked in the statutes of the nations whom the LORD had cast out from before the children of Israel, and of the kings of Israel, which they had made. Also the children of Israel secretly did against the LORD their God things that were not right, and they built for themselves high places in all their cities, from watchtower to fortified city. They set up for themselves sacred pillars and wooden images on every high hill and under every green tree. There they burned incense on all the high places, like the nations whom the LORD had carried away before them; and they did wicked things to provoke the LORD to anger, for they served idols, of which the LORD had said to them, "You shall not do this thing." (2 Kings 17:5-12)

The covenant people of God in Judah turned out to be the only nation-state able to resist the onslaught of the Assyrians during the 7th and 8th centuries BC. Sennacherib (ruling 705-681 BC) boasted of sacking eighty-nine cities and 820 villages and capturing 208,000 prisoners in his campaigns. This powerful monarch rebuilt the city of Nineveh and attempted an assault on Jerusalem. What he didn't count on was the omnipotent force of the true and living God, the Creator of heaven and earth. The most formidable kings in the world remain in the hands of God, and He raises them up for His own purposes and brings them down again when He is done with them.

Reigning from 726-697 BC, Judah's King Hezekiah proved himself to be a man of faith and brought reform to the nation. He restored temple worship, reinstated the Passover celebration, and "broke the sacred pillars in pieces, cut down the wooden images, and threw down the high places and the altars—from all Judah, Benjamin, Ephraim, and Manasseh—until they had utterly destroyed them all" (2 Chron. 31:1). For his faith and obedience to God, the Lord chose to delay judgment upon the southern kingdom of Judah, and He thwarted Assyria's attempts to capture Jerusalem in the most remarkable way.

As he prepared to take Jerusalem, the Assyrian king sent a threatening message laced with mockery and spite for Israel's God:

Thus says Sennacherib king of Assyria: "In what do you trust, that you remain under siege in Jerusalem? Does not Hezekiah persuade you to give yourselves over to die by famine and by thirst, saying, 'The LORD our God will deliver us from the hand of the king of Assyria'? Has not the same Hezekiah taken away His high places and His altars, and commanded Judah and Jerusalem, saying, 'You shall worship before one altar and burn incense on it'? Do you not know what I and my fathers have done to all the peoples of other lands? Were the gods of the nations of those lands in any way able to deliver their lands out of my hand? Who was there among all the gods of those nations that my fathers utterly destroyed that could deliver his people from my hand, that your God should be able to deliver you from my hand? Now therefore, do not let Hezekiah deceive you or persuade you like this,

Remnants of the Broad Wall in Jerusalem Built by King Hezekiah

> *and do not believe him; for no god of any nation or kingdom was able to deliver his people from my hand or the hand of my fathers. How much less will your God deliver you from my hand?" (2 Chronicles 32:10-15)*

As the scenario played out, Isaiah the prophet informed Hezekiah that the Lord would not take kindly to the blasphemies of Sennacherib or his captain, the Rabshakeh, and that this siege would go nowhere.

> *Do not be afraid of the words which you have heard, with which the servants of the king of Assyria have blasphemed Me. Surely I will send a spirit upon him, and he shall hear a rumor and return to his own land; and I will cause him to fall by the sword in his own land. (2 Kings 19:6-7)*

Accordingly, the Rabshakeh was called back to Assyria to address other military conflicts. However, later he returned to Judah, warning Hezekiah by letter:

> *Do not let your God in whom you trust deceive you. . . . Look! You have heard what the kings of Assyria have done to all lands by utterly destroying them; and shall you be delivered? Have the gods of the nations delivered those whom my fathers have destroyed, Gozan and Haran and Rezeph, and the people of Eden who were in Telassar? Where is the king of Hamath, the king of Arpad, and the king of the city of Sepharvaim, Hena, and Ivah? (2 Kings 19:10-13).*

It was at this point that Hezekiah spread out the letter before the Lord in the temple and lifted up this simple but powerful prayer:

> *O LORD God of Israel, the One who dwells between the cherubim, You are God, You alone, of all the kingdoms of the earth. You have made heaven and earth. Incline Your ear, O LORD, and hear; open Your eyes, O LORD, and see; and hear the words of Sennacherib, which he has sent to reproach the living God. Truly, LORD, the kings of Assyria have laid waste the nations and their lands, and have cast their gods into the fire; for they were not gods, but the work of men's hands—wood and stone. Therefore they destroyed them. Now therefore, O LORD our God, I pray, save us from his hand, that all the kingdoms of the earth may know that You are the LORD God, You alone. (2 Kings 19:15-19)*

The consequences that followed this prayer were abrupt, earthshaking, and history-making beyond any other event in the history of the great empires. We read from 2 Kings 19 that the "angel of the LORD went out, and killed in the camp of the Assyrians one hundred and eighty-five thousand; and when people arose early in the morning, there were the corpses—all dead." Importantly, this deliverance did not come through the ordinary means of Israel's natural defenses. It was accomplished by divine intervention from the covenant-keeping, sovereign, Almighty God of Israel.

In AD 1830, British Colonel R. Taylor uncovered one of the most significant archaeological finds in his excavations around ancient Nineveh. The Taylor Prism contains the Assyrian account of Sennacherib's siege of Jerusalem. While boasting loudly of his conquests over other lands in and around Canaan, this proud king could not bring himself to admit that he had lost this battle against Judah. Curiously, Sennacherib does point out that Hezekiah's armies refused to fight—yet it is plain from the reading that the Assyrians could not conquer them. In his account,

Sennacherib is careful to point out that he had "besieged and conquered" the surrounding nations. However, he forgets to mention that his entire army died at the gates of Jerusalem, probably from a mysterious plague. This was the one fight Assyria could not win. What follows is the script from the prism:

> *But Sidka, the king of Ashkelon, who had not submitted to my yoke, the gods of his father's house, himself, his wife, his sons, his daughters, his brothers, the seed of his paternal house, I tore away and brought to Assyria. Sharru-lu-dari, son of Rukibti, their former king, I set over the people of Ashkelon, and I imposed upon him the payment of tribute: presents to my majesty. He accepted my yoke. In the course of my campaign, Beth-Dagon, Joppa, Banaibarka, Asuru, cities of Sidka, who had not speedily bowed in submission at my feet, I besieged, I conquered, I carried off their spoil.*
>
> *The officials, nobles, and people of Ekron, who had thrown Padi their king, bound by oath and curse of Assyria, into fetters of iron and had given him over to Hezekiah, the Judahite—he kept him in confinement like an enemy—their heart became afraid, and they called*

Sennacherib's Prism

upon the Egyptian kings, the bowmen, chariots and horses of the king of Meluhha [Ethiopia], a countless host, and these came to their aid. In the neighborhood of Eltekeh, their ranks being drawn up before me, they offered battle. With the aid of Assur, my lord, I fought with them and brought about their defeat. The Egyptian charioteers and princes, together with the Ethiopian king's charioteers, my hands captured alive in the midst of the battle. Eltekeh and Timnah I besieged, I captured, and I took away their spoil.

I approached Ekron and slew the governors and nobles who had rebelled, and hung their bodies on stakes around the city. The inhabitants who rebelled and treated (Assyria) lightly I counted as spoil. The rest of them, who were not guilty of rebellion and contempt, for whom there was no punishment, I declared their pardon. Padi, their king, I brought out to Jerusalem, set him on the royal throne

Isaiah Before King Hezekiah

over them, and imposed upon him my royal tribute.

As for Hezekiah the Judahite, who did not submit to my yoke: forty-six of his strong, walled cities, as well as the small towns in their area, which were without number, by leveling with battering-rams and by bringing up siege-engines, and by attacking and storming on foot, by mines, tunnels, and breeches, I besieged and took them. 200,150 people, great and small, male and female, horses, mules, asses, camels, cattle and sheep without number, I brought away from them and counted as spoil. (Hezekiah) himself, like a caged bird I shut up in Jerusalem, his royal city. I threw up earthworks against him, the one coming out of the city-gate, I turned back to his misery. His cities, which I had despoiled, I cut off from his land, and to Mitinti, king of Ashdod, Padi, king of Ekron, and Silli-bl, king of Gaza, I gave (them). And thus I diminished his land. I added to the former tribute, and I laid upon him the surrender of their land and impost gifts for my majesty. As for Hezekiah, the terrifying splendor of my majesty overcame him, and the Arabs and his mercenary troops which he had brought in to strengthen Jerusalem, his royal city, deserted him. . . . To pay tribute and to accept servitude, he dispatched his messengers.[8]

Recent Discovery Verifies Historicity of Hezekiah and Isaiah

In AD 2015, clay impressions of seals were found in Jerusalem bearing the names of Hezekiah and the prophet Isaiah,[1] once again confirming the biblical records concerning these critical years in the history of Israel. The name "Isaiah" is transliterated "Yahweh saves." Hezekiah's seal appeared in Hebrew script as follows (and translated into English):

הדהי דלמ זחא [וב] והיקזחל

"Belonging to Hezekiah [son of] Ahaz king of Judah"

Assyria: 1200-612 BC

Stone Monument of Ashurbanipal II

Military State

Woe to Assyria, the rod of My anger
And the staff in whose hand is My indignation.
I will send him against an ungodly nation,
And against the people of My wrath
I will give him charge,
To seize the spoil, to take the prey,
And to tread them down like the mire of the streets. (Isaiah 10:5-6)

By God's absolute sovereign will, Assyria would reach the zenith of its power during the reign of Sennacherib's grandson, Ashurbanipal (reigning from 668 to 627 BC). Historian Will Durant describes the exhaustion felt by an empire entirely immersed in war for hundreds of years in these words: "It is a dull and bloody mess of war after war, siege after siege, starved cities and flayed captives."[9]

Ashurbanipal is pictured in royal tablets in hand-to-hand combat with lions. Apparently the king would perform in arenas, proving himself to be a "mighty hunter" and killing lions with knife or javelin. Another Assyrian king boasted of killing thirty elephants, 257 wild oxen, and 370 great lions.

The description of Assyrian tortures is grislier and gorier than any other records in all the history of empires. The kings seemed to relish in detailing stabbings, body mutilations, flaying, burnings, and dismemberments.[10] Civil punishments for crimes could involve up to one hundred lashes, pulling out tongues, impalement, drinking poison, etc. And the cruelty did not stop with the treatment of the empire's enemies. According to Scripture (as well as ancient Babylonian and Assyrian records), Sennacherib was murdered by his own son.

So Sennacherib king of Assyria departed and went away, returned home, and remained at Nineveh. Now it came to pass, as he was worshiping in the temple of Nisroch his god, that his sons Adrammelech and Sharezer struck him down with the sword; and they escaped into the land of Ararat. Then Esarhaddon his son reigned in his place. (2 Kings 19:36-37; Reference also 2 Chronicles 32:21).

At first, cruelty and fearsome, terror-inspiring techniques may give the impression that an empire has achieved an all-powerful and godlike status. However, these tough brutes and wicked tyrants will always meet their end along with every other proud person who refuses to submit to God. They may appear to prosper for a while, but they soon disappear.

Wait on the LORD,
And keep His way,
And He shall exalt you to inherit the land;
When the wicked are cut off, you shall see it.
I have seen the wicked in great power,
And spreading himself like a native green tree.
Yet he passed away, and behold, he was no more;
Indeed I sought him, but he could not be found. (Psalm 37:34-36)

Nineveh Warned

In God's providential dealings, He makes sure that the great empires of the earth are not exempted from prophetic warnings out of the mouths of His pastors, prophets, and teachers. The prophets of the Old Testament are continually issuing warnings against Egypt, Assyria, Moab, Tyre and Sidon, Philistia, Babylon, Persia, Greece, and Rome.

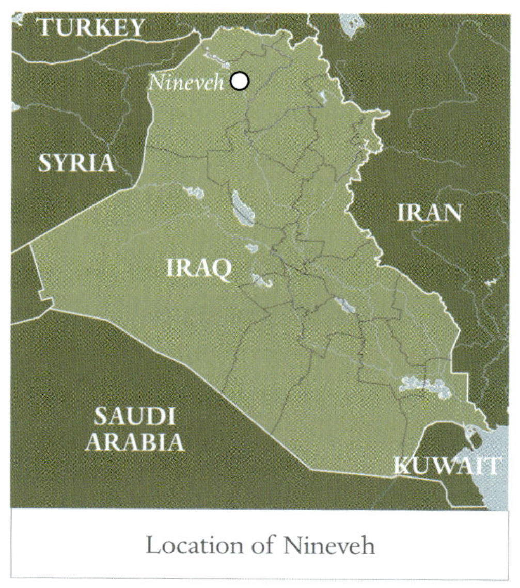

Location of Nineveh

During the reign of Jehoahaz, king of Israel (814-798 BC), the Israelites were oppressed by heavy taxes imposed on them by Hazael, king of Aram (Syria).

So Jehoahaz pleaded with the LORD, and the LORD listened to him; for He saw the oppression of Israel, because the king of Syria oppressed them. Then the LORD gave Israel a deliverer, so that they escaped from under the hand of the Syrians; and the children of Israel dwelt in their tents as before. (2 Kings 13:4-5)

Jonah Mercifully Delivered from the Giant Fish

Interestingly, the stele for King Adad-Nirari III mentions a military campaign he began against Syria in the fifth year of his reign (800 BC)—exactly the time when the Israelite King Jehoahaz needed some relief from Syria. The stele reads: "I gave the command [to march against Aram] to Mari [Ishutup] in Damascus, [his royal city] . . . I received 100 talents of gold and 1,000 talents of silver."[11]

This was also when Jonah was active as a prophet in Israel (2 Kings 14:25), about the time that God called him to prophesy against Nineveh. Jonah initially resisted, but after his encounter with the giant fish the prophet finally relented and hoofed the 400 miles to Nineveh to bring the word of warning.

> *And Jonah began to enter the city on the first day's walk. Then he cried out and said, "Yet forty days, and Nineveh shall be overthrown!" So the people of Nineveh*

Jonah Preaches in Nineveh

believed God, proclaimed a fast, and put on sackcloth, from the greatest to the least of them. Then word came to the king of Nineveh; and he arose from his throne and laid aside his robe, covered himself with sackcloth and sat in ashes. And he caused it to be proclaimed and published throughout Nineveh by the decree of the king and his nobles, saying,

"Let neither man nor beast, herd nor flock, taste anything; do not let them eat, or drink water. But let man and beast be covered with sackcloth, and cry

mightily to God; yes, let every one turn from his evil way and from the violence that is in his hands. Who can tell if God will turn and relent, and turn away from His fierce anger, so that we may not perish?"

Then God saw their works, that they turned from their evil way; and God relented from the disaster that He had said He would bring upon them, and He did not do it. (Jonah 3:4-10)

Jonah's visit probably occurred during the reign of Adad-nirari III (811-783 BC). For a brief time it does appear from historical records that Nineveh reverted to monotheism under Adad-nirari III—much like the Egyptian Pharaoh, Amenhotep IV. A temple erected in 787 BC contained a statue with a dedication to the king including the words: "Trust in Nabu, do not trust in any other god."[12]

The lesson from Jonah is poignant and relevant. God's mercy is always available, at any time, to any person, city, or nation who will humble themselves and repent before Him.

Nonetheless a century later, at or around 664 BC, the Lord over all nations was finished with Nineveh and the wicked Assyrian Empire. The entire book of Nahum was dedicated to pronouncing judgment upon Assyria. The prophet begins by reminding the nations that our God does not ignore sin. He is a righteous God and His wrath burns hot against those nations that persist in wickedness.

The burden against Nineveh. The book of the vision of Nahum the Elkoshite.
God is jealous, and the LORD avenges;
The LORD avenges and is furious.
The LORD will take vengeance on His adversaries,
And He reserves wrath for His enemies; . . . (Nahum 1:1-2)

The reason for God's judgment on Nineveh is given in chapter 3.

Woe to the bloody city!
It is all full of lies and robbery.
Its victim never departs. . . .
Because of the multitude of harlotries of the seductive harlot,
The mistress of sorceries,
Who sells nations through her harlotries,
And families through her sorceries. (Nahum 3:1, 4)

It was the violence, deceit, witchcraft, and sexual sin countenanced by the nation that finally brought down God's judgment upon them. The Lord would no longer permit this nation to make a prey out of nations or lions. These verses refer to the tendency of the kings of Assyria to hunt and kill lions in the arenas:

> *"Behold, I am against you," says the LORD of hosts, "I will burn your chariots in smoke, and the sword shall devour your young lions; I will cut off your prey from the earth, and the voice of your messengers shall be heard no more." (Nahum 2:13)*

Nineveh was destroyed fifty years after this prophecy.

The Last Kings of Assyria

The feasts celebrated by the Assyrian kings during the height of Assyria's power were shockingly extravagant. When Assurnasirpal king of Assyria inaugurated the palace in Calah (c. 883 BC), someone took the time to carve out a stele with a list of the courses in what was thought to be an epic feast.

> *A palace of joy, built with great ingenuity, he invited into it Assur (the Assyrian national god), the great lord and the gods of the entire country. He prepared a banquet of 1,000 fattened head of cattle, 1,000 calves, 10,000 stable sheep, 15,000 lambs—for my lady Ishtar (alone) 200 heads of cattle (and) 1,000 spring lambs, 500 stags, 500 gazelles, 1,000 ducks, 500 geese . . . 10,000 doves . . . 10,000 skins with wine . . . 1,000 wooden crates with vegetables, 300 containers with oil, 300 containers with salted seeds . . . 100 containers of fine mixed beer, 100 pomegranates, 100 bunches of grapes, 100 pistachio cones . . . . 100 with garlic, 100 with onions . . . 100 with honey, 100 with rendered butter, 100 with roasted . . . barley, 10 homer of shelled peanuts . . . 10 homer of dates . . . 10 homer of cumin . . . 10 homer of thyme, 10 homer of perfumed oil, 10 homer of sweet smelling matters . . . 10 homer of zinzimu-onions, 10 homer of olives. When I inaugurated the palace at Calah, I hosted for 10 days with food and drink 47,074 persons, men and women, who were bid to come from across my entire country, also 5,000 important persons, delegates from the country Sukhu, from Khindana, Khatina, Hatti, Tyre, Sidon, Gurguma, Malida, Khubushka, Gilzana, Kuma and Musasir (capital of Urartu), also 16,000 inhabitants of Calah from all ways of life, 1,500 officials of all my palace, altogether 69,574 invited guests . . . furthermore, I*

> *provided them with the means to clean and anoint themselves. I did them due honors and sent them back, healthy and happy to their own countries.*[13]

By the end of the empire, the Greek historian Diodorus noted that the Assyrian kings were giving way to homosexuality, sexual indulgence without restraint, and transgender tendencies.[14] These sorts of destructive practices were considered by the pagans as the "swan song" of empires and nations.

Crossing Over the Line of Despair

Every empire built upon the pride of humanist man will eventually cross over the line of despair. These empires are first established on pride and self-confidence in man. Their chief motive is always fame and the acclaim of men. Political leaders, sports stars, entertainment stars, and business leaders jockey for more and more acclaim. In the process, much is achieved in terms of infrastructure, buildings, roads, bridges, colosseums, castles, walls, militaries, schools, universities, literary works, and sports complexes are all provided for the glory of man. Then comes the day when the God of heaven brings it all crashing down. The collapse begins in the hearts and minds of the people. The nation turns pessimistic and walks over the line of despair, increasingly self-conscious of the futility and meaninglessness of everything. The wealth, the decadence, the perverted sexuality is all turned to destruction. Without God, man inevitably must admit all to be vanity, nothing but futility. Fifteen

Assyrian Terracotta Tile Showing the Assyrian King Surrounded by Guards and Attendants

Assyrian Games

years before the total collapse of the mighty Assyrian Empire (627 BC), King Ashurbanipal inscribed these words on a stele—fateful, depressing, honest words of a dying emperor for a dying empire. This testimony marked the end of the empire.

> *I did well unto god and man, to dead and living. Why have sickness and misery befallen me? I cannot do away with the strife in my country and the dissensions in my family; disturbing scandals oppress me always. Illness of mind and flesh bow me down; with cries of woe I bring my days to an end. On the day of the city god, the day of the festival, I am wretched. Death is seizing hold upon me, and wears me down. With lamentation and mourning I wail day and night, and groan, "O God! Grant even to one who is impious that he may see thy light!"*[15]

Civil wars and assaults from Babylon to the south brought this once-glorious empire to a crushing end by 612 BC. Nahum's prophecy was fulfilled. The big-talking, fierce, and cruel emperors of Assyria were no more. After the sovereign Lord had used this cruel military power to discipline His people Israel, He did away with it as He said He would. Speaking through the prophet Isaiah, God called Assyria "the rod of My anger and the staff in whose hand is My indignation," yet He pronounced a woe against this mighty nation (Isa. 10:5). Because these Assyrian kings were arrogant and viewed their victories as the accomplishments of their own sovereign power, Yahweh God promised to bring them down. They would not see themselves as tools in the hands of the ultimate sovereign, and so He destroyed them for their pride.

> *Therefore it shall come to pass, when the LORD has performed all His work on Mount Zion and on Jerusalem, that He will say, "I will punish the fruit of the arrogant heart of the king of Assyria, and the glory of his haughty looks." For he says: "By the strength of my hand I have done it, and by my wisdom, for I am prudent;" . . . So the Light of Israel will be for a fire, and his Holy One for a flame; It will burn and devour his thorns and his briers in one day. And it will consume the glory of his forest and of his fruitful field, both soul and body; and they will be as when a sick man wastes away. (Isaiah 10:12-13, 17-18)*

The prophet Nahum promised that Assyria's wound would "never heal" (Nah. 3:19). And it never did.

The Most Violent King of All

> *And you, being dead in your trespasses and the uncircumcision of your flesh, He has made alive together with Him, having forgiven you all trespasses, having wiped out the handwriting of requirements that was against us, which was contrary to us. And He has taken it out of the way, having nailed it to the cross. Having disarmed principalities and powers, He made a public spectacle of them, triumphing over them in it. (Colossians 2:13-15)*

With all their empire-building, warmongering, and cruel tyranny, the great kings of the earth do not come with the intent to destroy. They set out to build some glorious kingdom. They think of themselves as the great saviors and redeemers of mankind. They come to destroy the enemy and build a kingdom that will be the envy of all nations and the most glorious and wonderful place on earth. They always fail. Their kingdoms fail. In their wake is to be found destruction, cruelty, murder, adultery, treachery, envy, maliciousness, genocide, torture, and misery. These kings do not realize that the real problem with mankind is to be found in their own hearts.

Thanks be to God, there is a better King who comes to wage war. He comes to take vengeance on His enemies and to bring salvation to the earth. The Old

Testament prophets announce this King as the fulfillment of all the hopes and desires of the nations. He comes to make war, and He is the very essence of all that is just, righteous, and true. He brings about salvation and redemption for His people by the most violent means. He comes after the worst enemies of the human soul—the devil, sin, and death. He has no mercy upon these enemies, and He always wins His wars. The Lord Jesus Christ comes to crush His enemies, to save His people, and to build a kingdom that will never pass away. He came 600 years after the grand kingdom of Assyria failed.

Isaiah the prophet spoke of this great, violent, conquering King 700 years before He was born in Bethlehem of Judea.

Who is this who comes from Edom,
With dyed garments from Bozrah,
This One who is glorious in His apparel,
Traveling in the greatness of His strength?—

"I who speak in righteousness, mighty to save."

Why is Your apparel red,
And Your garments like one who treads in the winepress?

"I have trodden the winepress alone,
And from the peoples no one was with Me.
For I have trodden them in My anger,
And trampled them in My fury;
Their blood is sprinkled upon My garments,
And I have stained all My robes.
For the day of vengeance is in My heart,
And the year of My redeemed has come.
I looked, but there was no one to help,
And I wondered
That there was no one to uphold;
Therefore My own arm brought salvation for Me;
And My own fury, it sustained Me.
I have trodden down the peoples in My anger,
Made them drunk in My fury,
And brought down their strength to the earth." (Isaiah 63:1-6)

Timeline Review

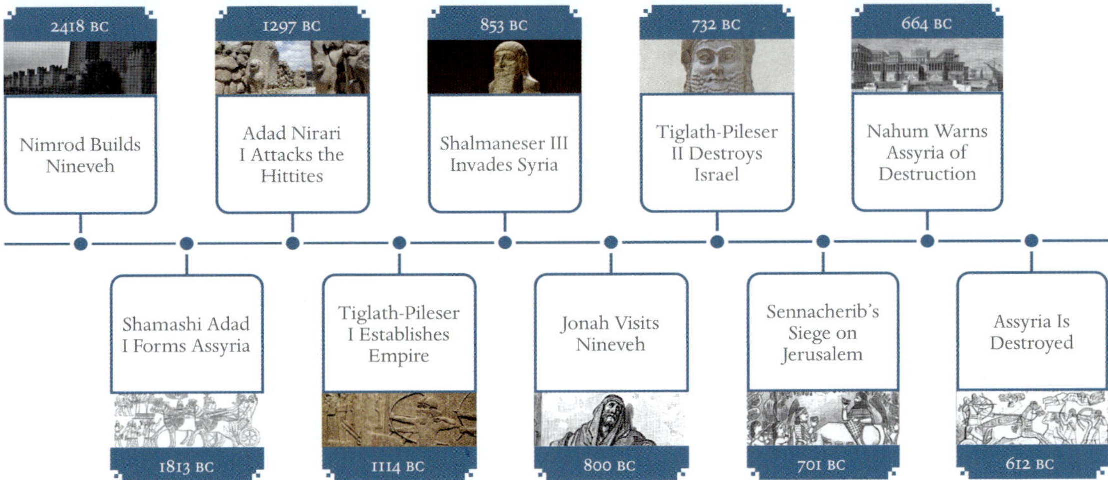

Chapter X Prayer

Our Father and God over heaven and earth,

You alone are worthy of all the praise, honor, and glory! The kings of the earth in their pride may try to usurp Your authority and glory, but all will be in vain. By cruelty and pride they think to establish the most wonderful kingdoms, but all is in vain. For by humility, by love, and by grace, Your King has come to establish another Kingdom that will endure forever! By stooping, He has conquered. By suffering and by subjecting Himself to the cruelty of men, He has brought vengeance against the enemy of sin and Satan at the cross. By His death, He has destroyed the enemy of death. His Kingdom brings eternal righteousness and peace. He is the ultimate Savior, the great Redeemer and the fulfilled Desire of the nations. Praise be to our King—the King of kings, the mighty Victor, eternal Lord, forever and ever.

Amen.

Babylonian Ruins Near Baghdad, Iraq

CHAPTER XI

Babylon Has Fallen (626-539 BC)

After these things I saw another angel coming down from heaven, having great authority, and the earth was illuminated with his glory. And he cried mightily with a loud voice, saying, "Babylon the great is fallen, is fallen, and has become a dwelling place of demons, a prison for every foul spirit, and a cage for every unclean and hated bird! For all the nations have drunk of the wine of the wrath of her fornication, the kings of the earth have committed fornication with her, and the merchants of the earth have become rich through the abundance of her luxury." (Revelation 18:1-3)

Of all the great cities and empires in the ancient world, the Bible refers particularly to Babylon as representative of the great city of man. This city was the quintessential picture of the fallen, sinful world in biblical accounts. Prophetic language and code language included in 1 Peter 5:13 and the Book of Revelation use the name "Babylon" to describe the city of Rome or any city built upon pride, covetousness, lust, power, dissipation, and money. The fall of Rome or any other city which idealizes luxury, wealth, decadence, and a life of sexual sin is described in Revelation 18. These Babylons always come crashing

Detail of a Limestone Monument in the British Museum Depicting King Hammurabi

down with astonishing speed. The prototype for this worldly city, or what the Christian author, John Bunyan called "Vanity Fair," was Babylon of Mesopotamia. The great, proud empire which was built around that city lasted only eighty-seven years.

After Hammurabi, Babylon was militarily unprepared to retain its status of power in the world. The city and region became vulnerable to greedy predators and plunderers such as the mountain tribe of the Kassites to the east. For about four hundred years, the Kassites alternately raided and ruled Babylon, further weakening the city. In the providence of God, these great power centers are often turned over to tribes who drain the capital and who are themselves incapable of developing infrastructure and expanding the economy.

During this period, the Babylonian god Marduk was seized in turn by the Hittites, the Assyrians, and the Elamites to the southeast. Apparently this god fashioned of gold was not very adept at defending himself—or protecting Babylon for that matter. It wasn't until Nebuchadnezzar I (ruled 1126-1104 BC) invaded Elam that Marduk was recaptured and returned to his temple in Babylon. Assyria gained ascendance during the reign of Adad-Nirari II around 900 BC, and would rule over Babylon the bulk of the time until 612 BC.

Prophesying around 700 BC, the prophet Isaiah mocked the Babylonian god Bel (Marduk) when he was carried off in the saddle bags of enemy warriors, thus proving himself worthless to help anyone else.

Bel bows down, Nebo stoops;
Their idols were on the beasts and on the cattle.
Your carriages were heavily loaded,
A burden to the weary beast.
They stoop, they bow down together;
They could not deliver the burden,
But have themselves gone into captivity. (Isaiah 46:1-2)

Babylon attempted to throw off Assyrian rule, but these efforts were quickly put down in 703 BC by Sennacherib, the same Assyrian king who attempted a siege of Jerusalem during the reign of Hezekiah. Babylon continued to cause problems, and Sennacherib responded by utterly destroying the city in 689 BC.

Babylon Defeats Assyria (627-605 BC)

I, wisdom, dwell with prudence,
And find out knowledge and discretion.
The fear of the LORD is to hate evil;
Pride and arrogance and the evil way
And the perverse mouth I hate. (Proverbs 8:12-13)

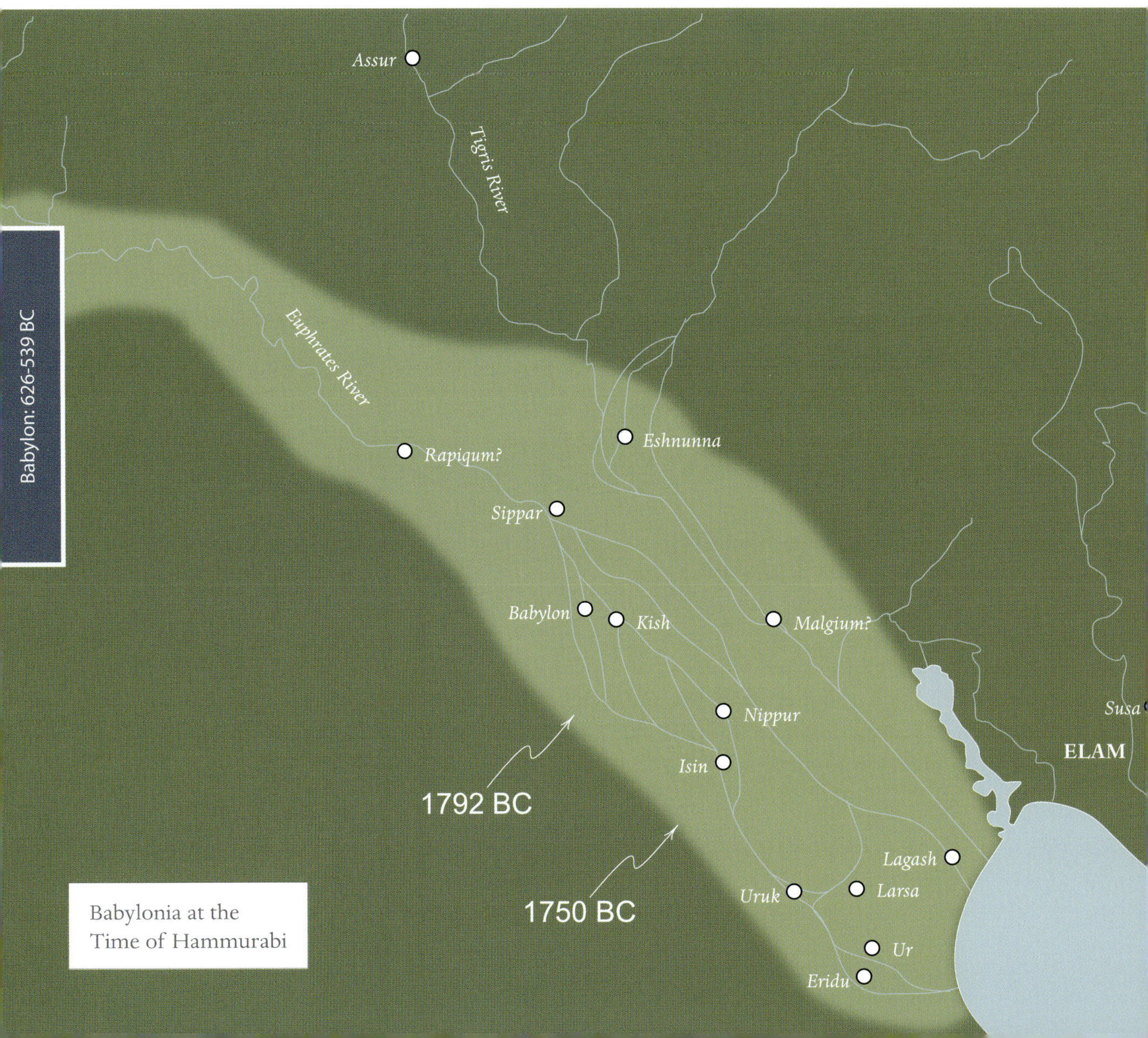

Babylonia at the Time of Hammurabi

Assyria had reached its zenith of power under King Ashurbanipal (668-627 BC). In common with all empires, the nation exalted in its wonderful intellectual pursuits. Ashurbanipal's palace included a library endowed with 30,000 clay tablets containing high literature, medical treatises, and historical essays. However, education cannot save a proud empire entirely void of the fear of God—as has been demonstrated by modern empires like Spain, Britain, and America.

Following Ashurbanipal's death in 627 BC, internal strife weakened that great empire. And so, the Babylonian King Nabopolassar took full advantage of this opportunity, joined forces with the Medes, and invaded the Assyrian-controlled cities of Nippur (615 BC), Ashur (615 BC), and Nineveh (612 BC). He pursued the Assyrian armies as far northeast as Harran (in Syria). Meanwhile the Egyptian Pharaoh Necho II united forces with the Assyrians. As he marched up through the land of Canaan he was met by King Josiah at the Battle of Megiddo. Josiah was killed in that conflict and the Egyptians pressed through, taking on the Babylonians at the Battle of Carchemish in 605 BC. The Medes and the Babylonians crushed the joint forces of the Egyptians and Assyrians, putting a final end to the remnants of these empires.

The death of King Josiah at the hands of Necho II is given in 2 Chronicles:

> *After all this, when Josiah had prepared the temple, Necho king of Egypt came up to fight against Carchemish by the Euphrates; and Josiah went out against him. But he sent messengers to him, saying, "What have I to do with you, king of Judah? I have not come against you this day, but against the house with which I have war; for God commanded me to make haste. Refrain from meddling with God, who is with me, lest He destroy you." Nevertheless Josiah would not turn his face from him, but disguised himself so that he might fight with him, and did not heed the words of Necho from the mouth of God. So he came to fight in the Valley of Megiddo. And the archers shot King Josiah; and the king said to his servants, "Take me away, for I am severely wounded." His servants therefore took him out of that chariot and put him in the second chariot that he had, and they brought him to Jerusalem. So he died, and was buried in one of the tombs of his fathers. And all Judah and Jerusalem mourned for Josiah. (2 Chronicles 35:20-24)*

Judah's King Josiah should have kept out of these intramural conflicts between pagan empires. God's people are often tempted to take sides in conflicts between

King Josiah's Death

two equally-bad positions. Perhaps Josiah realized that Babylon was on the ascent and Assyria was coming down. But godly leaders should not meddle with such power games. It would have been better to stay out of the conflict and trust in God to save His people from their foes.

The Neo-Babylonian Empire (605-539 BC)

Not long after the victory at Carchemish, King Nabopolassar died and left the Babylonian throne to his son, Nebuchadnezzar II. This twenty-nine-year-old king would become the longest reigning, most powerful potentate in Babylon's history. Around 605 BC, he returned from Syria, and the energy which the Assyrians had invested into perpetual warfare Nebuchadnezzar directed into building the great city of Babylon. If Assyria was the greatest and most powerful empire in the history of the world to date, Babylon was greater. This short lived kingdom would be known as the Neo-Babylonian Empire. Babylon funneled the wealth of the empire into a single city, and by the time Nebuchadnezzar had finished with it, it was the greatest city the world had ever seen. He rebuilt the Etemenanki Ziggurat to the grandeur it had possessed "at former times"—400 feet in height. He testified on the stele that this Ziggurat was to "reach the heavens" as the original builders of Babel said almost 1,800 years earlier.

The walls of Babylon were described by Herodotus as sixty miles in length and wide enough for a four-horse chariot to be drawn along their top—eighty-three feet thick and 330 feet high. The city was huge—200 square miles. In

Gates of Ancient Babylon

comparison, Sennacherib reported the walls surrounding Nineveh to be 7.5 miles in circumference, amounting to only about one seventh the area of Babylon.[1]

Located just south of the Ziggurat was the temple of Marduk, the special god of the Babylonians. And north of the Ziggurat was where Nebuchadnezzar erected his principal palace—a gigantic street lined with 120 massive sculptured lions led up to the palace. Near the palace Nebuchadnezzar built the famous Hanging Gardens for one of his wives missed the greenery of her native Media.. Called by the Greeks one of the seven wonders of the world, this garden was built seventy-five feet above ground level and covered about four square kilometers or 1.6 square miles. Among other public works projects, King Nebuchadnezzar built many canals and a reservoir 140 miles in circumference and about thirty miles in width and length. Agricultural projects also boomed at this time as farmers grew grains, nuts, and fruits including peaches, grapes, and cherries.

The Babylonian Exile of Judah (586 BC)

Meanwhile God's chosen people of the tribe of Judah were not doing well. After Josiah's death, four successive kings were all marked as evil in God's eyes—Jehoahaz, Jehoiakim, Jehoiachin, and Zedekiah. The Lord God of Israel brought Nebuchadnezzar's armies to the city of Jerusalem. The third time, in 586 BC, the Babylonians destroyed the city and temple and took the Israelites captive to Babylon. This final siege is recorded in Jeremiah 39:

> *In the ninth year of Zedekiah king of Judah, in the tenth month, Nebuchadnezzar king of Babylon and all his army came against Jerusalem, and besieged it. In the eleventh year of Zedekiah, in the fourth month, on the ninth day of the month, the city was penetrated.*
>
> *Then all the princes of the king of Babylon came in and sat in the Middle Gate: Nergal-Sharezer, Samgar-Nebo, Sarsechim, Rabsaris, Nergal-Sarezer, Rabmag, with the rest of the princes of the king of Babylon.*
>
> *So it was, when Zedekiah the king of Judah and all the men of war saw them, that they fled and went out of the city by night, by way of the king's garden, by the gate between the two walls. And he went out by way of the plain. But the Chaldean army pursued them and overtook Zedekiah in the plains of Jericho. And when they had captured him, they brought him up to Nebuchadnezzar king of Babylon, to Riblah in the land of Hamath, where he pronounced judgment on him. Then the king of Babylon killed the sons of Zedekiah before his eyes in Riblah; the king of Babylon also killed all the nobles of Judah. Moreover he put out Zedekiah's eyes, and bound him with bronze fetters to carry him off to Babylon. And the Chaldeans burned the king's house and the houses of the people with fire, and broke down the walls of Jerusalem. Then Nebuzaradan the captain of the guard carried away captive to Babylon the remnant of the people who remained in the city and those who defected to him, with the rest of the people who remained. But Nebuzaradan the captain of the guard left in the land of Judah the poor people, who had nothing, and gave them vineyards and fields at the same time.*

Nebuchadnezzar's Pride

> *Pride goes before destruction,*
> *And a haughty spirit before a fall. (Proverbs 16:18)*

Nebuchadnezzar's pride is no secret in the annals of history. On cuneiform inscriptions, this ruler was referred to as "the king of the universe." He spoke of himself as "Nebuchadnezzar, King of Babylon, the exalted prince, the favorite of the god Marduk, the beloved of the god Nabu . . ."[2] His prayer to his god was to receive "a heavy tribute of all mankind." He asked that "from the horizon of heaven to the zenith" he would have no enemies and that his descendants would live and rule over Babylon forever.[3] Upon a "dedication cylinder" found under one of the ancient Babylonian structures, the king boasts: "The fortifications of Esagila and Babylon I strengthened and established the name of my reign forever."[4] Thousands of ancient bricks recovered from ancient Babylon bear the stamp: "Nebuchadnezzar . . . the eldest son of Nabopolassar, King of Babylon, am I."[5] This king wanted his stamp on the whole city because, after all, from his perspective: "Is not this great Babylon, that I have built for a royal dwelling by my mighty power and for the honor of my majesty?" These were the proud words (recorded in Daniel 4:30) that precipitated Nebuchadnezzar's period of insanity.

Daniel the Prophet

The true and living God, Creator of heaven and earth and sovereign Lord of all, will never ignore the great empires of the earth. So to the Egyptians and the Assyrians, He sent His prophets Abraham, Moses, and Jonah. Similarly, in 605 BC He sent His prophet Daniel to the very center of the most powerful regime on earth—Babylon. These prophets of the true and living God always serve notice to the great kings of the earth so as to check them in their pride, to moderate their opposition against His people, and to remind them of the truth—even if only for a moment in history.

Daniel served as prophet to the Babylonians and the Persians alike, reminding them by his word and life of Yahweh God's absolute control over their empires and their rule. These kings would pretend to serve a weak god like Marduk, who was easily manipulated and possessed no sovereign control over anything. Yet these kings must still be told about the true God, the absolutely sovereign God, to whom they were totally accountable.

Daniel and his three friends were part of the first exile band taken out of Jerusalem by the Babylonians in 605 BC. In God's all-wise providence, Daniel would live through many kings and he would continue serving into the reign of Cyrus the Persian over 70 years later. If he was ten years old at the time of the exile, Daniel would have been in his eighties when Darius the Mede cast him into the lion's den.

Unbelieving scholars claim that Daniel's prophecies were written in the 2nd century BC. They refuse to believe that a prophet of God could accurately predict, in detail, events about future world empires, centuries before those events occurred. The ungodly are very opposed to humbling themselves before their Creator. They do not want to believe that God is in control because they are absolutely certain that man should be in control of his own destiny. Modern men are as proud as the proud kings of Babylon and Assyria.

Nebuchadnezzar Humbled

After building the city of Babylon and taking all the credit for it on almost every brick of the city, Nebuchadnezzar's pride was unrelenting and unrestrained. The king was especially proud of his images lining the street leading to his palace, all gold-plated—statues of lions, dragons, bulls, and flowers.[6] He set up another gold-plated statue, some ninety feet high, to which he commanded all his servants to bow down. Daniel's three friends, Shadrach, Meshach, and Abed-Nego, refused to submit to the idolatrous worship, and the king became enraged with them. The account is told in Daniel 3:

> *Then Nebuchadnezzar, in rage and fury, gave the command to bring Shadrach, Meshach, and Abed-Nego. So they brought these men before the king. Nebuchadnezzar spoke, saying to them, "Is it true, Shadrach, Meshach, and Abed-Nego, that you do not serve my gods or worship the gold image which I have set up? Now if you are ready at the time you hear the sound of the horn, flute, harp, lyre, and psaltery, in symphony with all kinds of music, and you fall down and worship the image which I have made, good! But if you do not worship, you shall be cast immediately into the midst of a burning fiery furnace. And who is the god who will deliver you from my hands?"*

The Fiery Furnace

Shadrach, Meshach, and Abed-Nego answered and said to the king, "O Nebuchadnezzar, we have no need to answer you in this matter. If that is the case, our God whom we serve is able to deliver us from the burning fiery furnace, and He will deliver us from your hand, O king. But if not, let it be known to you, O king, that we do not serve your gods, nor will we worship the gold image which you have set up." (Daniel 3:13-18)

This example of these three young men served as a sharp rebuke to the proud king. Nevertheless, he had the Judeans cast into the fiery furnace. They were unaffected by the flames, and in fact, they were joined by a fourth man in the fire, one who appeared as "the Son of God." Here is another prefigurement of the Messiah, the Savior who was to come about 600 years later.

The king was overcome with wonder at this miracle, a demonstration of the power of the true and living God. In an honest moment the king confessed, "Blessed be the God of Shadrach, Meshach, and Abed-Nego, who sent His Angel and delivered His servants who trusted in Him, and they have frustrated the king's word, and yielded their bodies, that they should not serve nor worship any god except their own God." Nebuchadnezzar was forced to admit that "there is no other god who can deliver like this" (Dan. 3:26-28). Nevertheless, this event was not enough to humble this king, the most powerful man on earth in the 6th century.

Daniel 4 relates the story of how Nebuchadnezzar was finally humbled in the most remarkable way. First, the king received a dream that troubled him, and Daniel interpreted the dream for him. It turned out to be a warning.

> *The tree that you saw, which grew and became strong, whose height reached to the heavens and which could be seen by all the earth, whose leaves were lovely and its fruit abundant, in which was food for all, under which the beasts of the field dwelt, and in whose branches the birds of the heaven had their home—it is you, O king, who have grown and become strong; for your greatness has grown and reaches to the heavens, and your dominion to the end of the earth.*
>
> *And inasmuch as the king saw a watcher, a holy one, coming down from heaven and saying, "Chop down the tree and destroy it, but leave its stump and roots in the earth, bound with a band of iron and bronze in the tender grass of the field; let it be wet with the dew of heaven, and let him graze with the beasts of the field, till seven times pass over him;" this is the interpretation, O king, and this is the decree of the Most High, which has come upon my lord the king: They shall drive you from men, your dwelling shall be with the beasts of the field, and they shall make you eat grass like oxen. They shall wet you with the dew of heaven, and seven times shall pass over you, till you know that the Most High rules in the kingdom of men, and gives it to whomever He chooses.*
>
> *And inasmuch as they gave the command to leave the stump and roots of the tree, your kingdom shall be assured to you, after you come to know that Heaven*

Nebuchadnezzar Humbled

> *rules. Therefore, O king, let my advice be acceptable to you; break off your sins by being righteous, and your iniquities by showing mercy to the poor. Perhaps there may be a lengthening of your prosperity."* (Daniel 4:20-27)

Nebuchadnezzar did not heed the warning, and one day as he contemplated the greatness of his own accomplishments, the hammer descended upon him:

All this came upon King Nebuchadnezzar. At the end of the twelve months he was walking about the royal palace of Babylon. The king spoke, saying, "Is not this great Babylon, that I have built for a royal dwelling by my mighty power and for the honor of my majesty?"

While the word was still in the king's mouth, a voice fell from heaven: "King Nebuchadnezzar, to you it is spoken: the kingdom has departed from you! And they shall drive you from men, and your dwelling shall be with the beasts of the field. They shall make you eat grass like oxen; and seven times shall pass over you, until you know that the Most High rules in the kingdom of men, and gives it to whomever He chooses." (Daniel 4:28-32)

The prophecy eventually came to pass, and Nebuchadnezzar took on the behavior of a grazing animal very much like a cow. Reduced to crawling on his hands and knees, the greatest king on earth was put out to pasture and fed on grass for a period of seven seasons.

Significantly, there is more information contained in the Old Testament Scriptures on the life of this great king and his empire than what is to be found in ancient Babylonian records. What we are to learn about this great empire is mostly that which is left us by God's inspired writings. This is the essential material He would have students of history to know—at least those who seek the truth, those who fear God and trust in Him. What little is found in secular historical records confirms both the pride and the humiliation of this great king of Babylon.

Finally, the most powerful man on earth, this man Nebuchadnezzar repented. He received the single most basic lesson which the God of heaven wanted to teach him: God is absolutely sovereign.

And at the end of the time I, Nebuchadnezzar, lifted my eyes to heaven, and my understanding returned to me; and I blessed the Most High and praised and honored Him who lives forever:

For His dominion is an everlasting dominion,
And His kingdom is from generation to generation.
All the inhabitants of the earth are reputed as nothing;
He does according to His will in the army of heaven
And among the inhabitants of the earth.
No one can restrain His hand

Or say to Him, "What have You done?"

At the same time my reason returned to me, and for the glory of my kingdom, my honor and splendor returned to me. My counselors and nobles resorted to me, I was restored to my kingdom, and excellent majesty was added to me. Now I, Nebuchadnezzar, praise and extol and honor the King of heaven, all of whose works are truth, and His ways justice. And those who walk in pride He is able to put down. (Daniel 4:34-37)

There is a little bit of this remarkable account to be found in secular records. An obscure clay cuneiform tablet excavated at Babylon was found to have recorded Nebuchadnezzar's frame of mind after the severe humbling he received at the hands of God. Parts of the writing are missing, but what was left on the tablet was translated in 1975 by A.K. Grayson:

[Nebu]chadnezzar considered
His life appeared of no value to [him, . . .]
And (the) Babylon(ian) speaks bad counsel to Evil-merodach [. . .]
Then he gives an entirely different order but [. . .]
He does not heed the word from his lips . . .
He does not show love to son and daughter [. . .]
. . . family and clan do not exist [. . .]
His attention was not directed towards promoting the welfare of Esagil [and Babylon]
He prays to the lord of lords, he raised [his hands (in supplication) . . .][7]

The tone of the king's own records changes perceptibly in his later inscriptions. For example, Building Inscription Number 15 demonstrates a humility and a tentativeness, a submission to the will of God and a fear of God not seen in other inscriptions.

Building Inscription Number 15

Without thee, Lord, what could there be
For the king thou lovest, and dost call his name?
Thou shalt bless his title as thou wilt,
And unto him vouchsafe a path direct.

I the prince obeying thee,
Am what thy hands have made.
'Tis thou who art my Creator,
Entrusting me with the rule of the hosts of men.
According to thy mercy, Lord, . . .
Turn into loving-kindness thy dread power,
And make to spring up in my heart
A reverence for thy divinity.
Give as thou thinkest best.[8]

Here, in this recently-discovered secular record we see that Nebuchadnezzar is now submitting himself to the will of God. Such writings indicate a monotheistic commitment—a sign that Nebuchadnezzar submitted himself to the sovereign will of one sovereign God.

God's mercy is surely witnessed here as the kings of the earth genuinely respond to His revealed warnings. Representatives from Egypt (Amenhotep IV—1350 BC), Assyria (Adad-Nirari III—800 BC), and Babylon (Nebuchadnezzar—560 BC) received a visitation and a revelation. They were given a message from God, and each of them demonstrated some willingness to humble themselves before the sole almighty and sovereign God of heaven and earth. This demonstrates the mercy of God and His concern for every tribe and nation, even before the coming of the Messiah—in whom all the nations of the earth would be blessed.

Belshazzar and the End of Babylon (539 BC)

"And this whole land shall be a desolation and an astonishment, and these nations shall serve the king of Babylon seventy years. Then it will come to pass, when seventy years are completed, that I will punish the king of Babylon and that nation, the land of the Chaldeans, for their iniquity," says the LORD; "and I will make it a perpetual desolation. So I will bring on that land all My words which I have pronounced against it, all that is written in this book, which Jeremiah has prophesied concerning all the nations. (For many nations and great kings shall be served by them also; and I will repay them according to their deeds and according to the works of their own hands.)" (Jeremiah 25:11-14)

The Babylonian Empire did not last long, probably because of its very poor moral fiber. Alexander the Great was shocked at the moral laxness he encountered in the city when he arrived there in the 330s BC. Great wealth, much like what Americans and Europeans have enjoyed in the last century, often results in very low morals. Babylon was no exception.

The Babylonian religion forced sexual immorality on its people, and every woman, rich or poor, was held to this expectation. The world would have to wait for the Christian influence brought with Constantine for the end of ritual prostitution in Babylon (c. AD 325). Pre-marital fornication was expected among Babylonian youth. Towards the end of the empire, Herodotus reports that the young men descended into "effeminate degeneracy," perfuming themselves and adorning themselves with earrings and makeup.[9] The Roman historian Quintus Curtius noted about Babylon: "Nowhere are things better arranged with a view to voluptuous pleasures."[10] By the end of the empire, fathers were selling their daughters to the highest bidder and husbands were killing their wives to prevent them from eating the last of their provisions.

Such conditions mark the modern world, at the end of the age of the western empires. This is the way it goes with the proud empires of men. Modern nations would do well to heed this warning.

Less than fifty years after Israel's Babylonian Exile of 586 BC, Persia invaded the city of Babylon. The Lord had assigned only seventy years for the Jewish exile. True to His word brought by the prophet Jeremiah around 600 BC, the Lord brought the Babylonian rule over His people to an end.

After Nebuchadnezzar's death in 562 BC, his sons and in-laws battled for the throne for several years. The rule eventually settled on Nabonidus, who was probably one of Nebuchadnezzar's sons-in-law. Nabonidus ruled from 556 BC until 539 BC, when Babylon fell to the Persians.

For many years unbelieving historians thought the Book of Daniel made a mistake when referring to Belshazzar. However, in 1854 the Nabonidus Cylinder was uncovered and, sure enough, Nabonidus's eldest son's name was Belshazzar. Beginning in 553 BC, for some reason Nabonidus turned the throne over to Belshazzar as a co-regent. For what could have been 14-15 years, Nabonidus took up residence in Teima, in Arabia. Thus it would have been Belshazzar who was ruling from Babylon when the Persians entered the city in 539 BC.

Nabonidus Cylinder

The Reasons for Babylon's Destruction

> *Then the men turned away from there and went toward Sodom, but Abraham still stood before the LORD. And Abraham came near and said, "Would You also destroy the righteous with the wicked? Suppose there were fifty righteous within the city; would You also destroy the place and not spare it for the fifty righteous that were in it? Far be it from You to do such a thing as this, to slay the righteous with the wicked, so that the righteous should be as the wicked; far be it from You! Shall not the Judge of all the earth do right?" So the LORD said, "If I find in Sodom fifty righteous within the city, then I will spare all the place for their sakes." (Genesis 18:22-26)*

In this passage Abraham clearly possesses complete confidence that the Judge of the earth, almighty Yahweh God, will always do that which is just and right. In this astounding exchange, Abraham is negotiating with God for the preservation of Sodom. He left off when the Lord agreed He would not destroy Sodom for ten righteous men in the city. Regrettably, there was only one man to be found. Not even Lot's sons-in-law feared God enough to leave the city. The complete absence of the fear of God and faith in the true God was the rule in these ancient cities.

The Fall of Babylon, 539 BC

Therefore they were fitted for destruction, especially when the cities flaunted the worst forms of sexual sin and unmitigated violence against the innocent.

Throughout the prophetic books of Isaiah and Jeremiah, Yahweh God promised violent and retributive destruction against the enemies of His people. Even though the Lord did use Babylon to chastise His people, He would still punish that wicked city for their treatment of Israel. Babylon would bear the guilt of its own sins, and God would bring His just judgment down upon this world power.

Yahweh God assigned destruction on Babylon for the "multitude of your sorceries . . . and the great abundance of your enchantments." As early as 700 BC, the Lord spoke to the Babylonians through the prophet Isaiah, saying, "You are wearied in the multitude of your counsels. Let now the astrologers, the stargazers, and the monthly prognosticators stand up and save you from what shall come upon you" (Isa. 47:9, 13). The king of Babylon would often consult images and examine the livers of dead animals to discern clues that might help him make wise decisions (Ezek. 21:21). This correlates perfectly with secular historians' understanding of the Babylonian mindset. The historian Will Durant reports, "Never was a civilization richer in superstitions. Every turn of chance from the anomalies of birth to the varieties of death received a popular, sometimes an official or sacerdotal, interpretation in magical or supernatural terms. Every movement of the rivers, every aspect of the stars, every dream, every unusual performance of man or beast, revealed the future to the properly instructed Babylonian. The fate of a king could be forecast by the movement of a dog . . ."[11]

Another reason offered for the destruction of Babylon in Isaiah's prophecy was a raw humanist, man-centered thinking:

> *For you have trusted in your wickedness; you have said, "No one sees me." Your wisdom and your knowledge have warped you; and you have said in your heart, "I am, and there is no one else besides me" (Isaiah 47:10).*

It was Babylon's pride that brought them down. It was too many pride marches that called for God's crushing hand to descend upon the Empire:

> *"Behold, I am against you,*
> *O most haughty one!" says the LORD God of hosts;*
> *"For your day has come,*
> *The time that I will punish you." (Jeremiah 50:31)*

Yet the foremost reason given for the destruction of Babylon comes in Jeremiah 51:24:

> *"And I will repay Babylon*
> *And all the inhabitants of Chaldea.*
> *For all the evil they have done*
> *In Zion in your sight," says the LORD. . . .*
> *The inhabitant of Zion will say,*
> *"And my blood be upon the inhabitants of Chaldea!" (Jeremiah 51:24, 35)*

For all of this, the Lord God promised that the land will be "desolate," Marduk will be "broken in pieces," the bars of her gates will be broken, her mighty men will act like women, and Babylon will "sink and not rise from the catastrophe that I will bring upon her" (Jeremiah 51:64).

As Scripture relates, King Belshazzar organized an epic feast for 1,000 of his lords—not unusual for the Assyrians and Babylonians. King Assurnasirpal threw a party for 70,000 guests in 883 BC, as mentioned earlier. This time, the Babylonians dragged out the gold vessels taken from the temple in Jerusalem some seventy years earlier—and they "praised the gods of gold and silver, bronze and iron, wood and stone" (Dan. 5:4).

Just then, a hand appeared, writing upon the wall the words: "Mene, Mene, Tekel, Upharsin." All the soothsayers and astrologers were unable to decipher the words, so Daniel the prophet was called upon to interpret the writing.

Daniel pointed out that Belshazzar's ancestor Nebuchadnezzar had humbled himself before Almighty God. Daniel reminded Belshazzar that "The Most High God rules in the kingdom of men and appoints over it whomever He chooses" (Dan. 5:21). Then Daniel went on to show that Belshazzar had not humbled his heart although he was well aware of his father's (or grandfather's) experiences.

Daniel Interprets the Handwriting

This young king refused to glorify "the God who holds your very breath in His hand and owns all your ways" (vs. 23). Daniel then translated the writing:

> ***Mene, Mene:*** *"God has numbered your kingdom and finished it. God has numbered your kingdom and finished it."*
>
> ***Tekel:*** *"You have been weighed in the balances and found wanting."*
>
> ***Upharsin:*** *"Your kingdom has been divided and given to the Medes and Persians."*

True to the word of prophecy, King Belshazzar was killed that very night, and the Persian armies took the city.

Babylon, the great city of man, had fallen.

This story of the rise and fall of the Babylonian Empire is more evidence that this and all nations are just "a drop in a bucket" and "the small dust on the scales" in God's eyes (Isa. 40:15). Although men will foolishly act as though they cannot be controlled by God, and though they will lift themselves up and oppose Him in pride, it is all a vain show. Surely He will quickly bring these proud nations down and toss them into the dust heap of history.

God permitted Belshazzar to rule for scarcely fifteen years. As it turns out, the most evil and powerful rulers of the last century didn't last very long either. Adolf Hitler controlled Germany for only eleven years, and Vladimir Lenin led the communist party in the Soviet Union for seven years.

> *I have seen the wicked in great power, and spreading himself like a native green tree. Yet he passed away, and behold, he was no more; indeed I sought him, but he could not be found. (Psalm 37:35-36).*

Yet the righteous rule of Jesus Christ, the Son of David, the King of kings and Lord of lords, still continues even 2,000 years after its commencement. His kingdom does not end. It only grows. To Christ our King be the glory, praise, and honor forever and ever! Amen.

The Plight of Man's Greatest Empires

> *Daniel answered in the presence of the king, and said. . . "This is the dream. Now we will tell the interpretation of it before the king. You, O king, are a king of kings. For the God of heaven has given you a kingdom, power, strength, and glory; and wherever the children of men dwell, or the beasts of the field and the birds of the heaven, He has given them into your hand, and has made you ruler over them all—you are this head of gold. But after you shall arise another kingdom inferior to yours; then another, a third kingdom of bronze, which shall rule over all the earth. And the fourth kingdom shall be as strong as iron, inasmuch as iron breaks in pieces and shatters everything; and like iron that crushes, that kingdom will break in pieces and crush all the others." (Daniel 2:27, 36-40)*

The age of empires began with Assyria and Babylon, yet this was only the beginning. For 1,300 years (800 BC-AD 476) man would produce his greatest kingdoms. Man would ascend to greater and greater heights of power. He would set himself against God and increasingly recognize himself to be god. As though anticipating the coming King, man would position himself in the most godlike and kingly position he could possibly achieve. It seemed as if nothing could compete with the glory of Babylon, Persia, Greece, and Rome—except for a Baby born in Bethlehem and a Boy raised in Nazareth of Galilee.

Before man had reached the ultimate summit of world power under Cyrus the Great, Alexander the Great, and Augustus Caesar, God gave the world a powerful and highly significant message through the prophet Daniel. He warned the nations of the futility of their grandest purposes and efforts. The revelations are found in Daniel 2 and Daniel 7. The first was a revelation made to Nebuchadnezzar II. The second vision came to the prophet Daniel during the reign of Belshazzar, his grandson.

The sovereign rule of God is seen throughout Nebuchadnezzar's experiences recorded in the book of Daniel. God's revelation and His condemnation of the greatest empires of men came directly to the greatest man of the day. It was a heads-up, a warning shot, a timely reminder that God's hand was firmly held over the most ambitious, most powerful, and most rebellious purposes of man and his empires. The ultimate God over heaven and earth will permit them to go so far, but no further. His sovereign control over these nations is total.

The image Nebuchadnezzar saw in his dream (recorded in Daniel 2) has a golden head, a chest and arms of silver, a belly of bronze, and feet of iron and clay. Daniel interprets the dream in this way:

- The gold head is Nebuchadnezzar.
- The silver chest is an inferior kingdom, probably the dynasty of Cyrus.
- The bronze belly is the kingdom that rules over all the earth, probably the Greek Empire. Made of bronze, it wasn't as wealthy as Babylon and Persia. Nonetheless, Alexander the Great would prove himself a mighty warrior and command control over the entire world from Persia to Egypt.
- The feet of iron and clay is a kingdom that will break in pieces and crush all others, probably the Roman Empire. However, this kingdom is weakened by a mixture of iron and clay. The constant division between the senate and the people, the emperor and the senate, and the murders and treacheries that constituted the long history of Rome would prove its undoing.

Then comes the prophecy concerning the King of kings and the kingdom that would never perish from the earth. After 2,000 years of failure from Sargon I to Nebuchadnezzar II, finally a kingdom was about to appear which would continue forever. This would happen sometime between 580 BC and AD 476—sometime in the days of these kings.

> *And in the days of these kings, the God of heaven will set up a kingdom which shall never be destroyed; and the kingdom shall not be left to other people; it shall break in pieces and consume all these kingdoms. Inasmuch as you saw that the stone was cut out of the mountain without hands, and that it broke in pieces the iron, the bronze, the clay, the silver, and the gold—the great God has made known to the king what will come to pass after this. The dream is certain, and its interpretation is sure. (Daniel 2:44-45)*

In a real sense, the Roman Empire had subsumed the Greek Empire, which had subsumed the Persian Empire, which had subsumed Babylon. Thus the kingdom of Christ would break in pieces and consume all these kingdoms. Truly it would be Christ and His kingdom that would bring an end to the power games, cruel colosseums, polytheism, emperor worship, infanticide, human sacrifice, and human pride and prestige that constituted Rome.

Daniel Interprets Nebuchadnezzar's Dream

Daniel adds in verse 35 that the stone that struck the image and destroyed it became a mountain and filled the whole earth. This is a picture of the kingdom of God and its worldwide influence which would come about over the following 2,000 years. By AD 2020, over two billion people in the world called themselves Christians. No other religion and no other empire could claim that many adherents. No other kingdom could claim a 2,000-year heritage and a worldwide influence like the Christian faith. No other King has ever been so successful at bringing down His enemies and perpetuating His kingdom like this one.

Would that all two billion professing Christians would praise their King, submit to His Lordship, and worship at His footstool today!

The revelation from Daniel 7 expands on the fourth kingdom, characterizing the kingdom as a beast. Pride and antagonism toward God are demonstrated in the most outrageous manner in the persecution of His saints. This seemingly unrelenting, long-term, and cruel persecution of Christians occurred under many of the Roman emperors from Nero until Diocletian. This persecution lasted (with interruptions) for 250 years. Nevertheless, the cruel kingdom of Rome was eventually subdued, and the church of the Lord Jesus Christ emerged victorious. This kingdom formed roots in Europe over about a thousand years. The powers of humanist empires and man's proud ideologies returned with a vengeance between AD 1200 and AD 2020. Persecution of God's people intensified between AD 1400 and AD 1600 in Europe and again in the 20th century, but it was never as prolonged and universal as what we find in the Roman Empire between AD 64 and AD 313.

> *He shall speak pompous words against the Most High, shall persecute the saints of the Most High, and shall attempt to change times and law. Then the saints shall be given into his hand for a time and times and half a time. But the court shall be seated, and they shall take away his dominion, . . . and the greatness of his kingdoms under the whole heaven, shall be given to the people, the saints of the Most High. His kingdom is an everlasting kingdom. And all dominions shall serve and obey Him. (Daniel 7:25-27)*

Lion on the Ishtar Gate

Timeline Review

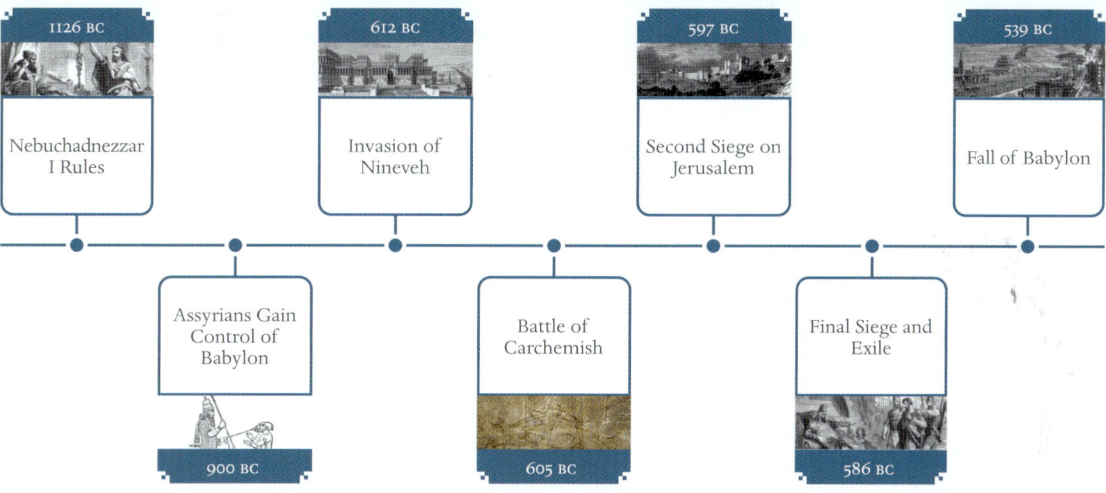

Chapter XI Prayer

Our Father and Almighty Sovereign God over all the nations,

We take great comfort in your sovereignty, in that you are well in control over all of the powerful nations of the earth. The wrath of man will praise you. You subject your own people to trial and tribulation, but only for their good and only for a short time. You raise up worldly powers to do Your sovereign will and then You bring them down when You are done with them. The most powerful man on earth was humbled by your mighty hand in the most extraordinary way. We are in awe of your works among the children of men! Oh that we would remain humble, ever fearing you, ever worshiping you, and ever loving you with heart, soul, mind, and strength!

In the Name of Jesus Christ, our Lord and Everlasting King,
Amen.

Ruins of Ancient Persepolis in Modern-Day Iran

CHAPTER XII

The Kingdom of the Medes and Persians (725-330 BC)

Now in the first year of Cyrus king of Persia, that the word of the LORD by the mouth of Jeremiah might be fulfilled, the LORD stirred up the spirit of Cyrus king of Persia, so that he made a proclamation throughout all his kingdom, and also put it in writing, saying,

Thus says Cyrus king of Persia:

"All the kingdoms of the earth the LORD God of heaven has given me. And He has commanded me to build Him a house at Jerusalem which is in Judah. Who is among you of all His people? May his God be with him, and let him go up to Jerusalem which is in Judah, and build the house of the LORD God of Israel (He is God), which is in Jerusalem. And whoever is left in any place where he dwells, let the men of his place help him with silver and gold, with goods and livestock, besides the freewill offerings for the house of God which is in Jerusalem." (Ezra 1:1-4)

The sovereign Lord over all the earth accomplished His purposes with Babylon and Assyria. All great empires, however, must quickly become corrupted because they are peopled by a sinful, fallen human race.

Zagros Mountains

Allowing the great kingdoms only a few generations to retain their exceptional powers, in time God will raise up another kingdom to displace them. Thus the Lord over the nations raised up the Medes and the Persians from the east to take the place of the age-old kingdom powers of Assyria, Babylon, and Elam.

The Ancient History of Elam and Persia (2418-725 BC)

The first settlements in Persia (or modern Iran) populated the far northeast corner of the Persian Gulf in the land of the Hamazi.

The Hamazi tribe most likely settled further north near the Zagros mountain range, somewhere around 2418 BC, following Nimrod's Tower of Babel. In fact, this tribe is mentioned in what may be the first secular reference to the Tower of Babel contained in a document called "Enmerkar and the Lord of Aratta." A portion is quoted as follows:

> *At such a time, may the lands of Cubur and Hamazi, the many-tongued, and Sumer, the great mountain of magnificence, and Akkad, the land possessing all that is befitting, and the Martu land, resting in security—the whole universe, the well-guarded people—may they all address Enlil together in a single language.*[1]

The complaint comes that the tribes are speaking in many different languages, and the author of this writing is vainly calling out for a re-unification under a single language. Following Babel, the first ruling dynasty in this land to the east was known as the Awan Dynasty, lasting from around 2418 BC to 2200 BC.

Not surprisingly, the earliest cuneiform record found in Elam corresponds with the oldest documents identified in Egypt and Sumer as well—around 2250 BC. This cuneiform record was a peace treaty drawn up between Sargon's grandson, Naram-Sin of Akkad, and the Awan governor, probably a man named Khita. As the Akkadian Empire broke down, Elam quickly extricated itself under the leadership of Kutik-Inshushinak (or Puzur-Inshushinak). However, the Sumerian

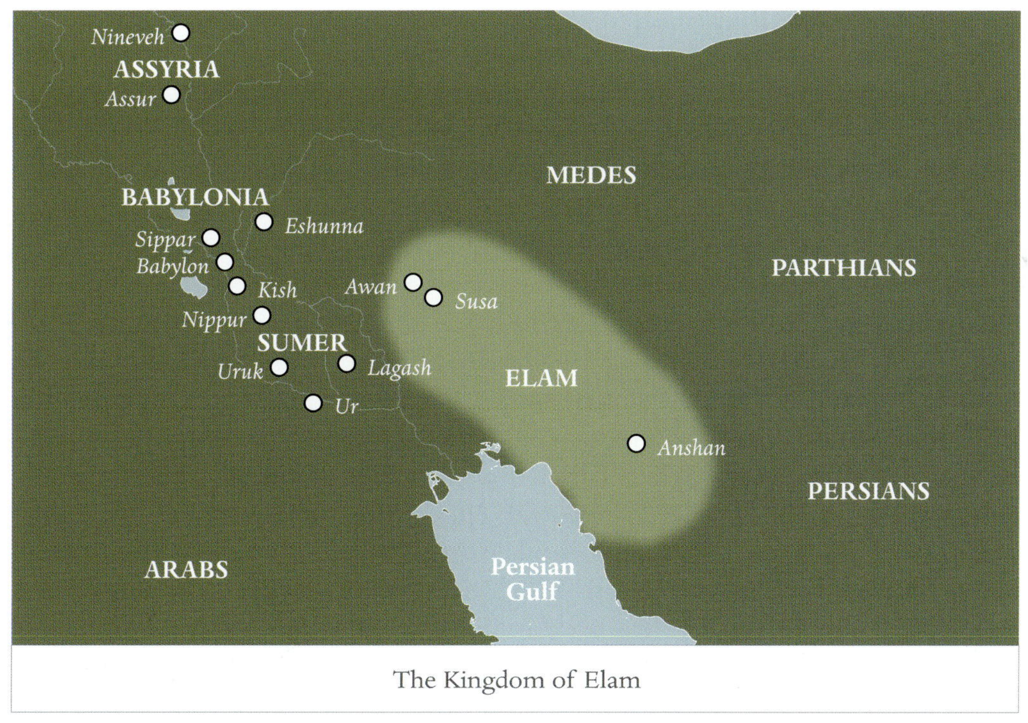

The Kingdom of Elam

king Ur-Nammu again conquered Elam around 2100 BC, putting an end to the Aran dynasty. The Shimashki dynasty ruled from 2100 BC to 1928 BC.

Elam became a kingdom of note by 1960 BC after a successful military campaign against the city of Ur. This was followed by the Sukkalmah dynasty, which lasted until 1760 BC when Hammurabi plundered the nation. Weakened by these military incursions, the nation entered into its own little dark age until the first Elamite empire formed around 1160 BC. The king Šutruk-Nakhunte successfully raided Babylon, returning home with the golden statue of Bel. The Elamites held on to the idol until Nebuchadnezzar I marched out and devastated the empire forty years later, retrieving his little god. Once again Elam faded into obscurity and never really recovered from the devastation caused by centuries of warfare with the many tribes of Mesopotamia.

A More Influential Monotheism

> *Truly, this only have I found: that God made man upright, but they have sought out many schemes. (Ecclesiastes 7:29)*

As the coming of Christ approached, the devil was active among the nations, developing and improving on counterfeits of the true faith. The old pagan polytheism was falling on hard times. New monotheistic lookalikes would arise through the years, including Islam, Arianism, and Zoroastrianism. At the same time, however, the common grace of God was working—creating a sense of expectation for a true salvation in the hearts of certain peoples.

In 2100 BC, Abraham had received the monotheistic faith, through an encounter with the one, true, and living God. Then Moses had laid down the commandments of God in writing by 1400 BC. Somewhere between 1000 and 600 BC, a man named Zarathustra received a vision from a spirit, revealing to him the tenets of Zoroastrianism. It was basically a monotheistic religion, but it pitted a good god against a bad god of equal power. These were the beginnings of humanist philosophy, a religion that would teach man to glory in himself. Zarathustra taught that man could save himself by choosing good thoughts and actions and thereby gain everlasting life. Unlike the God of the Bible, the Zoroastrian god Ahura-Mazda has no sovereign control over the free actions of men.

Zoroastrianism teaches a final judgment, a final resurrection, and eternal life. However, according to this system of thought, the evil power, Ahriman, will be forever engaged in a cosmic struggle against Ahura-Mazda. Both of these powers were said to have been "twin spirits," with Ahriman blamed as the source of all evil—which would include serpents, vermin, locusts, ants, darkness, crime, sin, and homosexuality.

Depiction of Zarathustra

While attempting to move towards a thoughtful monotheism, Zarathustra was deceived into accepting a god who was not sovereign, allowing only for the pretense that man's will was sovereign and capable of saving himself from evil. This would form the basis of later humanist philosophies, including the Greek philosophers who appeared around the turn of the 7th century BC (such as Thales around 600 BC and Pythagoras about 550 BC).

With the entrance of Zoroastrianism into Persia, human sacrifice ended. However, the Persians continued offering sacrifices to the sun, Ahura-Mazda, such as perfumes, flowers, fruit, bread, oxen, sheep, horses, donkeys, and deer. Zoroastrianism brought about little change to Persian life. The Persians continued to participate in divination and sorcery, the worst forms of incest were common, and the king's harem would sometimes number in the hundreds. However, similar to the Assyrians, abortion was a death penalty crime and

Ahura Mazda (Depicted on the Right)

homosexuality was frowned upon. The sacred writings of the Zoroastrians (the Avesta) call homosexuality a sin for which there is no forgiveness—"Nothing can wash it away."[2] The Persians were also punctilious about avoiding any appearance of adultery. According to the rules of the Avesta, women were not even allowed to visit with their nearest male relatives.

As with the Assyrians, the Persians did not stop short of severe, brutal treatment of their enemies. Crucifixion, dismemberment, selling women into harems, and similar atrocities were common practices among the kings. Yet they prided themselves on their integrity, their adherence to treaties, and the respect offered each other in public settings (similarly to the Chinese and the Japanese). Strict adherence to manners, such as bowing, embracing, and kissing, was expected of the various classes. Dogs were especially valued in Persian society—maltreatment of the furry creatures would warrant 200 to 1,400 stripes with a whip.

Heathen nations realized the tendency to destructive sins and disorder within their societies and, somewhat arbitrarily, would assign strict fences and laws to secure this social order. "These things indeed have an appearance of wisdom in self-imposed religion, false humility, and neglect of the body, but are of no value against the indulgence of the flesh" (Col. 2:23). Only in the Lord Jesus Christ would this world ever find substantial freedom from sin and victory over the powerful lusts of the flesh and the tendency to gross immorality.

Nevertheless, this was the worldview that shaped the great Medo-Persian Empire of the 6th to the 4th centuries before Christ. Through the strict moral program of Zoroastrianism, Cyrus and others were successful at building up a great kingdom. Yet, as in the case of the others erected on the wrong worldview, this empire came crashing down almost as rapidly as it arose.

The Beginnings of the Medes (725-560 BC)

After the flood and the fall of the Tower of Babel, some tribes moved due east of Mount Ararat towards modern-day Azerbaijan on the shores of the Caspian Sea. These were the Scythians and the origins of the Medes. When the great Assyrian king Shalmaneser III reached this area, he encountered twenty-seven distinct tribes of a people called the Madai or the Medes. Over hundreds of years these peoples moved southeast, settling in the Hamadan province of modern-day Iran, where they mined copper, iron, lead, gold, and silver, and developed their technology.

The Caspian Sea

Caspian Sea

The first king of any note among the Medes was Deioces (ruled around 725-675 BC), whom history remembers as a tyrant. He would not allow any common person in his presence and disallowed all laughing and spitting in court. He formed a rudimentary secret police called "The King's Eyes and Ears" to further incite a servile fear among the populace. Deioces built a castle on what is now known as Ecbatana Hill and surrounded it with seven walls; the outermost wall was white, the next black, then red, blue, red, copper, and gold. Five hundred miles to the northwest of Ecbatana, the Assyrians in Nineveh were growing a little nervous at the strengthening of this fledgling kingdom. King Sargon II entered the kingdom, exiled Deioces, and put his son in place as a regent ruler.

However, independence for the Medes came later under the leadership of Deioces' grandson, Cyaxares (ruled 625-585 BC). His father Phraortes had been killed in battle with the Assyrians, and Cyaxares committed himself to the independence of the kingdom. He allied himself with Babylon by marrying his daughter to Nebuchadnezzar II, son of then king Nabopolassar. The Babylon-Mede coalition succeeded in sacking Nineveh in 612 BC, making way for the Neo-Babylonian empire which would make way for the Medo-Persian not long after. In his last battles, Cyaxares gained control of Lydia (modern-day Turkey), extending his empire far to the west by 585 BC.

Cyaxares' son Astyages took the throne after his father's death, ruling the large empire from 585 BC to 550 BC in an uneasy alliance with his brother-in-law Nebuchadnezzar II.

The development of the empire of the Medes and Persians occurred through much treachery, wars, and power shifting. Despite all the evil purposes and means employed by its rulers, the Medo-Persian Empire's rise to power was ordained by God.

The king's heart is in the hand of the Lord,
Like the rivers of water;
He turns it wherever He wishes. (Proverbs 21:1)

Ecbatana Hill

Tomb of Cyaxares

Meanwhile, the kingdom of Persia had developed out of old Elam in the southeast. The Persians had wandered in from eastern Iran to settle in the Zagros mountains around 1000 BC. The kings of Persia Cyrus I and his son Cambyses I ruled under the lordship of the Medes between 625 and 559 BC following the destruction of Nineveh. In one of the most dramatic political power shifts in history, Astyages king of the Medes married his daughter Mandane to Cambyses I of Persia. Cambyses' and Mandane's son would become Cyrus the Great.

The Most Astounding Prophecy of Old Testament Scripture

> *Thus says the LORD your Redeemer, and He who formed you from the womb: "I am the LORD who makes all things, who stretches out the heavens all alone, who spreads abroad the earth by Myself; who frustrates the sounds of the babblers, and drives diviners mad; who turns wise men backward, and makes their knowledge foolishness; who confirms the word of His servant, and performs the counsel of his messengers; who says to Jerusalem, 'You shall be inhabited.'. . . who says of Cyrus, 'He is My shepherd, and he shall perform My pleasure . . ."*
>
> *Thus says the LORD to His anointed, to Cyrus, whose right hand I have held—to subdue nations before him and loose the armor of kings, to open before him the double doors, so that the gates will not be shut: "I will go before you and make the crooked places straight; I will break in pieces the gates of bronze and cut the bars of iron."* (Isaiah 44:24-45:2)

This passage from Isaiah has been referred to as the most amazing prophecy in the Bible. Fully 175 years before Cyrus appeared on the scene, Isaiah names him as the deliverer of God's people. In the passage, the Lord refers to this Persian king as "My servant" and "My shepherd." Then in Isaiah 45:13, the Lord informs the people of Israel that this king is raised up in righteousness to "build My city" and "let My exiles go free." This prophecy serves as an excellent illustration of the Lord Yahweh's absolute sovereignty over the most powerful kings of the earth. It also gives insight into His sovereign power to effect what He foretells. If the prophecy will be certainly fulfilled, then He must control all future contingencies which might prevent His purposes from coming about. For example, He must have control over Cyrus's mother's womb and the parents' thought processes as they make the decision to name their son "Cyrus." He must be in control of the decisions made by this powerful king in order to ensure the release of His people from captivity and to support the rebuilding of the city of Jerusalem.

Cyrus is called to the battlefield like a "bird of prey from the east" (Isa. 46:11). He will most certainly execute God's counsel because any other possibility would call God's sovereignty—God's very God-ness—into question. The Lord speaks: "I have spoken it. I will also bring it to pass. I have purposed it. I will also do it." The Persians will put an end to the Babylonian Empire because that empire showed God's people "no mercy" (Isa. 47:6).

This prophecy was provided to Judah well before the exile as a comforting assurance that the Lord was not finished with His people. Indeed, He would rescue them from exile and bring them back to their city, and He assured them of this by providing them with the very name of the king who would administer the plan at least 150 years before he was born.

Such prophecies have such a striking supernatural character to them that unbelieving historians cannot accept them. For the last two hundred years these unbelievers have worked very hard to date Isaiah's prophecy after Cyrus's ascension to the throne in an attempt to explain away the prophecy.

Cyrus the Great (600-530 BC)

Before Cambyses I died around 551 BC, his son took the throne (about eight years earlier). While Cyrus's father was the King of Persia, his grandfather on his mother's side was king of the Medes to the north. This young king would be known as Cyrus the Great—Cyrus II. At this time, the Persians were still under the control of the kingdom of the Medes, but King Astyages and the ruling class of the Medes had already grown lax. "The upper classes became the slaves of fashion and luxury, the men wore embroidered trousers, the women covered themselves with cosmetics and jewelry, the very horses were often caparisoned in gold."[3]

The king's revenge upon his general, Harpagus, backfired, and when Cyrus II rebelled against his grandfather, the Median military at least partially defected to the other side. By 550 BC, Cyrus II had captured the capital city of the Medes—Ecbatana.

Illustration of Cyrus

As the greatest king and conqueror in the history of the world thus far, Cyrus went on to conquer Lydia, Elam, Babylon, Lycia, Cilicia, and Phoenicia. This was the king whom the all-sovereign God raised up to return the Judean exiles and rebuild the house of God in Jerusalem.

The Cyrus Cylinder, discovered in 1879, contains Cyrus's own writings recorded in the first person. His easy conquest of Babylon is related as well as his interest in returning the people and their gods to their original places of residence. From the testimony on the cylinder, we learn that Cyrus was hoping that this equitable treatment of all gods would somehow provide for him "long life." The following is a portion of the cylinder translated into English:

> *I am Cyrus, king of the world, the great king, the powerful king, king of Babylon, king of Sumer and Akkad, king of the four quarters of the world, son of Cambyses, the great king, king of the city of Anshan, grandson of Cyrus, the great king, king of the city of Anshan; great-grandson of Teispes, the great king, king of the city of Anshan; eternal seed of royalty whose rule Bel and Nabu love, in whose administration they rejoice in their heart. When I made my triumphal entrance into Babylon, I took up my lordly residence in the royal palace with joy and rejoicing; Marduk, the great lord, moved the noble heart of the residents of Babylon to me, while I gave daily attention to his worship.*
>
> *My numerous troops marched peacefully into Babylon. In all Sumer and Akkad I permitted no enemy to enter. The needs of Babylon and of all its cities I gladly attended to. The people of Babylon [and . . .], and the shameful yoke was removed from them. Their dwellings, which had fallen, I restored. I cleared out their ruins. Marduk, the great lord, rejoiced in my pious deeds, and graciously blessed me, Cyrus, the king who worships him, and Cambyses, my own son, and all my troops, while we, before him, joyously praised his exalted godhead. All the kings dwelling in palaces, of all the quarters of the earth, from the Upper to the Lower sea dwelling [. . .] all the kings of the Westland dwelling in tents brought me their heavy tribute, and in Babylon kissed my feet.*
>
> *From [. . .] to Asshur and Susa, Agade, Eshnunak, Zamban, Meturnu, Deri, with the territory of the land of Qutu, the cities on the other side of the Tigris, whose sites were of ancient foundation—the gods, who resided in them, I brought back to their places, and caused them to dwell in a residence for all time, and the gods of Sumer and Akkad whom Nabonidus, to the anger of the lord of the gods,*

Cyrus Cylinder, Discovered in 1879

had brought into Babylon—by the command of Marduk, the great lord, I caused them to take up their dwelling in residences that gladdened the heart. May all the gods, whom I brought into their cities, pray daily before Bêl and Nabû for long life for me, and may they speak a gracious word for me and say to Marduk, my lord, "May Cyrus, the king who worships you, and Cambyses, his son, their [. . .] I permitted all to dwell in peace [. . .][4]

This testimony is substantiated by biblical records. Indeed, God had previously ordained Cyrus's clemency and generous treatment of His people taken captive in Babylon. While the Babylonians had used the sacred temple instruments for their wild parties, Cyrus carefully identified all 5,400 stolen articles and returned them to the Jewish exiles.

King Cyrus also brought out the articles of the house of the Lord, which Nebuchadnezzar had taken from Jerusalem and put in the temple of his gods; and Cyrus king of Persia brought them out by the hand of Mithredath the treasurer, and counted them out to Sheshbazzar the prince of Judah. This is the number of them: thirty gold platters, one thousand silver platters, twenty-nine knives, thirty gold basins, four hundred and ten silver basins of a similar kind, and one thousand other articles. All the articles of gold and silver were five thousand four

Tomb of Cyrus the Great

> *hundred. All these Sheshbazzar took with the captives who were brought from Babylon to Jerusalem. (Ezra 1:7-11)*

Cyrus was generous to peoples of various beliefs—his only interest was tribute and political subservience. Unlike the royal conquerors who came before him, Cyrus did not destroy temples or sack cities. He didn't follow a scorched-earth policy. Like Alexander the Great and Napoleon who came after him, Cyrus didn't know when to quit his military excursions, and he died on the battlefield—probably on the southern shores of the Caspian Sea.

Cyrus's grave is marked with an unusually modest script, unassuming for the great kings of his era—especially given the fact that he had turned his empire into the largest in the world. His tomb reads simply: "Cyrus, the mighty king, an Achaemenid." Plutarch the Greek historian records his epitaph: "Man, whoever you may be and wherever you may come from—for I know that you will come—I am Cyrus who won the Persians their empire. Do not then begrudge me the little bit of earth which covers my remains."[5]

Nevertheless, Cyrus's sons turned out to be a bitter disappointment for the empire, and they did not inherit their father's clemency and wise judgment. They copied his cruelty and failed to emulate any of his magnanimity. Cambyses II killed his own brother, sister, wife, and his son Prexaspes. In a far-fetched military campaign, he sent an army of 50,000 Persians to their deaths in the wilderness of Libya. While conquering Egypt, he desecrated the Egyptian gods and exhumed mummies from the revered tombs. Cambyses' reign lasted eight years—after which he either died of suicide or murder. His brother barely survived a few months as his successor, and Darius I took the throne in 522 BC.

> *I have seen the wicked in great power, and spreading himself like a native green tree. Yet he passed away, and behold, he was no more. Indeed I sought him, but he could not be found. (Psalm 37:35-36)*

Darius the Great (522-486 BC)

Darius the Great on the Behistun Rock

The first mention of Darius the Mede is found in Daniel 5:31 at the conquest of Babylon. While it is uncertain whether this is the same Darius that rules Babylon later (known as Darius I), it appears that Darius may have been involved as a military captain in the Babylonian conquest (with Cyrus I). During Persia's campaigns against Egypt, Darius acted as Cambyses' right-hand man and proved himself a competent soldier. Various stories explain how Cyrus's dynasty lost the throne and how Darius took it, all of which include some measure of treachery and murder. The official story tells of a Magian named Gaumata who killed Smerdis (Cyrus's younger son) and assumed his identity on the throne for a while. He slaughtered anyone who

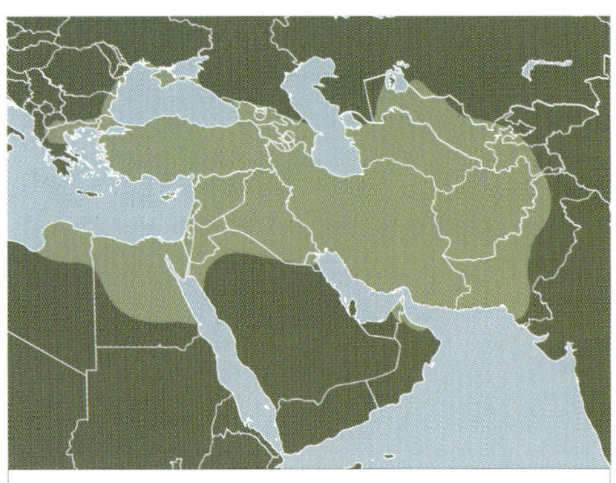

The Achaemenid Empire at Its Greatest Extent Under Darius the Great

had known the real Smerdis, and no one dared challenge him until Darius took a small band of friends, raided the stronghold, and killed the usurper.

Once in control of the empire, Darius extended its boundaries into Macedonia to the north and Pakistan and India (all the way to the Indus Valley) to the east. He established Aramaic as the official language of the empire and issued a universal, official coinage for the kingdom. Throughout his thirty-six-year reign, Darius kept busy quelling revolts among the Babylonians, Parthians, Persians, Armenians, and Elamites. At the height of its power, the kingdom of the Medes and Persians controlled 127 provinces from India to Ethiopia. It was the largest empire the world had ever known—by land mass three times larger than the Assyrian Empire of the 9th century BC and ten times larger than the Egyptian Empire of the 15th century BC.

To this day, a list of Darius's conquests can be seen on the Rock of Behistun. He writes in the first person, attributing his wins to the grace of the god of the Zoroastrians, a section of which is translated below:

> *These are the countries which are subject unto me, and by the grace of Ahuramazda I became king of them: Persia [Pârsa], Elam [Ûvja], Babylonia [Bâbiruš], Assyria [Athurâ], Arabia [Arabâya], Egypt [Mudrâya], the countries by the Sea, Lydia [Sparda], the Greeks [Yauna (Ionia)], Media [Mâda], Armenia [Armina], Cappadocia [Katpatuka], Parthia [Parthava], Drangiana [Zraka], Aria [Haraiva], Chorasmia [Uvârazmîy], Bactria [Bâxtriš], Sogdia [Suguda], Gandhara [Gadâra], Scythia [Saka], Sattagydia [Thataguš], Arachosia [Harauvatiš] and Maka [Maka]; twenty-three lands in all . . . These are the countries which are subject to me; by the grace of Ahuramazda they became subject to me; they brought tribute unto me. Whatsoever commands have been laid on them by me, by night or by day, have been performed by them . . . Within these lands, whosoever was a friend, him have I surely protected; whosoever was hostile, him have I utterly*

The Battle of Marathon, 490 BC

> *destroyed. By the grace of Ahuramazda these lands have conformed to my decrees; as it was commanded unto them by me, so was it done.*[6]

Darius and the Persian armies finally met their match in 490 BC at Marathon, about twenty-six miles northeast of Athens in Greece. Before the battle the Greeks sent a runner to Sparta to request support troops, but the Spartans refused to assist because of their celebrations of a religious festival underway at the time. The Greeks were outnumbered two to one in the battle, but they fought on their own turf and were far more ready to engage in hand-to-hand combat than their adversaries. The best explanation for why the Greeks were victorious was that they exhibited more courage in the heat of battle than the Persian soldiers did, and God wanted it to end that way.

All nations before Him are as nothing,
And they are counted by Him less than nothing and worthless.
To whom then will you liken God?
Or what likeness will you compare to Him?. . .
He brings the princes to nothing;
He makes the judges of the earth useless.
Scarcely shall they be planted,
Scarcely shall they be sown,
Scarcely shall their stock take root in the earth,
When He will also blow on them,
And they will wither,
And the whirlwind will take them away like stubble. (Isaiah 40:17-18, 23-24)

Darius and the Jerusalem Temple Project (520 BC)

Somewhere about 520 BC, Tattenai, a Persian provincial governor responsible for administering the area "across the river" (Syria and Israel), became concerned about the building of a temple over in Jerusalem. His name is recorded in various Babylonian cuneiform inscriptions and he is also mentioned in Ezra 5 and 6 in Holy Scripture. He interviewed the Judean governor, Zerubbabel, who reminded him of the mandate given the Jews by Cyrus in the previous administration. After this, Tattenai wrote King Darius, explaining his concern and the testimony of Zerubbabel. In response to the concern, King Darius confirmed the earlier decree and continued to support the work in Jerusalem, this time by financial reward. God's people and God's interests were well looked after by the most powerful kings of the earth. Then King Darius issued a decree, and a search was made in the royal archives. The records and the order of Darius are included in Ezra 6.

In the first year of King Cyrus, King Cyrus issued a decree concerning the house of God at Jerusalem: "Let the house be rebuilt, the place where they offered sacrifices; and let the foundations of it be firmly laid, its height sixty cubits and its width sixty cubits, with three rows of heavy stones and one row of new timber. Let the expenses be paid from the king's treasury. Also let the gold and silver articles of the house of God, which Nebuchadnezzar took from the temple which is in Jerusalem and brought to Babylon, be restored and taken back to the temple which is in Jerusalem, each to its place; and deposit them in the house of God"—

Now therefore, Tattenai, governor of the region beyond the River, and Shethar-Boznai, and your companions the Persians who are beyond the River, keep yourselves far from there. Let the work of this house of God alone; let the governor of the Jews and the elders of the Jews build this house of God on its site.

Moreover I issue a decree as to what you shall do for the elders of these Jews, for the building of this house of God: Let the cost be paid at the king's expense from taxes on the region beyond the River; . . . And may the God who causes His name to dwell there destroy any king or people who put their hand to alter it, or to destroy this house of God which is in Jerusalem. I Darius issue a decree; let it be done diligently. (Ezra 6:3-12)

Darius and Daniel

Daniel Caught Praying

The prophet Daniel would have been in his eighties by the time Darius was made king over the Medo-Persian Empire. Just as in the case of Moses in Egypt and Jonah in Nineveh, the Lord God would keep His prophet Daniel in a place of influence in the Medo-Persian Empire. He would never permit these powerful empires to go on without a check, a prophetic voice, and His man in place. Miraculously, Daniel's life had been preserved through the reigns of Nebuchadnezzar II, Nabopolassar, Belshazzar, Cyrus the Great, Cambyses II, and the revolutions that brought Darius to power. Some scholars believe that another

King Darius (known as Darius the Mede) ruled for a while before Cyrus I took control of the empire.

Daniel was given an important position directly under the king. He was assigned the office of one of three governors over 122 "satraps" or Persian procurators responsible for the various regions of the vast empire. It was at this stage of his life that Daniel was subjected to his most harrowing test. The governors and satraps conspired against him when they saw that he prayed to Yahweh God, the covenant God over Israel, three times a day.

As noted above, King Darius required all his rulers to worship the Persian god conjured up by the prophet Zarathustra centuries earlier. No less than seventy-six times in his Behistun "manifesto" Darius urged the worship of Ahura-Mazda for all the territories he had conquered! Unlike King Cyrus before him, this king was particularly jealous of the worship of the god of the Persians.

Daniel's political opponents obtained legislation signed by the king banning petitions or prayers to any god or man for thirty days (Dan. 6:7). That person violating the law would be cast into a den of lions. In steadfast faith, Daniel refused to comply. He continued to pray three times a day as was his habit. He was arrested and the king begrudgingly sentenced him to be thrown to the lions.

On the following day the man of God was still alive and well among the lions, and the king had him retrieved out of the den. In keeping with Persian severity, the king threw the conspirators, with their wives and children, into the den, and the lions quickly devoured them. Afterwards Darius issued an edict to his entire empire:

Then King Darius wrote:
To all peoples, nations, and languages that dwell in all the earth:
Peace be multiplied to you.
I make a decree that in every dominion of my kingdom men must tremble and fear before the God of Daniel.
For He is the living God,
And steadfast forever;
His kingdom is the one which shall not be destroyed,
And His dominion shall endure to the end.
He delivers and rescues,
And He works signs and wonders
In heaven and on earth,
Who has delivered Daniel from the power of the lions. (Daniel 6:25-27)

Ahasuerus: The Zenith of Persian Power (486-465 BC)

If there was a grand apex for the Achaemenid Empire, it would have been during the rule of Ahasuerus—or, in the Persian, "Khshayarsha." The Greeks pronounced the name "Xerxes." He was called the "handsomest man in the empire," and he became something of an "exemplar of sensuality."[7]

By this time, the Medo-Persian or Achaemenid Empire included four major capital cities: Susa, Persepolis, Ecbatana, and Anshan. Beginning with Darius the Great, the emperors would typically reside at Susa during the winter months.

It was in the third year of this Ahasuerus's reign at Susa (or "Shushan") that the events related in the Book of Esther probably transpired. When his wife Vashti dishonored him in the presence of his governors, the king shelved her and began the search for another wife. This became the providentially-arranged scenario in which the Jews were preserved from genocide at the hands of a tyrannical governor by the name of Haman. Evidently a rising anti-Jewish sentiment was spreading across the empire at this time. When Esther intervened and pleaded the cause of her people, the king relented. A letter was written enabling the Jews to destroy their enemies without interference from the ruling Persian authorities.

Esther Denouncing Haman

Mordecai Led Through the Streets of Susa by Haman

> *By these letters the king permitted the Jews who were in every city to gather together and protect their lives—to destroy, kill, and annihilate all the forces of any people or province that would assault them, both little children and women, and to plunder their possessions, on one day in all the provinces of King Ahasuerus, on the thirteenth day of the twelfth month, which is the month of Adar. A copy of the document was to be issued as a decree in every province and published for all people, so that the Jews would be ready on that day to avenge themselves on their enemies. The couriers who rode on royal horses went out, hastened and pressed on by the king's command. And the decree was issued in Shushan the citadel. (Esther 8:11-14)*

Fully 500 conspirators against the Jews were killed in Susa alone, including Haman's ten sons. The conspiracy must have been widespread in that a total of 75,000 enemies of the Jews were killed by the end of the conflict (Esth. 9:6-16).

Leading up to the critical battles in Greece, King Xerxes had worked his way down the Grecian Peninsula, conquering Thessaly, Phocis, Boeotia, Euboea, and Attica. He barely won the battle of Thermopylae in 480 BC, and that only at a tremendous loss of Persian lives. A mere 2,000 Spartans and Greeks defended the Thermopylae pass against 100,000 Persian troops. Down to using their fists and teeth, the Grecian forces killed about 20,000 Persians in the process. Inspired no doubt by the bravery of the Thermopylae warriors, the Greek alliance of Sparta, Athens, Corinth, and Megara decimated the remainder of the Persian army at the Battle of Plataea. Xerxes had met his Waterloo—it was thus far and no further for the Persian Empire.

When the Greeks later attempted an offensive thrust into the empire, Xerxes was distracted by his harem of women. Flush with success from early wins against the Persians, two hundred Greek ships coordinated an invasion of Caria in far western Anatolia (western Turkey). Xerxes sent his navy to defend his territory, but the battle was lost at the Eurymedon River in 466 BC.

Decadence always attending the decay of empires, it was the combined effect of sex scandals, jealousies, and political intrigue that brought King Xerxes down. He was murdered by a courtier, with a little help from a court eunuch named Aspamitres.

The Battle of Plataea, 479 BC

The Weakening and Collapse of the Medo-Persian Empire

The words of King Lemuel, the utterance which his mother taught him:
What, my son?
And what, son of my womb?
And what, son of my vows?
Do not give your strength to women,
Nor your ways to that which destroys kings.
It is not for kings, O Lemuel,
It is not for kings to drink wine,
Nor for princes intoxicating drink;
Lest they drink and forget the law,
And pervert the justice of all the afflicted. (Proverbs 31:1-5)

The hardiness characterized by the mountain tribes of the Medes and Persians did not last long after they had inherited the wealth of the greatest empire the earth had ever seen. The temptation to drunkenness, dissipation, and gluttony was just too much for them. At first the Persians partook of only one meal a day, but it wasn't long before this meal extended from noon until bedtime. The aristocracy stuffed themselves with a thousand delicacies, and cadres of chefs invented thousands of new sauces and desserts. The Greek historian Herodotus also pointed out that the Persians gave way to voluptuousness and "learnt from the Greeks" the practice of homosexuality.[8] It would prove to be their undoing.

When you come to the land which the LORD your God is giving you, and possess it and dwell in it, and say, "I will set a king over me like all the nations that are around me," you shall surely set a king over you whom the LORD your God chooses; one from among your brethren you shall set as king over you; you may not set a foreigner over you, who is not your brother. But he shall not multiply horses for himself, nor cause the people to return to Egypt to multiply horses, for the LORD has said to you, "You shall not return that way again." Neither shall he multiply wives for himself, lest his heart turn away; nor shall he greatly multiply silver and gold for himself. (Deuteronomy 17:14-17)

As the greatest of human empires declined, the Persian kings multiplied wives and concubines to themselves, in direct disobedience to the wisdom of Proverbs and Deuteronomy. Artaxerxes I (465 BC) produced one legitimate son and at least eighteen sons from his concubines. Sixty years later, Artaxerxes II (404 BC) claimed three legitimate sons and 150 by concubines.[9]

Murder and treachery ruled the day as the governance unraveled. The complex web of intrigue and murder present in the Persian court is illustrated by the following list of horrible crimes:

The Murder and Mayhem of the Persian Empire in Decline	
Xerxes I is murdered by his courtier and eunuch	465 BC
Xerxes' eldest son Darius is murdered by the same man	465 BC
The murderer of Xerxes I is murdered by Artaxerxes I	465 BC
Artaxerxes I rules	465-424 BC
Xerxes II is murdered by his half-brother	424 BC
Darius II murders Xerxes II's murderer	423 BC
Darius II rules	423-404 BC
Artaxerxes II rules, fights a war against his brother who is aided by the Greeks, and then kills his own son	404-358 BC
Artaxerxes III murders the rest of his family after three of his brothers had been executed, murdered, or committed suicide	358-338 BC
Artaxerxes III is poisoned by Bagoas the Younger	338 BC
Bagoas the Younger kills all of the king's sons but one	338 BC
Arses rules	338-336 BC
Bagoas kills Arses and his infant children	336 BC
Bagoas puts Darius III into power	336 BC
Darius III loses the empire to Alexander the Great	330 BC

Ancient Persian Ruins at Persepolis

At the end, it turned out to be a homosexual by the name of Bagoas the Younger who contributed to the chaos, murder, treachery, and demise of the Persian Empire. Bagoas turned the scepter of the kingdom over to a friend named Codomannus (Darius III), who brought the empire to an end six years later.

Darius III provides a fitting picture of the end of an empire. As reported by historian Quintus Curtius, the king rode into battle to meet Alexander the Great, dragging with him an entire procession of mother, "wife," children and governess, along with 365 concubines "also regally dressed and adorned." Much of this entourage fell into the hands of the enemy, along with 329 concubines who apparently "played musical instruments."[10] At the battle of Issus in 333 BC, the Macedonians under Alexander lost only 450 men to the Persian casualties of 40,000. Darius abandoned his mother, wife, and children, and ran from the scene. Two years later he returned with 100,000 troops against Alexander's 50,000 at the Battle of Gaugamela. Alexander defeated Darius again. Darius was eventually killed by a relative and the mighty Achaemenid Empire came to an end.

Thus another empire ended in shame, moral dissipation, and destruction. The judgment of God upon Persia was inescapable.

"Therefore wait for Me," says the LORD,
"Until the day I rise up for plunder;
My determination is to gather the nations
To My assembly of kingdoms,
To pour on them My indignation,
All My fierce anger;
All the earth shall be devoured
With the fire of My jealousy.

"For then I will restore to the peoples a pure language,
That they all may call on the name of the LORD,
To serve Him with one accord.
From beyond the rivers of Ethiopia
My worshipers,
The daughter of My dispersed ones,
Shall bring My offering." (Zephaniah 3:8-10)

Conclusion

Daniel's prophecy concerning Nebuchadnezzar's dream spoke of the Persian empire as "inferior" to Nebuchadnezzar's empire. In the end, the empire did not contribute much to the world except a few military victories under Cyrus and Darius.

As the dust settles on the Medo-Persians, one can't help but think how much futility is found in these kingdoms and empires of men! What is lasting of their contributions—their palaces, wars, murders, and harems? Why should we write stories of the conspiracies and intrigues—as if there was anything virtuous about a king who murders another who murders another?

We are thankful that through some of these civilizations, the Lord provides men with scientific innovation to take better care of the ground, animals, and fields. We are thankful for irrigation canals and roads that help to provide access to food and trade for the citizenry. But the greed, power struggles, pride, malice, and mass murder are always destructive and counter-productive in the long term. The sins of men always undo the progress made at the rise of the empires. With the accumulation of wealth and power, the thirst for leisure and decadence inevitably overcomes the contributions of hard work, honesty, and sacrifice. Self-interest always trumps charity in the end because of the sinful nature of man. Covetousness, envy, and competitions for fame and acclaim drown out the impulses to charity, gratefulness, and contentment.

These kingdoms will always sow the seeds of their own destruction. The world would have to wait until another kingdom came to destroy the chief enemies of the human soul. That kingdom arrived in AD 33.

The bigger story in all of this is God's purposes working in the background of history. Throughout the course of the Persian Empire the sovereign Lord used Xerxes, Darius, and Cyrus, the most powerful men on earth, to preserve His people and to preserve a Seed for a coming Savior and King in Israel.

Returning the people of Judah to Jerusalem was far more important than the great Persian military campaigns in Egypt, Greece, and India. The preservation of this little tribe during the reign of Xerxes was essential to all the world, to all eternity. While popular, political opinion was turning towards genocide against the Jews, with Haman at the lead, God used Esther to preserve a people in the highest courts of the land. He would preserve this tribe because a Child was coming—the Seed would come out of Judah in Bethlehem 400 years later.

And in that day there shall be a Root of Jesse,
Who shall stand as a banner to the people;
For the Gentiles shall seek Him,
And His resting place shall be glorious.

It shall come to pass in that day
That the LORD shall set His hand again the second time
To recover the remnant of His people who are left,
From Assyria and Egypt,
From Pathros and Cush,
From Elam and Shinar,
From Hamath and the islands of the sea.

He will set up a banner for the nations,
And will assemble the outcasts of Israel,
And gather together the dispersed of Judah
From the four corners of the earth. (Isaiah 11:10-12)

Lut Desert in Iran

Alamut Mountain Range in Iran

Timeline Review

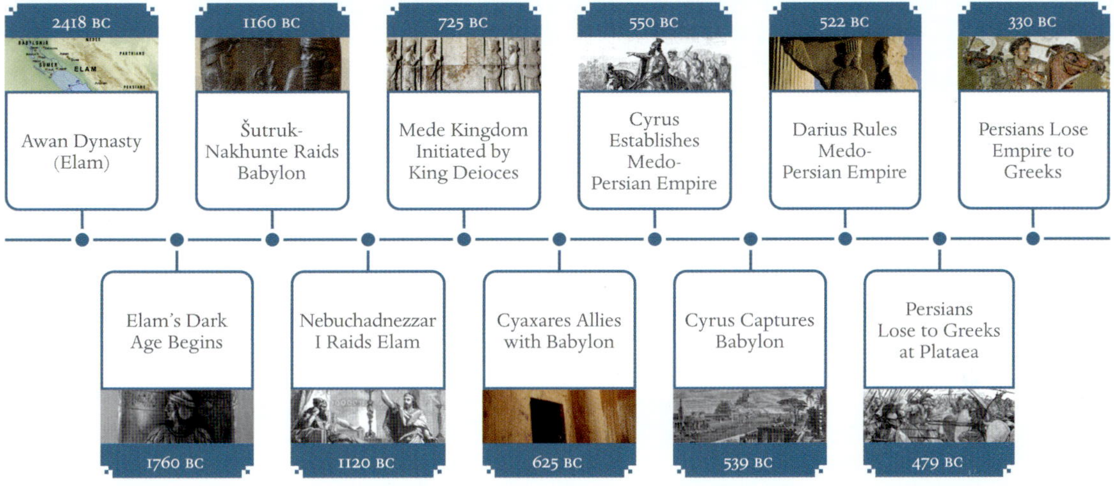

Chapter XII Prayer

Almighty God, and Father in Heaven,

What utter futility is found in the pride of men and the great empires of powerful kings who will not bow to your sovereignty! Babylon destroyed Nineveh. Persia destroyed Babylon. The Greeks destroyed Persia. But, You have destroyed them all. You have raised up these powers, and You brought them down. Through it all, You preserved Your people so as to preserve a Seed. Cyrus was Your servant. Darius was another servant of Yours. By Your sovereign power, these men returned the exiles of Israel and helped to rebuild the walls of Jerusalem—to prepare the world for Jesus, the Son of God, our Savior. We praise you for the perfection of your ways and the coming of the Kingdom of our Lord! It is a Kingdom that cannot fail forever and ever.

Amen.

The Parthenon, Athens, Greece

CHAPTER XIII

The Misguided Greeks and Alexander's Ill-Fated Empire (800-150 BC)

Now when they had passed through Amphipolis and Apollonia, they came to Thessalonica, where there was a synagogue of the Jews. Then Paul, as his custom was, went in to them, and for three Sabbaths reasoned with them from the Scriptures, explaining and demonstrating that the Christ had to suffer and rise again from the dead, and saying, "This Jesus whom I preach to you is the Christ." And some of them were persuaded; and a great multitude of the devout Greeks, and not a few of the leading women, joined Paul and Silas. (Acts 17:1-4)

To the north of the Mediterranean Sea lay the land of the Greeks—Athens, Corinth, Thessalonica, and Macedonia. Through the centuries these nations too would come to know the futility of man's kingdoms and the foolishness of his best philosophies. Then they would come to know Christ when the Apostle Paul reached them with the Gospel around AD 52.

The Scientific Contributions of the Greek Empire

Tremendous changes (which would impact the next 2,500 years of world history) came to the world through Greece and Rome. The influence of these cultures on future civilizations is undeniable—some was positive, although most was negative. The immorality of the Greeks was severe, and their world empire lasted barely seven years before it broke down in the wars of the Diadochi. After Alexander's death, his rival generals fought for control of his empire, and it broke up into several pieces.

With every civilization developing in Mesopotamia, Egypt, and China, opportunities for more "division of labor" opened up. While in small rural villages everyone would have to rely on basic farming to survive, in the larger cities men would take time to do the work required to develop medicine, science, mathematics, and technology.

For example, the Egyptians developed the door lock in 2000 BC, the potter's wheel somewhat early on, and glass-making around 1500 BC. The Mesopotamians have the record for the oldest map (dated around 2300 BC, not long after the flood). These early civilizations also produced the first sun dials, and they were the first to divide time units into sixty parts—which would lead to 60-second minutes and 60-minute hours. From what we can tell, the Sumerians and the Babylonians seemed to have preferred a base-60 mathematical system (unlike our base-10 system).

Pythagoras (c. 570 - c. 495 BC)

The Greek philosopher Anaximander provided the first map of the known world around 580 BC. Pythagoras, another Greek philosopher, helped develop geometry. He also proposed the heliocentric theory of the solar system, suggesting that the earth revolved around the sun. Greek engineers developed the water mill which could perform the arduous work of grinding grain into flour without human muscle power (around the 3rd century BC). The Greeks also developed the odometer and the first alarm clock.

It was the common grace of God that enabled these societies to continue long enough to provide the division of labor and innovative technological discoveries that have greatly helped mankind.

Medicine also made considerable progress in the large cities and more developed empires, where doctors could experiment with cures over the years. In the primitive world, false religions pointed their deceived followers to witchdoctors, false gods, demonic spirits, spells, and useless potions in hopes of achieving health and wealth. However, on occasion, some scientists and doctors would take notice of certain regular patterns, purposes, and order hard-wired into God's creation. Consequently, human society found uses for God's natural resources to solve man's scientific and medical problems.

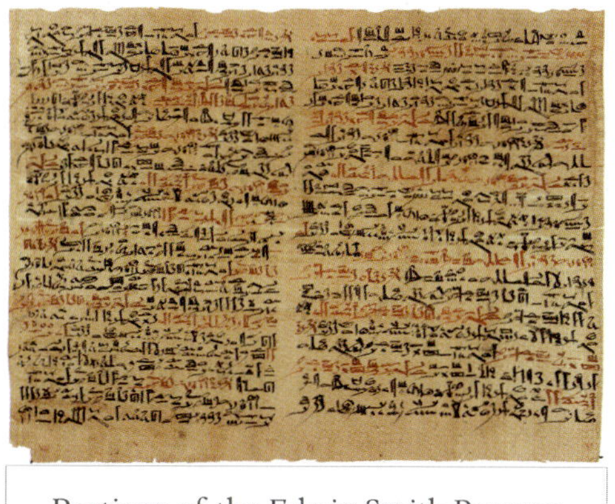
Portions of the Edwin Smith Papyrus

Egyptian doctors developed prosthetic toes. They discovered that garlic, radish, and onion contained natural antibiotics that could fight disease. The Edwin Smith papyrus from around 1600 BC describes various surgical methods used by these Egyptian doctors, including basic eye surgery. They learned that certain forms of blindness could be prevented by feeding the patient liver, which is strong in Vitamin A. Through the centuries, the Egyptians found that honey was a good antiseptic for wounds, willow could treat toothache (in the form of an ancient aspirin), mint could treat gastric problems, and pomegranate could treat parasitic worms; the tannin in the fruit actually paralyzes the worms.

The Greeks, on the other hand, did not improve medicine much. The Greek writer Homer considered the Egyptians the greatest in medical science. Greek scientists philosophized the four humors, which they believed needed to be kept in balance for good health. This philosophy of medicine misled the western world until Christians began developing science and medicine in the later Middle Ages.

The main problem with the Greeks was their philosophy, worldview, and literature. Their learning presented a pretense of intelligence, but underneath it all lay a foundation of falsehood and lies. Humanist thinking attempts to explain the ultimate questions of the universe by man's intuition, void of God's revelation. At first glance it has an appearance of wisdom. However, the thinking turns futile because it is not based in the fear of the Lord or in the understanding of the existence, power, and glory of the true and living God.

At first, very "smart" philosophers try to explain the world, the purpose of life, and ethics by their own ideas. They abandon the notion of the supernatural and a God or gods as relevant to the world and their understanding of the world. With all of their learning and academic institutions, these philosophers and teachers present themselves as quite intelligent and proud. After several hundred years of their writing and educational efforts, their schools will finally throw in the towel admitting to the futility of their intellectual efforts. At this point, the society crosses over from a mindset of proud intelligence to despair. What results is an intellectual suicide and a collapse of the civilization. That is the story of the early experiments in humanism with the Greeks and Romans.

> *"Vanity of vanities," says the Preacher, "All is vanity. . ." And further, my son, be admonished by these. Of making many books there is no end, and much study is wearisome to the flesh.*
>
> *Let us hear the conclusion of the whole matter: Fear God and keep His commandments, For this is man's all. For God will bring every work into judgment, including every secret thing, whether good or evil. (Ecclesiastes 12:8, 12-14)*

The History of Crete and the Early Greek States (2418-800 BC)

European civilization began in Crete more than anywhere else. Having the sea as natural protection against other mainland tribes probably enabled the island's long-term development. Stone tools discovered by archaeologists indicate that the first settlers had to use rudimentary implements as soon as they arrived around 2418 BC (after Babel). Eventually these Minoans would have to import copper from Cyprus, Canaan, and elsewhere. Archaeologists found what may have been the most well-developed civilization in the world among these Cretan Minoans, complete with superb palaces, sewer systems, houses, roads, paintings, and sculptures. After the volcanic eruption occurring in the 16th century BC, the Minoan culture disappeared, and the Mycenaean culture developed, dominating much of the Greek peninsula between 1550 BC and 1100 BC. This was the period of the ancient heroes recorded in mythic form by Homer and other Greek authors. These peoples were highly developed in their construction projects, which included bridges, fortifications, aqueducts, culverts, dams, and roads. The Mycenaeans left no written records, so much of their history is still obscure. However, they did leave a pantheon of gods, all of which dominated in Greece and Rome for the following 1,500 years. For the period coinciding with the Mesopotamian Dark

Map of Greece

Age, the Mycenaeans were militarily aggressive, fighting battles as far away as Troy, located on the northwest corner of modern-day Turkey.

Recently a tablet was discovered in Iklaina, Greece, dating from the 14th century BC. It was a government record of manufactured items obtained from certain persons in the city-state. Such evidence is the first indication that the Mycenaeans possessed political administration, bureaucracy, and economic organization—the first to be found in Europe.

There is not much to learn about these heroic peoples because Homer (and other Greeks) clouded their history in myth. The Mycenaean Kingdom broke down around 1100 BC, probably due to invasion from warring tribes, resulting in the European "Dark Age" which continued for about 500 years.

The earliest Grecian law code was found in Gortyn, a city-state in southern Crete, dating from the 600s BC. Upon reading it, we are immediately shocked at the lax moral standards upheld by the Greeks, at least in comparison to the Persians or Assyrians. Adultery results in a fine of only 100 staters (a Greek monetary unit), and rape requires a similar fine. The rape of a house-slave warranted a fine of only two staters, and infanticide was freely permitted. Here is an example of this early code:

> *A woman who gives birth to a child after leaving her husband having been divorced, she must have it taken to the husband's house before three witnesses. If he will not accept the child, it will be her right to decide whether to bring it up or expose it.*[1]

Law Code Fragments Found in Gortyn

The early Cretans loved their games. Boxing competitions equipped the combatants in helmets, cheek pads, and padded gloves. Acrobats would leap onto the backs of bulls, to the delight of spectators. For the next 4,000 years, the whole world would follow the Cretans and Greeks in sporting competitions of all sorts. The first Olympic Games were held every four years beginning in the year 776 BC—the events included running, jumping and throwing objects, boxing, wrestling, pankration (no-holds-barred punching, gouging, and wrestling), and chariot racing. From ancient carved reliefs, it appears that the Greeks also played something similar to field hockey as well as horseback dodgeball, handball, and lacrosse.

Athletes first competed in loin cloths, and then without clothes after 720 BC. The Greeks continued their immodest displays in the gymnasium into the 4th century AD. During the domination of Antiochus Epiphanes in Judea, some Jews, but not all, resisted the Greek sports in the nude (1 Macc. 1:14). The pagan Olympic Games finally came to an end in the Christian era, during the reign of the Roman emperor, Theodosius II (c. AD 420), after the Temple to the Olympian Zeus caught fire and burned down. The Olympic Games were revived in AD 1896. In the 20th century, immodesty returned to the Western world.

The pagan worldview shows off the body as if man is unashamed of sin, proud, and arrogant before God and man. However, the biblical worldview firmly holds that the uncovered body in public is a shame.

Pass by in naked shame, you inhabitant of Shaphir;
The inhabitant of Zaanan does not go out.
Beth Ezel mourns;
Its place to stand is taken away from you. (Micah 1:11)

Archaeological Site in Gortyn

Formal plays and large-scale entertainment originated with the early Cretans. As early as 1800 BC, theaters in ancient Crete could hold 500 spectators, offering dancing, music, and no doubt some form of drama. The Greeks loved their myths, fantasies, entertainment, and endless diversions. Thus man would seek meaning and joy in his literature and pastimes, but all to no avail. Well before the Greeks had perfected their sports and entertainment (around 1000 BC), King Solomon of Israel wrote of the ultimate futility of these pursuits.

> *I also gathered for myself silver and gold and the special treasures of kings and of the provinces. I acquired male and female singers, the delights of the sons of men, and musical instruments of all kinds.*
>
> *So I became great and excelled more than all who were before me in Jerusalem. Also my wisdom remained with me.*
>
> *Whatever my eyes desired I did not keep from them.*
> *I did not withhold my heart from any pleasure,*
> *For my heart rejoiced in all my labor;*
> *And this was my reward from all my labor.*
> *Then I looked on all the works that my hands had done*
> *And on the labor in which I had toiled;*
> *And indeed all was vanity and grasping for the wind.*
> *There was no profit under the sun. (Ecclesiastes 2:8-11)*

Homer (800 BC)

The Greeks began to break out of the dark age with the literature of the legendary Homer around 800 BC. The two greatest works attributed to him, the *Iliad* and the *Odyssey*, are centered around the siege of Troy, which took place some 380 years earlier. All Greek literature and schooling are rooted in the writings of this blind poet, and hundreds of volumes of commentary and literature have been written on what some consider to be one root of Western civilization.

The skillful weaving of webs and casting of spells through literature is seen in these very early works. They are the first super-hero tales. The gods are presented as fantastic yet morally compromised. They "quarrel like relatives, fornicate like fleas, and share with mankind the need for love and sleep; they do everything human but hunger and die."[2] They are both reverenced and then mocked. Their fantastic nature undermines belief in them. They are exactly what humanists want of their gods. They entertain. They fail—just like the men who try to emulate them. They create a starting point for humans who don't really want to believe in God but who would rather turn themselves into a god. The literature of the Greeks was both ingenious and depraved from its inception. The Christian pastor of the 5th century, Augustine of Hippo rightly referred to the writings of Homer as a "torrent from hell."[3]

Homer

In the providential workings of Almighty God, the Greeks would never organize a military or political state strong enough to govern an empire. However, the Greek culture, language, philosophy, and morals would have far more influence than other cultures on the entire Roman Empire in the centuries to follow.

The Greeks were soiled with the worst forms of sexual immorality early on, with veiled references to the sins of Sodom in Homer and explicit references in Solon (650 BC) and Sappho of Lesbos (600 BC). Somewhere around 514 BC, two homosexuals named Aristogeiton and Harmodius assassinated a civil leader and were executed—though they were later regarded as heroes by those who favored democracy.

In His laws for the Israelites, issued around 1400 BC, God Almighty had cautioned against these sins:

> *If a man lies with a male as he lies with a woman, both of them have committed an abomination. They shall surely be put to death. Their blood shall be upon them. . . . You shall therefore keep all My statutes and all My judgments, and perform them, that the land where I am bringing you to dwell may not vomit you out. And you shall not walk in the statutes of the nation which I am casting out before you; for they commit all these things, and therefore I abhor them. (Leviticus 20:13, 22-23)*

Homer Reciting *The Iliad*

The Rise of the Greeks (1000-480 BC)

How the powerful Mycenaean civilization collapsed is anybody's guess. The gross immorality of the Greeks always seemed to prevent their kingdoms and democracies from lasting very long. The simplest explanation is that God brought them down. Most likely this fun-loving, wealthy, and severely immoral civilization of the Mycenaeans became ready fodder for poorer, warring tribes.

During the dark age that spanned from 1000 BC to 600 BC, the Dorian and the Ionian tribes began settling in the major city-states of Athens and Sparta. Which of these tribes settled which states, where they came from, and when they settled Greece has never been settled by historians. Suffice it to say that by 600 BC four major states or power centers had developed: Macedon, Thessaly, Athens, and Sparta. Darius the Great of Persia invaded and took control of Thessaly and Macedon to the north. However, the Persians were never able to conquer Athens and Sparta further south on the peninsula.

Sparta and Athens would remain the two major Greek powers until the ascension of Philip II of the Argead Dynasty in Macedon in 359 BC. Sparta emerged as a significant power around 650 BC, at the time of King Lycurgus. This city-state's beginnings are important. For centuries the temple at Delphi was considered the most sacred pagan location in all the Grecian states. Men were known to have become possessed by spirits there, and some had disappeared into a cleft in the earth, according to the historian Diodorus. A witch who came to be known as "the Oracle of Delphi" was installed in the temple to communicate with the malevolent and deceptive spirits. She would convulse and speak in strange tones when functioning as the clairvoyant. This was the means by which Lycurgus received his revelation for a body of legislation for Sparta. And the result was the creation of the most evil civic power of the ancient world—at least in recorded history. Sparta would remain a city state conceived by a demon and controlled by a demonic system for about 300 years.

Here was yet another demonstration of the misery produced by sinful people, under the power of the devil himself, prior to the coming of the Savior Christ.

Sparta, Greece

We know that we are of God, and the whole world lies under the sway of the wicked one. (1 John 5:19)

After he had received the oracle and implemented it in Sparta, Lycurgus reputedly starved himself to death as an act of service to the evil state he had created.

At its peak, Sparta and surrounding areas were made up of 200,000 Helots and about 20,000 citizens. The Helots were a subservient tribe that had been conquered and basically enslaved by the Spartan people. The city installed a secret police who would spy on the citizens and kill the Helots at will. When the Helots assisted in fighting Sparta's wars, a city proclamation promised freedom for a select two thousand of them. However, not long afterwards they were all killed and, according to Thucydides, "no one ever knew how each of them perished."[4]

At the birth of every child born in Sparta, the father and a council of inspectors would determine if the offspring was worth keeping. Those infants not meeting the criteria were tossed off the cliff of Mt. Taygetus and left to die. The wicked Lycurgus even encouraged the cross breeding of Spartan wives to gain a "better stock."

The Spartans were known for their gross immodesty, especially among young men and women. Fornication was more or less expected of all, and marriage was delayed for men until they were thirty years of age, by law. Homosexuality was almost universally practiced. At the age of seven, boys were taken from their

Statue of Leonidas in Thermopylae, Greece

parents, never to see each other again. The youths were forced to sleep outside in the cold air with hardly any clothes through the cold winter months. Marriages were forced on young women, and it was expected that the choice of men would not meet with the agreement of the women.

Sickness in Sparta was considered a crime and could result in an early death. It was a cold, miserable, cruel, abusive, and de-humanizing life that could only have been concocted by Satan himself through the witch at Delphi. The goal was to produce a powerful state and a courageous military, but that really didn't happen.

A righteous man regards the life of his animal, but the tender mercies of the wicked are cruel. (Proverbs 12:10)

Like a roaring lion and a charging bear is a wicked ruler over poor people. (Proverbs 28:15)

By 550 BC the Spartans had stopped building and improving their city—they gave up on literature and art. Their tyranny created a static culture that could not build and grow. Over time the Greeks discovered that a focus on the unity of the corporate body was just as bad as the chaos of anarchy produced by an emphasis on the particulars. The Greek government would flip from tyranny to anarchy and would have a hard time finding a happy medium—which could only be secured by a Trinitarian, Christian faith.

The Spartans had a brave talk, and their institutions were geared to manufacture some sort of battlefield courage. Spartan mothers would tell their sons to come back with their shields or lying dead upon them. What they failed to realize was that courage has a hard time operating without love and loyalty. The Spartans refused to help Athens defend Greece from the Persians at the Battle of Marathon in 490 BC. Three hundred Spartans did demonstrate courage at Thermopylae (480 BC). But in 425 BC, a Spartan army surrendered to the Athenians at Sphacteria, and the city state virtually collapsed at the battle of Leuctra in 371 BC.

While courage was certainly not absent from our Savior Lord when He took on the enemies of death and sin at the cross, it was love that drove Him the hardest.

Therefore be imitators of God as dear children. And walk in love, as Christ also has loved us and given Himself for us, an offering and a sacrifice to God for a sweet-smelling aroma. (Ephesians 5:1-2)

Athens (800-428 BC)

Greece possesses an arid climate, with only sixteen inches of precipitation falling annually in Athens (equal to Denver, Colorado). Though the Greeks were successful at trade and the patient cultivation of the grape and olive, the soil is rocky, and only the hardiest of plants will grow and produce. Therefore this country was not a particularly attractive area for agriculture, and the peninsula turned into a refuge for those fleeing tribal warfare in the north.

Sometime between the 1200s and 800s BC, the various towns in the area of Attica were unified under a single government in Athens. Afterwards the political organization of Athens shifted from monarchy to oligarchy—the rule of a few men (probably around 800 BC). In 752 BC, the length of political service for the oligarchy was limited to ten years. A controversy arose around 632 BC when an Olympic champion and political leader named Kyron attempted to seize control of the government. The tyrant was chased out of town and his followers were executed, but this became the pretext for creating a written constitution or law code to which all would henceforth be held. The law code of Draco was issued around 620 BC.

The Acropolis, Athens, Greece

Solon (c. 630-560 BC)

Draco resorted to the death penalty for murder and almost every other crime he could think of. Even petty theft was punished with death. Twenty-five years later the Greeks considered his code too "draconian." Another lawmaker named Solon moderated the code. However, he retained the death penalty for intentional murder—unless the victim had forgiven his murderer before he died. Exceptions were also made for those who killed adulterers (out of jealousy), opponents in athletic competitions, or companions in battle.[5] A successful businessman himself, Solon freed those who had been jailed for political offenses, and he tried to incorporate the principle of "equal treatment under the law." This principle had been enacted by the Israelites 800 years earlier in Deuteronomy 1:

> *You shall not show partiality in judgment; you shall hear the small as well as the great; you shall not be afraid in any man's presence, for the judgment is God's. (Deuteronomy 1:17)*

Solon legalized and taxed prostitution. He assigned a moderate fine for raping a woman, limited the size of dowries, and made it a crime to speak evil of the dead. Solon further implemented a system of graduated property taxation in which the rich had to pay more and the poor paid less, contrary to biblical justice. He also canceled debts and set many slaves free.

Solon's law code is reflective of the modern bureaucratic systems in which he "catches the little flies and lets the big bugs escape." This was a criticism levied against him by Anacharsis of Scythia.[6] Nonetheless, Solon's law code remained in force in various forms for the next 500 years.

All said, Solon did what he could to avoid tyranny. He refused to continue in Athenian government as a dictator. Fair-minded, thoughtful men who did not give way to megalomania were extremely rare in ancient times. Yet this may have been the one sustaining element of Athenian life—all by the common grace of God. Common wisdom and God's basic laws require governments to punish premeditated murder, and little else. To recognize the limitations of civil government to accomplish much more than that is wisdom. To keep the government out of the hands of tyrants is about the best one can do. God's Word gives us the most basic principle of civil government in the simple word to Noah found in Genesis 9:6:

Pericles (c. 495-429 BC)

> *Whoever sheds man's blood,*
> *By man his blood shall be shed;*
> *For in the image of God*
> *He made man. (Genesis 9:6)*

Just as Draco had reacted to Kyron and Solon had reacted against Draco, democracy came about in reaction to another tyrant named Peisistratus. He seized control of Athens on three separate occasions between 561 BC and 527 BC, and took the side of the poor and the middle class against the rich. King Peisistratus confiscated large properties, taxed the rich, and redistributed wealth.

Violence, treachery, and moral scandal took over in Athens and everywhere else the Greeks ruled, almost always connected to the gross confusion of homosexuality. After Peisistratus' death, his younger son was killed by homosexual friends, and the elder son turned Athenian government into a tyranny. The banished

Ancient Theater in Miletus

aristocrats revolted, and with a little help from a Spartan invasion the dictatorship was overthrown. In 507 BC the aristocratic segment of Athens (led by Cleisthenes) formed the first democracy. Each tribe could name one general for the army and elect fifty members of the Council. The assembly could banish any rabble rouser by a vote, and over the next ninety years about ten people were exiled from Athens by democratic vote. This prevented the possibility of anarchy and revolution.

Democracy and the free press have their "drawbacks" to the public men who lead. Moral scandals are more quickly spread around, and the reputations of leaders are quickly ruined. Kings and dictators are usually a little more adept at squelching gossip and maintaining rule and order for a little longer. Pericles, for example, became one of the most honored leaders in Athens during the heyday of Greek democracy (between 467 BC and 428 BC). He enriched the state by taxes and created a large bureaucracy. He built the cultural center of Hellas and richly adorned the Acropolis. In the end, however, Pericles became embroiled in a scandal in which he divorced his wife and took in a live-in girlfriend from Miletus. He died a broken man.

The Greek Philosophers (624-322 BC)

Beware lest anyone cheat you through philosophy and empty deceit, according to the tradition of men, according to the basic principles of the world, and not according to Christ. (Colossians 2:8)

Greek philosophy did not begin in Greece. It began in Miletus in Lydia (located in modern northwestern Turkey). Miletus was the wealthiest city on the Mediterranean, and this increase of wealth meant leisure time to think, write, paint, and entertain. Moreover, Miletus was a metropolitan trading town. Egyptian, Babylonian, and Assyrian mathematics, astronomy, and philosophy were accessible to them. Milesian philosophy was eventually exported to Athens and then to Macedon.

Thales is typically seen as the first of the Greek humanist philosopher-mathematicians. Born in 624 BC in Miletus, he received part of his education in Egypt. He turned geometry into more of a deductive science and successfully predicted an eclipse of the sun for May 28th, 585 BC.

Philosophically, Thales edged towards scientific naturalism. As most humanist scientists would do for the next 2,600 years, this early philosopher dismissed the power of the gods or God. He believed that individual parts of nature had power (and perhaps even souls) in themselves. Thus he did not attribute earthquakes to the power of God or the "gods." He drew the hypothesis that the earth floated on water and that earthquakes occurred when the waves became tempestuous. It wasn't so much the hypothesis that mattered. What really mattered was that this new scientist was dismissing the power of the gods.

The fool has said in his heart,
"There is no God."
They are corrupt,
They have done abominable works,
There is none who does good. (Psalm 14:1)

None of these early scientists and mathematicians of repute were from Greece proper. Anaximander (611-549 BC), also from Lydia (a city of Ionia), thought the sun and moon revolved around the earth. He is the first of the Lydian scientists to

Aesop Was Not a Greek

Of all the literature associated with the Greeks, Aesop's Fables offer some wisdom for life, and even Christians have found them useful. However, Aesop was not a Greek. He was a slave from Lydia (in modern-day northwest Turkey). Many historians think he might have originated from Egypt since his writings show him to be familiar with African animals. He also professed to be "black." Regrettably, Aesop was killed by the Greeks at the demonic, sacred place of Delphi around 564 BC.

propose that man evolved out of less complex life forms. Pythagoras (570-495 BC) also came from Lydia, and it is clear that his mathematical training was obtained in Egypt. He is best known for producing the Pythagorean theorem, a method of determining the length of the hypotenuse of a right triangle. Democritus also came from Teos in Ionia (modern-day Turkey), and he was educated in Egypt and Persia. He was the first to propose the atom as a building block for material creation. Anaxagoras (510-428 BC) was also raised in Lydia (in the city of Clazomenae) while the country was under the control of the Persian Empire. He was a prototypical

Delphi, Greece

humanist scientist, known for founding the study of meteorology, explaining the geometry of eclipses, and postulating that the moon reflects the light of the sun. While he got some things right, Anaxagoras made some fatal errors. Assuming the worldview of naturalism and rejecting the creative power of God, Anaxagoras believed the world and its lifeforms evolved by themselves. Also, both Anaxagoras and Thales believed the earth to be flat. Thus a little scientific knowledge can produce pride, and that pride results in wrong conclusions. As these kind of men manufacture more of their hypotheses, they overstate the case and get some things very wrong.

Professing Themselves to Be Wise, They Become Fools

> *For the wrath of God is revealed from heaven against all ungodliness and unrighteousness of men, who suppress the truth in unrighteousness, because what may be known of God is manifest in them, for God has shown it to them. For since the creation of the world His invisible attributes are clearly seen, being understood by the things that are made, even His eternal power and Godhead, so that they are without excuse, because, although they knew God, they did not glorify Him as God, nor were thankful, but became futile in their thoughts, and their foolish hearts were darkened. Professing to be wise, they became fools, and changed the glory of the incorruptible God into an image made like corruptible man—and birds and four-footed animals and creeping things. Therefore God also gave them up to uncleanness, in the lusts of their hearts, to dishonor their bodies among themselves. (Romans 1:18-24)*

Describing the pagan Greek and Roman world in starkly accurate terms, the apostle points out in Romans 1 how man denies God the Creator and then descends into homosexuality and philosophical foolishness. With these words, he describes the Greek and Roman world to perfection.

Science attempts to answer questions about the world around us. But science cannot answer the ultimate questions. Where did everything come from? What is man's basic problem? What is real? How do we know truth, and how can we be sure that something is true? As man through science began to explain nature and

Socrates (c. 470-399 BC)

the natural processes occurring around him, he became very sure of himself. He thought he could answer the ultimate questions all by himself. That became the business of the philosophers.

The first of the philosophers was Xenophanes (570-475 BC) of Ionia. He was critical of the Greek gods and suggested that there must be "One god, greatest among gods and humans, like mortals neither in form nor in thought."[7] He also deduced from the existence of fossils around the world that a flood must at one time have covered the whole world.

Parmenides came next (born around 515 BC) and was possibly tutored by Xenophanes in his younger years. Like Xenophanes, he rejected the Greek gods as real beings; however, neither of these early philosophers distinguished God from everything else in the universe. Parmenides' basic philosophy (or religion) was simply this: "All things are one, and never change." Thus he rejected the idea that anything could move. Of course, this is foolishness. We see movement all around us.

Parmenides' student Zeno agreed that motion was not possible if everything is one unity—one gigantic fixed blob of matter. Zeno thought motion could not exist because distance is made up of an infinite number of sub-distances, and it would take an infinite amount of time to travel across these infinite sub-distances. But dividing reality into many disconnected pieces like this would deny the unity of reality. There are problems with a conception of reality as being fragmented pieces, but there is also a problem with a conception of reality being motionless and an absolute unity. Only the Trinitarian view of reality, in which God is one and God is three persons, could resolve this impossible conundrum. However, the humanist mind could not come up with this explanation without God's revelation.

Heraclitus (535-475 BC) proposed something the complete opposite of Parmenides. He suggested that everything is moving constantly and "nothing remains still."

Long after the early mathematicians and scientists had done their work in Lydia, Greek philosophy proper finally came to its own with Socrates (470-399 BC), who was raised near Athens and spent his entire life philosophizing and teaching in the city of Athens. Socrates did not claim to possess a fundamental philosophy. He did not adhere to any particular view of reality. He was mostly a skeptic, although he acted like he was searching for answers in the fields of ethics and politics. "Professing to be wise, they became fools" (Rom. 1:22). Socrates occasionally even admitted to knowing nothing.

Alcibiades Being Taught by Socrates

Socrates opposed the idea of democracy, preferring that society be run by wise philosophers. Yet he questioned philosophers. His method of learning was by the "Socratic method" of question and answer. He pushed for clarity in definitions of terms. He insisted on consistency in thought, and set himself up to weed out contradictions in the thinking of his students. He liked to classify things and organize thoughts from the general to the more specific, and then identify specific distinctions.

Socrates comes across as a relativist—not settling for anything as really true. He was supportive of homosexuality, if not a homosexual himself. He was accused of "questioning and confuting everybody."[8] To which Socrates replied, "The god compels me to be a midwife, but forbids me to bring forth."[9] This means that he could not discover any knowledge for himself but hoped he could help someone else bring it forth.

Socrates' troubles began when his friend asked the witch at Delphi who was the wisest man in Athens. The witch pointed to Socrates. For a while Socrates seriously wrestled with this. He knew he was ignorant, and he finally had to conclude that everyone else in Athens must have been extremely ignorant (if he was to be the wisest of them). This did not bode well with the prominent, proud Athenians who were pretty sure they were smart, and the philosopher was put on trial. He was convicted of dishonoring the gods of the city and was sentenced to death by poison.

Despite all that is known of this Greek philosopher, humanists still choose to regard Socrates as the foundation piece of Western civilization and philosophy. Sadly, Socrates' students were not able to bring forth knowledge either. Only by the revelation of God could true knowledge be found to understand reality, ourselves, our world, ethics, and salvation. Three deformed schools developed in Athens out of the teaching of Socrates—all wrong, all wandering about seeking ultimate truth or at least professing to seek for it.

Illustration of Diogenes (c. 412-323 BC)

Diogenes (412-323 BC) developed the philosophy of the Cynics. These misguided people were similar to modern hippies. They rejected marriage and would only associate with prostitutes. They lived like animals and preferred death over life as well as suicide as a means of death. Like Socrates, Diogenes denied the possibility of answering the ultimate questions relating to reality. His was a hopeless philosophy.

Plato (428-348 BC) tried to better understand reality, which he believed to be composed only of ideas. In Plato's view, the material world is only a shadow—not real. God is only an idea, not a person. He is not three persons and one God. There is flux in the world of sense (the physical world), but this world is not real. There is no motion, only changelessness in the realm of ideas.

Plato (428-348 BC)

When it came to ethics and politics, Plato suggested a utopian, bureaucratic government—one that orders all things like the communist and socialist governments of the 20th century. He theorized a society in which men and women come together for temporary relationships—not marriage. Children would be raised and educated by the bureaucrats, and in his words, "no father shall know his child, and no child shall know his father."[10] Plato also proposed the squelching of all free speech, and he wanted an egalitarian society in which men and women are all employed by a government run by philosopher kings. The family is abolished and only the state remains. This was supposed to be the great salvation of the human race. Of course, all of this is based on the assumption that man does not have a problem with sin. Therefore Plato hoped that very smart bureaucrats given absolute power to control a nation would produce the most beautiful utopia on earth. The opposite turned out to be the case. All of this philosophy did Athens no good, for the Peloponnesian wars had decimated the Greek city states by 401 BC.

Professing themselves to be wise, they became fools.

> *For Jews request a sign, and Greeks seek after wisdom; but we preach Christ crucified, to the Jews a stumbling block and to the Greeks foolishness, but to those who are called, both Jews and Greeks, Christ the power of God and the wisdom of God. Because the foolishness of God is wiser than men, and the weakness of God is stronger than men. (1 Corinthians 1:22-25)*

Aristotle's (384-322 BC) philosophy was probably worse than Plato's. Martin Luther, the Christian reformer of the 16th century, referred to him as a "devil" incarnate.

Aristotle (384-322 BC)

Two thousand years before Charles Darwin wreaked his damage on the modern world, Aristotle spoke of the ape as an intermediate form between man and other animals. He wrote that "Nature proceeds little by little from things lifeless to animal life . . ."[11] He was as wrong about that as he was about eels generating spontaneously and mice dying from drinking water in the summertime. Aristotle preferred a form of knowledge that rested entirely upon scientific observation. This is insufficient knowledge, however—especially when it comes to determining right and wrong, political rights, human psychology, and interpreting scientific data.

Although he spoke of god as a "First Cause Uncaused," Aristotle could not distinguish god from the material creation. He taught that god is energy and that all forces in the universe are a continuation of this god force. By failing to distinguish God from the created world, this new worldview became worse than the old polytheistic form. Before long man begins to think of himself as not distinct from god. And when man comes to think of himself as god, this becomes the most dangerous doctrine of all.

Aristotle's ethics are likewise bad. He defined that which is good and right as that which makes man happy. This is a slippery definition and entirely unhelpful. What is happiness? How do we know what would make us happy or what would produce the most good? Of course, without God's revelation, we would have no sure way of knowing.

His work on ethics allowed for homosexuality. Winning fame and honor was the highest end for man, according to Aristotle, and he said, "modesty [humility] is not a virtue."[12] The fear of God was not important, and humility was to be discarded. When it came to ethics, Aristotle got it wrong.

By humility and the fear of the LORD are riches and honor and life. (Proverbs 22:4)

Like Plato, Aristotle wanted to turn education of children over to the state, and he stated that "All [citizens] belong to the state and are each of them a part of the state."[13]

All of these Greek philosophers concluded that man is the measure of all things and that man is the ultimate determinant of his own truth. This is the religion of humanism, and it is usually preached in the religious temples called "colleges and universities." Conversely, the Christian faith teaches that God is the measure and the ultimate source of truth, reality, and ethics. We learn what is true and what is right and wrong from His Word revealed to us in the Old and New Testaments.

Sanctify them by Your truth. Your word is truth. (John 17:17)

The entirety of Your word is truth,
And every one of Your righteous judgments endures forever. (Psalm 119:160)

The Greek Worldview

In the end, however, it is always the cynicism, skepticism, relativism, and satire that wins out in humanist societies. Although a facade or pretense of optimism may continue for a while, pessimism always inevitably comes to dominate.

When society admits there is no possibility of knowing any truth for sure, then the literature and the stage plays will eventually be reduced to satire. Entertainers will mock everything in the comedy. This is what we see with Aristophanes. Then the tragic dramatists like Sophocles (495-405 BC) and Euripides (480-406 BC) present a world where fate rules the day. Man is reduced to a helpless pawn moved around on a chessboard by the greater powers of the universe. It is a cheap and easy way to remove human responsibility for sin. It is a philosophical sleight of hand to dispense with guilt for our sin. Man is seen as unaccountable for his sins and a victim of amoral forces. The humanist's perspective ultimately produces a despairing, hopeless world.

Could the final words of any stage play be more depressing than these from Sophocles' *Oedipus Rex*?

Chorus: All the generations of mortal man add up to nothing!
Show me the man whose happiness was anything more than illusion
Followed by disillusion.
Here is the instance, here is Oedipus, here is the reason
Why I will call no mortal creature happy . . .

Oedipus the Blind King Commends His Children to the Gods

What fate has come to me? . . .

Chorus: Unspeakable to mortal ear,
Too terrible for eyes to see.

Oedipus: O dark intolerable inescapable night that has no day! . . .

Chorus: Sons and daughters of Thebes, behold: this was Oedipus,
Greatest of men; he held the key to the deepest mysteries;
Was envied by all his fellow-men for his great prosperity;
Behold, what a full tide of misfortune swept over his head.
Then learn that mortal man must always look to his ending,
And none can be called happy until that day when he carries
His happiness down to the grave in peace.[14]

Such tragedies and satirical comedies were revived in the modern humanist renaissance with William Shakespeare, Christopher Marlowe, and others. Most modern stage plays, movies, and television programs also replicate this anti-Christian worldview.

Christian literature cannot and will not descend into tragedy. We cannot assume that the universe is hostile to man. We cannot relieve man of moral responsibility by blaming everything on the "fates" as the Greeks did. We must never think that evil can conquer good. Indeed, God can turn that which is evil towards a good end by His sovereign will while still allowing for the free actions of men. This is what He did at the cross of Christ, which could have been described as the arch crime of history, the most evil deed ever performed upon the most righteous man who ever lived. What some could have thought to be the worst week in the history of the world turned out to be the greatest. That was not a tragedy. It was the greatest victory in all the universe, in all of history!

> *Men of Israel, hear these words: Jesus of Nazareth, a Man attested by God to you by miracles, wonders, and signs which God did through Him in your midst, as you yourselves also know—Him, being delivered by the determined purpose and foreknowledge of God, you have taken by lawless hands, have crucified, and put to death; whom God raised up, having loosed the pains of death, because it was not possible that He should be held by it. (Acts 2:22-24)*

The Gross Immorality of the Greeks

As a result of intellectual pride and pseudo-philosophical justification of wicked behavior, the Greeks turned out to be the most immoral of the major ancient civilizations.

Civil war was the constant norm. Murder and treachery never ceased over centuries of Greek governance. After defeating the Persians, the Greeks immediately turned on themselves in the Peloponnesian Wars. They killed each other by a thousand battles—as one secular historian put it, this was one "prolonged national suicide."[15]

The Greeks tolerated all forms of prostitution in practically every city. Girls and boys were sold like dogs in the slave markets. The perversion of homosexuality

Ruins of Apollos Temple in Corinth

was everywhere—openly accepted in Sparta, Crete, Thebes, Athens, and Macedon, and endorsed by Plato and just about every other Greek writer.

Directly between Sparta and Athens, the city of Corinth resided on the Gulf of Corinth. There on the cliff overlooking the ocean waters sat the Temple of Aphrodite—where a thousand religious prostitutes would collect money for the false goddess. "Corinthian" was a word known around the Mediterranean as synonymous with prostitution.

Such was the pitch blackness of the world before Christ, the Light of the world, arrived. These were the conditions from which the Ephesian and Corinthian Christians would be redeemed.

> *. . . in which you once walked according to the course of this world, according to the prince of the power of the air, the spirit who now works in the sons of disobedience, among whom also we all once conducted ourselves in the lusts of our flesh, fulfilling the desires of the flesh and of the mind, and were by nature children of wrath, just as the others. (Ephesians 2:2-3)*

Do you not know that the unrighteous will not inherit the kingdom of God? Do not be deceived. Neither fornicators, nor idolaters, nor adulterers, nor homosexuals, nor sodomites, nor thieves, nor covetous, nor drunkards, nor revilers, nor extortioners will inherit the kingdom of God. And such were some of you [Corinthians]. But you were washed, but you were sanctified, but you were justified in the name of the Lord Jesus and by the Spirit of our God. (1 Corinthians 6:9-11)

The Collapse of Athens and Sparta (466-192 BC)

As soon as Xerxes conceded his loss at Eurymedon in 466 BC, the Greek states were consumed by inner conflicts with rebellions in Aegina (457 BC), Euboea (446 BC), and Samos (440 BC). The Peloponnesian Wars fought between the tiny Athenian Empire and that of Sparta and the Peloponnesian League lasted from 431-404 BC. At the same time Sparta was dealing with revolts from the Helots.

Towards the end, the Spartans led by Lysander won a key sea battle against the Athenians. The Greek democracies were overthrown and oligarchic governments were installed. Athens itself was besieged, and after three months the city was taken. With the death of Socrates, freedom of speech and thought declined, and the Golden Age of Greece was over. Two-thirds of its citizens had been killed. The government was bankrupt. The olive trees were burned to the ground. God brought an end to this proud, humanist experiment in the ancient world. Henceforth Greece would open itself to domination from Macedon—and the Romans.

Sparta burned out soon after its ill-gotten victories over Athens. The Spartan army tried invading Thebes in 371 BC, but the attempt was a disastrous failure. This wicked city slowly declined until it was conquered by the Romans in 146 BC.

Macedon (547-336 BC)

Abram dwelt in the land of Canaan, and Lot dwelt in the cities of the plain and pitched his tent even as far as Sodom. But the men of Sodom were exceedingly wicked and sinful against the LORD. (Genesis 13:12-13)

With the breakdown of the Babylonians, Persians, and Greeks, there wasn't much character left among these peoples to unite the Mediterranean world west to east.

However, enough of the Greek military discipline still remained to wage war and develop a little more of the empire that Cyrus and Darius had built 200 years earlier. According to the purposes and workings of God, power would transfer to the hands of Macedonia for a short time.

However, the beginnings of the Macedonian Empire looked a lot like the end of the Persian Empire—the details are sordid and wicked through and through. Alexander the Great wasn't very great. He was a one-hit wonder. He came and went. He had his fifteen minutes of fame. His empire lasted about seven years.

The political evils surrounding the development of the Macedonian Empire were more heinous and horrific than Sparta or Athens, if that were possible.

King Amyntas I ruled from 547 BC to 498 BC. When the Persians threatened to attack and required him to return "earth and water" (a symbol of submission) to the "King of kings" (Darius), Amyntas quickly complied. Alexander I then took the throne in 498 BC and ruled for forty-five years in Macedon. He joined forces with Xerxes I to fight against Athens in the Battle of Plataea in 479 BC. It was a victory for the Greeks, a humiliation for the Macedonians, and the beginning of the end for the Persian Empire.

Alexander I went on to play the Persians against the Greeks and vice-versa for years until he was finally assassinated in 454 BC.

His son Perdiccas took the throne, ruling from 454 BC to 413 BC. Depending on which alternative was more politically expedient, he aligned himself with different sides in the Peloponnesian Wars between Athens and Sparta. He too was murdered by an illegitimate son, Archelaus, in which homosexual allegiances were involved.

After that, Archelaus was also murdered by a homosexual cohort in 399 BC during a hunting expedition. More murder and mayhem continued in the Macedonian court in the successive reigns of Orestes (399-398 BC), Aeropus II (398-395 BC), Amyntas II (395-394 BC), Amyntas III (393-370 BC), Alexander II (370-367 BC), Ptolemy (367-365 BC), and Perdiccas III (365-359 BC). Almost all were assassinated. Alexander II was murdered by his cousin Ptolemy, who was then killed by Perdiccas (Alexander's brother). Three years later, Perdiccas III was killed in battle. Philip II (Alexander and Perdiccas' brother) had to eliminate two of his half-brothers before he could secure his place on the throne of Macedonia. By the time Philip took the throne in 359 BC, he had figured out that the only way to avoid assassination would be to involve the nation in some imperialistic war in

Coinage Depicting Alexander the Great (356-323 BC)

which attention was diverted to the killing of other tribes and peoples. Philip II was finally murdered in the midst of yet another homosexual tryst in 336 BC. This was the terrible family situation into which Alexander the Great was born.

> *Do not envy the oppressor,*
> *And choose none of his ways;*
> *For the perverse person is an abomination to the LORD,*
> *But His secret counsel is with the upright.*
> *The curse of the LORD is on the house of the wicked,*
> *But He blesses the home of the just. (Proverbs 3:31-33)*

Alexander and Aristotle

Alexander received his education from Aristotle, who himself was born in Macedon. Having grown up with Philip, Alexander's father, Aristotle departed for Athens at seventeen years of age. He studied under Plato and pursued a teaching career for twenty years before returning to Macedonia. This tutor taught the young Alexander philosophy, ethics, politics, observational science, and basic medical skills. Later Alexander would erect a monument to his teacher, on which he inscribed these words:

Alexander set up this portrait of the divine Aristotle, son of Nicomachus, fountain of all wisdom.[16]

Such statements illustrate just how proud and how certain these men were of their own wisdom and learning. Ascribing deity to man and the source of knowledge to a human philosopher is the fount of all foolishness and evil. Only Christ Jesus the Lord is the fount of all wisdom:

. . . in [Christ] are hidden all the treasures of wisdom and knowledge. (Colossians 2:3)

The Macedonian Empire Under Philip II (359-336 BC)

Phillip II of Macedon (c. 382-336 BC)

The beginnings of the Macedonian Empire arrived with Philip II and his military-mindedness and preparedness. He drilled his soldiers relentlessly and developed the military formation called the Phalanx. The phalanx placed the infantry men marching in front of the archers, who marched in front of the catapults and battering rams; if one of these platoons was unable to overcome the enemy, they would leave the task for the others. It was a formidable battle strategy, and quite successful for the Macedonians.

While Athens was overcome by more civil wars and revolts with surrounding city states, Philip took full advantage of the situation and began grabbing control of the other cities throughout Macedonia. Philip fought successful battles against the Illyrians to the north and the Thracians to the northeast (359-356 BC). He conquered the Thracian city of Crenides in 356 BC and changed its name to Philippi. Four hundred years later the Apostle Paul would plant a church in this city. One of his epistles is also addressed to the Philippians.

In 353 BC Philip moved south through Thessaly, and by 338 BC he had reached the gates of Thebes, forty miles to the northwest of Athens. Philip allowed his eighteen-year-old son Alexander to lead the cavalry in the ensuing battle, and the Greeks didn't stand a chance. The Macedonian king treated the Athenians with fairness and a degree of mercy. He enforced an autonomy for each city to ensure that they would not unify against Macedonia, and he required that each city state provide men and arms for the Macedonian army.

Philip's reign did not last long. Shortly before his death, he drew a sword on his son in a drunken party—almost killing him. The two things Alexander's father taught his son were to kill and to drink. Both of these Alexander accomplished with a reckless and unrelenting zeal during the few years that followed—before he drank himself to death.

Alexander "The Great" (356-323 BC)

To this day, Alexander III of Macedonia is considered by many as the greatest man in history. Indeed, he is fallen man's ideal man. Some call him the greatest military general who ever lived. There are more biographies written on this man than any other in history. Alexander wanted to rule the world, but even more so he wanted to fight. The most literate people of the Mediterranean world, the Greeks, ensured that the stories of Alexander were told everywhere for a very long time. He became a legend and is still known the world over as "Alexander the Great."

However, Alexander of Macedonia was not great. He fought wars against broken-down, worn-out empires like Persia and the Greeks. He fought more primitive tribes in India. His rule over what used to be the Persian empire was brief and inconsequential. He was a drunkard, a violent man prone to losing his temper, an arrogant narcissist, a cruel tyrant, and probably a homosexual. As one historian put it, "if he were alive today, he would be condemned as a war criminal."[17] Alexander preferred war over everything else, and "his mind never knew an hour of peace."[18] More than anything else in the world, Alexander hated to lose.

Detail from Mosaic Below

As soon as he ascended to power, Alexander decapitated his political enemies and marched off to Thebes in order to quell any potential revolts in Greece. He slaughtered an Illyrian army that attempted to shake off Macedonian control. When Thebes rebelled in 336 BC, he burned the city to the ground and sold off the remaining inhabitants as slaves. All of Greece acknowledged allegiance to him except Sparta. Returning to Macedon, Alexander discovered the state treasury empty. He then borrowed 800 talents ($5 million) and set off with his army of 50,000 men to conquer the world.

Mosaic from Pompeii, Depicting Alexander at the Battle of Issus (333 BC)

Alexander handily beat Darius III and his Persian army of 60,000 men at Issus (in modern-day Turkey) in 333 BC. Moving further south, he laid siege to Tyre. It was a grueling battle that resulted in the destruction of this thousand-year-old city. There Alexander's men massacred 8,000 citizens and sold 30,000 into slavery. At the siege of the Philistine city of Gaza, he killed every man in the city and dragged the king about by his chariot until he was dead. He was welcomed in Egypt as a great liberator from the Persians and later, equally welcomed into Elam where he helped himself to Darius's vaults of 50,000 talents of gold ($300,000,000).

After Alexander refused three diplomatic offers from Darius III, the Persians came against him once more at Gaugamela (in modern-day Iraqi Kurdistan) on October 1st, 331 BC. Once more the Macedonians were outnumbered, but Alexander's superior light cavalry won the day. Darius III fled the battle scene before the battle was ended, and in the end was killed by one of his own relatives. This was the decisive battle securing Persian territory for Alexander.

When he attempted to overcome the Scythians and Sogdians at the far northeastern corner of Persia (or modern Iran), he met considerable resistance from men attempting to defend their homelands. Out of pure spite, Alexander burned the villages and killed both women and children by the thousands. These campaigns were nothing new for empires. Cyrus the Great had already subdued the Sogdians in campaigns waged between 536 BC and 549 BC. Not much more was accomplished by the Macedonian troops some 200 years later.

To comfort himself after two years of fruitless battles on the frontier of the Persian Empire (329-328 BC), Alexander would hold drunken parties with his men long into the night. One evening the young soldiers began mocking Alexander's father, Philip, and his soldiers as weak and ineffective. Alexander was spoken of as incomparably better than his father. An older soldier, Cleitus, rose to protest, and as the argument grew more heated, Alexander himself ran the old man through with a spear. Sadly, this was the same old general who had intervened at the battle of the Granicus River as a Persian satrap crept up behind Alexander to deal him a death blow. Cleitus had leaped on the Persian and severed his arm, saving the young commander's life. This was the faithful soldier whom Alexander killed in a drunken rage.

Alexander moved into India in 327 BC. He defeated King Porus on the Indus River and hoped to press on over the Ganges, where he would have faced off with the burgeoning Maurya Empire. This, however did not happen. Alexander's

Alexander Standing Over the Body of Darius After the Battle of Gaugamela

soldiers refused to continue with what appeared to be a wasteful crusade. On the way back from India, plodding through the Gedrosia desert (located in modern Pakistan and Iran), at least ten thousand of his men perished of thirst. When someone discovered a little water, Alexander poured it out on the ground in front of his troops. By this time he was half insane, maddened and frustrated at his failure to realize his dreams. He would not rule the world. God would not let him.

Upon returning to Persia, Alexander married the daughters of Darius III and Artaxerxes, and eighty of his officers also married into Persian families in hopes of uniting the empires. He declared himself to be a god, the "son of Zeus." This was a sacrilege even the pagan Greeks and Persians were reticent to support, but they were too fearful of Alexander not to comply. He sat on a golden throne in Susa dressed in sacred garments. Meanwhile his less-than-impressed army was disintegrating amid conspiracies and resignations.

> *So on a set day Herod, arrayed in royal apparel, sat on his throne and gave an oration to them. And the people kept shouting, "The voice of a god and not of a man!" Then immediately an angel of the Lord struck him, because he did not give glory to God. And he was eaten by worms and died. (Acts 12:21-23)*

Sometime in the summer of 324 BC, Alexander moved his entourage to Ecbatana, where his homosexual cohort Hephaestion died. Terribly distressed by this tragedy, Alexander killed his friend's physician. For hours he cast his own body over the dead corpse, weeping, and for days refused to eat. He sacrificed a tribe of

Cossaeans to Hephaestion's spirit in his attempts to deify the dead man. For the following year he abandoned himself to alcohol, drinking as much as six quarts of wine at a time. After one such drunken evening, Alexander got sick, and he died eleven days later. He wasn't quite thirty-three years of age.

Alexander had reigned over his empire for barely a year when God took his life. At the time of his death, there wasn't much to appreciate about the dissipated emperor, whether judged by Greek or Persian, pagan or Christian. He was a despicable man even to his closest compatriots. He was a megalomaniac, more insane than arrogant at the end.

How often is the lamp of the wicked put out?
How often does their destruction come upon them,
The sorrows God distributes in His anger?
They are like straw before the wind,
And like chaff that a storm carries away. (Job 21:17-18)

This is what the greatest heroes of fallen, natural man look like. What a contrast with the Son of Man in His greatness, mercy, compassion, righteousness, wisdom, and power! Man seeks a true Savior, a true Hero, a true King, and this we find with the Son of God who was to come—324 years later. Whereas Alexander was educated in the paradigm of falsehood and was characterized by pride and wickedness, this King would arrive on a humble donkey's colt and champion the cause of truth, righteousness, and humility. And He would ride prosperously and always win His battles against the ultimate enemies of the human soul. There would be nothing so beautiful, triumphant, or majestic as this true King of kings and His glorious Kingdom.

My heart is overflowing with a good theme;
I recite my composition concerning the King;
My tongue is the pen of a ready writer.

You are fairer than the sons of men;
Grace is poured upon Your lips;
Therefore God has blessed You forever.
Gird Your sword upon Your thigh, O Mighty One,
With Your glory and Your majesty.

And in Your majesty ride prosperously because of truth, humility, and righteousness;
And Your right hand shall teach You awesome things.
Your arrows are sharp in the heart of the King's enemies;
The peoples fall under You.

Your throne, O God, is forever and ever;
A scepter of righteousness is the scepter of Your kingdom.
You love righteousness and hate wickedness;
Therefore God, Your God, has anointed You
With the oil of gladness more than Your companions.
All Your garments are scented with myrrh and aloes and cassia,
Out of the ivory palaces, by which they have made You glad.
Kings' daughters are among Your honorable women;
At Your right hand stands the queen in gold from Ophir. (Psalm 45:1-9)

On the other hand, the life and times of Alexander are perfectly illustrated in the words of the Apostle Paul as he describes the Romans (and Greeks) in Romans 1:

Therefore God also gave them up to uncleanness, in the lusts of their hearts, to dishonor their bodies among themselves, who exchanged the truth of God for the lie, and worshiped and served the creature rather than the Creator, who is blessed forever. Amen.

For this reason God gave them up to vile passions. For even their women exchanged the natural use for what is against nature. Likewise also the men, leaving the natural use of the woman, burned in their lust for one another, men with men committing what is shameful, and receiving in themselves the penalty of their error which was due.

And even as they did not like to retain God in their knowledge, God gave them over to a debased mind, to do those things which are not fitting; being filled with all unrighteousness, sexual immorality, wickedness, covetousness, maliciousness; full of envy, murder, strife, deceit, evil-mindedness; they are whisperers, backbiters, haters of God, violent, proud, boasters, inventors of evil things, disobedient to parents, undiscerning, untrustworthy, unloving, unforgiving, unmerciful; who, knowing the righteous judgment of God, that those who practice such things are deserving of death, not only do the same but also approve of those who practice them. (Romans 1:24-32)

The Decline of Greece

In God's good providence, the man-glorifying Grecian world would prove itself a miserable failure well before the coming of the true Messiah of God. The ideas produced by the best and brightest of the proud philosophers would turn out futile and bankrupt.

By the 200s BC, Greece had given way to an extremely toxic, skeptical atheism much like the 20th century West following the humanist renaissance. Popular opinion held that Zeus had died in the Cretan wars. As the kings deified themselves and were deified in the minds of their citizens, the gods became less important to Greek society. Weird mystery religions predominated.

What little interest there was in real observational science faded quickly. Astrology replaced astronomy. Effeminacy became the rule of the day. Men shaved their beards. Homosexuality was even more common. The pursuit of pleasure was all that mattered now, especially for the upper class. Women sought emancipation from motherhood, and abortion became socially acceptable. The majority of infants were killed or left out to die. Poseidippus reported that, "Even a rich man always exposes a daughter."[19] This was the practice of 99% of Greek families. This pattern has been repeated throughout the world since the mid 20th century, with the legalization of abortion.

The birth rate among the ancient Greeks dropped below the replacement level to 1.85 in Miletus, a phenomenon that has returned to the Western world in the early 21st century. "At Eretria only one family in twelve had two sons, hardly any had two daughters."[20] The philosophers of the day almost universally spoke favorably of infanticide in order to control population.

Around 150 BC, Polybius recorded that "The whole of Greece has been subject to a low birth rate and a general decrease of population, owing to which cities have become deserted and the land has ceased to yield fruit, . . . men had fallen into such a state of luxury, avarice, and indolence that they did not wish to marry, or, if they married, to rear the children born to them, or at most but one or two of them . . ."[21]

Thus abortion, infanticide, birth implosions, and homosexuality become the marks of a hopeless, dying humanist culture. However, this would not be the end of Greece. A true Savior was to come, and the Gospel would reach Athens by the preaching of the Apostle Paul around AD 52. The inevitable conclusion

Acropolis of Lindos, Greece

to these many accounts of broken cultures and bankrupt civilizations was this: only the Messiah of God could save them. With the coming of the Christian age, the predominance of abortion and homosexuality would disappear for nearly two thousand years. Indeed, Christ came to save individuals from sin and the devil, but He also came to save peoples and nations as they are made His disciples over the centuries. He came to save, not by civil government, but by the Gospel. In the words of the apostle:

> *For I am not ashamed of the gospel of Christ, for it is the power of God to salvation for everyone who believes, for the Jew first and also for the Greek. (Romans 1:16)*

Corfu, Greece

Timeline Review

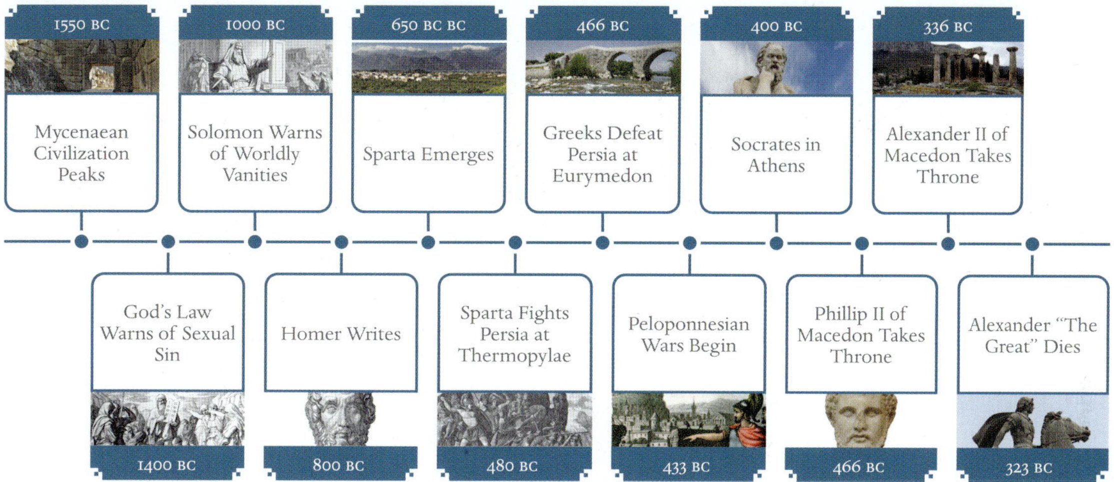

Chapter XIII Prayer

Almighty God, and Father in Heaven,

Our Father in Heaven, almighty sovereign God over the nations, we praise Your majestic and holy Name. You raise up the humble and You bring down the proud. The wisdom of men is but foolishness in Your eyes. The foolishness of our God is infinitely wiser than man. What a vain and useless thing it is for man to exalt himself against You! For the kingdoms of men survive hardly a year, or even a second from Your vantage point! All the while, You still reside in eternity, the source of all life, unchangeable, still and always infinite in power, wisdom, and goodness. Of the increase and the glory of the Kingdom and government of Your Son there will be no end. Hasten the glorious consummation of this kingdom, and bring down every enemy that opposes His rule. Preserve our families, our churches, and our communities from the destruction that comes by man's pride. While nations crumble around us, strengthen Your church, and may Christ's Kingdom prevail!

In His Name we lift up these petitions and praises,
Amen.

Sunrise Over Masada Fortress
in the Judaean Desert

CHAPTER XIV

The Hellenistic Kingdoms (323-63 BC)

In the third year of the reign of King Belshazzar a vision appeared to me—to me, Daniel—after the one that appeared to me the first time. I saw in the vision, and it so happened while I was looking, that I was in Shushan, the citadel, which is in the province of Elam; and I saw in the vision that I was by the River Ulai. Then I lifted my eyes and saw, and there, standing beside the river, was a ram which had two horns, and the two horns were high; but one was higher than the other, and the higher one came up last. I saw the ram pushing westward, northward, and southward, so that no animal could withstand him; nor was there any that could deliver from his hand, but he did according to his will and became great.

And as I was considering, suddenly a male goat came from the west, across the surface of the whole earth, without touching the ground; and the goat had a notable horn between his eyes. Then he came to the ram that had two horns, which I had seen standing beside the river, and ran at him with furious power. And I saw him confronting the ram; he was moved with rage against him, attacked the ram, and broke his two horns. There was no power in the ram to withstand him, but he cast him down to the ground and trampled him; and there was no one that could deliver the ram from his hand.

> *Therefore the male goat grew very great; but when he became strong, the large horn was broken, and in place of it four notable ones came up toward the four winds of heaven. . . .*
>
> *Then it happened, when I, Daniel, had seen the vision and was seeking the meaning, that suddenly there stood before me one having the appearance of a man. And I heard a man's voice between the banks of the Ulai, who called, and said, "Gabriel, make this man understand the vision." So he came near where I stood, and when he came I was afraid and fell on my face; but he said to me, "Understand, son of man, that the vision refers to the time of the end."*
>
> *Now, as he was speaking with me, I was in a deep sleep with my face to the ground; but he touched me, and stood me upright. And he said, "Look, I am making known to you what shall happen in the latter time of the indignation; for at the appointed time the end shall be. The ram which you saw, having the two horns—they are the kings of Media and Persia. And the male goat is the kingdom of Greece. The large horn that is between its eyes is the first king. As for the broken horn and the four that stood up in its place, four kingdoms shall arise out of that nation, but not with its power." (Daniel 8:1-8, 15-22)*

To assure His people of His sovereign power over the great empires of the earth and their wicked machinations, the Lord provided relevant prophecies concerning the fate of Babylon, Persia, Greece, and Rome through His holy prophets. Daniel is the last of these prophets, receiving God's plans for Persia and Greece in the inter-testamental period concerning events taking place between 400 BC and 100 BC. These prophecies served as a comfort to the people of God to assure them that all things would indeed play out according to His purposes. Even the tyranny of the Seleucids would be well within the plan of our sovereign God.

The Seleucids could very well be referred to as junior tyrants, opposing God and acting out their malice towards God's people in terrible ways. They can hardly compare, however, to the devilish tyranny that would come under Nero and the seven persecutions unleashed upon Christians during the first three centuries of the church.

The interpretation of Daniel's dream in Daniel 8 provided during the reign of Belshazzar of Babylon is pretty straightforward, and may be easily applied to the world events playing out during the period of the Greeks and the Seleucids.

1. The Medo-Persian Empire was made up of two powers—Media to the northwest and Persia to the south. The Median kings Deioces and Cyaxares formed the first empire which was soon overtaken by Cyrus the Great, the Persian from Pasargadae to the south. These were the two horns on Daniel's ram, the second and highest horn belonging to Cyrus and his dynasty.
2. The male goat is the kingdom of Greece—the explicit interpretation is given in verse 21. The horn protruding from the head of this goat is Alexander the Great. He comes quickly and runs at Persia with a "furious power," handily defeating Darius IV at Gaugamela (in modern-day Iraqi Kurdistan). He came so quickly, like a blitzkrieg, that it appeared as if his feet hardly touched the ground—seizing control of what used to be the mighty Persian Empire.
3. However, when Alexander the Great (the male goat's horn) is at the very zenith of his power, he breaks into pieces—dead at thirty-two years of age.
4. After Alexander's death, his generals and assorted other powerful interests fight for control of the empire (323-275 BC). These were known as the Diadochi wars. It was a chaotic, bloody mess for forty-seven years. Alexander's newborn son was installed as king, but he was killed in 309 BC. By the turn of the 3rd century before Christ, the empire had split into fourteen kingdoms. At the battle of Ipsus (located in central Turkey) in 301 BC, Antigonus I Monophthalmus of Phrygia and his son Demetrius I of Macedon led their troops against three of Alexander's other generals: Cassander of Macedon, Lysimachus of Thrace, and Seleucus I Nicator, governor of Babylonia and Persia at the time. Both sides used the formidable strategy of the phalanx which had proved so useful in the wars conducted by Alexander and his father, Phillip of Macedon. In these battles, both sides were equipped with war elephants, cavalry, and about 75,000 men each. The side of Antigonus and Demetrius lost, and the victors divided the empire into four parts. Cassander took over Macedonia, Ptolemy ruled Egypt, Lysimachus was given Asia Minor to rule, and Seleucus ruled Persia, Syria, and Israel. These circumstances are recorded by the historians Diodorus and Plutarch and are considered indisputable.
5. Out of the fourth horn of Seleucus would arise a relatively little horn—a tyrant who would defile the temple of God in Jerusalem and cause the sacrifices to cease. He would do his best to destroy "the holy people" of God (Dan. 8:11, 24). His name was Antiochus Epiphanes (175-164 BC).

The Prophet Daniel

Daniel's prophecy turned out to be absolutely accurate, and during these periods of serious upheaval, the people of God were comforted to know that all of these world events were playing out exactly as the Lord God had planned.

The parts of the empire including eastern Persia, India, and Afghanistan were quickly lost, as they had never really been secured by Alexander anyway.

The flimsy empire of Alexander "the Great" was no more. However, these four fragments of the empire would drag along for 265 years. Conflicts would ravage the Mediterranean nations, especially from Syria to Egypt, for almost the whole time. These were no easy times, as Israel would be ground zero, the center of the conflict for these great powers. Both the spiritual and physical condition of the people of God would deteriorate during this inter-testamental period.

Pre-Seleucid Israel

Ezra Reads the Law

First work on the temple rebuilding project in Judea got under way in 536 BC, but this didn't last long due to opposition from the Samaritans (Ezra 3:8-13; 4:1-24; 5:16). Sheshbazzar was appointed governor over Judah (Ezra 1:7-8). However, interest in the temple quickly waned, and the prophets Haggai and Zechariah addressed this religious indifference in their prophetic rebukes. The temple was finally completed in 516 BC, thanks to the leadership of Zerubbabel, the governor appointed by Cyrus to rule over the returned exiles (Ezra 6:15-22).

During the reign of Artaxerxes I (the son of Xerxes), Ezra was commissioned by the Persian king to beautify the worship of God and was given gold and silver contributions from the king for the Jewish temple. Assurances were provided the priests and Levites that they would be exempted from taxation in this decree contained in Ezra 7:

Artaxerxes, king of kings,
To Ezra the priest, a scribe of the Law of the God of heaven:
Perfect peace, and so forth.

I issue a decree that all those of the people of Israel and the priests and Levites in my realm, who volunteer to go up to Jerusalem, may go with you. And whereas you are being sent by the king and his seven counselors to inquire concerning Judah and Jerusalem, with regard to the Law of your God which is in your hand; and

> *whereas you are to carry the silver and gold which the king and his counselors have freely offered to the God of Israel, whose dwelling is in Jerusalem; and whereas all the silver and gold that you may find in all the province of Babylon, along with the freewill offering of the people and the priests, are to be freely offered for the house of their God in Jerusalem—now therefore, be careful to buy with this money bulls, rams, and lambs, with their grain offerings and their drink offerings, and offer them on the altar of the house of your God in Jerusalem. (Ezra 7:12-17)*

Thus, in the year 458 BC, Ezra brought the second major group of exiled Jews back to Jerusalem (Ezra 7:1ff). About this time, the prophet Malachi was warning God's people of their tendency to return to synthesis with the world. Also, Artaxerxes I commissioned his cupbearer, a Jew named Nehemiah, to lead yet another group back into Judea to rebuild the walls of Jerusalem (Neh. 2:1-11; 5:14). Artaxerxes continued his rule until 423 BC. Meanwhile Nehemiah instituted reforms in Judea relating to Sabbath-keeping, the enslavement of fellow Jews, and mixed marriages around 432 BC.

For a period of 130 years no history of the Jews, either secular or sacred, is available to us. When Alexander the Great marched through Judea, it appears that the Jews did their best to stay on friendly terms with him. At first the Samaritans towards the north (the Jews who had intermarried with various tribes and settled in Samaria) submitted to Alexander. Later, however, they rebelled and burned Alexander's governor alive. The Macedonian king did not take kindly to this—he returned and burned their city to the ground.

Seleucus Nicator (c. 358-281 BC)

Seleucus Nicator was probably the most renowned of Alexander's generals, and he built a city at the junction of the Tigris and Euphrates rivers. Seleucia became a major city. Seleucus Nicator also founded the city of Antioch in Syria, which he made his capital.

His attempt to take on the formidable Maurya Empire of India (305-303 BC) was soundly defeated. He tried to expand his rule over Macedon and Thrace but was assassinated during the campaign in 281 BC. His sons and grandsons would continue ruling the Seleucid Empire, all the while feuding with the Ptolemies in Egypt over the land of Israel. Daniel 11 prophesies about the warfare between kings of the North (Seleucids) and the kings of the South (Ptolemies).

Seleucus' son Antiochus Soter reigned from 281 to 261 BC and referred to himself as the Savior and Ruler of the Universe. Following Antiochus Soter comes Antiochus II Theos or "Antiochus the God" (ruling from 261 to 246 BC). Titles for the kings were becoming increasingly arrogant and blasphemous as these men pretended to take the place of the Christ who was to come. Applying to these wicked kings the titles of the true Messiah, it seems that the devil was offering the world a counterfeit savior and god in the form of the state. Later, the Roman Empire would begin to use similar terms for their emperors. Antiochus II Theos did not act very much like a "god." He was almost perpetually drunk. He divorced his wife, but she later returned to murder his new wife and their newborn son. The God of heaven does not take kindly to these outrageously proud men who fancy themselves gods.

Coin Depicting Antiochus II Theos

> *Let no one deceive you by any means; for that Day will not come unless the falling away comes first, and the man of sin is revealed, the son of perdition, who opposes and exalts himself above all that is called God or that is worshiped, so that he sits as God in the temple of God, showing himself that he is God. . . whom the Lord will consume with the breath of His mouth and destroy with the brightness of His coming. (2 Thessalonians 2:3-4,8)*

Ptolemy II (c. 308-246 BC)

The Jews Under the Ptolemies and the Seleucids (312-142 BC)

From 312-198 BC, Judea was subject to the Ptolemies who ruled from Egypt. During this time, the Jews were given the right of self-government with their own senate and supreme court. However, Greek culture seeped into Judea as well as into Samaria, Gaza, Escalon, Joppa, Damascus, and other surrounding cities. Greek schools and gymnasiums dotted the landscape. The language of the people shifted to Greek. Young Jewish boys were tempted to join in the nude games. The world's temptations had always been a lure to God's people in the Old Testament era, and things weren't any different when it came to the temptations that came with the Greek humanistic philosophy and life.

Ptolemy II obtained a temporary peace with Antiochus II, giving his daughter to the Seleucid in marriage. This did nothing to secure any lasting peace, however (as was previously ordained and foretold in Daniel 11:6).

> *And at the end of some years they shall join forces, for the daughter of the king of the South shall go to the king of the North to make an agreement; but she shall not retain the power of her authority, and neither he nor his authority shall stand; but she shall be given up, with those who brought her, and with him who begot her, and with him who strengthened her in those times. (Daniel 11:6)*

Ptolemy III gained a little ground against the Seleucids but then lost a key battle, as prophesied in Daniel 11:7-10. After him Ptolemy IV won a key battle at Raphia against Antiochus III on June 22nd, 217 BC, as was prophesied in Daniel 11:11-12.

> *And the king of the South shall be moved with rage, and go out and fight with him, with the king of the North, who shall muster a great multitude; but the multitude shall be given into the hand of his enemy. When he has taken away the multitude, his heart will be lifted up; and he will cast down tens of thousands, but he will not prevail. (Daniel 11:11-12)*

Finally, in 198 BC, Antiochus III (grandson of Antiochus II) defeated Ptolemy V and united Judea with the Seleucid empire. This was predicted in Daniel 11:13-14. At first the Jews were supportive of Antiochus, thinking he would release them from their Egyptian yoke. Antiochus III attempted an invasion of Greece but was thwarted by the Romans. This is mentioned in verse 19 of Daniel 11: "Then he shall turn his face toward the fortress of his own land; but he shall stumble and fall, and not be found."

Antiochus IV Epiphanes usurped the throne and killed the rightful heir, an infant at the time, in accordance with verse 21 of Daniel 11: "And in his place shall arise a vile person, to whom they will not give the honor of royalty; but he shall come in peaceably, and seize the kingdom by intrigue."

Then Antiochus Epiphanes invaded Egypt in 170 BC, capturing Ptolemy VI before being expelled by the Romans. It is this man who would bring severe persecution upon the Jews between 170 and 164 BC, as prophesied in Daniel 11:28-32:

> *While returning to his land with great riches, his heart shall be moved against the holy covenant; so he shall do damage and return to his own land. At the appointed time he shall return and go toward the south; but it shall not be like the former or the latter. For ships from Cyprus shall come against him; therefore he shall be grieved, and return in rage against the holy covenant, and do damage. So he shall return and show regard for those who forsake the holy covenant. And forces shall be mustered by him, and they shall defile the sanctuary fortress; then they shall take away the daily sacrifices, and place there the abomination of desolation. Those who do wickedly against the covenant he shall corrupt with flattery; but the people who know their God shall be strong, and carry out great exploits. (Daniel 11:28-32)*

Returning from Egypt after his humiliation, Antiochus Epiphanes set out to "Hellenize" the Jewish people. The book of Second Maccabees, written around 100 BC, testifies to the easy progress made with a people who were not committed to God.

> *[Antiochus Epiphanes] went so far as to found a gymnasium at the very foot of the Citadel, and to fit out the noblest of his young men in the petasos. Godless wretch that he was and no true high priest, Jason set no bounds to his impiety; indeed the hellenizing process reached such a pitch that the priests ceased to show any interest in serving the altar; but, scorning the Temple and neglecting the sacrifices, they would hurry, on the stroke of the gong, to take part in the distribution, forbidden by the Law, of the oil on the exercise ground; setting no store by the honours of their fatherland, they esteemed hellenic glories best of all.* (2 Maccabees 4:12-15)

Antiochus IV Epiphanes (c. 215-164 BC)

The writer of 2 Maccabees admits that these were God's chastisements on the Jews for their infidelity to Him: "Antiochus did not realise that the Lord was temporarily angry at the sins of the inhabitants of the city, hence his unconcern for the holy place" (2 Macc. 5:17).

Antiochus proceeded to crucify all Jews who insisted on circumcising their sons and observing the Sabbath. Worst of all, he set up the "abomination of desolation" in the temple—profaning the ceremonial purity of God's worship. The wicked ruler ordered a daily sacrifice of a swine upon an altar he erected, and dragged other forms of pagan worship into the temple at Jerusalem, as reported in 2 Maccabees 6.

> *The Temple was filled with reveling and debauchery by the gentiles, who took their pleasure with prostitutes and had intercourse with women in the sacred precincts, introducing other indecencies besides. The altar of sacrifice was loaded with victims proscribed by the law as profane. No one might either keep the Sabbath or observe the traditional feasts, or so much as admit to being a Jew. People were driven by harsh compulsion to take part in the monthly ritual meal commemorating the king's birthday; and when a feast of Dionysus occurred, they were forced to wear ivy wreaths and walk in the Dionysiac procession. (2 Maccabees 6:4-7)*

Of course this dastardly insult to their traditions greatly angered the Jews. However, this "abomination of desolation" was, at root, a symbol of God's displeasure with Israel (referenced in Daniel 11:31). The impurity of the heart of Israel after the return from the exile had already been revealed by the prophet Malachi. The Jews were more concerned about the pig than they were about their adulteries (Mal. 3:5), divorces (Mal. 2:16), half-hearted worship of God (Mal. 1:6), oppression of the widow (Mal. 3:5), failure to tithe (Mal. 3:8), and marriages with unbelievers (Mal. 2:11). None of these sins are mentioned in the books of Maccabees. This would become the thrust of Jesus Christ's message to the nation 200 years later. He would condemn the Jews for their externalistic religion, their hardness of heart, their failure to reckon with the heart of God's law, and their displacing God's law with their own traditions. And they would kill the Messiah of God for speaking the truth. These are the words used by Christ to describe these people:

> *Woe to you, scribes and Pharisees, hypocrites! For you pay tithe of mint and anise and cummin, and have neglected the weightier matters of the law: justice and*

mercy and faith. These you ought to have done, without leaving the others undone. Blind guides, who strain out a gnat and swallow a camel! Woe to you scribes and Pharisees, hypocrites! For you cleanse the outside of the cup and dish, but inside they are full of extortion and self-indulgence!" (Matthew 23:23-25)

Upon hints of revolt, Antiochus Epiphanes returned to Judea and unleashed an even worse persecution on the Jews, as recorded in 2 Maccabees 5:

When the king came to hear of what had happened, he concluded that Judaea was in revolt. He therefore marched from Egypt, raging like a wild beast, and began by storming the city. He then ordered his soldiers to cut down without mercy everyone they encountered, and to butcher all who took refuge in their houses. It was a massacre of young and old, a slaughter of women and children, a butchery of young girls and infants. There were eighty thousand victims in the course of those three days, forty thousand dying by violence and as many again being sold into slavery. Not content with this, he had the audacity to enter the holiest Temple in the entire world, with Menelaus, that traitor to the laws and to his country, as his guide; with impure hands he seized the sacred vessels; with impious hands he seized the offerings presented by other kings for the aggrandizement, glory and dignity of the holy place. Holding so high an opinion of himself, Antiochus did not realize that the Lord was temporarily angry at the sins of the inhabitants of the city, hence his unconcern for the holy place. (2 Maccabees 5:11-17)

The persecution of the Jews and this "abomination of desolation" in the temple lasted from 170 to 164 BC—a total of 2,300 days or 6.3 years, according to the prophecy given to Daniel (Dan. 8:13-14). Antiochus Epiphanes died in 164 BC. In 167 BC, a priest named Mattathias and his sons took up arms to resist this horrendous persecution. Mattathias soon died, and was succeeded by his son Judas Maccabee. A brilliant general, Judas won many victories against superior Seleucid armies. But in 161 BC, he made the fateful step of allying his people with the rising power of Rome. The terms of this agreement are recorded in 1 Maccabees 8:

Judas chose Eupolemus, the son of John and grandson of Accos, and Jason son of Eleazar and sent them to Rome to make a treaty of friendship and alliance with the Romans. He did this to eliminate Syrian oppression, since the Jews clearly saw that they were being reduced to slavery. After a long and difficult journey, Eupolemus and Jason reached Rome and entered the Senate. They addressed the assembly in these terms:

> *"Judas Maccabeus, his brothers, and the Jewish people have sent us here to make a mutual defense treaty with you, so that we may be officially recorded as your friends and allies."*

The Romans accepted the proposal, and what follows is a copy of the letter which was engraved on bronze tablets and sent to Jerusalem to remain there as a record of the treaty:

> *May things go well forever for the Romans and for the Jewish nation on land and sea! May they never have enemies, and may they never go to war! But if war is declared first against Rome or any of her allies anywhere, the Jewish nation will come to her aid with wholehearted support, as the situation may require. And to those at war with her, the Jews shall not give or supply food, arms, money, or ships, as was agreed in Rome. The Jews must carry out their obligations without receiving anything in return.*
>
> *In the same way, if war is declared first against the Jewish nation, the Romans will come to their aid with hearty support, as the situation may require. And to their enemies there shall not be given or supplied food, arms, money, or ships, as was agreed in Rome. The Romans must carry out their obligations without deception. (1 Maccabees 8:17-28)*

When it came to trusting God for their safety and defense, Israel would fail the test time and time again. Throughout the Old Testament history of the covenanted people of God, they would look to their alliances with the Assyrians, Egyptians, or Romans instead of trusting in God. The words of Isaiah in 700 BC and Jeremiah in 600 BC were just as applicable in 161 BC:

Thus says the LORD:
"Cursed is the man who trusts in man
And makes flesh his strength,
Whose heart departs from the LORD.

Eleazar in Battle (1 Maccabees 6)

For he shall be like a shrub in the desert,
And shall not see when good comes,
But shall inhabit the parched places in the wilderness,
In a salt land which is not inhabited. (Jeremiah 17:5-6)

"Do not be afraid of the king of Babylon, of whom you are afraid; do not be afraid of him," says the LORD, "for I am with you, to save you and deliver you from his hand. And I will show you mercy, that he may have mercy on you and cause you to return to your own land." But if you say, "We will not dwell in this land," disobeying the voice of the LORD your God, saying, "No, but we will go to the land of Egypt where we shall see no war, nor hear the sound of the trumpet, nor be hungry for bread, and there we

will dwell"—Then hear now the word of the LORD, O remnant of Judah! Thus says the LORD of hosts, the God of Israel: "If you wholly set your faces to enter Egypt, and go to dwell there, then it shall be that the sword which you feared shall overtake you there in the land of Egypt; the famine of which you were afraid shall follow close after you there in Egypt; and there you shall die." (Jeremiah 42:11-16)

Woe to those who go down to Egypt for help,
And rely on horses,
Who trust in chariots because they are many,
And in horsemen because they are very strong,
But who do not look to the Holy One of Israel,
Nor seek the LORD! . . .
Now the Egyptians are men, and not God;
And their horses are flesh, and not spirit.
When the LORD stretches out His hand,
Both he who helps will fall,
And he who is helped will fall down;
They all will perish together. (Isaiah 31:1, 3)

After Judas Maccabee was killed in battle in 160 BC, his brother Jonathan took over and was appointed high priest by a Greek governor. After Jonathan was killed in battle, a third brother, Simon Maccabee, was made king of Judah. The Maccabees won independence for the Jews from Greek tyranny. But they wrongly united the offices of high priest and king in one person. Simon's son John ruled from 135-104 BC. He expanded the borders of his Jewish kingdom, forcibly converting the Edomites to Judaism. Herod the Great would be one of these converted Edomites or Idumeans.

By 100 BC two political parties were vying for power in Judea—the Pharisees and the Sadducees—both representing compromised systems of faith. The Sadducees had been most influenced by the Greeks, and they rejected the idea of an afterlife and a resurrection. Theirs was a humanist faith in the here and now—the present material world only of any real importance. This was a materialistic, naturalistic worldview very similar to what is taught by the secular humanists in schools and universities everywhere today. John Hyrcanus, the son of Simon Maccabee, was a Sadducee.

Death of Judas Maccabeus (190-160 BC)

By 66 BC the Jews reverted to civil war, with Hyrcanus and his brother Aristobulus competing for the throne. Both brothers appealed to Rome for help. The Roman General Pompey intervened, siding with the weaker Hyrcanus against Aristobulus. In 63 BC, Pompey stormed Jerusalem, entered the temple, and placed Judea under tribute to Rome. Once again, the Jews had lost their political independence and were ruled by a foreign power.

When the Christ finally arrived a hundred years later, He did not come as a military commander who would chase the Romans out of Jerusalem. The Jews had bigger problems than political subjugation to a foreign power. Sadly, this nation did not recognize their more radical problem. They told Jesus, "We are Abraham's descendants, and have never been in bondage to anyone" (John 8:33). But He told them, "He who commits sin is a slave of sin" (John 8:34). Then He lowered the boom and defined the real and fundamental problem.

> *A slave does not abide in the house forever, but a son abides forever. Therefore if the Son makes you free, you shall be free indeed. (John 8:35-36)*

What Israel (and the entire world) needed was to be set free from sin. Though the Romans were a tremendously oppressive power, they still allowed some measure of self-rule for the Jews. But sin and Satan were the Tyrant of tyrants, and only the Son of God could set His people free from them.

Conclusion

Thus vast changes transformed the world between 1000 BC and 1 BC. The Mediterranean civilization had turned from a primitive, pagan polytheism into a man-centered, state-worshiping humanism. And God's people had moved from compromising with pagan polytheism to a thin-coated moralism and compromise with the ideologies of humanist Greek philosophers.

After 4,000 years of futile and vain attempts, man had proven to himself the utter failure of every idea and kingdom produced by man. There was no hope to be found in the innumerable false gods of the nations. There was no hope to be found in man and his impressive empires. There was no hope to be found with the covenanted people of God and their kingdom and temple rituals. The only hope for true faith, a sustainable kingdom, real salvation from man's problems, and a

Coastline of the Dead Sea, Israel

transformation of the evil heart of man would be found in the Messiah of God, the true Savior, born about the year AD 1.

> *For unto us a Child is born,*
> *Unto us a Son is given;*
> *And the government will be upon His shoulder.*
> *And His name will be called*
> *Wonderful, Counselor, Mighty God,*
> *Everlasting Father, Prince of Peace.*
> *Of the increase of His government and peace*
> *There will be no end,*
> *Upon the throne of David and over His kingdom,*
> *To order it and establish it with judgment and justice*
> *From that time forward, even forever.*
> *The zeal of the LORD of hosts will perform this. (Isaiah 9:6-7)*

For God's people, these were the years of darkness. This was the true "dark age" in the history of the world. In fact, this would be the third in a series of dark ages, in which revelation ceased and true faith declined. Between 1840 BC and 1440 BC, the Israelites were more or less exiled and enslaved under the powerful Egyptians. After a brief but potent period of revelation of God's power and Word under the ministration of Moses, once again God's people entered a period of darkness. Between 1400 BC and 1000 BC, again the children of Israel synthesized with the pagan religions, and they were dominated by small but powerful nation states. However, with the prophetic age of Samuel, David, Elijah, Isaiah, and the others, there came an age of small revivals. The Kingdom of David initiated. Once more however, after the prophet Malachi revelation is silenced, and the people of God enter a third era in which darkness descended over the world. During this time, the remnant of Judah would find themselves exiled and dominated by the large empires of Babylon, Persia, Greece, the Seleucids, and the Romans.

Each of these dark ages was interrupted by a singular act of divine providence in which a woman had a baby. After 400 years in Egypt, the Book of Exodus opens up with a woman having a baby. The seed of the woman would become the greatest threat to the serpent. The serpent responded by killing the male children in Egypt. Then once again, after 400 years of domination under the surrounding nation-states, in 1 Samuel 1 another woman had a baby. Hannah gave birth to the prophet Samuel, officially opening up a new age of prophecy and the kingdom of David. Following the final dark age extending from 400 BC to AD 1, the Gospels of Matthew, Mark, and Luke open with another woman, Mary, pregnant with a Baby. This time, the Seed of the woman would certainly crush the head of the serpent as was promised.

> *Now in the sixth month the angel Gabriel was sent by God to a city of Galilee named Nazareth, to a virgin betrothed to a man whose name was Joseph, of the house of David. The virgin's name was Mary. And having come in, the angel said to her, "Rejoice, highly favored one, the Lord is with you; blessed are you among women!" But when she saw him, she was troubled at his saying, and considered what manner of greeting this was. Then the angel said to her, "Do not be afraid, Mary, for you have found favor with God. And behold, you will conceive in your womb and bring forth a Son, and shall call His name Jesus. He will be great, and will be called the Son of the Highest; and the Lord God will give Him the throne of His father David. And He will reign over the house of Jacob forever, and of His kingdom there will be no end." (Luke 1:26-33)*

The Sea of Galilee

Timeline Review

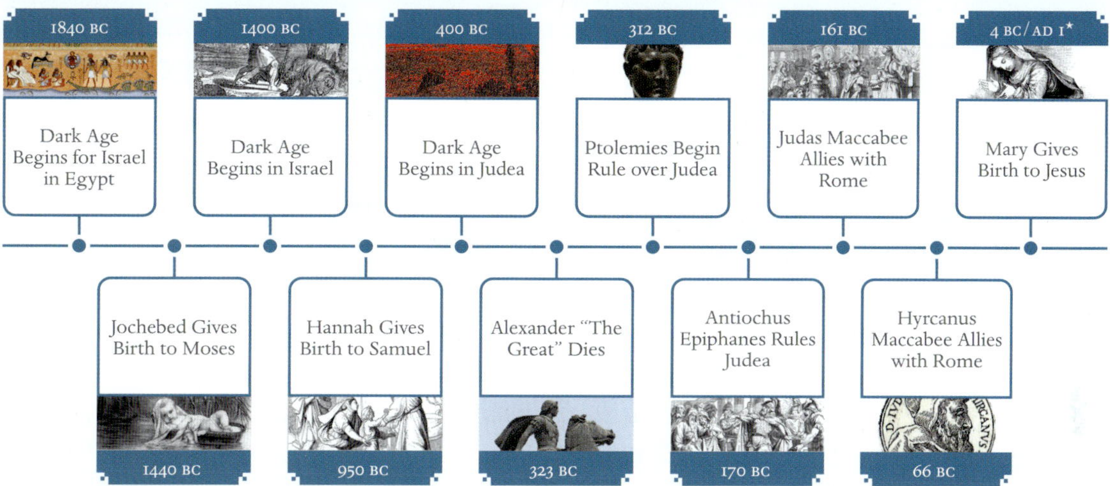

* Historians are divided on what is the most likely date of Christ's birth. Both are included on this timeline.

Chapter XIV Prayer

Our Father, Almighty Sovereign God over all,

We thank You this day that you purposed a tremendous redemption for this world. Not for a moment would the world sink into hopelessness. Indeed, Your promise would always be fulfilled. When prophecy was silent, there was always hope. The seed of the woman always appeared, and the devil could not overcome this. Your plan was being accomplished all through history. Your true redemption was certain, and it would come with the incarnation of Your Son, Your only begotten Son, in the womb of the virgin Mary. Only Your Christ could save us from religious compromise, wicked kingdoms, and the slavery of sin. Today, we praise you for Your salvation! We do not look to human princes and governments to save us. For You are our strength and song, and You have become our salvation. Jesus is our King and He has already come to save us from the enemy of sin, death, and hell. We acknowledge Your King, and we worship Him now!

Amen.

Roman Forum

CHAPTER XV

The Romans: Reaching the Zenith of the Empires (753 BC - AD 33)

But the following night the Lord stood by him and said, "Be of good cheer, Paul; for as you have testified for Me in Jerusalem, so you must also bear witness at Rome." (Acts 23:11)

The gathering spiritual darkness of the pre-Christ world culminated in one particular city and one final empire before the coming of the Messiah. The dragon unleashed his ultimate fury against the Seed by this great power, but he would not prevail. Finally, Christ would prevail against the power of Rome, and the Gospel would come to the city by way of an apostle, in chains.

World history before the coming of Christ consists of a series of rises and declines of the great empires of men. As one empire died out, another would take its place, building off of what the previous kingdom had left. The great statute in Nebuchadnezzar's dream was one entity that subsumed all the kingdoms. As the Egyptian empire rose and fell, God was preparing the Assyrians to take their place. As the Assyrians were gathering strength and then losing strength, in the providence of God the Babylonians were preparing to take their place. As the Babylonians became arrogant and decadent while persecuting God's people, the Lord was staging the Persians to take their place. Then, as the Persians were corrupted, He introduced the Greeks to take their place. And finally, as a fractured Greek empire fumbled with the reins of power, the Romans came in to take their place. And, all the while, the land mass that made up this empire base was increasing in size.

The Expansion of the Great Empires of Man (1700 BC - AD 100)

Empire	Square Miles	Square Kilometers	Approx. Zenith
Babylonian	0.10 million	0.25 million	(1700 BC)
Egyptian	0.14 million	0.39 million	(1400 BC)
Assyrian	0.54 million	1.4 million	(700 BC)
Medo-Persian	2.12 million	5.5 million	(500 BC)
Seleucid	1.5 million	3.9 million	(300 BC)
Roman	1.93 million	5 million	(AD 100)

Then I wished to know the truth about the fourth beast, which was different from all the others, exceedingly dreadful, with its teeth of iron and its nails of bronze, which devoured, broke in pieces, and trampled the residue with its feet; and the ten horns that were on its head, and the other horn which came up, before which three fell, namely, that horn which had eyes and a mouth which spoke pompous words, whose appearance was greater than his fellows.

I was watching; and the same horn was making war against the saints, and prevailing against them, until the Ancient of Days came, and a judgment was made in favor of the saints of the Most High, and the time came for the saints to possess the kingdom.

Thus he said:

"The fourth beast shall be
A fourth kingdom on earth,
Which shall be different from all other kingdoms,
And shall devour the whole earth,
Trample it and break it in pieces.
The ten horns are ten kings
Who shall arise from this kingdom.
And another shall rise after them;
He shall be different from the first ones,
And shall subdue three kings.
He shall speak pompous words against the Most High,
Shall persecute the saints of the Most High,
And shall intend to change times and law.
Then the saints shall be given into his hand
For a time and times and half a time.
But the court shall be seated,
And they shall take away his dominion,
To consume and destroy it forever.
Then the kingdom and dominion,
And the greatness of the kingdoms under the whole heaven,
Shall be given to the people, the saints of the Most High.
His kingdom is an everlasting kingdom,
And all dominions shall serve and obey Him." (Daniel 7:19-27)

Daniel 7 lays out a prophecy similar to that given to Nebuchadnezzar in Daniel chapter 2. This fourth kingdom, following Babylon, was to be "strong as iron: for as much as iron breaks in pieces and subdues all things, and as iron breaks all these, shall it break in pieces and bruise" (Dan. 2:40). Rome would be the strongest kingdom of all. This kingdom would persecute the saints of the most High for a time. And no power of man on earth would have been so accomplished at changing the times and the laws as the great institutions of Rome.

Far beyond what Babylon, Persia, or Greece ever achieved, Rome perfected the art of ruling an empire. Indeed, this kingdom ruled the whole Mediterranean

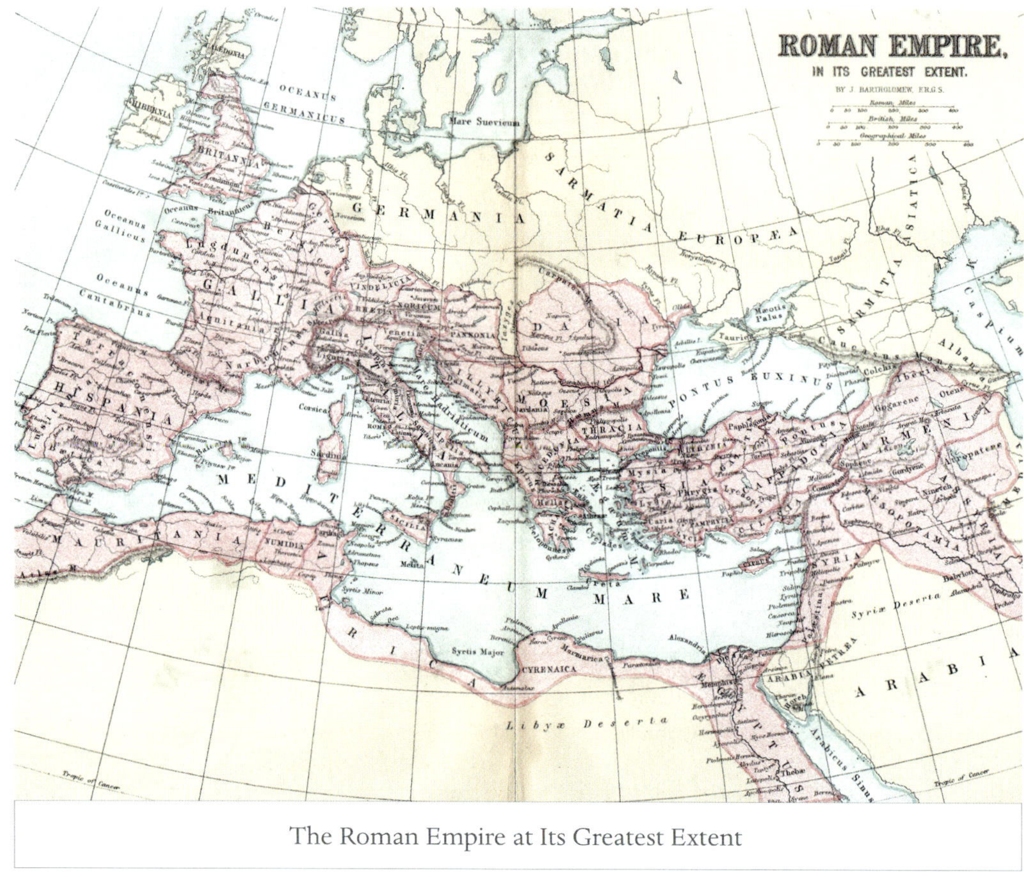

The Roman Empire at Its Greatest Extent

world with an iron hand. The Romans managed to keep the empire going for about 500 years, dwarfing the seven-year reign of Alexander and the eighty-year longevity of the Babylonian Empire. Rome centralized power over its districts like no one else. The Roman roads provided Roman bureaucracy with improved accessibility to every corner of the empire. Cruel tortures, persecutions, and forms of tyrannical control invented by former kings and emperors were mass produced and universalized by the Romans in every nook and cranny of the empire.

Cain Revisited in Rome's Foundations (753-509 BC)

> *Now Cain talked with Abel his brother; and it came to pass, when they were in the field, that Cain rose up against Abel his brother and killed him. . . . And he built a city . . . (Genesis 4:8, 17)*

The most telling commentary concerning the wicked character of this great city and its empire is found in its inception. It is a shameful, horrible story of which the Romans greatly boasted. It is difficult to tell which part of the tale is legend and which is truth, yet these origins formed the basic world and life view of the Roman mind.

As the story goes, twin brothers named Romulus and Remus, abandoned by their mother, were cared for by a she-wolf until they were discovered by a shepherd. Later on, the two young men set out to build a city at the location where they were rescued. They began to argue, and Romulus killed his brother. The story is reminiscent of Cain who killed his brother, wandered in the wilderness east of Eden, and then built his city. In the biblical account, Cain is not a hero. In the city of man, however, Romulus remains a hero and a role model for all future leaders. Preeminence and power trump all other virtues and values in the city of man. Fallen man's heroes are biblical villains.

Romulus, Remus, and the She-Wolf

It should be obvious that Christians cannot cast their admirations upon the wicked city of man. Those who glory in these great empires and admire the founders of such kingdoms are too much like them. They come to emulate the things they admire. Rome's foundations were evil, and over time she would collect the power to replicate this evil all over the world.

Actually, the ancient legend of the Romans begins at the battle of Troy (in modern-day Turkey). As the Greeks burned Troy to the ground, Aeneas escaped by boat with other Trojan fugitives. They settled in central Italy, and generations later a king's daughter named Rhea is found pregnant with the twins. They are

Tiber River

thrown into the Tiber River, where the wolf later finds them in a dry spot. The city of Rome was formed on the south side of the Tiber River, a strategic location for trading with other peoples further upstream. Whereas the lands settled by the Greeks were less favorable to agriculture, both the western and eastern sides of the Italian peninsula were fruitful plains.

Roman history records Romulus as the first of seven kings ruling from 753 BC to 509 BC (244 years). Distinguishing himself throughout his career as both deceptive and wicked, Romulus invited people from surrounding areas into his city for a festival. Then his men kidnapped their young women in what became known as "the Rape of the Sabine Women."

Romulus fought a war with the Sabines after the tribe had been ravaged of its women. Years later a truce was called, and together they formed a government. Romulus shared the monarchy with the Sabine king and appointed 100 "patricians" as an advisory council for himself. In the end, Romulus was torn in pieces by the senators, and that became the fate of many if not most of the kings of Rome.

But You, O God, shall bring them down to the pit of destruction;
Bloodthirsty and deceitful men shall not live out half their days;
But I will trust in You. (Psalm 55:23)

Location of Rome Within Modern-Day Italy

Simultaneous with the establishment of the city of Rome, two civilizations appeared on the Italian Peninsula—the Etruscans and the Greeks. Between 750 and 550 BC, Greek colonists settled the fruitful plains on the eastern side of the country, and they built the city states of Cumae, Reggio Calabria, Crone, Naples, Sybaris, and Taranto. The Etruscans appeared in the fruitful valleys to the northwest. This rich cultural group got its start as far back as the 10th century, probably migrating from ancient Germanic tribes in the north. They became a highly developed civilization after 750 BC, with beautiful art (including a well-developed bronze sculpturing), monogamous families, and a written language. The Romans took their gods Juno, Minerva, and Jupiter from the Estruscans, and others from the Greek pantheon. As early as the 5th century BC, the Greek culture would come to dominate on the Italian Peninsula.

History records at least ten wars between the Etruscans in the north and the Romans on the south side of the Tiber River between 750 and 351 BC.

By 500 BC, three major civilizations dominated the western Mediterranean—the Carthaginians, the Etruscans, and the Greeks. These expanding political powers were pretty much out of reach of Persia in the east. Since the Persians were never able to capture Athens and Sparta, they did not pursue anything further west. About this time, Etruscan power was waning as Rome gained ascendancy. The Gauls from the north also pressed into Etruscan territory, and around 390 BC the Gaulish armies sacked Rome.

Between 367 and 272 BC, the Romans fought successive battles with the Etruscans to the north, the Latins to the south, and the mountain peoples called the "Samnites." Inch by inch, the Romans achieved victory over their neighbors, after which they would build roads proceeding to all the places of their dominions. Thus, "all roads lead to Rome" as the saying goes. About this time, Rome began stationing a garrison of its troops in some of the maritime cities they had conquered. Of the conquered peoples, three classes developed:

1. Full citizens of Rome and those who settled as colonists in other parts of the growing empire.
2. Passive citizens who could intermarry with Romans. These peoples were granted self-government if they lived in their own cities.
3. Allies who would furnish soldiers for the Roman armies and accept Roman coinage. The Jews would trade in Roman money at the time of Christ, as He pointed out to the religious leaders in Mark 12.

Then they sent to [Jesus] some of the Pharisees and the Herodians, to catch Him in His words. When they had come, they said to Him, "Teacher, we know that You are true, and care about no one; for You do not regard the person of men, but teach the way of God in truth. Is it lawful to pay taxes to Caesar, or not? Shall we pay, or shall we not pay?"

But He, knowing their hypocrisy, said to them, "Why do you test Me? Bring Me a denarius that I may see it." So they brought it.

And He said to them, "Whose image and inscription is this?" They said to Him, "Caesar's."

And Jesus answered and said to them, "Render to Caesar the things that are Caesar's, and to God the things that are God's." (Mark 12:13-17)

The Greco-Roman wars began around 280 BC and continued until 146 BC. At first, King Pyrrhus of Epirus (from the western coast of Greece) was called upon to defend the colonists on the eastern coast of Italy from the Roman armies. Pyrrhus was second cousin to Alexander the Great, and he thought he could overcome the Romans with better military technology and the use of elephants—an added weapon of war obtained from previous campaigns in India. Pyrrhus defeated the Romans in initial battles, but his limited troops and lack of support from the Italian Greeks prevented him from sustaining control of the peninsula. The Romans kept a seemingly endless supply of troops coming into successive battles, and eventually Pyrrhus had to acknowledge defeat. It is from these wars that we get the term "a Pyrrhic victory."

Pyrrhus of Epirus (c. 319-272 BC)

The Roman Republic (509-50 BC)

While the monarchy continued in Rome from 750 BC until 509 BC, the kings governed with a senate of patricians and a general assembly made up of any and all military men. These fellows would not bother with deliberating on matters, but only indicated their support or opposition to a measure by shouting or brandishing their swords and spears.

The last of the kings of Rome were Etruscan, the most important of which was Lucius Tarquinius Priscus (ruling 616-579 BC). He won battles against the Sabines to the north and the Latins to the south, but he is best known for introducing the Circus Maximus, organized on an annual basis and featuring chariot races, wrestling, and boxing. When men aren't fighting wars, they usually resort to mock battles and sports competitions. These games become increasingly elaborate as the empires that sponsor them are enriched, and Rome became the world leader in the industry. Tarquinius Priscus used the booty collected during his wars to fund his sports programs.

Despite the success of the kings at building Rome's power base, the Romans would not tolerate the

The Roman Forum, Seat of the Roman Republic

View of the Ancient Roman Chariot-Racing Stadium, the Circus Maximus

tyranny that came with it. Tarquinius' grandson, Tarquinius the Proud (ruling 535-509 BC) is blamed for the demise of the monarchy and the rise of a republican form of government. This tyrant wrested power by killing the ruling king (his own father) and not a few senators. However, after his son raped the noblewoman Lucretia, Tarquinius and his whole family were chased out of the kingdom.

Like a roaring lion and a charging bear
Is a wicked ruler over poor people.
A ruler who lacks understanding is a great oppressor,

But he who hates covetousness will prolong his days.
A man burdened with bloodshed will flee into a pit;
Let no one help him. (Proverbs 28:15-17)

Lawless kings will encourage anarchical unrest and violent revolution, and Rome serves as an exemplar for these proverbial warnings. The revolution against the monarchy was instigated mostly by a man consumed by bloodshed by the name of Junius Brutus. Every evil was justified in the name of the revolution, and Brutus himself murdered his own sons and brothers-in-law who were not sufficiently supportive of this "great and righteous" cause. This was the beginning of the great "Roman Republic." However, given the state of depravity that characterizes the hearts of men representing all the political parties, it was hardly an improvement. Changing forms of government or dictatorships would always transfer the country out of one frying pan, into another, and then into the fire. This happened time and time again in Roman history. The Republic is one long record of murder and mayhem, assassinations and civil wars, and mobs and massacres.

Brutus' revolution marked the beginning of the Roman aristocratic-republican form of government. The patricians (or the upper class) participated exclusively in the rule, leaving the plebeians (or the commoners) without representation. The plebeians protested their lot and threatened to build another city in 494 BC. After some negotiations with the patrician leadership, the commoners gained two representatives in the council.

At first the patricians tried to keep the laws ruling the city secret, but in 450 BC the plebeians finally persuaded the council to publish the common laws. This was a breakthrough for liberty in that public access to the laws discouraged the government from acting arbitrarily and providing unequal treatment by the courts. This was the basic instruction for a judicial system provided by Moses in Deuteronomy.

Then I commanded your judges at that time, saying, "Hear the cases between your brethren, and judge righteously between a man and his brother or the stranger who is with him. You shall not show partiality in judgment; you shall hear the small as well as the great; you shall not be afraid in any man's presence, for the judgment is God's." (Deuteronomy 1:16-17)

Below are portions of this first Roman law or "The Twelve Tables of Law":

Patria Potestas

- Monstrous or deformed offspring may be put to death.
- The father shall, during his whole life, have absolute power over his legitimate children. He may imprison the son or scourge him, or keep him working in the fields in fetters, or put him to death, even if the son holds highest offices of state, and were celebrated for his public services. He may also sell his son. If a father thrice surrenders a son for sale the son shall be free from the father.

Other Laws

- Marriage by 'usage' (*usus*): If a man and woman live together continuously for a year, they are considered to be married; the woman legally is treated as the man's daughter.
- If any person has sung or composed against another person a song (*carmen*) such as was causing slander or insult . . . he shall be clubbed to death.
- If a person has maimed another's limb, let there be retaliation in kind, unless he agrees to make compensation with him.
- If a patron shall defraud his client, he must be solemnly forfeited (killed).
- Whoever is convicted of speaking false witness shall be flung from the Tarpeian Rock.
- No person shall hold meetings in the city at night.
- The penalty shall be capital punishment for a judge or arbiter legally appointed who has been found guilty of receiving a bribe for giving a decision.
- Putting to death . . . of any man who has not been convicted, whosoever he might be, is forbidden.

By biblical standards, the laws of the Romans were generally unjust and severe. Death was about the only sanction, even for taking a bribe, failing to repay a debt, or insulting some person in a song. There was a curtailing of the right to assembly at night. Reasonable retribution—fitting the punishment to the crime—seemed a foreign concept to the Romans. Also the basic civil law God gave to Noah in Genesis 9:6 appears absent from these early records.

The empowerment given to the family jurisdiction—and to the father specifically, under the *patria potestas*—was nothing short of outrageous. A father could kill his family member at will. On the one hand, the Romans recognized the necessity of a strong nuclear family to maintain any kind of a human social system. However, they took it too far, openly permitting murder, abortion, and infanticide at the whim of the head of household. This countenanced gross immoralities that would undermine the integrity of the family, contribute to murder and assassinations at the highest levels of government, and generally destabilize the Roman state over time. Contrary to unjust Roman law, the Scriptures require death or some other civil punishment for a father who kills a member of his household in the case of a slave, and certainly in the case of a son or daughter.

> *If a man beats his male or female servant with a rod, so that he dies under his hand, he shall surely be punished. (Exodus 21:20)*

The father in the Roman family was considered the priest of the home, in charge of performing sacrifices to the gods for the family. The fires on the altar were always to be kept burning, usually a slavish responsibility fulfilled by members of the household. In a similar manner, the king or emperor was usually considered the high priest of the nation itself.

While each family was given room for a small garden, a larger portion of land was held in common by the community. The family therefore laid claim to the crop produced, but had no right to the land itself.

The Governmental Organization of the Roman Republic

Until the monarchy was abolished, the Roman Senate was responsible for choosing a new king (upon the death of a king). The Senate also served in an advisory capacity to the king. However, during the years of Republican governance, two consuls (governors) were elected on an annual basis for the administration of the government of Rome. Each could veto the other's actions. Only patricians could serve as consuls until 367 BC, at which time the office was open to plebeians. The Senate, then, still operated as an advisory council for the consuls, issuing semi-authoritative decrees and controlling the state budget. On occasion, especially during times of war, the government would be turned over to a dictator who would lead the country until the time of national crisis was over.

Carthage and the Punic Wars (270-146 BC)

For over 200 years, Carthage in North Africa and Rome maintained friendly relations. After all, the two great powers were only separated by about 100 miles of ocean. A treaty signed somewhere around 509 BC specified that Roman citizens in the Carthaginian province of western Sicily would "enjoy all rights enjoyed by others." The Carthaginians promised to "build no fort in Latium; and if they enter the district in arms, they shall not stay a night therein."[1] Nonetheless, by 270 BC a tug-of-war picked up once more over the island of Sicily, finally resulting in the Punic Wars.

These two Mediterranean powers had very different strengths and weaknesses. Carthage was proud, opulent, and not really battle tested. As such, the nation would find great elation with initial wins and then sink into depression upon the loss of a battle. Rome, on the other hand, was far more resilient to loss and "possessed a fortitude which neither success nor failure could shake."[2] Rome had been fighting wars almost constantly for 500 years.

With its robust system of economic trading, Carthage had amassed an abundance of gold from Spanish mines, but the nation lacked fighting men. Her conquered territories were reluctant to support the mother country, especially when tax rates would sometimes exceed 50% of the annual yield. On the other hand, Rome's government lived hand-to-mouth, but almost every man in the city and district knew how to fight. Carthage had a much better navy—the best in the world. When Rome found a wrecked Carthaginian galley, their shipbuilders reverse-engineered the boat and then began building something comparable to it. They constructed 100 ships in two years, and by 260 BC a great naval battle was fought on the northeastern coast of Sicily. The Romans emerged victorious.

Rome made the mistake of being too aggressive in the first Punic War and took a fleet of 330 ships into Africa, where they were soundly defeated. For the next six years, the Romans lost battle after battle over Sicily to the Carthaginian general Hamilcar. However, not to be discouraged, the citizens of Rome rallied, and by 241 BC Carthage was ready to talk terms of surrender. They agreed to leave Sicily to Roman control, pay Rome 2,200 talents of gold (worth about $3 billion in today's money), and release all prisoners of war without ransom.

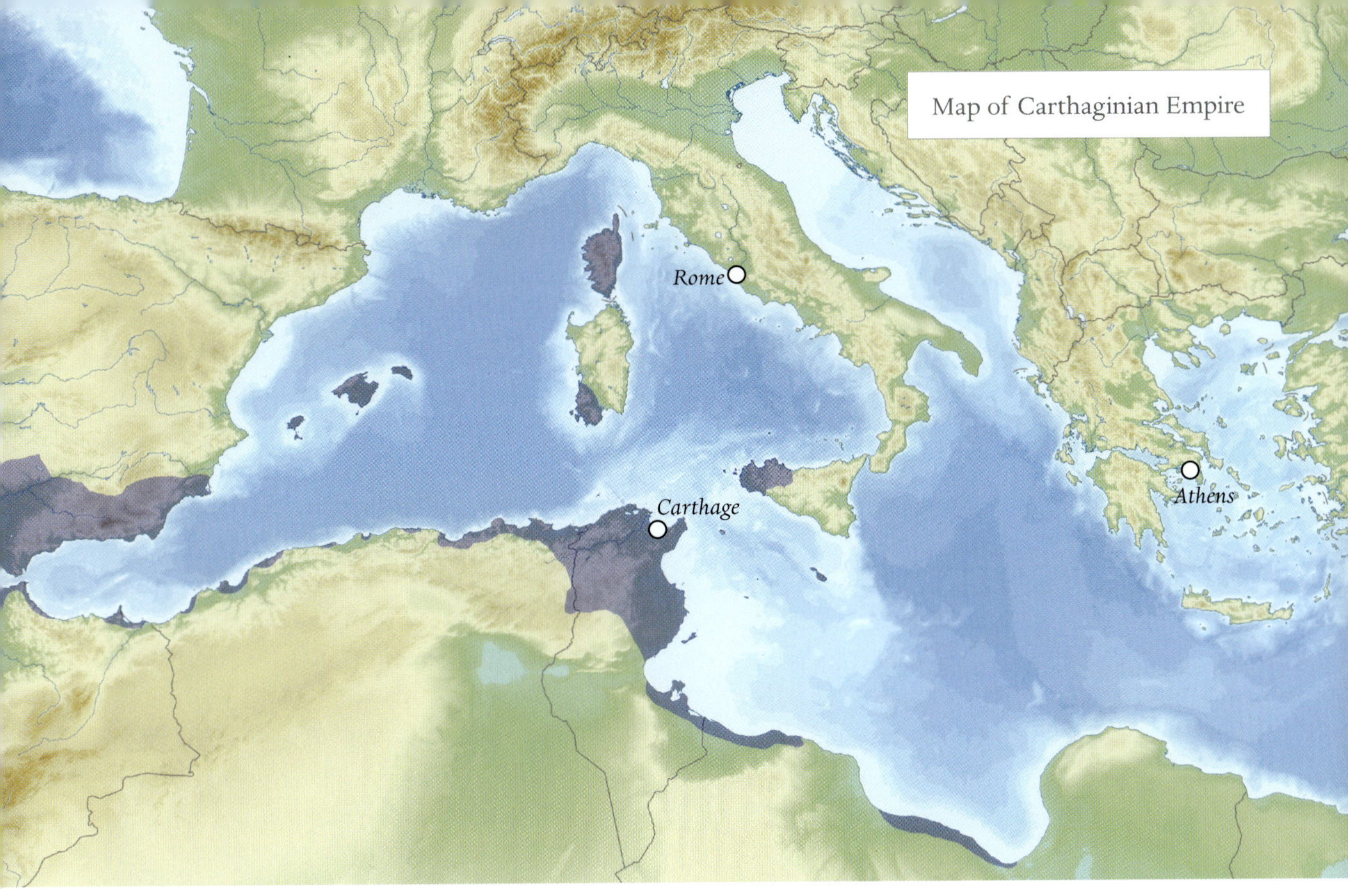

Carthage's leading general, Hamilcar, carried a grudge over the war to his grave. He pressed into Spain in hopes of securing more gold to pay his mercenaries from the previous war with Rome. Many of the Carthaginian rulers were not interested in pursuing any further war with Rome—they wanted to retain peace for purposes of trade and financial profit. However, egos were at stake, and the pride of man knows no bounds.

By pride comes nothing but strife,
But with the well-advised is wisdom. (Proverbs 13:10)

After Hamilcar was assassinated in Spain by one of his own men, his son Hannibal took up the grudge and the challenge to prosecute a war against Rome. He was committed to making Rome pay for the humiliation brought upon his father twenty years earlier.

Hannibal set out from Spain with 90,000 infantry, 12,000 cavalry, and 58 elephants, making his way over the Pyrenees Mountains and then across the

Hannibal Crossing the Alps

Rhone River. As winter approached, he fought his way across the snowy Alps, finally arriving in the Po Valley with 20,000 infantry and a mere 6,000 cavalry.

His perseverance paid off, and the Carthaginian general quickly succeeded in subduing the Romans in their own backyard throughout 217 and 216 BC. At the battle of Cannae, Hannibal was outnumbered 80,000 to 30,000 troops, yet succeeded in utterly destroying the Roman army. By this time, the Romans had lost 20% of their population in this Second Punic War. Yet in the final analysis, the Carthaginians failed to take into account the undying tenacity of the Romans. Only in the direst extremities would the true pluck of the Romans reveal itself.

Meanwhile, back in Carthage, the aristocracy was dragging its heels when called to support their general in the field. They figured that since Hannibal had gotten himself into the conflict, he would have to get himself out of it. Spain failed to help him with troops, and Philip V of Macedonia was busy fighting his own wars in Greece. At times coming within three miles of the walls of Rome, Hannibal continued burning down villages and carrying off the booty of crops and cattle to feed his men.

Meanwhile, the Roman General Cornelius Scipio was waging successful warfare in Spain. In 204 BC he crossed the Mediterranean and took the war to Hannibal's backyard. He won the battle of Zama, in which the Carthaginian army was destroyed and that ended the war. The terms of peace turned Spain over to Rome, the Carthaginians were forced to burn almost all their beautiful ships, and an annual tribute was levied against them.

In the final war with Carthage in 146 BC, the Romans utterly destroyed the city, killing 650,000 men, women, and children, and selling the remaining 50,000 into slavery. Actually, this marked the end of the proud and decadent Phoenician Empire which had its beginnings in Tyre and Sidon some 1,000 years earlier. Phoenicia had introduced Baal worship into Canaan, and King Ahab brought the travesty into Israel by way of his Sidonian wife, Jezebel. This demonically-invented god Baal required sacrifices wherein the victims (wearing a smiling mask) were placed on the arms of the idol set over a fire, and then rolled into the fire to be consumed. Children in particular were included in these horrible rites.

Tens of thousands of remains of children have been uncovered in burial grounds called Tophets in ancient Carthage as well as in Carthaginian territories in Malta, Sardinia, and Sicily.[3] Since 1963, excavators have discovered at least 3,000 bodies of children from one month to four years old in a Tophet located in Sardinia.

Ruins in Carthage

Archaeologists have discovered that child sacrifice among the Carthaginians actually increased in regularity with each century from the 8th to the 3rd century BC.[4]

The Old Testament prophets referred to these terrible places:

> *"For the children of Judah have done evil in My sight," says the LORD. "They have set their abominations in the house which is called by My name, to pollute it. And they have built the high places of Tophet, which is in the Valley of the Son of Hinnom, to burn their sons and their daughters in the fire, which I did not command, nor did it come into My heart. "Therefore behold, the days are coming," says the LORD, "when it will no more be called Tophet, or the Valley of the Son of Hinnom, but the Valley of Slaughter; for they will bury in Tophet until there is no room. The corpses of this people will be food for the birds of the heaven and for the beasts of the earth. And no one will frighten them away." (Jeremiah 7:30-33)*

Archaeologists have uncovered dedications to the gods inscribed on stone over the cremated remains of small children where parents claimed that "the gods heard my voice and blessed me."[5] More than anything, the Carthaginians desired material wealth, and they thought the gods would reward them if they offered up their children. Since 1960, the modern world has embraced convenience abortion and abortifacient birth control pills for similar reasons—as a means of living a wealthy and trouble-free lifestyle. Between one and two billion babies have been killed through these means in modern times, dwarfing the sins of ancient Carthage.

Carthage was doomed to destruction, and the annihilation of the abomination of Baal worship was inevitable. Surely, the true and living God would not tolerate such shedding of innocent blood indefinitely. The prophecies of the Lord God of Israel against Phoenicia came to pass in full measure when Carthage burned to the ground in 146 BC. A full 350 years earlier the prophet Zechariah had promised this sea power would be destroyed and devoured by fire.

The burden of the word of the LORD
Against the land of Hadrach,
And Damascus its resting place
(For the eyes of men
And all the tribes of Israel
Are on the LORD);
Also against Hamath, which borders on it,
And against Tyre and Sidon, though they are very wise.
For Tyre built herself a tower,
Heaped up silver like the dust,
And gold like the mire of the streets.
Behold, the LORD will cast her out;
He will destroy her power in the sea,
And she will be devoured by fire. (Zechariah 9:1-4)

No doubt the destruction of Tyre at the hands of Alexander the Great in 314 BC and the razing of Carthage were still on the minds of the Jews when Christ made this pronouncement in AD 33:

Woe to you, Chorazin! Woe to you, Bethsaida! For if the mighty works which were done in you had been done in Tyre and Sidon, they would have repented long ago, sitting in sackcloth and ashes. But it will be more tolerable for Tyre and Sidon at the judgment than for you. (Luke 10:13-14)

Ultimate Evil Unleashed

> *When He opened the fifth seal, I saw under the altar the souls of those who had been slain for the word of God and for the testimony which they held. And they cried with a loud voice, saying, "How long, O Lord, holy and true, until You judge and avenge our blood on those who dwell on the earth?" Then a white robe was given to each of them; and it was said to them that they should rest a little while longer, until both the number of their fellow servants and their brethren, who would be killed as they were, was completed. (Revelation 6:9-11)*

No greater evil in all the world could be invented than the demonic persecution of the people of God. This is the devil's best attempt to thwart Christ, for it is the ultimate insult to the groom to abuse His bride. The persecutions of Christians ordered by Satan at the hands of the Romans would continue for 300 years after the resurrection of the Lord Jesus Christ. In the words of Revelation 12, "The dragon was enraged with the woman, and he went to make war with the rest of her offspring, who keep the commandments of God and have the testimony of Jesus Christ" (Rev. 12:17). Never again was there another sustained, thorough-going persecution like this in church history following the Roman assault on Christ.

Well before this persecution arrived, the Romans and their empire were being conditioned by demonic influences to embrace senseless, sustained, cruel violence against the innocents. This came in the form of "the games."

The roots of the gladiatorial killing games are found in Etruria and the Etruscans. Human sacrifices were offered for the dead at funerals. A scene is portrayed in a fresco at the Tomb of the Augers from about 520 BC, in which gladiators are wrestling to their deaths.[6] The cultural practice from Etruria must have been carried on in Rome, with the first recorded gladiatorial competition conducted around 264 BC in honor of the dead. Decimus Junius Brutus Scaeva organized three gladiatorial fights to the death as an "honor" to his dead father, Brutus Pera.

Julius Caesar opened the floodgates to this cursed evil, inviting 300 pairs of combatants to enter the arena in one showing. He dug out an enormous lake in the middle of the arena to stage mock battles between warships, in which hundreds were killed. All of this only served to awaken the blood lust of the Romans, resulting in an unceasing demand for more and more victims. The crowds especially loved to see the slaughter of dwarves, women, children, and of course Christians.

The Roman Colosseum

Tens of thousands of animals were used to satisfy the blood lust of the crowds, including lions, panthers, elephants, wolves, hippopotami, bison, hyenas, and giraffes. Augustus Caesar sponsored his own gladiatorial events, explaining:

> *Three times in my own name and five times in that of my sons or grandsons, I have given gladiatorial exhibitions. . . . Twenty-six times in my own time or in that of my sons and grandsons, I have given hunts of African wild beasts in the circus, the forum, the amphitheaters, and about 35,000 beasts have been killed.*[7]

The games were universally applauded by Roman historians, philosophers, and politicians alike, and universally decried by Christians and almost no one else. Augustine of Hippo, the great Christian theologian of the 5th century, described the games in his *Confessions* as "a bloody pastime," "intoxicating," and "a cruel and savage evil."[8]

Roman Gladiators

Entertainment in Rome

When the Romans were not entertaining themselves at the games, they availed themselves of the bathhouses. Like hotels and resorts of our day, they offered legitimate services—but often were used for immoral activities by both men and women. By the fourth century, there were some 856 public bathhouses in Rome—roughly one for every 1,000 persons. Some could accommodate over 1,000 people, equipped with saunas, perfumeries, massage rooms, and hair salons. In one bathhouse, fifty furnaces consumed approximately ten tons of wood on a daily basis to keep the floors well heated. Mosaics and carvings depicted immodest and sensual figures on the walls.

The Romans and the Greeks were notorious for presenting their gods and heroes unclothed. They wanted an imaginary, idealistic world where no shame and no guilt was recognized—a flat-out denial of man's fall into sin. This immodesty and shameless art and statuary communicates a lie. The Scriptures define shameful nakedness minimally as the display of the buttocks in 2 Samuel 10:4-5. Public display of generic nude bodies of females or males would cast shame on females or males in general. Christians are careful not to publicly shame others by revealing unclothed male or female images—and they plainly do not pretend a world without shame, guilt, and sin.

Statue of Jupiter the Roman God

> *Then the LORD God called to Adam and said to him, "Where are you?" So he said, "I heard Your voice in the garden, and I was afraid because I was naked; and I hid myself." And He said, "Who told you that you were naked? Have you eaten from the tree of which I commanded you that you should not eat?" Then the man said, "The woman whom You gave to be with me, she gave me of the tree, and I ate." (Genesis 3:9-12)*

Roman Worldviews

The Roman worldview was based on a pagan idea of an impersonal polytheism. Religious worship was strictly a quid-pro-quo business arrangement. *Do ut des* was the common religious confession—"I give so that you will give me back." No relationship, no mercy, no emotion, and no adoration necessarily belonged in this arrangement with the gods.

The first temple in Rome was built to Vesta, the goddess of fire and warmth. The decor of the temple involved licentious displays in keeping with just about every pagan religion in the world. The enslavement of the pagan mind to the sensual is particularly clear from their religious worship. Six vestal virgins would serve in the temple for thirty-year stints, and if they failed to keep their virginity, they were buried alive.

Salvation by the State and the Breakdown of the Republic (148-50 BC)

Immediately after concluding its wars with Carthage, Rome faced internal social upheaval. The great empires of men almost universally and completely ignore the wisdom of the Proverbs. For example:

> *Wealth gained by dishonesty will be diminished,*
> *But he who gathers by labor will increase. (Proverbs 13:11)*

The sudden inflow of wealth and slaves into Rome from Carthage did the Romans no good. It produced inflation in the Roman economy (the false appearance of wealth), and then it destroyed the character of the rich and eroded the middle class—always the healthiest element of a society. Large slave-based plantations drove the small farmer out of business. The poor began to live off of government aid and the rich collected their rewards from the war booty and the empire. Thus social upheaval continued from 135-129 BC, beginning with a slave revolt in Sicily.

To compensate for these problems, Rome turned to political solutions. Somehow men want to believe that the government can salvage the imploding character of a nation. This is one of the greatest mistakes socialist governments, powerful governments, and modern governments have made.

Tiberius Sempronius Gracchus was a plebeian tribune who tried to bring social reform by forcibly limiting the size of estates and redistributing lands. His plan was not well received, and he was subsequently murdered. His younger brother Gaius stepped in and introduced welfare programs and mass extension of citizenship for almost all immigrants. He too was murdered, along with 3,000 of his followers.

Augustine comments on these horrible insurrections and wars that characterized Rome during these years:

Augustine of Hippo (AD 354-430)

> *What a sea of Roman blood was shed, what desolations and devastations were occasioned in Italy by wars social, wars servile, wars civil! . . . What slaughter ensued when shortly, after the younger brother met the same fate [as Gracchus]! For noble and ignoble were indiscriminately massacred; and this not by legal authority and procedure, but by mobs and armed rioters.*[9]

What Rome (and Greece) came to understand was that humanist democracy always degrades into the welfare state, where politicians will seek to make voters happy by redistributing wealth from the rich to the poor. Covetousness, envy, and stealing is the default position for the voting base, whose hearts are depraved and corrupted by sin. Populist candidates then appeal to these sinful inclinations of the heart. And thus the "reform" policies of Rome further destroyed the character of the nation and brought about instability and chaos, which then surrendered to dictatorship.

The people appointed Gaius Marius general of the Roman army. He formed a professional fighting force and won important battles against tribes in German territory and Numidia, North Africa. This military hero held almost total political control over Rome as consul until 100 BC. His nephew Julius Caesar would gain an even larger reputation in military accomplishments and political leadership.

Another social reform was attempted by Marcus Livius Drusus in 91 BC, but this too failed when Drusus was murdered and Italy broke out into another civil war. That was quelled by the granting of universal citizenship to more immigrants and conquered peoples. When foreign wars broke out with Mithridates of Pontus, the Romans assigned Lucius Cornelius Sulla to lead the troops against him. Around the same time, Rome was torn apart by more civil wars (88-82 BC). General Gaius Marius returned to power in 87 BC and initiated a bloody revolution against the aristocracy. In the killing spree that followed, senators were murdered in cold blood, and women and children were not spared. Before he could do any more damage, Marius died of natural causes in his bed (at seventy years of age). Shortly thereafter, the military commander Sulla returned to assume dictatorial rule over all of Rome between 82 BC and 79 BC.

When the righteous rejoice, there is great glory;
But when the wicked arise, men hide themselves. (Proverbs 28:12)

If Marius beat Rome with whips, Sulla would beat Rome with scorpions. These were days that prefigured the horrors of the 18th century French Revolution or the Bolshevik Revolution in the 20th century. Blood ran freely in the streets again—no one was safe from Sulla's wrath. He would place a list of the names of those he wanted dead on the Forum, and then he would offer a bounty to the killer, which usually included the dead man's property. In this way Sulla disposed of thousands of his enemies, among whom were the followers of Marius. Even young Julius Caesar, now nineteen years of age, was not exempt during these terrible years. Sulla pressed Caesar, Pompey, and other young leaders to divorce their wives because of their family connections (belonging to the wrong political party). The young men complied, except for Caesar. His name was added to the hit list on the Forum, and he fled to the Sabine Mountains to the south. In 78 BC, Sulla was dead, eaten by worms (like King Herod, as related in the Book of Acts).

The non-stop murders and madness in the governments of ancient pagan empires come as a shock to those born into Christian nations. Occasional assassinations appear in European and American governments, but the rule of law generally predominates. Most Christian nations shudder to think that the government might be turned over to a dictator like Lucius Cornelius Sulla, for example.

Thus democracy was quickly breaking down into anarchy. . . and dictatorship. The chaos that came through social reform, welfare programs, redistribution of land, and price controls on grain inevitably moved the nation towards the dictatorship of the Caesars.

Once again, man had failed to establish righteousness by playing with the form of his civil government. The monarchy had failed, but so had the Republic. In the words of Augustine, who wrote his masterpiece *City of God* as the Roman Empire was collapsing in the 5th century AD:

> *Rome never was a republic, because true justice had never a place in it. . . . But the fact is, true justice has no existence save in that republic whose founder and ruler is Christ, if at least any choose to call this a republic.*[10]

Julius Caesar—The Most Powerful Man in the World (100-44 BC)

> *Now there was also a dispute among them, as to which of them should be considered the greatest. And He said to them, "The kings of the Gentiles exercise lordship over them, and those who exercise authority over them are called 'benefactors.' But not so among you; on the contrary, he who is greatest among you, let him be as the younger, and he who governs as he who serves. For who is greater, he who sits at the table, or he who serves? Is it not he who sits at the table? Yet I am among you as the One who serves." (Luke 22:24-27)*

Certainly, the study of the greatest empires and leaders of the world offers living illustrations of what the Lord said about them in Luke 22. These great kings really did see themselves as "benefactors" while they tyrannized the people with their governments. Ultimately they were motivated by an unquenchable thirst for power over all. Augustine, the Christian theologian of the 5th century, summarized the misery brought about by these empires in these words: "The lust of sovereignty disturbs and consumes the human race with frightful ills."[11] He pointed out that both Greeks and Romans were constantly motivated by this lust for power. Then he quotes the Roman historian Sallust (b. 86 BC), who had to admit that a mere lust for sovereignty was "a sufficient ground for war." And he said, "the greatest glory consisted in the greatest empire."[12]

Bust Depicting Julius Caesar (100-44 BC)

When modern historians set out to identify the most powerful men in the world, they will usually point to Alexander the Great, Julius Caesar, and Genghis Khan. All were men of war, fiercely ambitious men who really wanted to conquer the world and then rule the world. It was Julius Caesar who turned the Roman Republic into an empire led by a single powerful dictator. The impulse to centralize power and turn the state into a god increases in intensity when man has one-upped the gods (or God) in his own mind. And so, the Romans took over where the Greeks left off, hoping to establish man as ultimate and the state as the savior of mankind. All of this came about just before the arrival of the Son of God, the true Savior of the world.

At twenty-five years of age, Julius Caesar was on his way to Rhodes to study rhetoric when his ship was waylaid by pirates. The outlaws were delighted to find they had captured one of the aristocracy, and suggested a ransom price of twenty talents. Caesar laughed it off and insisted they raise it to fifty talents. His captors thought he was joking when he told them he would have them all crucified. While waiting for the money to arrive, Caesar entertained them by composing poetry and playing their athletic games. When his men returned with the money, he was released, but promptly returned with a militia he had commandeered. He arrested the pirates and had them all crucified.

Julius Caesar finally made it to Rhodes, when Mithradates of Pontus, the formidable enemy of the Romans, stirred up another military campaign in Asia Minor. The local Roman army was offering a lackluster response to the enemy, so Caesar assumed control of the army and drove Mithradates out of the Roman province.

In 73 BC, a gladiator named Spartacus initiated a slave revolt, assembling for himself an army of thousands. The Romans sent an army against the slaves led by Crassus and Pompey—Caesar no doubt playing a part in the war as well. When the revolt was put down, six thousand slaves were crucified on the Appian Way, one every hundred feet from Capua to Rome, a non-too subtle message to all future would-be revolutionaries. Although Crassus and Pompey were competitors for the glory of the Spartacus War, they joined political forces and were both elected

Death of Spartacus

as consuls in 70 BC. Caesar united himself with the two generals to support the plebeians against the aristocracy, a triumvirate of power that continued for several years. This would be the fastest way to dictatorship since the aristocracy was always the first to oppose dictatorships. It was at this time that Julius Caesar was elected to the Senate.

Leaving Rome in 67 BC, Pompey was intent on making a name for himself by fighting a war against piracy, destroying the armies of Mithradates, interfering in the Judean civil war, and gaining control of Armenia. For the time being, the Jews were left to govern themselves in a rather small geographical area surrounding Jerusalem (and a little more territory around the sea of Galilee).

Back in Rome, Caesar was gaining popular recognition, particularly after he was put in charge of public festivals. He vastly increased the killing games in the Colosseum and hosted spectacular stage productions. He knew what would delight the masses, and he gave it to them. All the while, he was running the city into massive debt. Risking popular opposition and a political loss, Julius publicly glorified the dead Marius, his uncle, despite all of the bloodshed the man brought upon Rome (particularly upon the aristocracy).

After serving ten years as a religious priest for the official state religion of Rome, Julius Caesar presented himself as a candidate for Pontifex Maximus (the high priest) in 63 BC. This was a major political move for the young politician. He bribed his way in and effectively bought the office. After driving himself and the city deep into debt, Caesar was finally forced to leave town mainly as a way to escape his creditors—taking on the governorship of Spain.

Meanwhile, Pompey returned to Rome as a great military victor. Thankfully, he decided not to march his armies into town, kill his political enemies, and rule as dictator, as his predecessors had done. However, his proposals and policies for the Senate were snubbed, and he became a political nothing as a consequence.

Bound and determined to make his mark, Caesar fought a war against mountain bandits in Spain, chasing them into the sea and killing them to the last man. Seen now as a military conqueror and popular with the plebeians, he was elected one of the consuls in 59 BC. About this time Caesar solidified the triumvirate, a political alliance of three of Rome's most powerful men—himself, Pompey, and Crassus.

During his stint as consul, Julius Caesar proved himself competent at administering the ever-expanding empire. What became known as the "Julian law of extortion" would turn into the basic legal code used to govern the empire for the following centuries. His carefully constructed one hundred chapters of rules directed the prosecution of crooked governors, the administration of the provinces, and the banning of bribes. Such legislative leadership was daring, and the traditionalists fought him tooth and nail. His enemies were waiting to pounce on him after his year in the consulship ended. Before his time in office was over, however, his friends in power strategically offered him the governorship of Gaul and Illyricum (modern-day France, Switzerland, southern Germany, and Austria). Caesar left Rome in December of 59 BC with the intent of establishing Roman rule over unruly Gaul.

By the next summer, Julius Caesar had defeated the German tribes on the east side of the Rhine River and the Helvetii tribe on the west side. Meanwhile, back in Rome, the consul Clodius had turned Rome into a full-fledged welfare state, handing out grain free of charge to the lower classes and gaining a great deal of popular support.

However, in 58 BC, Caesar was to take on another challenge—the Belgae (in modern-day northern France and Belgium). The battle that took shape pitted 30,000 Romans against an enormous Belgae army of 150,000 fighting men. Caesar defeated them handily at the Aisne River. His armies also conquered the Nervii tribe, killing all but 500 of a host of 60,000. Battles were fought and won against the tribe at Octodurus (in modern-day Switzerland), as well as the Veneti and the Osismi tribes near modern-day Normandy (northern France). The Veneti rebelled in 57 BC, but Caesar subdued them again in a fierce sea battle at summer's end.

Between 56 BC and 54 BC, Julius Caesar set out across the English Channel to conquer Britain. His men built 626 ships, and 20,000 men were transported over the sea to invade Britain. He found that these British "barbarians" would dye their skin blue, and they refused to eat birds and rabbits (for they were considered sacred). Caesar had no problem subduing the Britons as far north as the Thames River.

The severity of Caesar's imperialistic campaigns intended to subdue western Europe is not to be minimized. Altogether he counted a million deaths of men, women, and children—combatants and non-combatants alike. Hundreds of thousands were sold into slavery, and fields and forests were laid waste in his scorched-earth wars. It was all for the sake of stability—the cruel and "wonderful" *Pax Romana*. The tender mercies of the wicked are cruel, and the peace of man is only won by more war.

Roman Invasion of Britain

Crossing the Rubicon (49 BC)

As the year 50 BC came to a close, the power struggle within the triumvirate had reached its climax. Crassus had died and two military commanders were staring each other in the face. Pompey had his armies that had been waging war in the south, and Caesar had his armies claiming new lands for the republic in the north. Fearing a civil war or bloodshed in the streets similar to what had happened with previous dictators, the Senate asked both men to surrender their armies. Caesar replied that he would if Pompey would agree. Pompey was not willing to cooperate. So, on January 10th, 49 BC, Caesar made the momentous decision to cross the Rubicon River with a legion of several thousand soldiers. This commenced the Roman civil war that would turn him into the first emperor of the rising empire. For the next five years, Caesar busied himself killing off his political enemies. When Rome was not killing the empire's enemies, the Roman leaders were occupied with killing each other off in power struggles. Such is the horrible life of a fallen, sinful world. These were just more of the works of the flesh, mass-produced, magnified, and enabled by powerful empires and armies.

> *Now the works of the flesh are evident, which are: adultery, fornication, uncleanness, lewdness, idolatry, sorcery, hatred, contentions, jealousies, outbursts of wrath, selfish ambitions, dissensions, heresies, envy, murders, drunkenness, revelries, and the like; of which I tell you beforehand, just as I also told you in time past, that those who practice such things will not inherit the kingdom of God. (Galatians 5:19-21)*

Julius Caesar Crosses the Rubicon

Julius Caesar had the title "dictator," and was in full control of the Roman government in 49 BC. Armed with a much smaller force, he fought a cat and mouse war with Pompey for a full year. By the end of the summer of 48 BC, Caesar had defeated his opponent in Greece. He later pursued Pompey to Egypt, only to find his nemesis murdered. He had the assassins put to death.

While in Egypt, Caesar fought the Pharaoh's armies, taking sides with the sister, wife, and co-regent queen, Cleopatra. (The Egyptians and the Ptolemies were known to marry their sisters well into the 1st century BC.) In what is perhaps his most celebrated public sin, Julius Caesar committed adultery with this woman. His reign barely survived three years after giving way to this adulterous affair.

Can a man take fire to his bosom,
And his clothes not be burned?
Can one walk on hot coals,
And his feet not be seared?
So is he who goes in to his neighbor's wife;
Whoever touches her shall not be innocent. (Proverbs 6:27-29)

Wrapping things up in 46 BC, Caesar fought the battle of Thapsus (in Tunisia) against Metellus Scipio and Cato the Younger (who committed suicide). He then defeated Pompey's sons at the Battle of Munda in March of 45 BC.

Cleopatra (69-30 BC)

The next year Julius Caesar brought Cleopatra to Rome. By this time, she had borne him a son named Caesarion. The senators were beginning to warm to the "godhood" of Caesar, but it was this celebrated paramour, this new "incarnate goddess" from Egypt whom they refused to accept. The senator Cicero exclaimed: "I detest Cleopatra. . . . I cannot even describe the insolence of this queen in her gardens across the Tiber without bursting into anger."[13] Well did Solomon's mother warn him:

What, my son?
And what, son of my womb?
And what, son of my vows?
Do not give your strength to women,
Nor your ways to that which destroys kings. (Proverbs 31:2-3)

Julius Caesar's pride and celebrations went on and on. He threw parties for tens of thousands of people at a time. He was installed as dictator for an unprecedented ten-year period. The Senate lavished him with titles, including the highly ironic title of "Master of Morality." They declared a forty-day celebration of thanksgiving to him and treated him as a god. Caesar announced to the Senate that "men ought to speak to me more courteously and treat my word as law."[14] He cut the free-food recipient list from 320,000 to 150,000. He outlawed the organization of clubs and guilds in Rome to prevent any threat to his power, though he exempted the Jews who were still meeting in synagogues. He restricted the use of certain forms of clothing and jewelry. He expanded citizenship throughout Italy, laying the foundation for the modern large country. Then he exported some 80,000 Roman citizens into colonies in Africa, Gaul, and Greece. Importantly for the modern-day, he created the Julian Calendar, which he aligned to the true solar year of 365 days, including an extra day every four years in February.

While he had condemned the pagan sacrifices of the Gauls, Julius Caesar reintroduced human sacrifice by ritually killing two soldiers and hanging their heads on the Regia. Such was a rare event for the Romans at this point in their history, but, after all, Caesar was the chief priest of the nation, and such were the ways of the tyrant.

By 45 BC, the Senate had bestowed on Caesar the title "Dictator for Life." He was given a golden chair in the Senate and allowed to dress in purple, as had the previous kings of Rome some 500 years earlier. In a final act of attributing deity to the man, the Senate allowed his ivory statute to be included in the procession of the gods. In the temple of Quirinius, a statue of Caesar was placed with the inscription "To the Unconquered God." Such pride and blasphemy would not long be tolerated by the God of heaven.

Death of Caesar—March 15th, 44 BC

The conspirators who organized to murder Caesar included some of his friends, the enemies he had conquered, and those Romans who wanted a return to the Republic. Chief among them was the Senator, Brutus, an advocate for the old Republic, and also the son of Caesar's long-term mistress. This flagrant wickedness could not be ignored even by pagans living in the darkest regions of the Satanic kingdom. Moreover, it was Brutus' forefather Lucius Junius Brutus who had overthrown the tyrant king in 509 BC to establish the Republic at the beginning.

Caesar began laying plans to lead a campaign against the Parthians, remnants of the ancient Persians still opposing Rome and aiding Syria in its resistance. On March 15th (the Ides of March), 44 BC, Caesar entered Pompey's Theater to the west of the Forum to meet with the Senate. First the senator Casca attempted to stab him in the neck. He missed, but the other senators in the conspiracy swarmed the man who would be god, and it was Brutus who stabbed him last. Julius Caesar's last words were: "Kai su, teknon?" or in English, "You also, my child?"

But Jesus said to [Judas], "Friend, why have you come?"
Then they came and laid hands on Jesus and took Him. And suddenly, one of those who were with Jesus stretched out his hand and drew his sword, struck the servant of the high priest, and cut off his ear.
But Jesus said to him, "Put your sword in its place, for all who take the sword will perish by the sword." (Matthew 26:50-52)

Thus the cycle of never-ending violence continues in the kingdoms of men as they always seek for a better world by wars, murders, and treacheries. Seventy-five years after Caesar collapsed onto the floor in Pompey's Theater, the Lord spoke these words and exposed the utter futility of the sinful kingdoms of men. Indeed, Christ's kingdom is better, for it is won by His sacrificial death—not by joining in the endless cycle of wars, massacres, and assassinations.

The Rise of Augustus

Seventeen-year-old Octavius joined Julius Caesar in his campaign through Spain as he was chasing down Pompey's sons in 46 BC. Octavius was shipwrecked on the way and fought through hostile territory to reach his uncle's camp. Caesar was so impressed that he named the young man his successor.

Upon the death of Julius in 44 BC, Octavius took on Caesar's name, joined forces with Mark Antony, and began slaughtering his enemies, including Cicero. When Mark Antony divorced Octavius' sister, Octavia Minor, in preference for Cleopatra, the relationship broke down between Mark Antony and Octavius, resulting in another civil war. Both Cleopatra and Mark Antony ended up committing suicide after Octavius won the Battle of Actium in 31 BC. Octavius solidified his place as the second Caesar, ruling the entire Roman Empire—and preparing the way for another King and a kingdom that would never pass away.

The dark treacheries, sexual sins, murders, wicked intrigues, twists and turns, and political machinations occurring at this time are the stuff of which novels and plays are written. Men and women are less and less horrified by these details and more and more enamored by the high crimes and sinful behavior of powerful men and women. This too is a fleshly response from depraved hearts, "who not only do these things but take pleasure in them that do them."

The great Christian thinker of the 5th century, Augustine, soundly shamed the Romans for their insane civil wars and attributed them to the influence of pagan gods or demons upon the minds of Rome's leaders.

These bloody civil wars, more distressing, by the avowal of their own historians, than any foreign wars, and which were pronounced to be not merely calamitous, but absolutely ruinous to the republic, began long before the coming of Christ, and gave birth to one another; so that a concatenation [chain] of unjustifiable causes led from the wars of Marius and Sylla to those of Sertorious and Cataline . . . from this to the war of Pompey and Caesar, of whom Pompey had been a partisan of Sylla, whose power he equalled or even surpassed, while Caesar condemned Pompey's power because it was not his own, and yet exceeded it when Pompey was defeated and slain. From him the chain of civil wars extended to the second Caesar, afterwards called Augustus, and in whose reign Christ was born. For even Augustus himself waged many civil wars; and in these wars many of the foremost men perished, among them that skillful manipulator of the republic, Cicero.[15]

Augustus Caesar (63 BC - AD 14)

And it came to pass in those days that a decree went out from Caesar Augustus that all the world should be registered. This census first took place while Quirinius was governing Syria. So all went to be registered, everyone to his own city. Joseph also went up from Galilee, out of the city of Nazareth, into Judea, to the city of David, which is called Bethlehem, because he was of the house and lineage of David, to be registered with Mary, his betrothed wife, who was with child. So it was, that while they were there, the days were completed for her to be delivered. And she brought forth her firstborn Son, and wrapped Him in swaddling cloths, and laid Him in a manger, because there was no room for them in the inn. (Luke 2:1-7)

Despite the dissipation and immorality that characterized Rome, the empire's life would be extended for five centuries. In the common grace and mercy of God, the Roman world was granted a stay of execution. This would allow enough time for the kingdom of Christ to expand throughout the known world, in both the West and the East.

Augustus Caesar (63 BC - AD 14)

What destroys nations is that which is destroying America, Europe, Russia, and elsewhere in the 21st century—the breakdown of the family, abortion, and divorce. Augustus Caesar, by God's common grace, was able to discern this as the dry rot that was destroying Rome. He therefore instituted laws that made it very difficult to obtain a divorce. He granted tax breaks to families with three or more children. According to the Lex Julia laws incorporated between 18 BC and AD 9, adultery was treated as a criminal offense—which resulted in the exile of Augustus' own daughter and granddaughter. In AD 11, he is recorded as reprimanding unmarried singles at the Forum: "You are betraying your country by rendering her barren and childless!"[16] He would not allow unmarried young men and women to participate in entertainment so they would be more serious about getting married and getting on with life. A heavy penalty was levied against any young person who would attempt to watch the games or attend the shows. He also exiled Ovid, well-known for his literary works advocating sexual immorality. Ovid was only recovered in the modern world by William Shakespeare and Christopher Marlowe at the turn of the 17th century. However, the religious worship of Jupiter, Apollo, and Vesta was supported by the state. Augustus restored eighty-two temples to the false gods of

Rome. As would be expected, the humanist thinking of the Greeks continued to seep into Roman schools and political life.

Augustus conducted a census of Roman citizens, counting 4,230,000 persons throughout the empire. He also expanded the games to massive naval battles, one of which involved 3,000 men fighting for their lives to the pleasure of the Roman crowds. He moved battalions of soldiers into twenty-eight regions, including Spain, Africa, Asia, Syria, Judea, and Pisidia.

The accolades showered on this new emperor knew no bounds. A town called Priene (in Turkey) issued a decree in 9 BC, calling on the world to begin dating the year at the birth of Augustus Caesar. The tablets were discovered in the 19th century, and in this translation of the Priene Calendar, Caesar is referred to as a "god" and "savior" who brings a "gospel" to the world.

It is extraordinary that such a pronouncement of an explicitly counterfeit gospel should be made in 9 BC, just nine years before the birth of the Messiah, the true Savior of God, who would bring the true Gospel to the whole world! It is even more remarkable that the world did not pick up on this decree, but instead established an annual date from the birth of the real Savior of the world.

A denarius coin struck about the time of the birth of our Lord bears the image of Augustus Caesar. He is lauded by the laurel around his head in the picture, and the inscription reads: CΛESΛR ΛVGVSTVS DIVI F PΛTER PΛTRIAE, translated "Augustus Caesar, son of god, father of the nation." The title is the same as the one ascribed to the Child who was born in a stable in Bethlehem about the same time.

> *When He had been baptized, Jesus came up immediately from the water; and behold, the heavens were opened to Him, and He saw the Spirit of God descending like a dove and alighting upon Him. And suddenly a voice came from heaven, saying, "This is My beloved Son, in whom I am well pleased." (Matthew 3:16-17)*

While it would have been blasphemous for Augustus and Julius Caesar to declare themselves god, it was not so for Christ. The Jews would have been rightly concerned that their emperor had done this, but they should have accepted Christ, the true Son of God, as equal to God.

The Priene Calendar Inscription

Decree of the Greek Assembly in the province of Asia, on motion of the High Priest Apolionios, son of Menophilos, of Aizanoi—Whereas Providence that orders all our lives has in her display of concern and generosity in our behalf adorned our lives with the highest good: Augustus, whom she has filled with arete [virtue] for the benefit of humanity, and has in her beneficence granted us and those who will come after us a Saviour (σωτῆρα) who has made war to cease and who shall put everything in peaceful order; and whereas Caesar, [when he was manifest], transcended the expectations of [all who had anticipated the good news], not only by surpassing the benefits conferred by his predecessors but by leaving no expectation of surpassing him to those who would come after him, with the result that the birthday of our God (τοῦ θεοῦ) signaled (ἦρξεν δὲ τῶι κόσμωι τῶι δι' αὐτὸν εὐαγγελίων ἡ γενέυλιος ἡμέρα τοῦ θεοῦ) the beginning of Good News for the world because of him; . . . (proconsul Paul Fabius Maximus) has discovered a way to honor Augustus that was hitherto unknown among the Greeks, namely to reckon time from the date of his nativity; therefore, with the blessings of Good Fortune and for their own welfare, the Greeks in Asia decreed that the New Year begin for all the cities on September 23rd, which is the birthday of Augustus; and, to ensure that the dates coincide in every city, all documents are to carry both the Roman and the Greek date, and the first month shall, in accordance with the decree, be observed as the Month of Caesar, beginning with 23 September, the birthday of Caesar.[17]

The Priene Calendar Inscription

Therefore the Jews sought all the more to kill Him, because He not only broke the Sabbath, but also said that God was His Father, making Himself equal with God. (John 5:18)

It is plain from this that man's desires and hopes for a savior had reached extreme levels of desperation by this time. Both the great Chinese Han Empire and the Roman Empire were attempting to present their governments as the solution to man's problem by the time of the birth of the Christ. Man's problems were manifest, crippling, devastating, exhausting, unrelenting, and without remediation. Each and every human messiah had proven to be a complete failure and even counterproductive to peace, righteousness, and wellbeing. Only God could save the world now, and only by His only begotten Son. The fullness of time had finally come.

But when the fullness of the time had come, God sent forth His Son, born of a woman, born under the law, to redeem those who were under the law, that we might receive the adoption as sons. (Galatians 4:4-5)

Postscript: When Jesus Came to the Roman Empire

The pride that arrived with the great empires and the glorification of man's mind that came through humanist philosophers was the dry rot of the Greek and Roman world. First, the Greeks declined into skepticism and immorality in the centuries before Christ. After Augustus, the Roman world turned into a moral cesspool. Caligula (ruled AD 37-41) was a complete profligate who thought of himself as a god and murdered and raped at will. He was assassinated by the Praetorian Guard. Nero became the first world leader to advocate the travesty of homosexual marriage. He murdered his own mother and wife and then burned down much of Rome, finally committing suicide in AD 68. Then Emperor Domitian (ruled AD 81 to 96) forced his niece to abort her child, and she died in the process. The worst of all, Elagabalus (ruled AD 218 to 222), married and divorced five times, and then was the first Roman Emperor to pursue the destructive lifestyle of homosexuality and transgenderism.

The Arch of Constantine in Rome

However, before the Greeks and Romans completely destroyed themselves by their abortion, infanticide, birth implosions, and homosexuality, the Gospel of Christ was carried by the Apostles Peter and Paul (and others) into the far reaches of the Empire. Thousands were converted, institutions changed, and the rule of law was restored again and again throughout the centuries.

Nevertheless, compromise with humanist ideologies returned to Italy and Greece during the Renaissance. State control of the church and a power-intoxicated church government increasingly contaminated these nations through the centuries. Neither Greece nor Rome received much of the influence of the Protestant Reformation in the 16th and 17th centuries. Therefore the influence of Christ waned greatly in these nations, and there is but a shadow of this influence still remaining in the 21st century after Christ's coming. Moreover, the influence of the Muslims in Turkey, Syria, Albania, and elsewhere washed out the Christian influence and produced some of the most impoverished and corrupt nations in the world.

Mediterranean Nation	Corruptions Rating[18]	Freedom Rating[19]	Prosperity Rating[20]	Percent Christian[21]
Slovenia	36	78	36	0.3% Protestant - 73% Catholic
Italy	53	80	33	0.6% Protestant - 78% Catholic
Greece	67	106	50	0.3% Protestant - 90% Orthodox
Macedonia	93	33	81	0.7% Protestant - 70% Orthodox
Albania	99	52	95	0.2% Protestant - 12% Catholic
Armenia	105	47	106	1% Protestant - 93% Armenian Apostolic
Turkey	178	68	52	0.02% Protestant - 0.3% Catholic
Syria	78	n/a	159	0.2% Protestant

The Economy of Southern Europe and Asia Minor

Turkey's proximity to Christianized Europe enabled it to retain a stronger economy, although it remains a very corrupt nation on the Transparency International scale. Also, Greece and Italy have both degraded economically very badly over the last century. These countries have increasingly abandoned much of the Christian heritage they received, embracing the pagan humanism of the ancient Greeks and Romans. However, abortion and homosexuality are not as popular among these states as they are in the rest of Europe, as of 2020.

Country	Major Resource / Exports
Slovenia	motor vehicles, furniture and household electrical equipment, pharmaceutical products and clothes
Italy	petroleum, pharmaceuticals, cars, gold, valves, leather shoes
Greece	petroleum, aluminum, electrical equipment, pharmaceuticals, plastics, cotton, rice, pistachios, figs, almonds
Macedonia	reaction and catalytic products, centrifuges ($602M), insulated wire, vehicle parts, buses
Albania	leather footwear, chromium ore, ferroalloys
Armenia	copper ore, rolled tobacco, hard liquor, gold, aluminum foil
Turkey	cars, gold, delivery trucks, vehicle parts, and jewelry
Syria	spice seeds, pure olive oil, apples and pears, nuts, cotton yarn

Interior of the Colosseum

Timeline Review

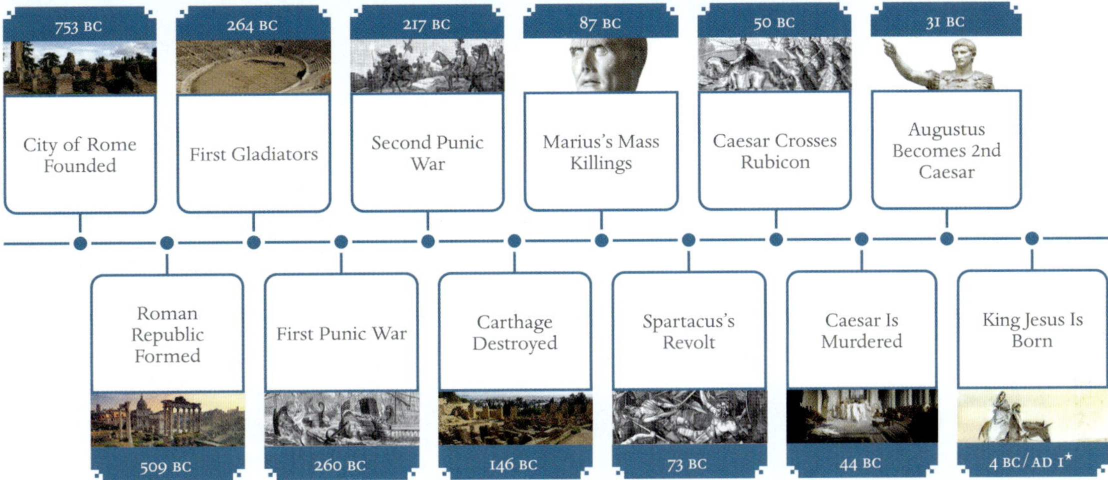

* Historians are divided on what is the most likely date of Christ's birth. Both are included on this timeline.

Chapter XV Prayer

Almighty God, and heavenly Father,

What heights to which man builds great empires! What great pride and faith he places in his kings and emperors! What tremendous expectations he places in his auspicious works and powerful systems! Yet it is all futility and all yields failure. What a contrast between the great Roman empire and the Kingdom of the Lord Jesus Christ! How the ultimate pride of man come down in total ignominy! Yet, this humble Child who was born in a stable, crucified by the Roman powers, has established His eternal Kingdom that can never fail! The Caesars are long gone, but the true Son of God will be King forever, King of kings, and Lord of lords. Of the increase of this Kingdom of peace and righteousness there is no end. He is the true Savior, the ultimate and final Savior of the world. May all other false gods and all false saviors be revealed for what they are and destroyed. And, may the Name of Jesus Christ our Lord be lifted up, honored, and praised by all tribes and nations the world over.

Amen.

Mount of Olives Near Jerusalem

CHAPTER XVI

Preparing the World for Jesus: Jerusalem (73 BC - AD 33)

Again, the devil took [Jesus] up on an exceedingly high mountain, and showed Him all the kingdoms of the world and their glory. And he said to Him, "All these things I will give You if You will fall down and worship me." Then Jesus said to him, "Away with you, Satan! For it is written, 'You shall worship the Lord your God, and Him only you shall serve.' " (Matthew 4:8-10)

The war that rages in the hearts of men and among the principalities and powers of this world is a spiritual conflict. The battle is fought out over ideas and matters of authority. Who will be worshiped? Whose word is essential, and who speaks with ultimate authority in our lives? At root, all wars in the world are reduced to a power struggle. Man wants power and authority that does not belong to him. Like the ancient Assyrians and Babylonians, man in his fallen state will always covet the title "King of the Universe" and "King of kings." Ultimately, sinful man is seeking to take the place of God.

This battle played out with the Roman emperors, and it was intensely waged in the life of Herod "the Great"—a key figure who was instrumental in the fulfillment of prophecy and in preparing the way for Jesus.

Herod, a descendant of Esau (of the Edomites), was born in 73 BC, about ten years before Augustus Caesar's birth. He was raised as a Jew, and his father worked in the administration of Hyrcanus II, the grandson of John Hyrcanus and great grandson of Simon the Maccabee. When John Hyrcanus defeated Edom fifty years earlier, he had forced all Edomites to convert to Judaism and submit to circumcision.

It was this Hyrcanus II who entered into conflict with his brother Aristobulus and then called in the Romans to defend his right to rule. Hyrcanus II served as high priest almost continuously from 76 BC to 40 BC, and he held the title of "King of Judea" from 67 BC to 66 BC and the title Ethnarch (ruler) from 47 BC through 40 BC.

About 40 BC, the Parthians interrupted the scene in Judea and appointed Antigonus Mattathias (Hyrcanus II's nephew) as puppet king. Earlier in 53 BC, the Parthians had won a major battle against Rome at Carrhae (present-day Harran, Turkey). And, in God's providence, the Parthians allied with supporters of Cassius and Brutus in 40 BC and conquered the Roman armies in Syria. Temporarily, Rome lost complete control of the entire eastern part of their empire. The Roman civil wars had weakened the empire until Caesar Augustus gained ascendance. These Parthians were famous for installing kings in their territories—they called themselves "kingmakers." Thus, their interference with Judean politics was not unusual.

Ruins in Harran, Turkey

Upset with the appointment of Antigonus as king, and still supporting Hyrcanus II, Herod traveled to Rome with a request for help from the Senate. Surprisingly to all, including himself, the Senate made Herod "King of the Jews." He then married Hyrcanus' granddaughter and discarded his first wife—in hopes this would legitimize his rule over the Jews. By 37 BC, Herod had joined forces with the governor of Syria and collected an army large enough to capture Jerusalem, with a little help from Mark Antony. The Parthian-appointed king, Antigonus, was executed, and that ended the Hasmonean (Maccabee) Dynasty.

Herod the Great (73-4 BC)

With Herod's appointment by the Roman Senate, the Judean leadership was now totally controlled by Rome, preparing the way for the coming of the Messiah thirty-seven years later.

Who Will Be King?

Now after Jesus was born in Bethlehem of Judea in the days of Herod the king, behold, wise men from the East came to Jerusalem, saying, "Where is He who has been born King of the Jews? For we have seen His star in the East and have come to worship Him."

When Herod the king heard this, he was troubled, and all Jerusalem with him. And when he had gathered all the chief priests and scribes of the people together, he inquired of them where the Christ was to be born.

So they said to him, "In Bethlehem of Judea, for thus it is written by the prophet:
'But you, Bethlehem, in the land of Judah,
Are not the least among the rulers of Judah;
For out of you shall come a Ruler
Who will shepherd My people Israel.' "

> *Then Herod, when he had secretly called the wise men, determined from them what time the star appeared. And he sent them to Bethlehem and said, "Go and search carefully for the young Child, and when you have found Him, bring back word to me, that I may come and worship Him also."*
>
> *When they heard the king, they departed; and behold, the star which they had seen in the East went before them, till it came and stood over where the young Child was. When they saw the star, they rejoiced with exceedingly great joy. And when they had come into the house, they saw the young Child with Mary His mother, and fell down and worshiped Him. And when they had opened their treasures, they presented gifts to Him: gold, frankincense, and myrrh.*
>
> *Then, being divinely warned in a dream that they should not return to Herod, they departed for their own country another way. (Matthew 2:1-12)*

The men referred to as "Magi" in the Greek who came to Jerusalem looking for the king of the Jews were the kingmakers or the priestly class of the Medes and Persians (or the Parthians). Of all the nations in the earth, these Persians were the people who had access to the records of Daniel the prophet. As referenced in the Greek Septuagint rendition of Daniel 2:10 and 2:48, Daniel was appointed head over the wisemen and the "Magi" in Babylon. There is one highly significant prophecy that Daniel records in his prophetic book, and that is the coming of a King and a kingdom that will last forever (Dan. 2 and 7).

The Greek historian Strabo, writing around the time of the birth of Christ (10-5 BC), notes that "The council of the Parthians is composed of two classes, one of relatives, (of the royal family,) and another of wise men and Magi, by both of which kings are chosen."[1] That is, Antigonus II would not have been appointed king without the approval of the Magi.

By God's common grace, He reaches into the darkest corners of this world and shines His truth into the hearts of men of His choosing. He would choose Gentiles instead of Jews to welcome His Son, the King. At the birth of Christ, the Lord God communicated a message to these Magi about a King who was worthy of their worship.

However, Herod was troubled and all Jerusalem with him upon the arrival of these Magi from Parthia. Surely he remembered that these were the kingmakers who had placed Antigonus on the throne almost forty years earlier. Moreover, at this point, Rome was in complete control of Judea, and the Parthians would have possessed no influence on the kingdom of Judea, from Herod's point of view. Herod would brook no competition and neither would Rome.

While Jerusalem rejected her King, the Son of David and the Son of God, these foreigners from the East came to worship Him. They rejoiced with exceeding joy when they saw the star. What was it about this star and the coming King that caused them to respond with this great joy? Given that their business was to identify the king who would rule with perfect wisdom and righteousness, God must have revealed to them the coming of the ultimate King—the great Desire of all nations. Here was a King better than Nebuchadnezzar, better than Cyrus, better than Alexander and all the others. This was a King who would put an end to all of the cruel disappointments and crushed expectations of the ages. Indeed, here in Bethlehem was born a special King—One whose kingdom would never fail, never suffer loss, and always increase in glory, right rule, and peace. Finally, after all the disappointments of the millennia, here was a King truly worthy of worship by men.

For 2,000 years, men's hopes were set on kings, only to be dashed to pieces. For 500 years, the Magi had watched kings come and go in Persia. They had seen empires rise and fall. No doubt after all that time a raw, undiluted, uncompromising, cynicism would have set in. Optimism must give way to hopeless pessimism after continual letdowns over the centuries. From man's point of view, there was no more reason for hope or for any wonder and praise in the works of man. But then the star appeared, associated with the prophetic word that the King had come. So these men had come to Bethlehem to behold the King and to worship Him. To a world of failed kings, failed empires, failed wars, and failed everything else, came God's King. This is the greatest, most wondrous event in all of human history. God's eternally begotten Son was joined to human flesh to become our Savior and King.

> *I urge you in the sight of God who gives life to all things, and before Christ Jesus who witnessed the good confession before Pontius Pilate, that you keep this commandment without spot, blameless until our Lord Jesus Christ's appearing, which He will manifest in His own time, He who is the blessed and only Potentate, the King of kings and Lord of lords, who alone has immortality, dwelling in unapproachable light, whom no man has seen or can see, to whom be honor and everlasting power. Amen. (1 Timothy 6:13-16)*

The Worst King in the World and His Temple

It is highly significant that Herod was king of the Jews when Jesus was born, because he was one of the most evil rulers on earth. During his 37-year reign, Herod "the Great" gained a terrible reputation throughout the whole world. He married ten women. He killed at least one of his wives and two sons. Augustus Caesar said of Herod, "It is better to be Herod's pig than his son."[2] He played the "game" of political intrigue, murder, and adultery as well or better than the pagan Romans.

After the Magi returned home from Bethlehem, Herod proceeded to kill all the children in the city two years old and under. A man who wouldn't think twice of killing his own sons would have little trouble killing other people's children. Yet there is a spiritual force working here as well. The serpent-devil was well aware that the Seed of the woman would crush his head. This was the first promise of God's deliverance given four thousand years earlier in the Garden of Eden. Thus the serpent makes war with the seed. He would destroy this woman's child in Bethlehem if he could. However, Joseph was warned in a dream to leave Herod's

Modern-Day Bethlehem

jurisdiction for Egypt, where the child Jesus would be protected until the evil king had died.

> *Then Herod, when he saw that he was deceived by the wise men, was exceedingly angry; and he sent forth and put to death all the male children who were in Bethlehem and in all its districts, from two years old and under, according to the time which he had determined from the wise men. Then was fulfilled what was spoken by Jeremiah the prophet, saying:*
>
> > *"A voice was heard in Ramah,*
> > *Lamentation, weeping, and great mourning,*
> > *Rachel weeping for her children,*
> > *Refusing to be comforted,*
> > *Because they are no more." (Matthew 2:16-18)*

Like many of the "great men" of the Gentiles, Herod left a legacy of massive construction projects. He began building the magnificent temple in Jerusalem around 20 BC. The major structures for the project were finished forty-six years later (around AD 26). Significantly, the Lord Jesus would leave another temple for His people after the destruction of Herod's temple in AD 70. When Christ visited the temple in Jerusalem, He described another building project underway, even more important than Herod's:

> *Now the Passover of the Jews was at hand, and Jesus went up to Jerusalem. And He found in the temple those who sold oxen and sheep and doves, and the money changers doing business. When He had made a whip of cords, He drove them all out of the temple, with the sheep and the oxen, and poured out the changers' money and overturned the tables. And He said to those who sold doves, "Take these things away! Do not make My Father's house a house of merchandise!" Then His disciples remembered that it was written, "Zeal for Your house has eaten Me up."*
>
> *So the Jews answered and said to Him, "What sign do You show to us, since You do these things?"*
>
> *Jesus answered and said to them, "Destroy this temple, and in three days I will raise it up."*

Depiction of Herod's Temple in a Model in Jerusalem

Then the Jews said, "It has taken forty-six years to build this temple, and will You raise it up in three days?"

But He was speaking of the temple of His body. Therefore, when He had risen from the dead, His disciples remembered that He had said this to them; and they believed the Scripture and the word which Jesus had said. (John 2:13-22)

Herod's temple was probably the greatest architectural accomplishment of the 1st century BC. It was magnificent. The largest stones used in the construction measured 44.6 feet by 11 feet by 16.5 feet and weighed approximately 600 tons. King Herod called on architects from Greece, Rome, and Egypt to plan the construction. The Western Wall (the Wailing Wall) is part of a 500-meter-long retaining wall that was designed to hold a huge man-made platform that could accommodate twenty-four football fields. When it was completed, it was the world's largest functioning religious site, and until today it remains the largest man-made platform in the world. There was enough room in the temple courts to accommodate between six and seven million Jews and proselytes who would gather in Jerusalem from around the Empire for the annual feasts.

The outbuildings for Herod's Temple were finally finished in AD 62, eight years before it was destroyed by the Romans in one of the most devastating judgments in the history of the world.

Jesus's disciples were amazed at the beauty and magnificence of the great stones in the temple construction, as recorded in Luke 21. But, the Lord warned them that this temple would be utterly destroyed within a generation.

> *Then, as some spoke of the temple, how it was adorned with beautiful stones and donations, He said, "These things which you see—the days will come in which not one stone shall be left upon another that shall not be thrown down. . . Assuredly, I say to you, this generation will by no means pass away till all things take place." (Luke 21:5-6, 32)*

Cave of the Patriarchs, Hebron, an Example of Herodian Architecture

Corrupted Faith

Hypocrites! Well did Isaiah prophesy about you, saying:
"These people draw near to Me with their mouth,
And honor Me with their lips,
But their heart is far from Me.
And in vain they worship Me,
Teaching as doctrines the commandments of men." (Matthew 15:7-9)

These were the words of Jesus Christ following hundreds of years of shallow, half-hearted, externalistic religion on the part of the Pharisees and Sadducees. While the Jews made it a point not to give in to the gross idolatry of the pagan nations around them during the inter-testamental period, they still failed to trust God and shed themselves of humanist ideas. They had created for themselves a thin facade of man-made religion devoid of a heart of faith and love for God. Some had bought into the materialist worldview of the Greeks. Sexual sin, divorce, fraud, bribery, dishonor for parents, and other works of the flesh were rampant in 1st century Judea. There wasn't much difference between the day-to-day moral condition of the Jews and that of the pagans around them.

Herod the Great's son Archelaus took the throne when his father died and immediately began tyrannizing the Jews. In AD 6, Augustus deposed Herod Archelaus and placed Judea under the direct control of the Romans. Beginning at this time, the Romans assumed the power to appoint the high priest who would head up the religious worship in Herod's temple. Annas was appointed to the office and served from AD 6 to 15. He learned quickly how to play the political game with the Roman authorities, and his influence over temple politics and civil politics continued until his death around AD 40.

Annas had five sons and many grandsons, and from AD 15 until the fall of Jerusalem in AD 70, this unprincipled household dominated the high priestly office. The Jewish historian Josephus describes Annas' son as "a great hoarder up of money."[3] They would go as far as to beat people with rods to extort money or to confiscate the hides of sheep and goats from them. When Jesus drove out the money-changers (Matt. 21:10-11), the sons of Annas were apparently among them, if not key players in the racket. In 2016, archaeologists came upon what they believe to have been Annas' house. It was filled with luxuries only found

Sea of Galilee

in the house of Herod, including such things as Murex dyes and royal bathtubs. Clearly, Annas and Herod were the richest, most powerful, and the most politically-connected people in Judea.

It was this Annas and his son-in-law Caiaphas who ordered the arrest of the Son of God, our Savior.

> *Then the detachment of troops and the captain and the officers of the Jews arrested Jesus and bound Him. And they led Him away to Annas first, for he was the father-in-law of Caiaphas who was high priest that year. Now it was Caiaphas who advised the Jews that it was expedient that one man should die for the people. (John 18:12-14)*

Annas was haughty, audacious, and cruel. He was deposed by the Procurator Gratus "for imposing and executing capital sentences which had been forbidden by the imperial government."[4] That is, as the high priest, he had secured the reputation of remanding those whom he didn't like to execution, without the benefit of a court trial before a magistrate. Even the pagan Romans considered

Titus Flavius Josephus (AD 37 - c. AD 100)

Year	Event
AD 33	Annas recommends the crucifixion of Jesus Christ
AD 33/34	Caiaphas, Annas' son-in-law, presided over the first trial of the apostles
AD 34	Caiaphas presided over the second trial of the apostles
AD 36/37	Jonathan, son of Annas, presided over the murder of Stephen and others
AD 43	Matthias, son of Annas, presided over the murder of the Apostle James
AD 62	Ananus the Younger, son of Annas, presided over the murder of James (brother of Jesus and pastor in the church of Jerusalem)

men like Herod the Great, Herod Archelaus, and Annas to be excessively cruel. Moreover, historians have noted that every bloody persecution against Christians in Judea occurred during a period of time that a member of the house of Annas served as high priest in Jerusalem.

Such was the political situation in Jerusalem when Jesus was born and during that time He conducted His ministry in Galilee and Judea. The religious leadership could best be described as nothing less than a "pit of vipers," using the words of our Lord.

> *Woe to you, scribes and Pharisees, hypocrites! For you are like whitewashed tombs which indeed appear beautiful outwardly, but inside are full of dead men's bones and all uncleanness. Even so you also outwardly appear righteous to men, but inside you are full of hypocrisy and lawlessness.*
>
> *Woe to you, scribes and Pharisees, hypocrites! Because you build the tombs of the prophets and adorn the monuments of the righteous, and say, "If we had lived in the days of our fathers, we would not have been partakers with them in the blood of the prophets."*

> *Therefore you are witnesses against yourselves that you are sons of those who murdered the prophets. Fill up, then, the measure of your fathers' guilt. Serpents, brood of vipers! How can you escape the condemnation of hell? Therefore, indeed, I send you prophets, wise men, and scribes: some of them you will kill and crucify, and some of them you will scourge in your synagogues and persecute from city to city, that on you may come all the righteous blood shed on the earth, from the blood of righteous Abel to the blood of Zechariah, son of Berechiah, whom you murdered between the temple and the altar. Assuredly, I say to you, all these things will come upon this generation. (Matthew 23:27-36)*

These were the religious and political powers which would bring about the arch crime in history—the crucifixion of the Son of God. To this point in human history, the covenanted people of God and the Jewish religious leadership had proven themselves to be morally and religiously bankrupt. The great empires had proven a moral failure. They could never save mankind from his troubles.

This salvation would have to come by the death and resurrection of the Son of God. It would be a salvation that would overcome the

The Old City of Jerusalem

devil himself, death, the power of the world, and the sin principle which ruled in the hearts of men.

The devil would not win this war. The evil intentions of the Romans and Jews could not thwart the ultimate good accomplished by the purposes of God. The greatest crime ever committed in history was the crucifixion of the Son of God, but this would yield the greatest good by atoning for sin and redeeming sinners from eternal destruction. Christ's victory over the devil and all the powers of darkness was secured by His death, and by His resurrection. This King conquered the greatest enemies of the human soul, and established His Kingdom in the hearts of His people—a Kingdom that will never pass away. All praise be to God, forever and ever! Amen.

> *Men of Israel, hear these words: Jesus of Nazareth, a Man attested by God to you by miracles, wonders, and signs which God did through Him in your midst, as you yourselves also know—Him, being delivered by the determined purpose and foreknowledge of God, you have taken by lawless hands, have crucified, and put to death; whom God raised up, having loosed the pains of death, because it was not possible that He should be held by it.* (Acts 2:22-24)

Timeline Review

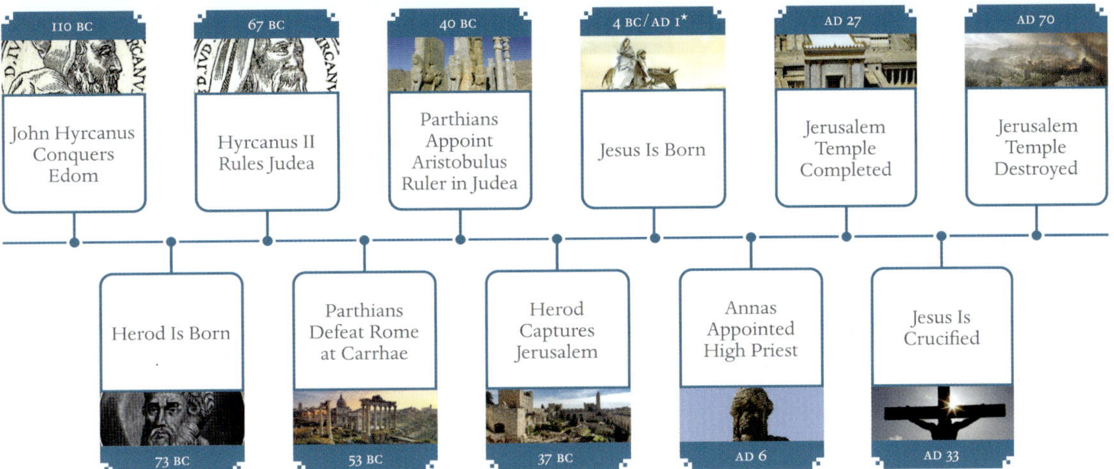

* Historians are divided on what is the most likely date of Christ's birth. Both are included on this timeline.

Chapter XVI Prayer

Our Father and Sovereign God Over All,

We are struck by the moral bankruptcy of the nations, of human religions, and of all of us. More than anything, today we can see the desperate, crying need for the Messiah, our Savior, your Son, and His work of salvation. Man's best works are nothing but filthy rags and useless garbage. Please grant to us your salvation, your righteousness, and your kingdom through Jesus Christ our Lord. With the Magi from the east, we recognize this One, the King for whom the nations have waited through the millennia. We receive this King, now on the right hand of the Father on high, and we worship Him. What a contrast between the magnificent temple constructed by the evil hands of wicked men, and the true Temple of the Body of our Lord Jesus Christ! He is the perfect Temple of God and the best revelation of God's glory. He is God with us. He is where the presence of God is known and enjoyed by those who are in Him. We praise you for the conquest of the devil and sin at the cross! We praise you for your heavenly kingdom which shines in our hearts and has spread all over this world! We praise you for Christ Jesus, our Lord and King, and we gladly submit to His rule.

In His name, Amen.

End Notes

CHAPTER I

The Creation and the Global Flood

1. The Septuagint would put the date of the flood between 3298 and 3168 BC, depending on whether one accepts the addition of Cainan into the Noah-Abraham genealogy, (which did not appear in the earlier LXX copies). Of the lower estimates of the date of the flood, Bishop James Ussher provided a date of 2348 BC. More recently, some creationists have suggested a flood date of 2532 - 2518 BC. This allows for 60 years between the birth of Abraham and Terah's firstborn, a full 400 years for the Israelites' dwelling in Egypt, some room for the differences in birth dates between fathers and sons, and assumes Solomon's death in 931 BC. For a full discussion on the date of creation and the flood, see https://creation.com/images/pdfs/tj/j31_1/J31_1_120-127.pdf.
2. John Woodmorappe, "How Could Noah Fit the Animals on the Ark and Care for Them?" *Answers in Genesis*, October 15, 2013, https://answersingenesis.org/noahs-ark/how-could-noah-fit-the-animals-on-the-ark-and-care-for-them/.

3. Malcolm W. Browne, "Whale Fossils High In Andes Show How Mountains Rose From Sea," *New York Times*, March 12, 1987,
4. https://www.nytimes.com/1987/03/12/us/whale-fossils-high-in-andes-show-how-mountains-rose-from-sea.html.
5. Albert, "Fossils of Mount Everest", *Volcano Café*, July 6, 2018, https://www.volcanocafe.org/fossils-of-mount-everest/.
6. Plutarch, *Moralia*, 5.26.
7. John D. Morris, "Why Does Nearly Every Culture Have a Tradition of Global Flood?" *Institute for Creation Research*, BTG No.153b, September 2001.
8. "Eridu Genesis," *Livius*, https://www.livius.org/sources/content/oriental-varia/eridu-genesis/.
9. Sir James G. Frazer, *Folk-Lore in the Old Testament*, Vol. 1 (London: Macmillan, 1919), 327.
10. Theodor H. Gaster, *Myth, Legend, and Custom in the Old Testament* (New York: Harper & Row, 1969), 120–121.
11. Edgar A. Truax, "Genesis According to the Miao People," *Institute for Creation Research*, April 1, 1991, https://www.icr.org/article/genesis-according-miao-people/.
12. Bill Cooper, *After the Flood* (Chichester, UK: New Wine Press, 1995), http://www.ldolphin.org/cooper/appen12.html.

CHAPTER II

The Whole Pagan World: Darkness Prevails (2518 BC - AD 33)

1. Arthur C. Custance, *The Doorway Papers*, Vol. 4 (Grand Rapids: Zondervan, 1984), https://custance.org/Library/Volume4/Part_II/chapter1.html.
2. Ibid.
3. Ibid.
4. Quoted in John Eidsmoe, *Historical and Theological Foundations of Law*, Vol. 1 (Powder Springs, GA: American Vision, 2012), 27.

5. Quoted in Will and Ariel Durant, *The Story of Civilization*, Vol. 1, *Our Oriental Heritage* (New York: Simon & Schuster, 1942), 65.
6. Matilda Battersby, "Prostitutes of god," *UK Independent*, September 20, 2010, https://www.independent.co.uk/news/world/asia/prostitutes-of-god-2082290.html.
7. Durant, 66.
8. Ruth A. Tucker, *From Jerusalem to Irian Jaya: A Biographical History of Christian Missions* (Grand Rapids: Zondervan, 1983), 201.
9. Quoted in Durant, 38.
10. Ibid.
11. John Angell James, *Female Piety* (New York: Robert Carter and Brothers, 1853), 34.
12. Durant, 50.
13. Helen L. Ball and Catherine M. Hill, "Reevaluating 'Twin Infanticide'," *Current Anthropology* 37, no. 5 (1996): 856-63, https://www.jstor.org/stable/2744421.
14. Naia Carlos, "Cannibalism Actually Happened in Spain 10,000 Years Ago," *Nature World News*, March 23, 2017, https://www.natureworldnews.com/articles/36646/20170323/cannibalism-actually-happened-spain-10-000-years-ago.htm; Nicola Davis, "Prehistoric cannibalism not just driven by hunger, study reveals," UK Guardian, April 6, 2017, https://www.theguardian.com/science/2017/apr/06/prehistoric-cannibalism-not-just-driven-by-hunger-study-reveals;
    Elizabeth Culotta, "Neanderthals Were Cannibals, Bones Show," *Science Mag*, October 1, 1999, https://science.sciencemag.org/content/286/5437/18.2.
15. Peter Hammond, *The Greatest Century of Missions* (Capetown, South Africa: Christian Liberty Books, 2002), 8.
16. Tucker, 202.
17. Rudyard Kipling, "The Gods of the Copybook Headings."
18. Durant, 361.
19. Ibid., 374.

20. Ibid., 376.
21. Quoted in Durant, 373.
22. Durant, 275.
23. Ibid.
24. Stephen Ambrose, *Undaunted Courage: Meriwether Lewis, Thomas Jefferson, and the Opening of the American West* (New York: Simon & Schuster, 2003), 341.
25. Anton J.L. Van Hooff, "Ancient Euthanasia: 'Good Death' and the Doctor in the Greco-Roman world," *Social Science & Medicine* 58 (2004): 975–985, https://pdfs.semanticscholar.org/f0fb/c8cc5afad83e96569120bc78e1b870224261.pdf.
26. Tomoko Otake, "Suicides down, but Japan still second highest among major industrialized nations, report says," *Japan Times*, May 30, 2017, https://www.japantimes.co.jp/news/2017/05/30/national/social-issues/preventive-efforts-seen-helping-2016-saw-another-decline-suicides-japan-21897/#.XRFZjZNKiu4.
27. Quoted in Ambrose, 285.
28. Ibid.
29. Ibid., 340.
30. Durant, 493.
31. Quoted in Arvind Sharma, et. al., *Sati: Historical and Phenomenological Essays* (Delhi: Motilal Banarsidass, 1988), 8.
32. "Corruption Perceptions Index 2018," *Transparency International*, https://www.transparency.org/cpi2018.
33. Transparency International, Corruptions Perception Index 2018.
34. Heritage Foundation Freedom Index, 2019.
35. Gross Domestic Product per Capita, International Monetary Fund, 2018.
36. Estimated Protestant Christian Population - Pew Templeton Global Religious Futures Project.

CHAPTER III

Babel and the Futility of the Kingdoms of Men

1. Two timelines are presented at the end of the early chapters of his text, covering the range of dates conservative biblical students would put for the Flood and the Tower of the Babel. The major variant is whether the Israelite sojourn in Egypt lasted 430 years or 215 years. The clearest indication of a 430-year sojourn is found in Exodus 12:40-41, in which the sons of Israel (Jacob) were said to have sojourned in Egypt for 430 years. However, Galatians 3:17 speaks of how the Abrahamic Covenant (mentioned as a promise made to Abraham in verse 16) was confirmed 430 years before the giving of the law at Sinai. The debate continues over whether the covenant was confirmed just once, or whether it was confirmed many times in the lifetime of Abraham, Isaac, and Jacob.
2. "The Tower of Babel, King Nebuchadnezzar II and the Schøyen Collection," *Archaeology & Arts*, December 29, 2011, https://www.archaeology.wiki/blog/2011/12/29/the-tower-of-babel-king-nebuchadnezzar-ii-and-the-sch%C3%B8yen-collection/.
3. Andrew R, George, "The Tower of Babel: Archaeology, History and Cuneiform Texts," *Archiv für Orientforschung* 51 (2005/2006): 75–95, https://eprints.soas.ac.uk/3858/2/TowerOfBabel.AfO.pdf.
4. Robert W. Carter, "Adam, Eve and Noah vs Modern Genetics," *Creation Ministries International*, May 11, 2010, https://creation.com/noah-and-genetics.

CHAPTER IV

First Empires in Mesopotamia (2360-1750 BC)

1. George Modelski, *World Cities: -3000 to 2000* (Washington, DC: Faros, 2003), 6.
2. "Chronicle of Early Kings," *Livius*, https://www.livius.org/sources/content/mesopotamian-chronicles-content/abc-20-chronicle-of-early-kings/.
3. Susan Wise Bauer, *The History of the Ancient World: From the Earliest Accounts to the Fall of Rome* (New York: W.W. Norton, 2007), 95.

4. Carl S. Ehrlich, ed., *From an Antique Land: An Introduction to Ancient Near Eastern Literature* (Lanham, MD: Rowman & Littlefield, 2009), 40.
5. "The Instructions of Shuruppag," *Electronic Text Corpus of Sumerian Literature*, http://etcsl.orinst.ox.ac.uk/section5/tr561.htm.
6. Ibid.
7. "The Liberty Cones of Urukagina," *Sumerian Shakespeare*, http://sumerianshakespeare.com/70701/79201.html.
8. Ibid.
9. Elizabeth Meier Tetlow, *Women, Crime and Punishment in Ancient Law and Society*, Vol. 1,*The Ancient Near East* (New York: Continuum International, 2004), 9-10.
10. "A Praise Poem of Shulgi," *Electronic Text Corpus of Sumerian Literature,* http://etcsl.orinst.ox.ac.uk/section2/tr24201.htm.
11. "Chronicle of Early Kings," *Livius*, https://www.livius.org/sources/content/mesopotamian-chronicles-content/abc-20-chronicle-of-early-kings/.
12. Although unbelieving archaeologists have attempted to dismiss the Ebla Tablets, the Ca' Foscari University of Venice has made the texts available online at http://ebda.cnr.it/word/list?q=i.
13. Bryant G. Wood, "The Discovery of the Sin Cities of Sodom and Gomorrah," *Associates for Biblical Research,* April 16, 2008, https://biblearchaeology.org/research/patriarchal-era/2364-the-discovery-of-the-sin-cities-of-sodom-and-gomorrah.
14. Ibid.
15. Chris Chase-Dunn, et al., *Institute for Research on World Systems*, March 20, 2008, https://pdfs.semanticscholar.org/6a8f/2f82208e205974a35a44f016ff26a59a29bf.pdf.
16. "The Code of Hammurabi," *The Avalon Project*, https://avalon.law.yale.edu/ancient/hamframe.asp.
17. Ibid.
18. "Evangelical Growth," *Operation World*, http://www.operationworld.org/hidden/evangelical-growth.

CHAPTER V

The Egyptian Empire (2450-332 BC)

1. Alan Gardiner, *Egypt of the Pharaohs* (Oxford: Oxford University Press, 1964), 53.
2. Cf. Darrell White and Kenneth Griffith, *A Chronological Framework of Ancient History*, manuscript prepublication.
3. George Rawlinson, *The Origin of Nations* (New York: Scribner, 1881), 13.
4. Quoted in William J. Duiker and Jackson Spielvogel, *The Essential World History* (Belmont, CA: Thomson & Wadsworth, 2008), 15.
5. Lesley Smith, "The Kahun Gynaecological Papyrus: Ancient Egyptian Medicine," November 8, 2010, https://srh.bmj.com/content/familyplanning/37/1/54.full.pdf.
6. Quoted in Patrick V. Reid, ed., *Readings in Western Religious Thought: The Ancient World* (New York: Paulist Press, 1987), 35.
7. Quoted in Michael Kerrigan, *The Ancients in Their Own Words* (London: Amber, 2019), 61.
8. Quoted in E.A. Wallis Budge, *Egyptian Ideas of the Future Life* (London: Kegan Paul, Trench, Turner & Co., 1908), 23-24.
9. Quoted in Will and Ariel Durant, *The Story of Civilization,* Vol. 1, *Our Oriental Heritage* (New York: Simon & Schuster, 1942), 194-195.
10. Ibid., 195.
11. Cf. White and Griffith
12. David Down and John Ashton, *Unwrapping the Pharaohs: How Egyptian Archaeology Confirms the Biblical Timeline* (Green Forest, AR: Master Books, 2006), 83.
13. Ibid.
14. Peter F. Dorman, et al., *Egypt and the Ancient Near East* (New York: The Metropolitan Museum of Art, 1987), 26.
15. Flavius Josephus, *Antiquities of the Jews*, 2.232.

16. Quoted in J. Randall Price and H. Wayne House, *Zondervan Survey of Biblical Archaeology* (Grand Rapids: Zondervan, 2017), 86.
17. Ibid.
18. Flavius Josephus, *Against Apion*, 1.14.
19. Flavius Josephus, *Antiquities of the Jews*, 8.6.5.
20. Down and Ashton, 134.
21. Ibid.
22. Quoted in Kerrigan, 59.
23. "The world`s oldest autograph by a Christian is in Basel," *University of Basel*, July 11, 2019, https://www.unibas.ch/en/News-Events/News/Uni-Research/The-world-s-oldest-autograph-by-a-Christian-is-in-Basel.html.
24. Transparency International, Corruptions Perception Index 2018.
25. Heritage Foundation Freedom Index, 2019.
26. Gross Domestic Product per Capita, International Monetary Fund, 2018.

CHAPTER VI

The Special People of God

1. J. Randall Price and H. Wayne House, *Zondervan Handbook of Biblical Archaeology* (Grand Rapids: Zondervan, 2017), 101.
2. "Sennacherib Prism, Column 2," http://www.kchanson.com/ANCDOCS/meso/sennprism2.html.
3. *Book of Jubilees*, 29.11.
4. Bryant G. Wood, "Did the Israelites Conquer Jericho? A New Look at the Archaeological Evidence," *Associates for Biblical Research*, May 1, 2008, https://biblearchaeology.org/research/conquest-of-canaan/2310-did-the-israelites-conquer-jericho-a-new-look-at-the-archaeological-evidence.
5. Quoted in Price and House, 110.
6. Amarna Tablets, EA 292:28-29.
7. Amarna Tablets, EA 271:10-11, 13-16.

8. Amarna Tablets, EA 274.
9. Amarna Tablets, EA 288:33-40.
10. Amarna Tablets, EA 289:21-24.
11. David G. Hansen, "Shechem: Its Archaeological and Contextual Significance," *Associates for Biblical Research*, https://biblearchaeology.org/research/new-testament-era/2365-shechem-its-archaeological-and-contextual-significance.
12. Kristin Romey, "Ancient DNA may reveal origin of the Philistines," *National Geographic*, July 3, 2019, https://www.nationalgeographic.com/culture/2019/07/ancient-dna-reveal-philistine-origins/.
13. Quoted in Michael Kerrigan, *The Ancients in Their Own Words* (London: Amber, 2019), 80.

CHAPTER VII

Western and Eastern Europe After the Flood (2518 BC - AD 33)

1. M.D.R. Evans and Jonathan Kelley, "National Pride in the Developed World: Survey Data from 24 Nations," *International Journal of Public Opinion Research*, 14, no. 3 (September 1, 2002): 303–338, https://academic.oup.com/ijpor/article/14/3/303/678035.
2. James Morgan, "Dig Pinpoints Stonehenge Origins," *BBC*, September 21, 2008, http://news.bbc.co.uk/2/hi/science/nature/7625145.stm.
3. "Ancient genomes indicate population replacement in Early Neolithic Britain," https://www.nature.com/articles/s41559-019-0871-9.
4. Chris Ciaccia, "500-year-old frozen bodies are 'North America's best preserved mummies,'" *Fox News*, https://www.foxnews.com/science/500-year-old-frozen-bodies-north-america-mummies.
5. Phillip Freeman, *St. Patrick of Ireland* (Simon & Schuster, 2004), 99.
6. Julius Caesar, *Commentaries on the Gallic War*, 6.13, 16.
7. Herodotus, *The Persian Wars*, 4.108.
8. Transparency International, Corruptions Perception Index 2018.
9. Heritage Foundation Freedom Index, 2019.

10. Gross Domestic Product per Capita, International Monetary Fund, 2018.

11. Estimated Christian Population.

CHAPTER VIII

India Waiting for the Coming of Christ (2200 BC - AD 33)

1. Rohan Venkataramakrishnan, "Who was here first? A new study explains the origins of ancient Indians," *Quartz India*, April 3, 2018, https://qz.com/india/1243436/aryan-migration-scientists-use-dna-to-explain-origins-of-ancient-indians/.

2. Rig Veda, 3.34.9.

3. Rig Veda, 1.100.18.

4. Alden Bass, "An Investigation of Hindu Scripture," *Apologetics Press*, https://www.apologeticspress.org/apcontent.aspx?category=8&article=1410.

CHAPTER IX

The Far East Before the Coming of Christ (2300 BC - AD 33)

1. John Wu, "Readings from Ancient Chinese Codes and Other Sources of Chinese Law and Legal Ideas," *Michigan Law Review*, Vol. 19, No. 5 (March, 1921), 502-536, https://www.jstor.org/stable/pdf/1276932.pdf.

2. Ibid.

3. Ibid.

4. Ibid.

5. "Inscriptions found in Shanghai pre-date 'oldest Chinese language by 1,400 years,'" *UK Guardian*, July 10, 2013, https://www.theguardian.com/world/2013/jul/10/inscriptions-predate-oldest-chinese-language.

6. "Oracle-Bone Inscriptions of the Late Shang Dynasty, http://afe.easia.columbia.edu/ps/cup/oracle_bone_general.pdf.

7. "Announcement of Tang," *Chinese Text Project*, https://ctext.org/shang-shu/announcement-of-tang.

8. "Wen Wang," *Chinese Text Project*, https://ctext.org/book-of-poetry/wen-wang.
9. Quoted in Zhengyuan Fu, *Autocratic Tradition and Chinese Politics* (Cambridge: Cambridge University Press, 1993), 177.
10. Quoted in Steven W. Mosher, *Bully of Asia: Why China's Dream Is the New Threat to World Order* (Washington DC: Regnery, 2017), 36.
11. Ibid., 37.
12. Ibid., 38.
13. Ibid.
14. Ibid., 39.
15. Ibid.
16. Ibid.
17. Ibid.
18. Ibid.
19. Ibid.
20. Ibid., 44-45.
21. Confucius, *The Great Learning,* http://classics.mit.edu/Confucius/learning.html.
22. Quoted in Will and Ariel Durant, *The Story of Civilization*, Vol. 1, *Our Oriental Heritage* (New York: Simon & Schuster, 1942), 674.
23. John Wu, 502-536.
24. Ibid.
25. Quoted in Durant, 699.
26. "Historical Abortion Statistics, Japan," http://www.johnstonsarchive.net/policy/abortion/ab-japan.html.
27. "The Bamboo Annals," *Chinese Text Project*, https://ctext.org/searchbooks.pl?if=en&searchu=%E7%AB%B9%E6%9B%B8%E7%B4%80%E5%B9%B4.
28. Ibid.

29. Ibid.
30. Ibid.
31. Transparency International, Corruptions Perception Index 2018.
32. Heritage Foundation Freedom Index, 2019.
33. Gross Domestic Product per Capita, International Monetary Fund, 2018.
34. Estimated Protestant Christian Population.

CHAPTER X

The Assyrian Empire: Power by Cruelty (1200-612 BC)

1. "The Edict of Telepinu," Quoted in Marc Van De Mieroop, *A History of the Ancient Near East ca. 3000 - 323 BC* (Malden, MA: Blackwell Publishing, 2007), 120.
2. "Old Hittite Law Code," https://lrc.la.utexas.edu/eieol/hitol/40.
3. Ibid.
4. Aleksandar Mishkov, "Egyptian Hittite Peace Treaty - One of the Oldest Treaties in the World," http://www.documentarytube.com/articles/egyptian-hittite-peace-treaty--one-of-the-oldest-treaties-in-the-world.
5. "Queen Nefertari Meryetmut," https://mathstat.slu.edu/~bart/egyptianhtml/kings%20and%20Queens/Queen_Nefertari.html.
6. Quoted in Daniel D. Luckenbill, *Ancient Records of Assyria and Babylonia* (Chicago: University of Chicago Press, 1927), 1:27.
7. Marco De Odorico, "Compositional and Editorial Processes of Annalistic and Summary Texts of Tiglath-Pileser I," https://www.academia.edu/8308416/Compositional_and_Editorial_Processes_of_Annalistic_and_Summary_Texts_of_Tiglath-Pileser_I.
8. Quoted in Luckenbill, 2:119-121.
9. Will and Ariel Durant, *The Story of Civilization,* Vol. 1, *Our Oriental Heritage* (New York: Simon & Schuster, 1954), 268.
10. Erika Belibtreu, "Grisly Assyrian Record of Torture and Death,"

Biblical Archaeology Society, https://pdfs.semanticscholar.org/f4af/bb82f1b7920fa9444e29eb128bd13832cd46.pdf.

11. Marc Madrigal, "Adad-Nirari III: Jonah's Assyrian King?" *Evangelical Focus*, January 10, 2018, http://evangelicalfocus.com/blogs/3168/AdadNirari_III_Jonah_Assyrian_King_Old_Testament.
12. Quoted in John H. Walton, ed., *Zondervan Illustrated Bible Backgrounds Commentary*, Vol. 4 (Grand Rapids: Zondervan, 2009), 155.
13. "Ashurbanipal Quotes From Texts, Sitchin Books, etc.," http://www.mesopotamiangods.com/ashurbanipal-quotes-from-texts-sitchin-books-etc/.
14. Didorus Siculus, *Library of History*, 2.23.
15. Quoted in Durant, 282.
16. https://www.smithsonianmag.com/smart-news/seal-prophet-isaiah-180968255/

CHAPTER XI

Babylon Has Fallen (626-539 BC)

1. Charles Halton, "How Big Was Nineveh?: Literal versus Figurative Interpretation of City Size," *Bulletin for Biblical Research* 18.2 (2008): 193–207, https://www.ibr-bbr.org/files/bbr/bbr18b01_halton.pdf.
2. Nebuchadnezzar, "The East India House Inscription," https://research.britishmuseum.org/research/collection_online/collection_object_details.aspx?objectId=367114&page=1&partId=1&searchText=East%20India%20House%20Inscription.
3. Ibid.
4. "The Madness of King Nebuchadnezzar," https://biblereadingarcheology.com/2017/09/25/the-madness-of-king-nebuchadnezzar/.
5. "Brick Stamped with the Name of Nebuchadnezzar II," https://www.ancient.eu/image/5240/brick-stamped-with-the-name-of-nebuchadnezzar-ii/.
6. Quoted in Michael Kerrigan, *The Ancients in Their Own Words* (London: Amber, 2019), 40.

7. "Is it reasonable to believe that Nebuchadnezzar went mentally insane like an animal?" http://www.evidenceunseen.com/bible-difficulties-2/ot-difficulties/daniel-amos/dan-433-is-it-reasonable-to-believe-that-nebuchadnezzar-went-mentally-insane-like-an-animal/.
8. Quoted in Will and Ariel Durant, *The Story of Civilization*, Vol. 1, *Our Oriental Heritage* (New York: Simon & Schuster, 1942), 241.
9. Ibid., 248.
10. Ibid.
11. Ibid., 244.

CHAPTER XII

The Kingdom of the Medes and Persians (725-330 BC)

1. "Enmerkar and the Lord of Aratta," *Electronic Text Corpus of Sumerian Literature*, http://etcsl.orinst.ox.ac.uk/section1/tr1823.htm.
2. Quoted in Will and Ariel Durant, *The Story of Civilization*, Vol. 1, *Our Oriental Heritage* (New York: Simon & Schuster, 1942), 374.
3. Ibid., 351.
4. "The Cyrus Cylinder," https://www.bible-history.com/archaeology/persia/cyrus-cylinder.html.
5. Quoted in Michael Kerrigan, *The Ancients in Their Own Words* (London: Amber, 2019), 103.
6. "The Behistun Inscription," *Livius*, https://www.livius.org/articles/place/behistun/behistun-3/.
7. Durant, 352.
8. Ibid., 374.
9. "Harem i. in Ancient Iran," *Encyclopedia Iranica*, http://www.iranicaonline.org/articles/harem-i.
10. Ibid.

CHAPTER XIII

The Misguided Greeks and Alexander's Ill-Fated Empire (800-150 BC)

1. Quoted in Michael Kerrigan, *The Ancients in Their Own Words* (London: Amber, 2019), 129.
2. Will and Ariel Durant, *The Story of Civilization*, Vol. 2, *The Life of Greece* (New York: Simon & Schuster, 1942), 211.
3. Augustine, *Confessions*, 1.16.
4. Quoted in Durant, 81.
5. "The Homicide Courts of Ancient Athens," *University of Pennsylvania Law Review*, https://scholarship.law.upenn.edu/cgi/viewcontent.cgi?article=7670&context=penn_law_review.
6. Quoted in Durant, 117.
7. Quoted in Nicholas Laos, *Methexiology: Philosophical Theology and Theological Philosophy for the Deification of Humanity* (Eugene, OR: Pickwick, 2016), 216.
8. Quoted in Durant, 368.
9. Plato, *Theaetetus*, 150.
10. Plato, *The Republic,* Book 5.
11. Quoted in Durant, 530.
12. Aristotle, *Nicomachean Ethics*, 2.7.
13. Aristotle, *Politics*, 8.1.
14. Sophocles, *Oedipus Rex*.
15. Durant, 296.
16. Quoted in Kerrigan, 140.
17. Quoted in Simon Adams, *Alexander: The Boy Solider who Conquered the World* (Washington, DC: National Geographic Society, 2013), 23.
18. Durant, 540.
19. Ibid., 567.

20. Ibid., 568.
21. Ibid.

CHAPTER XV

The Romans: Reaching the Zenith of the Empires (753 BC - AD 33)

1. Polybius, *Histories*, 3.22.
2. J.K. Brennan, et al., eds., *The World's Progress*, Vol. 3 (Chicago: The Delphian Society, 1913), 441.
3. Katelyn DiBenedetto, "Analyzing Tophets: Did the Phoenicians Practice Child Sacrifice?" *Anthropology*, May 2012, https://scholarsarchive.library.albany.edu/cgi/viewcontent.cgi?article=1004&context=honorscollege_anthro.
4. Malcolm W. Browne, "Relics of Carthage Show Brutality Amid the Good Life," *New York Times*, Sept. 1, 1987, https://www.nytimes.com/1987/09/01/science/relics-of-carthage-show-brutality-amid-the-good-life.html; The ratio of child sacrifice to animal sacrifice increased from 3:1 to 10:1 between the 8th century BC and the 3rd century BC.
5. "Ancient Carthaginians really did sacrifice their children," *University of Oxford*, January 23, 2014, http://www.ox.ac.uk/news/2014-01-23-ancient-carthaginians-really-did-sacrifice-their-children.
6. Sybille Haynes, *Etruscan Civilization: A Cultural History* (Los Angeles: Getty Publications, 2000), 232-233.
7. Quoted in J.K. Brennan, et al., eds., *The World's Progress,* Vol. 4 (Chicago: The Delphian Society, 1923), 12.
8. Augustine, *Confessions*, 6.8.
9. Augustine, *City of God*, 3.23-24.
10. Ibid., 2.21.
11. Ibid., 3.14.
12. Ibid.

13. Quoted in Philip Freeman, *Julius Caesar* (New York: Simon & Schuster, 2008), 334.
14. Ibid., 333.
15. Augustine, *City of God*, 3.30.
16. Cassius Dio, *Roman History*, 56.5.
17. "The Priene Calendar Inscription," https://web.archive.org/web/20170722070724/http://www.masseiana.org/priene.htm.
18. Transparency International, Corruptions Perception Index 2018.
19. Heritage Foundation Freedom Index, 2019.
20. Gross Domestic Product per Capita, International Monetary Fund, 2018.
21. Estimated Protestant Christian Population.

CHAPTER XVI

Preparing the World for Jesus: Jerusalem (73 BC - AD 33)

1. Strabo, *Geography*, 11.9.3.
2. Macrobius Ambrosius Theodosius, *Saturnalia*, 2.4.11.
3. Flavius Josephus, *Antiquities of the Jews*, 20.9.2.
4. Taylor G. Bunch, *Behold the Man!: A Review of the Trials and Crucifixion of Jesus* (Nashville: Southern Publishing Association, 1946), 48.

Name Index

B

C

F

G

H

N

O

P

Q

R

S

T

U

V

W

X

Y

Z

Subject Index

B

C

D

E

F

G

H

I

J

K

L

O

P

Q

R

S

T

U

V

W

Y

Z

List of Images

CHAPTER I

The Creation and the Global Flood

CHAPTER II

The Whole Pagan World: Darkness Prevails (2518 BC - AD 33)

7. Fragment from the Temple of Inanna | Wikimedia Commons | Public Domain
8. King Pomare of Tahiti | Wikimedia Commons | Public Domain
9. Marco Polo (1254-1324) | Wikimedia Commons | Public Domain
10. Madagascar | iStock.com
11. Fiji | iStock.com
12. Tablet Containing Code of Hammurabi | Wikimedia Commons | Public Domain
13. Darius I (522-486 BC) | Wikimedia Commons | Public Domain
14. Widow-Burning (Sati) | Wikimedia Commons | Public Domain
15. Mt. Kilimanjaro | iStock.com

CHAPTER III

Babel and the Futility of the Kingdoms of Men

1. Tower of Babel | iStock.com
2. Modern-Day Syria (a Possible Location of the Tower of Babel) | Wikimedia Commons | Public Domain
3. Example of a Ziggurat | iStock.com
4. Chichen Itza Mayan Temple in Mexico | iStock.com
5. Great Pyramid of Giza | iStock.com
6. Exhibit of Göbekli Tepe in Instanbul Airport, Istanbul, Turkey | Image taken by author in Instanbul Airport, March 2020

CHAPTER IV

First Empires in Mesopotamia (2360-1750 BC)

1. Euphrates River | iStock.com
2. Map of Syria and Mesopotamia | iStock.com
3. Victory Stele of Sargon | Wikimedia Commons | Public Domain
4. Image of Ishtar | Wikimedia Commons | Public Domain
5. Naram Sin's Reign | Wikimedia Commons | Public Domain
6. Victory Stele of Naram Sin | Wikimedia Commons | Public Domain
7. *Instructions of Shuruppak* | Wikimedia Commons | Public Domain
8. Bronze Helmet from 1st Dynasty | Wikimedia Commons | Public Domain
9. Fragment of the Urukagina Code | Wikimedia Commons | Public Domain
10. Brick Stamped with "Ur-Nammu" | Wikimedia Commons | Public Domain
11. Abraham's Journey from Ur to Canaan | Wikimedia Commons | Public Domain
12. Restored Ziggurat in Ancient Ur | iStock.com
13. Possible Remnants of Sodom or Gomorrah | Wikimedia Commons | Public Domain
14. *The Destruction of Sodom and Gomorrah*, by John Martin | Wikimedia Commons | Public Domain
15. Relief of Hammurabi | Wikimedia Commons | Public Domain
16. Code of Hammurabi | Wikimedia Commons | Public Domain
17. Map of Middle East | Wikimedia Commons | Public Domain
18. Flock of Sheep on the Tigris River | iStock.com

CHAPTER V

The Egyptian Empire (2450-332 BC)

1. Pyramids | iStock.com
2. Djoser's Step Pyramid | iStock.com
3. Seneferu's Bent Pyramid | iStock.com
4. Great Pyramid of Giza | iStock.com
5. The Great Sphinx of Giza | iStock.com

CHAPTER VI

The Special People of God

CHAPTER VII

Western and Eastern Europe After the Flood (2518 BC - AD 33)

CHAPTER VIII

India Waiting for the Coming of Christ (2200 BC - AD 33)

CHAPTER IX

The Far East Before the Coming of Christ (2300 BC - AD 33)

CHAPTER X

The Assyrian Empire: Power by Cruelty (1200-612 BC)

CHAPTER XI

Babylon Has Fallen (626-539 BC)

CHAPTER XII

The Kingdom of the Medes and Persians (725-330 BC)

CHAPTER XIII

The Misguided Greeks and Alexander's Ill-Fated Empire (800-150 BC)

CHAPTER XIV

The Hellenistic Kingdoms (323-63 BC)

CHAPTER XV

The Romans: Reaching the Zenith of the Empires (753 BC - AD 33)

CHAPTER XVI

Preparing the World for Jesus: Jerusalem (73 BC - AD 33)